THE ROSSLYN HOAX?

Viewing Rosslyn Chapel from a new perspective

THE ROSSLYN HOAX?

Viewing Rosslyn Chapel from a new perspective

Robert L. D. Cooper

LEWIS

Dedication: For my wife, Yvonne

WORCESTERSHIRE COUNTY COUNCIL	
730	
Bertrams	18.07.07
366.109411	£7.99
MA	

First published in hardback 2006
This paperback edition first published 2007

ISBN (10) 0 85318 281 7
ISBN (13) 978 0 85318 281 8

Published by Lewis Masonic

an imprint of Ian Allan Publishing Ltd, Hersham, Surrey KT12 4RG.
Printed in Great Britain by TJ International, Padstow, Cornwall

Code: 0706/D

Visit the Lewis Masonic website at www.lewismasonic.co.uk

Front cover: Rosslyn Chapel. *Antonia Reeve Photography*

Contents

Preface

Because I have received innumerable enquiries over many years on a whole host of subjects as diverse as: the Knights Templar, Rosslyn Chapel, the St Clair family and their possible connections with Freemasonry (particularly Scottish Freemasonry) I have not only accumulated a great deal of material on these subjects but also have gained some insights on matters that are of interest to some people. Since the success of the novel, *The Da Vinci Code* by Dan Brown the number of enquires I receive has increased dramatically and I therefore confess to having a selfish motive in writing this book – to try to reduce my workload! Despite Freemasonry being a very small part of the novel it has created a great deal of interest in the Craft, especially its Scottish dimension. The repetitive nature of many of the questions being asked makes it clear that most people do not have sufficient *Masonic* knowledge and/or information with which to differentiate between fact and fiction. This book is intended to provide such material which might be used to assess the work, not only of novelists who write about the subjects previously mentioned, but also to provide material with which to assess the work of 'popular' historians. It is a matter of some Scottish pride that Dan Brown's novels are the latest in the *genre* of the historical novel which were 'invented' by another Freemason – Sir Walter Scott. However, I digress. In order to assist the reader in determining the type of books that are works of academic history, fiction or popular history, I have divided the bibliography (at the rear of the book) into these three categories. Please be aware that the bibliography is not intended to be comprehensive (although it is extensive) but I am confident that it provides a clear indication of the three 'types' in question.

Other considerations have an effect - one common problem is the ignorance regarding the history and origins of Freemasonry, and the common belief that Freemasonry *per se* is much the same everywhere in the world. This assumption is made by very many authors who assume that Freemasonry has a 'commonality' to the point that, as far as they are concerned, there is no difference whatsoever between Freemasonry in Scotland, and that in any other country.[1] It is therefore possible, when reading the work of 'popular' historians who discuss Scottish Freemasonry, to recognise fundamental weaknesses. Even those authors who claim to be Freemasons display little acquaintance with Scottish Masonic custom and practice. That may be partly due to what Professor David Stevenson describes as an 'anglo-centric' approach to the study of the history of Freemasonry.

Although the main purpose of this book is to discuss: 'Has modern Freemasonry any connection with the Medieval Order of the Knights Templar, Rosslyn Chapel and the St. Clair family?' (a more detailed version of the hypothesis is posited in Chapter 1) I have taken the opportunity, where relevant, to discuss associated subjects. The suggestion that there is such a link has been discussed in the works of a variety of popular writers over the last twenty years. One way of examining the validity of their claims is to examine what Scottish Freemasons themselves thought their history and origins to be. Non-Masons and Freemasons alike of the 18th and 19th centuries wrote a great deal on this subject and today little has changed. What did our Masonic forebears have to say? What evidence did they produce? Is any of it relevant today? The first part of the book therefore examines their beliefs about the history of Freemasonry in Scotland and traces the numerous additions and elaborations to their core beliefs over those two centuries. The opportunity has also been taken to discuss, briefly, subjects which arise as a consequence, such as: the structure of Freemasonry, Masonic ritual and anti-Masonry.

Zealous, often over zealous, writers frequently turn a blind eye to inconvenient evidence and this usually manifests itself in major contradictions within a particular hypothesis or theory. This common practice, with some examples, will be discussed. However, this book should not be seen as a deliberate attempt to debunk popular mythology regarding the Knights Templar etc. but it is very definitely an attempt to bring some clarity to an often confused and contradictory debate on the subject. It is also a positive attempt to examine the myth itself in the context of Scottish (Masonic) history for the first time and that by that very examination shed some light on why the myth holds such a strong attraction. The exponents of the Popular or Alternative Approach have brought forward evidence, and their interpretation of it, in support of particular hypotheses and theories. That evidence forms the other major part of the book and the discussion is therefore 'themed' – e.g. The Kirkwall Scroll, Rosslyn Chapel, the Battle of Bannockburn etc. The number of such themes is large and some, such as Rosslyn Chapel, has a number of sub-themes. It is not possible to address every single one of these and so I have opted to examine those which feature most prominently in popular works.

Another major aim of the book is to provide more information regarding the history Scottish Freemasonry. With the honourable exception of the books (published almost 20 years ago) by David Stevenson there is little generally available.[2] In this respect I have included transcripts of some of the rare documents of Scottish Freemasonry (such as the so called St. Clair 'Charters') as Appendices. Many of these documents have been previously available only in specialist publications and certainly have not been accessible by a mass audience. It is one of the curious facts that such documents although available to *bona fide* scholars, researchers and authors, not one of the Popular or Alternative approach has, during my tenure as Curator of the Grand Lodge of Scotland Museum and Library, examined these various documents which are housed within Freemasons' Hall, Edinburgh. It is difficult to understand why this should be, although I have made some suggestions in the first chapter, but in reproducing these documents in the public domain here I hope to achieve two things. Firstly, it is simply not possible for the Grand Lodge of Scotland to allow all who are interested, to examine such old and rare documents. By transcribing the text (not in facsimile) then those with an interest in them will now be able to gain some insight as to their content and meaning.[3] The second benefit is, I hope, that those who have been unable to read these documents due to distance or unavailability will no longer labour under that deficit.

Freemasonry in general is much misunderstood and I hope that this book will go some way to explaining why Freemasonry, particularly Scottish Freemasonry, has come to be in that position. In doing so, I offer my own opinions only. It is extremely important for the reader to understand that no one individual can speak 'for' Freemasonry because it has no dogma and therefore it is for the individual to interpret and not for any Freemason, or group of Freemasons, to impose their opinion on fellow Freemasons. Despite that fact many, and for purposes best known to themselves, occasionally organisations of which they are a member, use comments made by individual Freemasons to suggest that they are, in fact, speaking for all Freemasons. I therefore emphasize that the observations, deductions and opinions (and the errors) in this book are mine and mine alone. This work does not represent the views of any Masonic body of which I may or may not be a member.

Acknowledgements

Extending thanks to all those who have assisted in preparing a book is common practice but I hesitate to do so because I shall forget someone. Had I taken notes as I went along perhaps this problem would not exist. However, I did not and so must live with the consequences. First and foremost my thanks must go to my wife, Yvonne, for putting up with all the additional hassle that comes from having someone writing a book and doing none of the housework! I am also grateful for all her assistance regarding the photographs contained within this book. My son, Owen, has also been very supportive – of his mother! In a professional capacity I am indebted to members of staff at Freemasons' Hall, Edinburgh, all of whom have assisted to a greater or lesser extent. The recently retired Grand Secretary, C. Martin McGibbon, has always been supportive as has his successor, David M. Begg. Members of the Grand Lodge of Scotland in general and the Publications Committee (subsequently the Information and Communications Committee) in particular have, without exception, been encouraging ever since I took up this post more 13 years ago. Past chairman of the Publications Committee, J. Mark Garside and Robert S. Tait together with Walter Sneddon of the ICC, stand out as individuals who have wished me well in my endeavours. Angus MacInnes, editor of the Ashlar magazine, kindly supplied me with out of print editions of the magazine. Michael Baigent, Julian Rees and Yasha Beresiner of the Masonic magazine, Freemasonry Today, have all been helpful in numerous ways, together with the Masonic magazine, The Square. The staff at The Library and Museum of Freemasonry, London, particularly the Director, Diane Clements, and Librarian Martin Cherry, have been very helpful on a number of matters including illustrative material. My Brothers in Quatuor Coronati Lodge, No.2076, including the Master (at the time), James Daniel, John Hamill, PM, and A. Trevor Stewart. P.M, and many, many others have provided valuable assistance and have made many helpful suggestions.

Overseas, Mark Tabbert of the George Washington National Monument, Alexandria, Virginia, was the first person to encourage me to produce this work. His enthusiasm and assistance were invaluable especially at an early stage. S. Brent Morris of the Scottish Rite Research Society, Washington DC, in his own inimitable manner, has been of great service. Without doubt the individual who first caused me to think more deeply about Freemasonry is my friend and Brother Richard F. Driver of Phoenix, Arizona. He always believed that I should write more substantial works to share with others because: '*Above all else Freemasonry is essentially a cerebral activity*' – an opinion I happen to share. Also in the USA, my namesake John L. Cooper III and his lovely wife Heather, Adam Kendall, Paul Rich and Norm Lepper, all of California, were most enthusiastic that this work be produced. My good friends Jerry Ward (and his delightful wife, Agnes), Steve Ellis and William Harker, all of the Walter F. Meier Lodge of Research, Seattle, have all shown interest in my research and have been especially kind when my wife, Yvonne, and I have visted. Then there are the members of the Australian

New Zealand Masonic Research Council (ANZMRC) who kindly organised the round the world tour in 2005. Kent Henderson and Tony Pope being the principal organisers and whose kindness and assistance stands out in my memory. In Europe there are also a number of people to whom I am most grateful principally to Prof. Jan Snoek of the University of Heidelberg whose insightful, even clinical, observations have occasionally come as a shock but were very welcome none-the-less. Pierre Mollier, Paris, and Evert Kwaadgrass, The Hague, The Netherlands, have both been supportive and have kindly provided information from their respective libraries.

In Edinburgh, the staff at the National Library of Scotland; the Royal Commission on the Ancient and Historical Monuments of Scotland (RCAHMS); the Scottish Library and Edinburgh Room of the City of Edinburgh Council's Central Library and Historic Scotland have never failed to provide information and assistance when requested.

The opportunity has also been taken to correct a number of errors contained within the first edition and I thank those who have brought these to my attention.

Robert L. D. Cooper

Edinburgh

May 2007

---

[1] It is suspected that many writers on Scottish Freemasonry rely on non-Scottish reference material such as, Masonic Encyclopaedias in the mistaken belief that they accurately present Scottish Masonic custom and practice.

[2] Stevenson's books: *The First Freemasons – Scotland's Early Lodges and their Members* and *The Origins of Freemasonry – Scotland's Century 1590 – 1710* were both published in 1988. A testament to their importance lies in the fact they remain in print today. It is a mystery, and disappointment, that hardly any other academic historians have followed his ground breaking work.

[3] I am acutely conscious that these old documents ought to be reproduced in facsimile and translated form. This is a project I hope to undertake in due time.

Chapter 1
Introduction

The Power of Myth[1]

During the last 20 years there have been a number of books by popular authors who have suggested that modern Freemasonry derives from the medieval Order of the Poor Fellow-Soldiers of Christ and the Temple of Solomon (otherwise known as the Knights Templar and hereinafter referred to as KT) and attempt to chart that lineage, mentioning, specifically, Scotland as a place where this synthesis took place.[2] We owe a debt of gratitude to all those authors in their various endeavours. They have created a most interesting debate that would not have otherwise existed and which has led to many questions that would not also otherwise have been asked. This very positive process, however speculative, is important if for no other reason than that of stimulating Freemasons to seek more understanding of the unique organisation of which they are members. Non-Freemasons, although handicapped by not having an 'inside view' of this most Ancient and Honourable Order, have also enjoyed the work of these authors as evidenced by the huge number of these books which have been sold.

It is the task of historians to engage in that debate and to respond to those questions and, it is to be hoped that by doing both, we extend our knowledge and understanding of the past as it relates to Freemasonry, specifically Scottish Freemasonry.

There are, presently, at least two main approaches to the study of Freemasonry's origins and development:

The Academic Approach
The Popular or Alternative (also described as the Mythological) Approach.

The former might define 'history' thus:

'… *the interpretations of historians* [are] *based on the critical study of the widest possible range of relevant sources, every effort having been made to challenge, and avoid the perpetuation of, myth.*'[3]

As new ideas are created, and new evidence comes to light, analytical methods are used to examine existing theories of what constitutes the past. In this continuous process all aspects of the past, including myths, are re-considered. This approach to history constantly seeks to challenge accepted theories, including myths, and can be represented diagrammatically thus:[4] (See below.)

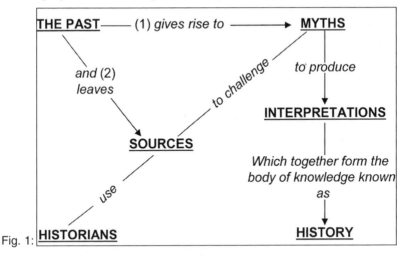

Fig. 1:

The other, contrasting, Popular Approach is also a continuous and never ending process. However, the most important difference is that during its continuous re-assessment and re-examination, the central features of myths are seldom ever challenged, at least not substantially. When challenges are made they never seriously damage the basis of the myths and always serve, ultimately, to support them — albeit in the guise of 'correcting' errors or providing 'new' material. In this way myths may be re-interpreted continuously but they never change fundamentally. Another distinctive feature of this approach is that it does not deal with the past *per se* but with the past only from its own interpretative point of view, thereby reinforcing itself.

The Popular Approach, based on myth, might usefully be defined as:

> '...*a traditional story, especially one concerning the early history of a particular group of people or organization or one that explains a natural or social phenomenon.*'[5]

It too is a continuous and never ending process and might also be represented as a diagram. As can be seen this is a 'closed' system of examination, which does not introduce the elements that are an essential part of the process in the Academic Approach. (see over)

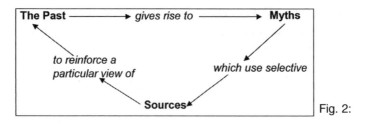

Fig. 2:

There are some specific techniques which can reveal that the work is by a practitioner of the Alternative Approach and it is worthwhile briefly outlining these here in order that they might be anticipated while considering the variety of works available.

One of the greatest difficulty in considering the work of those of the Popular or Alternative Approach is that their 'rules', if any, are never explained.[6] To explain this simply can be done by analogy. Wherever one goes in the world one expects a certain standard of training for professionals engaged in their field of expertise. Thus, when one visits a dentist in virtually every country one can be certain that the dentist concerned will have undergone internationally accepted standards of training before being permitted to practise the profession. Writing about the past is different. Not everyone who does so is a qualified historian — and just as well too, otherwise some fascinating material and insights would simply not come to the attention of the public. However, it is possible to identify certain techniques which suggest a writer is not an historian in the academic sense and which might cause problems. It is stressed here that the discussion regarding the Popular and Academic approaches in no way implies criticism. The purpose is rather to assist the reader in deciding which approach a particular author is adopting. One means to this end is to indicate particular techniques common within the Popular Approach and discuss their potential weaknesses. Throughout this book where specific examples of these techniques are used they will be identified.

Negative = positive

Using a negative to prove a positive can, at first glance, appear to be acceptable and logical. However, it is rarely explained in these terms as it is often disguised with a host of 'facts', which make the technique difficult to spot especially in a lengthy and detailed piece of writing. The technique is frequently the one employed when there is no evidence available to support a particular point of view. In essence the argument goes like this. Because there is no evidence that fugitive Knights Templar sailed to Argyll and hid there for seven years before appearing on the field of battle at Bannockburn does not mean that they did not do these things. This technique is based on a false premise — that the absence of evidence that something took place means that it could have taken (which often quickly becomes 'did take') place. This reasoning is quite common and underlies many arguments for which there is no supportive evidence. The attraction of this logic lies in the fact that it can be used to support *any* claim for which there is no evidence.

Legitimisation

Everyone wishes their work to be accepted as accurate, useful, well written and thoroughly researched — in other words that the finished article is a legitimate piece of historical writing. One method of enhancing the legitimacy of one's work is to ensure that experts, known authorities, on the subject are quoted. This form of endorsement legitimises the work even if the expert's involvement is minimal.[7] Listing the works of experts in a bibliography at the rear of a book also adds legitimacy as it implies that these works have been consulted, and I have no doubt that they would have been, although there are occasions for doubt where a crucial fact, argument or observation contained within a work listed in the bibliography is not discussed by the author in the main text.

Retrospective Application

Many people view the past from the standpoint of their own lives and experiences. This is quite natural but can be very dangerous for an untrained historian. This is because, without due care, one can impose one's own beliefs, prejudices and emotion on the past when it is quite inappropriate to do so. Additionally the use of evidence, and especially its interpretation, and applying it to the past can also lead to erroneous conclusions.

Our understanding of modern society, and our place in it, cannot be applied to the past without caution. For example, the place of children in modern society is quite different from their place in past societies. Many will be familiar with the statement: 'Children should be seen and not heard.' This concept of the child originated in the Victorian age but certainly does not apply today. Similarly, suggesting that children had the same rights and privileges in the 19th century as they do today would be equally inaccurate. Further back in time the concept of childhood hardly existed at all and children were treated merely as small adults. Simply because we, today, have knowledge and experience of today does not mean that we can apply that knowledge to the past without a great deal of thought.

This way of looking at the past does not, generally, produce 'good' history — e.g. 'A Rolls-Royce is a motor car. Motor cars existed in the past therefore in the past all motor cars were Rolls-Royces!' It is much better to investigate the past by examining contemporary evidence (that is evidence from the same time) which ought to provide us with an understanding of that period from the point of view of those who were then alive. In that way *they* tell something of their time rather than us trying to impose upon them, their society and their culture *our* beliefs, prejudices, etc. Once an understanding of the past has been obtained, comparing it with our modern experiences can, it is to be hoped, highlight significant differences. This process will often reveal why examining the past using entirely our own experiences and modern evidence is not the best way to 'see' the past. This is a most important point which shall be discussed in greater detail later with reference to the subject matter of this book. Meantime it is sufficient to note that there are a huge number of examples of the retrospective imposition of modern knowledge and experience on the past which are quite inappropriate.

Self Imposed Ignorance

The academic historian is bound to, or at least must attempt to, examine all evidence relevant to the hypotheses in question even when such evidence may be 'uncomfortable'. This part of the process has been described at the beginning of this chapter. However, during the process of research, material might not be included, or consulted, because the researcher is unaware of its existence. Investigating subjects on which a great deal has been written, such as the Knights Templar, Freemasonry and Rosslyn Chapel and related matters, means that genuine ignorance of relevant material, especially primary source material, is unlikely.

In relation to the subject matter of this book there is a great deal of material which is not used or discussed by many of the Popular School. However, the existence of such material is widely known and modern writers in particular cannot have failed to come across references to it during the course of their research. This curious situation, where the most important material is not analysed, in modern popular works raises important questions not only because it may present a distorted view to the readers but also suggests that there is another factor at work — emotion.

As has been seen earlier, the way in which some writers frame their hypotheses (if they do so at all) before conducting their research predisposes them towards certain outcomes. Here we have returned to the debate regarding 'open' and 'leading' questions. For example, the question 'What are the similarities between Rosslyn Chapel and King Solomon's Temple?' inherently means that there *are* some similarities — they merely have to be found. With such closed questions some material simply cannot be used in the research because to do so would reveal that the question was inherently biased. However, those posing closed questions must, sooner or later, confront (or be confronted with) the problem that some relevant material has not been considered. Claims by the researcher that they did not know of the importance of the material are usually unsustainable because the material *is* often of central importance and, what is more, is widely accepted as being of such importance. This defence is weak and does nothing to inspire confidence in the quality of the research.

The other, frequent, claim is that the author was unaware of the existence of the material. This defence too is weak and also undermines any reason to accept the research as rigorous and valid. One of the principal points of research is, after all, to discover and analyse all relevant sources and material and, at the very least, the most important of these. How and why is ignorance of important material used as defence? The matter of the 'closed' question aside, the claim to ignorance is considered to be better than no defence at all. However, this still fails to answer the question satisfactorily. As implied above the emotional aspect cannot be discounted. Belief is a strong emotion and the desire for one's beliefs to be proved can be almost overwhelming. The historian is trained to try to eliminate emotion from the research process. That does not mean that emotion has no part to play but where it does it ought to be clearly highlighted so that it is not disguised. The reason for this is because most of us are not able to analyse the emotions in the work of others (or not able to do so well). The powerful desire to have one's belief's supported and proved by evidence means that material which would do the exact opposite simply cannot be used. The claim of ignorance is about the only defence available in this situation. This kind of ignorance (as opposed to a genuine lack of knowledge) is what I describe as 'self imposed ignorance'. Specifically I mean those instances where it is almost impossible for a writer to be unaware of the existence of material but a decision (perhaps unconsciously) is taken not to deal with such 'unhelpful' evidence. Self imposed ignorance, by its very nature, can be difficult to spot and it is frequently only by dialogue that it is revealed. Statements, regarding material of prime importance, such as '*I did not know about that*'; '*I have not got round to reading that yet*'; '*It is too difficult to access*' or '*That has already been discussed many times*' *may* all be indicative of self imposed ignorance.

There are several pertinent examples of this which are relevant to the subjects discussed in this book. The so-called St. Clair Charters, considered in detail later, are a case in point. These manuscripts are the property of the Grand Lodge of Scotland. Dated *c*.1601 and *c*.1628 they are crucial pieces of evidence regarding the role of the St. Clair family and their alleged connection with Scottish Freemasonry. Yet not one modern exponent of the Popular Approach has examined the original documents! It may be claimed that there are other reasons for this, an inability to understand the language perhaps, but without having first viewed the documents it is difficult to see how even that claim can be legitimate.

Deliberately Imposed Ignorance

Self imposed ignorance can be, as suggested above, an unconscious act albeit one that can be anticipated and guarded against. Deliberately imposed ignorance is similar but is a conscious decision to be or to remain ignorant. This 'tactic' is used when an author knowingly wishes to present a biased view or opinion. This can be a legitimate tactic to present a view quite at odds with all other opinion in order to throw it into sharp relief — usually in order to criticise that view. In that case the writer is *acting* as wilfully ignorant in order to make a particular point. Other instances of deliberately being ignorant appear to be in order to make sensational claims on a particular subject. This is quite different from suggesting that an author who does this is being untruthful. This too is a tactic designed for a specific purpose but it is one that this writer cannot envisage an academic historian ever employing. The example below is provided for the sole reason of allowing the reader to consider this particular 'tactic' and to come to a judgement as to whether, or not, this is a case of 'self imposed ignorance' or 'deliberately imposed ignorance' and, if so, the intended purpose of employing the technique.[8]

'Membership of that controversial and secret Order, in all its forms, has long been an indispensable key to high office. For instance every Prime Minister in England [sic] from Walpole [1676–1745] to Ramsey [sic] MacDonald [1866–1937] in the twentieth was a Grandmaster of the Freemasons. This pattern of power was repeated throughout Europe. The same situation also existed in America where every President until John F. Kennedy, was a Freemason of high degree. This domination of power was not just restricted to the Heads of State but also permeated throughout the entire power structure of the judiciary, the police, the armed services and civil administration throughout the Western World. And, in this manner,

Freemasonry continues to exercise profound influence, on all aspects of society today.'[9]

This means that, according to this author, from the time Robert Walpole entered Parliament in 1701 until 1935 when Ramsay MacDonald ceased to be Prime Minister, the United Kingdom has had a Freemason at the head of government. This is extraordinary and in order to demonstrate the sheer scale of that claim below is a list of the names of all the Prime Ministers stated, without any suggestion of doubt, to be not only Freemasons but also Grand Masters.

	Name of 'Masonic' Prime Minister	**D.o.B.–D.o.D.**
1	Robert Walpole	1676–1745
2	Spencer Compton	1673–1743
3	Henry Pelham	*c*.1695–1754
4	Thomas Pelham-Holles	1693–1768
5	William Cavendish	1720–1764
6	James Waldegrave	1715–1763
7	John Stuart	1713–1792
8	George Grenville	1712–1770
9	Lord Charles Watson-Wentworth	1730–1782
10	William Pitt, Snr.	1708–1778
11	Augustus Henry FitzRoy	1735–1811
12	Frederick North	1732–1792
13	William Petty	1737–1805
14	William Henry Cavendish Bentinck	1738–1809
15	William Pitt, Jnr.	1759–1806
16	Henry Addington	1757–1844
17	William Wyndham Grenville	1759–1834
18	Spencer Perceval	1762–1812
19	Robert Banks Jenkinson	1770–1828
20	George Canning	1770–1827
21	Frederick John Robinson	1782–1859
22	Arthur Wellesley	1769–1852
23	Charles Grey	1764–1845
24	William Lamb	1779–1848
25	Robert Peel	1788–1850
26	John Russell	1792–1878

27	Edward Geoffrey Smith-Stanley	1799–1869
28	George Hamilton Gordon	1784–1860
29	Henry John Temple	1784–1865
30	Benjamin Disraeli	1804–1881
31	William Ewart Gladstone	1809–1898
32	Robert Arthur Talbot Gascoyne-Cecil	1830–1903
33	Archibald Philip Primrose	1847–1929
34	Arthur James Balfour	1848–1930
35	Henry Campbell-Bannerman	1836–1908
36	Herbert Henry Asquith	1852–1928
37	David Lloyd George	1863–1945
38	Andrew Bonar Law	1858–1923
39	Stanley Baldwin	1867–1947
40	J. Ramsay MacDonald	1866–1937

This means that, if the statement is correct, all of the above were Freemasons and all Britain's governments from 1721 (when Robert Walpole became Prime Minister) until 1935 when (J. Ramsay MacDonald stepped down as Prime Minister) were led by Grand Masters. Needless to say, this claim that for 215 consecutive years there was a continuous succession of Masonic Prime Ministers is simply not true.

Membership records of any organisation (except, of course actual secret societies!) are usually available to *bona fide* researchers.[10] Any historian, author, etc. knows this and all of those working in the field of Masonic research are aware that Masonic membership records are generally available. The above quote is emphatic: '*every Prime Minister in England* [*sic*] *from Walpole… to Ramsey* [*sic*] *MacDonald… was a Grandmaster*'. This statement means, if true, that during 1721–1935, Britain had governments led by Prime Ministers who were Freemasons.

Furthermore, according to the author, all 40 English [*sic*] Prime Ministers were also Grand Masters no less! This means that all of these Prime Ministers were Grand Masters of a Grand Lodge. There are only three Grand Lodges within Britain and Ireland — Scotland, Ireland and England — and the Grand Masters of each are a matter of public record.[11] The author does not state which Grand Lodge(s) these Prime Ministers were Grand Masters of, but the names of all the Grand Masters of all three Grand Lodges are well known. Needless to say, none of the 40 Prime Ministers listed above was a Grand Master of any of the three Grand Lodges.

Here 'deliberately imposed ignorance' can be seen. The author provides no supportive evidence whatsoever for any of the claims made. It must be considered doubtful, therefore, that the Masonic membership records held in Edinburgh, London and Dublin were consulted on this matter. Had that been done the quotation above could not realistically have been published. The question must be: 'What was the purpose of stating that 40 Prime Ministers of Great Britain were Freemasons?' What was the purpose in stating that each and every one of them was a Grand Master?'

The statement that no fewer than 40 consecutive Prime Ministers have been Grand Masters is nothing less than startling. For the record, only two of the above were Freemasons — The Duke of Wellington and George Canning. Neither were at any time Grand Masters of any Grand Lodge.[12] The author makes another equally startling statement, one which is equally unambiguous and without any trace of doubt — that *every* President of the United States of America up to, but not including, John F. Kennedy (1917–1963), was a Freemason of '*high degree*'. Listed below are the Presidents concerned:

	Name of 'Masonic' Presidents	Period
1	George Washington*	1789–1797
2	John Adams	1797–1801
3	Thomas Jefferson	1801–1809
4	James Madison	1809–1817
5	James Monroe*	1817–1825
6	John Q. Adams	1825–1829
7	Andrew Jackson*	1829–1837
8	Martin Van Buren	1837–1841
9	William H. Harrison	1841
10	John Tyler	1841–1845
11	James Polk*	1845–1849
12	Zachary Taylor	1849–1850
13	Millard Fillmore	1850–1853
14	Franklin Pierce	1853–1857
15	James Buchanan*	1857–1861
16	Abraham Lincoln	1861–1865
17	Andrew Johnson*	1865–1869
18	Ulysses S. Grant	1869–1877
19	Rutherford B. Hayes	1877–1881

20	James A. Garfield*	1881
21	Chester Arthur	1881–1885
22	Grover Cleveland	1885–1889
23	Benjamin Harrison	1889–1893
24	Grover Cleveland	1893–1897
25	William McKinley*	1897–1901
26	Theodore Roosevelt*	1901–1909
27	William H. Taft*	1909–1913
28	Woodrow Wilson	1913–1921
29	Warren G. Harding*	1921–1923
30	Calvin Coolidge	1923–1929
31	Herbert Hoover	1929–1933
32	Franklin D. Roosevelt*	1933–1945
33	Harry S. Truman*	1945–1953
34	Dwight Eisenhower	1953–1961
35	John F. Kennedy	1961–1963

Those who were Freemasons, although by no means all were of '*high degree*', have been indicated by an asterisk following the name. Inherent in citing these men as Freemasons is the suggestion that it is in some way bad. The statement: '*Membership of that controversial and secret Order* [Freemasonry], *in all its forms, has long been an indispensable key to high office*' perhaps provides the best clue as to the reason why the technique was used.

Self quoting
Researchers tend to become specialists in a particular field if they are involved long enough and deeply enough. The accumulation of knowledge ensures that their work can be referred to regularly as an expert source. It is almost certain that they will require to cite and to quote evidence, arguments and material they themselves have previously produced. However, it is bad practice to quote earlier supposition, speculation or mere opinion, in subsequent work, as if it was actual fact. In doing this authors are suggesting that their earlier work has been substantiated when it has not. Most people would not take the time and trouble to read the previous work to ascertain the accuracy, or otherwise, of later statements and so, in this situation, quoting one's previous work becomes self-serving.

Inter-quoting

Specialists in particular fields inevitably quote each other *because* they are specialists. This is normal practice and, as with the need to consider all relevant evidence, a writer in a particular field must attempt to consider all material produced by other specialists in the same field. This is true regardless of whether the other specialist's research supports, or otherwise, one's own research. Failure to consider such other research is considered to be a weakness. This point becomes much more acute in respect of the work of pre-eminent researchers in any particular field. When important work is not considered legitimate questions arise as to why and what purpose is served by not using important published research. This is 'cherry picking' the work of authors. This is similar to 'cherry picking' evidence — there is a strong tendency only to use evidence and arguments which support one's own views. The effects are to reinforce one particular view and to exclude material which has the potential to damage that point of view.

Closely associated with the retrospective application of modern knowledge, material and experience etc. on the past (discussed briefly above) is what I shall call 'forced contemporary evidence.' This occurs when a modern author will make a comment, observation or deduction about the past and then place it into the period under investigation. This occurs when a speculative comment is made, which is not an accepted fact, is forced into the past as if it was a contemporary fact — that is, one that originated from the time it has now been placed. One example will suffice to illustrate this point. An author claims that James II (1437–1460, b.1430) made William St. Clair of Rosslyn Hereditary Grand Master of the Scottish Masons. Another author writing about the life and times of James includes this 'fact' in his work. The 'fact' is a modern creation but now appears in the chronology of the past — it now has the appearance of being contemporary evidence. This technique means that 'contemporary evidence' can be mistakenly manufactured and often inadvertently appears to legitimately support a particular point of view. If repeated often enough and without being challenged such 'evidence' can lead to it being universally accepted as true.[13] There are a variety of examples relevant to the subject of this book which shall be discussed in succeeding chapters. Challenging the basis of a myth, 'forced contemporary evidence' being but one example of myth sustaining practice, is one of the principal duties of an historian and which has been previously explained at the beginning of this chapter.

Ignore Quoting

'Ignore quoting' is simply the implication that other sources, evidence or the work of other authors has been consulted. This can occur when material is cited in a bibliography, foot or endnotes or mentioned in promotional literature but is not used or discussed. This gives the appearance that all relevant material has been given due consideration when it has not.

Conspiracy theory

This appears occasionally in published matter on the various subjects covered by this book. It can be simply explained. The underlying assumption is that something does exist and which takes a variety of forms from the existence of a 'blood line' to physical artefacts such as the 'treasure' of the Knights Templar. No proof is produced to support the assumption as there is no need to have such evidence because there is a conspiracy at work. The conspiracy is designed to keep the existence of 'something' secret and may be a conspiracy by those who hold the secret because they do not wish their secret become public knowledge or it may be that others (often described as 'enemies' who are not named) do not wish the secret to be revealed because this would destabilise the existing order of things. Occasionally a 'secret' is revealed despite the best efforts of all concerned to stop that from happening. When no secret is revealed that is proof that there is a conspiracy at work and when a secret is revealed that is proof that there was a conspiracy which has now been revealed. This tautological argument simply means that those claiming knowledge of the existence of some secret, secret knowledge, hidden treasure or blood line etc. always have someone else to blame for their inability to produce evidence in support of their claims.

Simple errors

No one is immune from making the occasional error. It must immediately be stated that this is not a 'technique' employed by those of the Popular or Alternative approach nor is the discussion, here, of simple error a criticism in any way. It is a matter of ensuring that everyone is aware that errors do occur and must be guarded against. It is a matter of professional courtesy to point out errors in order that they may be corrected in future as well as to alert others to their existence and allowing them to be taken into account by readers of the text concerned.

Apart from typographical, grammatical and spelling errors, and like everyone else this author suffers from these just as much as anyone else, the more serious problems relate to omission or inaccurate quotation.

Selective use of sources

Another important difference between these two approaches concerns sources. The practitioners of the Academic Approach are bound to consider all relevant evidence no matter how difficult or awkward such evidence might be to various hypotheses or theories. Those who adopt the Popular Approach are not hampered in this way. Because the conclusion has already been pre-determined (that is, the myth itself is not subject to challenge) only evidence that tends to support that view is used. If other evidence is used it is with the intention of its neutralisation. Examples of this selective use of sources and evidence will become evident.

Misquoting

Similar to the selective use of material which only suits or supports one's particular point of view is the misquoting of the work of others. There is no evidence that this is done deliberately or systematically but where this has happened it can give a very misleading result (often the exact opposite of what the person being quoted intended). It noticeable that only deceased authors are misquoted and that living authors do not appear to suffer from this problem.[14] Closely allied to misquoting is 'non-quoting' — that is, ignoring the work of living authors. Not using such work (which is very often the result of recent research on a subject) means that contradictions are created and that the writing of those holding to the Alternative Approach is often out of date.

Speculation into Fact

Speculating about the past is a part of writing about the past — after all that is essentially what a hypothesis or theory is (albeit refined to exclude the impossible and fantastic). Here, however, I am referring to how a speculation can be turned into a fact without anything else being involved in that process. This too is difficult to spot as the change from speculation to fact can be subtle. The change may go unnoticed because very few words are used to make the change. The change can also be obscured when a great many words are used. Once an erroneous 'fact' has been created this way it is often repeated as being true, using some, or all, of the techniques mentioned above. The most obvious occasion when this is done is where a writer will speculate often quite legitimately but will later state something like 'as we have previously shown' etc. and as few people go back to check this can be difficult to spot. If the 'fact' refers to a speculation in another book then the difficulty in checking is increased. There are a few examples of this which will be mentioned later in the book.

Methodology

It is important that authors explain the historiographical methods being used. One general criticism of some of those who use the Alternative or Popular Approach to Masonic historiography is that they rarely explain their methods. Consequently, that approach can, unwittingly, be perceived to be academic history.

All these techniques or devices are best illustrated using actual examples and rather than repeat these here they will be highlighted at the appropriate point in the text.

The Hypotheses

Following this slight digression I now wish to make the point of this book very clear by stating the principal hypothesis. This book discusses some Scottish aspects of a popular myth of the origins of Freemasonry from a Scottish perspective and seeks to examine the following question:

> *'What evidence is there that members of the medieval Order of KT fled from France and settled in Scotland, assisted Robert the Bruce at the Battle of Bannockburn (1314) and, that as a reward for their services, he created an 'underground organisation' — Freemasonry — within which they could hide their true identity and preserve their "treasure" and esoteric knowledge?'*

There are two subsidiary, but very important, questions:

> *'What part, if any, did the St. Clair family and Rosslyn Chapel play in the alleged continuance of the KT (in the guise of being Freemasons) in Scotland?'* And,

> *'Is there any other extant physical evidence which supports any of the above?'*

Summary of the Main Elements of the Modern Myth:

What follows is therefore an examination and discussion of these questions (the hypothesis) and, to make it clear what exactly they are intended to address, below are the principal elements of the modern myth to be examined:

- Some members of the KT had foreknowledge of the impending mass arrest of the KT in France (13 October 1307) ordered by the King of France, Philip IV (1285-1314, b.1268).
- Having been so forewarned these KT fled to La Rochelle where the KT fleet (occasionally stated to be 18 ships) lay at anchor. The ships left the harbour before the arrests took place taking with them the KT 'treasure'. The fleet divided into two groups: one sailed to Portugal and the other to the west coast of Scotland, specifically Argyll. A later elaboration of the myth suggests that this second group also divided and, in addition to Argyll, the other section had Midlothian as its destination.
- The fugitive KT came to Scotland because Robert I (1306–1329, b. 1274) had been excommunicated by Pope Clement V (1305–1314, b. 1264), and, therefore, Papal law did not apply in Scotland.
- Argyll was chosen as a destination because it was an isolated and thinly populated part of Scotland where fugitives could easily hide. Midlothian was chosen because the main KT Preceptory in Scotland was at Ballantradoch.[15]
- At the Battle of Bannockburn these fugitives appeared at a crucial point in the fighting and swung the balance in favour of the Scottish army. The KT intervened in support of Robert I because he had given them sanctuary. By their timely intervention Scotland obtained its independence.
- Following Bannockburn Robert I wished his newly independent country to be re-admitted into European Christendom but could not do so whilst 'heretic' KT were at large in Scotland. He resorted to the subterfuge of creating the Order of Freemasonry (variously described as 'the Royal Order of Scotland', the 'Knights of Heredom' or 'Freemasonry') into which the medieval KT integrated discreetly. In this way he could claim that the KT no longer existed in Scotland.
- As Robert I created, for fugitive KT in Scotland, the Order of Freemasonry, modern Freemasonry is directly descended from those fugitive KT.
- This continuation from 1314 was encouraged by the Sinclair family who built Rosslyn Chapel, Midlothian, in order to house the KT 'treasure' brought to Scotland in 1307.[16]
- There is extant physical evidence of the existence of fugitive KT in Scotland from 1307.

The main purpose of this book is to examine the Popular or Alternative view of the origins of Freemasonry, but all should be aware that there are other hypotheses and theories relating to this subject and these must be, albeit very briefly, detailed here if for no other reason than for comparison purposes and to facilitate the reader in investigating these further.[17]

The King Solomon's Temple Theory

The Temple built (*c*.962-*c*.959 BC) by King Solomon as related in 1 Kings Ch. 5-8 and 2 Chronicles Ch. 3 of the Old Testament features prominently within Freemasonry. This theory (more correctly, a hypotheses) argues that King Solomon's Temple was the first stone building in history and was built by stonemasons who later metamorphosed into Freemasons. This is based on the assumption that the people and events are accurately portrayed within Kings and Chronicles and as they are only main source (other than Masonic lore itself) for this theory, it has advanced little, until that is, it became part of the KT myth which is the principal subject of this book.

The Transition or Guild Theory

This theory is probably the most powerful alternative to that promoted by the Popular or Alternative writers. In essence it is claimed that stonemasons, all over Europe, who were responsible for building the great cathedrals of the Middle Ages were organised into guilds (either by the church, kings or themselves) which offered some protection from the vagaries of life. As most stonemasons were illiterate, exactly how they had the ability to make some of the western world's most awe inspiring buildings was seen by many as verging on the miraculous. Stonemasons working in all corners of the continent, frequently travelling from building site to building site, must have had some secret knowledge known only to themselves. This secret knowledge, handed down from generation to generation over eons of time allowed them not only to build the great cathedrals of Europe but also to obtain work even in places where they were not known. In dismissing this theory two popular authors explained:

> "… *despite rigorous searching, we were completely unable to find any records to show that medieval stonemasons' guilds existed at all in England. Had they existed we felt certain that some trace would still remain; in many European countries they certainly did exist and there is plenty of evidence of their activities. Gould's History of Freemasonry*

carries page after page of crests of the guilds of stonemasons across Europe, but none is British!"[18]

The book in which this statement appears deals in large measure with Scotland and Scottish Freemasonry. The idea that English history is British history can lead to some major errors, as in this instance.[19] A least one Scottish stonemason's Incorporation continues to exist and has a continuous recorded existence since it came into being during the 15th century.[20] Although now essentially charitable institutions, their written records are a valuable source of information. It will be a revelation therefore to some that Scottish stonemasons' Incoporations have a recorded existence since 1475 and that their Incorporations have a continous existence to this day.[21]

The first written records of a Scottish Lodge commence in January 1599.[22] These are the Minute Books of Lodge Aitcheson's Haven and are the records of a stonemasons' Lodge.[23] Other early Scottish Lodge records include, for example, those of the Lodge of Edinburgh (Mary's Chapel), No.1, dating from July 1599.[24]

During the 17th century the 'Mason Word' was referred to on a number of occasions.[25] These references, Masonic or not, make no mention of the KT. Even if there were some connection with the medieval Order of KT these records would be unlikely to mention them given the paucity of detail they contain. However, according to the myth at least, these early lodges were direct descendants of the KT, yet there is nothing within their records to support that view. More damaging for the maintenance of the myth is that the analysis of the membership records of such lodges shows that the stonemason members were ordinary working men who were illiterate, or semi-literate, and hardly likely to form the ideal repository of secret knowledge and to be guardians of sacred treasure for the previous 292 years.[26]

The range of material, good and bad, relating to Freemasonry, the Knights Templar, Rosslyn Chapel, etc. is huge and it is not possible for every book and article to be discussed here. Instead I have attempted to show one way that material might be assessed — by examining the methods and techniques used by writers. Even this attempt to allow for such assessments to be made must be acknowledged as an elementary one. A comprehensive account as to how writing about the past can be critically analysed would take a book on that subject alone.

Having briefly looked at how the two main groups (the Alternative and the Academic Approaches) write about the past and some of the methods used, the hypothesis that this book seeks to examine has been stated in some detail. In order to make clear what the hypothesis is to examine, the main elements of the myth have been given in some detail but shall be expanded upon during the relevant discussion.

All myths have a starting point and this book is an attempt to find when this particular myth came into being and to trace its development. Because the myth claims that there is a link between the Medieval Order of the Knights Templar and Freemasonry in Scotland (as detailed above) it is Scottish Masonic sources that are examined for evidence of such a link. What did past generations of Scottish Freemasons consider their origins to be? By analysing their writing, their rituals and their records light may be shed on where the alleged link between the KT and Freemasonry first appeared and hopefully suggest *why* it was created. However, the evidence to be examined will not be limited solely to Masonic material.

Lastly, although this book is intended to examine one particular theory of origin — that Freemasonry derives from the medieval Order of Knights Templar — other competing theories have been very briefly mentioned, not for the purpose of any detailed analysis but merely to highlight their existence and because some may wish to read further in that regard.

The myth is analysed in order not to destroy it but to understand it and its dynamics. In the process, hopefully, it may be possible to gain an insight to the origins of Freemasonry and the motives of some key individuals responsible for much of what has been written about Freemasonry.

[1] *The Power of Myth*. Joseph Campbell. 1988.

[2] One of the first, and most popular of these was *The Temple and The Lodge* by Michael Baigent and Richard Leigh. 1989

[3] *The Nature of History, The,* Marwick, Arthur, 3rd edn. (Macmillan, 1989), p. 13.

[4] *The Nature of History, The,* Marwick, Arthur, 3rd edn. (Macmillan, 1989), p. 13.

[5] *After* Marwick.

[6] I am aware that this is a generalisation.

[7] I have been thanked several times, in print, for answering 'yes' to a question!

[8] It must be stressed that this example was chosen for its powerful illustration of this point and as an academic exercise rather than any partiality.

[9] *Templar Legacy and the Masonic Inheritance within Rosslyn Chapel, The,* Wallace-Murphy, T., p. 31.

[10] This is one reason why describing Freemasonry as a secret society is grossly inaccurate.

[11] The correct title of the Grand Master of the Grand Lodge of Scotland is Grand Master Mason.

[12] As a young man, the Duke of Wellington was initated in to Freemasonry, when in Ireland. It meant so much to him that when he was asked in the 1820s if he was a Freemason he replied that he could not remember! Canning died after being Prime Minister for only 6 months. He was a member of two Lodges in London (the Lodge of Antiquity, No.2 and Royal Somerset House and Inverness Lodge, No.4) but was not particularly active.

[13] A similar and quite legitimate technique (because the 'forcing' of the evidence is acknowledged) is to be found in *The Knights Templar Chronology* by George Smart.

[141] To prove that this is a frequent occurrence within the Alternative Approach would require a detailed analysis which is beyond the scope of this work.

[15] Now Temple (Midlothian). The existing church and graveyard are not medieval.

[16] The incorporation of the Sinclair family and Rosslyn Chapel into the myth is relatively recent and a detailed discussion of those, and other, modern facets cannot be undertaken here, although it is hoped that a full examination will be presented at a later date.

[17] Freemasons who are interested in Masonic research in general may wish to consider joining the Correspondence Circle of Quatuor Coronati Lodge, No.2076, the Premier Lodge of Research in the world.

[18] *The Hiram Key*, by Knight, C. and Lomas R. 1996. p. 20.

[19] In relation to Freemasonry, Prof. David Stevenson describes this way of looking at history as 'Anglo-centric'.

[20] In Scotland such Guilds are typically referred to as Incorporations. The continued use of the term 'Guild' by authors demonstrates their ignorance of Scottish historical terminology. The Trades House of Glasgow is the meeting place of not only the Incorporation of Masons but many others including Baxters, Wobsters, Fleshers, etc.

[21] The Lodge of Edinburgh is mentioned in this year and continues to meet in the city.

[22] This later became a Masonic Lodge in the modern sense.

[23] There is a translation of parts of the early minutes of this lodge on the Grand Lodge of Scotland website at www.grandlodgescotland.com

[24] The records of Lodge Mother Kilwinning, No. 0, do not commence until 1642 but that Lodge was known also to have existed from at least 1599 as evidenced by the Second Schaw Statute of 28 December 1599.

[25] *The First Freemasons*

Chapter 2
18th Century and Earlier

The Grand Lodge Era

Although work on Rosslyn Chapel began in 1446 there was no published material available before the short description and engraving by John Slezer in 1693.[1,2] The work of Father Hay (see below) was not generally available until Maidment printed and published Hay's work in 1835.[3]

Father Richard A. Hay (1661–c.1736)

About 1690 Father Richard Augustine Hay, Prior of St. Pierremont, whose widowed mother, Jean Spottiswood, married (*c.*1667) James St. Clair of Rosslyn, examined all that family's records then held in Rosslyn Castle. He was the arch-propagandist of the Sinclair family and credited them with the most obscure titles and meticulously copied the family's charters, deeds and other transactions. The results of his labours are contained within three large manuscript volumes.[4] Hay does not appear to have been a Freemason. He did not reproduce any evidence suggesting a connection between the family and the KT nor did he ever mention Freemasonry. When one is aware that he also wrote a very brief, sympathetic, history of the medieval KT one can only conclude there was evidently no connection for him to find.[5] What Hay did was bring to light two documents which, at first glance, had much to do with Scottish Freemasonry and the Sinclair family. In their totality these charters, deeds and petitions, etc. detail the family's activities from *c.*1067, when one '*Sir William Sinclare, second son to Woldonius or Wildernus in France*' arrived in Scotland, until the time of being written, *c.* 1700. These MSS were edited and published, anonymously, by James Maidment (?1795–1879) in 1835.[6] It is the work of Hay that provided the base on which the modern myth was created and his work continues to be quoted today as a source of evidence, and proof, for the involvement of the Sinclair family with Scottish Freemasonry and the KT.

Hay's work is that of a propagandist. He elevates the Sinclair family to the highest levels of Scottish society. This he does by reproducing the various family charters and deeds in support of his claims on behalf of the family.[7] The accuracy of his claims are not for debate here but rather the use to which his material has been put must be considered. The charters transcribed by Hay include one, for example, entitled: '*Charta Walteri de Maleville de Temple Land*'. This charter concerns land, called Tempelland, belonging to (c.1290) Walter, son of Stephen de Maleville, and now being transferred to Lord William de Saint Clair.[8] The use of material which mentions KT from a source so intimately concerned with the Sinclairs without translation and with no regard to the historical context could so easily lead to incorrect conclusions. (See pages 85, 103-104 and 287-288.)

However, Hay's most significant contribution to the history of Scottish Freemasonry is his revelation of the existence of the so-called 'St. Clair Charters' (Hay entitles them both: *Charter[s] granted by the Masons to William Saintclair*) of c.1601 and 1628.[9] In fact these are letters, not charters, and Hay's description of them as charters is most unfortunate as this carries misleading connotations of legitimacy and authority. These letters are, in effect, 'begging' letters and provide the first link of the Sinclair family, not with Freemasonry, but with stonemasons of early 17th century Scotland. Curiously Hay makes nothing of these 'charters', simply copying them without comment — an indication perhaps of their perceived value and importance in relation to the other documents he transcribed. The 'charters' were used at the formation of the Grand Lodge of Scotland, in 1736, to enhance the antiquity of the Scottish Craft and therefore Grand Lodge's pedigree. It did so in a novel way. Those responsible for the creation of the new Grand Lodge were well aware that Grand Lodges had been formed in England 19 years previously and 11 years earlier in Ireland. Hay's work brought to the attention of Scottish Freemasons the existence of these 'charters', which appeared to prove a connection with an earlier period of Scottish history. In order to understand the attraction in using these documents in this way we must first consider what the charters actually are and what was their purpose.[10]

The document dated c.1601 (Plate 1) begins by stating that the masons (that is stonemasons) of Scotland, with the consent of the King's Master of Work, William Schaw (c.1550-1602), acknowledge that they (the masons) had long recognised the Sinclairs of Roslin to be their *'Patrons and Protectors'*.[11] (Appendix IV) It is explained that because of their negligence masons have allowed that association to lapse and that by this letter they hope to re-instate the family once again as their *'Patrons and Protectors'*. This lapse means that the hereditary 'line' had been broken and further indicates just how important both parties considered it to be — assuming of course that it ever existed. The masons are candid about the motive for their request — they cannot go to court to have internal disputes resolved because of their poverty and the time the legal system takes to reach a judgment. They are asking William St Clair of Roslin to become their *'patrone and judge'*; in other words they wish him to become the arbitrator of their internal disputes. The writers of the document use flattery and a little emotional blackmail to try to create the sympathy that they hope will convince Sinclair to agree. It said by these stonemasons, and no one else, that they ask Sinclair to become their patron and protector and that this position is hereditary to all his heirs. The letter bears the signatures of William Schaw (as Master of Work) and representatives of five stonemasons' Lodges.

In 1628 the stonemasons of Scotland again sought a patron and protector from the family. A second letter was addressed to William Sinclair, the son of the Sinclair addressed in the first letter. (Plate 2) This document is essentially the same as the earlier one, using much the same language. (Appendix V) It is twice the length of the former and it is twice as repetitious. This document repeats much of the first, especially the theme that the Sinclair family was considered by *'masons'* (stonemasons) to be their *'Patrons and Protectors'*, and that, again, through their own negligence that patronage had been allowed to lapse. Once again it is not the alleged *'Hereditary Patron'*, William Sinclair, who is seeking to re-assert the family's 'rights'. This perhaps indicates just how important the Sinclair family considered this position.

However, the differences between the two documents demonstrate that, even at this very early stage, changes and elaborations were being made in order to support a particular interpretation of the past, in this instance the past as it was desired to be — by Scottish stonemasons. It is alleged that:

'... *they* [the Sinclair family] *had letters of protection and other rights granted by his Majesty's most noble progenitors of worthy memory together with sundry others of the Lairds of Roslin his writings were burnt in a flame of fire within the Castle of Roslin in an* [*sic*] . . . [blank].'[12] (Translated)

The stonemasons make two claims:

- That a Scottish monarch had granted 'letters of protection' of stonemasons to the Sinclair family.
- That these 'letters of protection' had been destroyed by fire.

These claims are embellishments. They are not mentioned in the first letter to Sinclair. The name of the monarch who allegedly granted these rights is not mentioned nor is a date provided. The 'rights' allegedly so granted are not specified — something unheard of given that that is exactly the intention of such 'charters.' The fire that consumed the *'letters of protection'* is not mentioned in the first document (*c*.1601). A space has been left for the date of the fire, suggesting that the date was unknown, or more probably, that the writers had no wish to be too specific.

Internal evidence reveals that these MSS cannot be considered to be charters in the accepted sense. The stonemasons of Scotland sought out William Sinclair and it was they who asked him to take on the duties of arbitrator, or using their terminology *'Patron and Protector'; 'patron and protector and overseer'; 'patrone and judge'.*[13] Sinclair is to receive nothing in return. He is not described as a Grand Master and there is no suggestion that he is expected to join a stonemasons' lodge. He is, in effect, an outsider whose duties are simple and clear and which are set out in the document. This letter has nothing to do with a charter or deed from a monarch, the allusion to the past involvement of the family with stonemasons is vague and again, it is stonemasons, not the Sinclair family, who claim such a connection — *'…from aige to aige it has been observit amangis that the Lairds of Rosling has ever been Patrons and Protectors…'* [from age to age it has been observed amongst us that the Lairds of Roslin have always been Patrons and Protectors — Trans.]. There is no indication in these letters, or elsewhere, that the Sinclairs of Rosslyn knew of, or even acknowledged, the stonemasons' claim that they were arbiters of the internal disputes of stonemasons. The letters say nothing whatsoever about Freemasonry.

A great deal has been made of these documents with little consideration given to what they mean in their historical context. Many quote them, or refer to them, without any analysis. The first document reveals that it was stonemasons, not the Sinclair family, who considered the family to have hereditary rights as *'Patrons and Protectors'.* From the first then, there are major problems in accepting the 'charters' at face value. If the Sinclairs were, by *c*.1601, already hereditary Patrons of stonemasons it was they who had forgotten their duties. It required a letter to bring their 'negligence' to the family's attention. The stonemasons do so rather adroitly, claiming that it was their negligence, not the family's. There is nothing to suggest any connection between the Sinclair family and Freemasonry or that Sinclair was a 'Grand Master', nor are there any references to stonemasons' lodges or Sinclair's involvement with any such lodges. The reasons for the letter, principally the stonemasons' need for an arbiter of their internal disputes (a *'Patrone'*) is ignored. The stonemasons make it obvious a Patron is needed to save the time and expense of more normal methods of resolving disputes — action in courts of law. The documents were written by stonemasons, for stonemasons; the content is therefore biased and their interpretation should be considered accordingly.

When four Edinburgh Lodges sought to form a Grand Lodge for Scotland they not unreasonably looked for relevant documents much as Anderson and Desaguliers had done when establishing the Grand Lodge of England, in 1717, and which culminated in the *'The Constitutions of the Free-Masons'* (1723).[14, 15] (Plate 3) (Hereinafter described as the *Constitutions*) The St. Clair 'Charters' were a boon to those who sought to form a Grand Lodge as they apparently provided a lineage stretching back almost 140 years earlier. One might suspect that, if for no other reason, the documents were accepted uncritically because they served the purpose of providing an appearance of antiquity which otherwise would have been lacking.

James Anderson (*c*.1678–1739)

The first published evidence of the presence of the myth, and its development, in relation to Scotland, is contained within the *Constitutions* of 1723. Anderson was born in Aberdeen and his father was Master and Secretary of the Lodge there, a number of times.[16] Anderson was, therefore, brought up in a household with strong links to the local lodge which had existed prior to his birth and continued after he had settled in London. As yet, it is not known if he was a member of the Lodge of Aberdeen, as the early records could not be examined at the time of writing. His *Constitutions* for the nascent Grand Lodge of England contain information for the regulation of lodges, songs and music and 48 pages devoted to a fantastic history of 'Masonry'.[17, 18] The Dedication to the Duke of Montagu, then Grand Master, states:

'I need not tell your Grace what Pains our Learned Author has taken in compiling and digesting this Book from the old Records, and how accurately he has compar'd and made every thing agreeable to History and Chronology, so as to render these New Constitutions as just and exact Account of Masonry from the Beginning of the World to your Grace's Mastership.

J. T. Desaguliers
Deputy Grand-Master'

Anderson and Desaguliers, therefore, claim authentic sources for the 'history' which commences: '*Adam, our first Parent, created after the Image of God, the great Architect of the Universe...*' and traces the development of Freemasonry through the Old Testament, mentioning important building projects such as the Tower of Babel, King Solomon's Temple and the Hanging Gardens of Babylon. Anderson follows the dispersion of Freemasonry throughout the Greek and Roman empires, the latter bringing it to southern England. Thereafter, Freemasonry was patronised by the Anglo-Saxon Kings and subsequently by the Normans. From then he traces those kings (i.e. Athelstan (*fl*.924–939), and Henry VI (1422–1461 and 1470–1471, b.1421) who either were Grand Masters or who 'patronised' the craft of Freemasonry, mentioning, for example, Charles I (1625–1649, b.1600) — patron of Inigo Jones (1573–1652) and also a Grand Master; Charles II (1660–1685, b.1630) — an '*Accepted Free-Mason*' — and William III (of Orange) (1689–1702, b.1650) ('*who by most is reckon'd a Free-Mason*').

He devotes only two pages to 'Masonry' in Scotland but since he was producing his book for the Grand Lodge of England his limited references to Scotland are unsurprising, i.e.:

'*The Kings of Scotland very much encouraged the Royal Art; from the earliest Times down to the Union of the Crowns, as appears by the Remains of glorious buildings in that ancient Kingdom, and by the Lodges there kept up without Interruption many hundred Years, the records and Traditions of which testify the great Respect of those Kings to this honourable Fraternity, who gave always pregnant Evidence of their Love and Loyalty, from whence sprung among the old Toast among Scots Masons, viz, God Bless the King and the Craft!*'

'*Nor was the royal Example neglected by the Nobility, Gentry and Clergy of Scotland, who join'd in every thing for the good of the Craft and Brotherhood, the Kings being often the Grand Masters, until, among other things, the Masons of Scotland were impower'd to have **a certain fix'd Grand Master** and Grand Warden, who had a Salary from the Crown, and also an acknowledgement from every New Brother in the Kingdom at Entrance, **whose Business was not only to regulate what might happen amiss in the Brotherhood, but also to hear and finally determine all Controversies between Mason and Lord, to punish the mason, if he deserv'd it, and to oblige both to equitable Terms: At which Hearings, if***

the Grand Master was absent (who was always nobly born) the Grand Warden presided. *This Privilege remain'd till the Civil Wars* [1642–1651], *but is now obsolete; nor can it well be receive'd until the King becomes a Mason, because it was not actually exerted at the Union of the Kingdoms* [1707].'[19]

In 1721 Anderson had been asked by the Grand Lodge of England to '. . . *digest the old Gothic Constitutions in a new and better method'* which resulted in the *Constitutions* of 1723, and the part, above, relating to Scotland indicates that Anderson may have had access to, or was aware of, the 'charters' transcribed by Hay. Those parts, above, in bold type have strong resemblance to the tone and sense of the 'charters'.

There is more than a little suggestion of pride in being Scottish as Anderson specifically links Scotland with the preservation of '*true Masonry*', in Scotland, until it could be revived in England. The revival of 'Masonry', in England, was instigated by a '*Mason King'* — James VI of Scotland (James I of Great Britain) (reigned 1567–1625 Scotland, and Great Britain 1603–1625, b.1566). Anderson comments:

'*Yet the great Care that the Scots took of true Masonry proved afterwards very useful to England; for the learned and magnanimous Queen Elizabeth,* [of England 1558–1603, b.1533] *who encourag'd other Arts, discourag'd this; because, being a Woman, she could not be made a Mason, tho', as other great Women, she might have much employ'd Masons, like Semiramis and Artemisia.*

Upon her Demise, King James VI of Scotland, succeeding to the Crown of England, being a Mason King, reviv'd the English Lodges; and as he was the First King of Great Britain, he was also the First Prince in the World that recover'd the Roman Architecture . . .'[20]

These pages represent the earliest reference to Scottish 'Masonry'. Anderson's brief, but emphatic, reference to the importance of Scotland in the origin and revival of 'Masonry' ensured that the Scottish aspect could never be entirely ignored, although its contribution would always be presented and discussed ambiguously thereafter. Anderson does not mention the KT, but he does state:

'*Nay, if it were expedient, it could be made appear, that from this ancient fraternity, the Societies or Orders of the Warlike Knights, and of the Religious too, in the process of time, did borrow many solemn Usages; for none of them were better instituted, more decently install'd, or did more sacredly observe their Laws and Charges than the Accepted Masons have done...'[21]*

It cannot be assumed that this is a reference to the KT (medieval or otherwise). It is important to note that he places Freemasonry first and that *'Orders of the Warlike Knights, and of the Religious too . . .'* borrowed from that ancient fraternity. This shows that in the early 18th century 'Masonry' was considered to have preceded chivalric and religious Orders and that it was they who had borrowed *'many solemn Usages'* from 'Masonry' rather than the other way around. This vague reference to *'Warlike Knights'* is not found in his brief piece on Scottish 'Masonry'.

Chevalier Andrew Ramsay (*c.*1687–1743)

Consider next, Ramsay's *Oration (*Appendix VIII). Ramsay, the son of a baker, was born in Ayr, Scotland. Ramsay studied at the University of Edinburgh for three years, having entered at the age of 14. Thereafter he became tutor to the two sons of the Earl of Wemyss. About 1706 he went to Flanders where he served in Marlborough's army. He met François Fénelon (1651–1715), who was Archbishop of Cambrai, in 1710. Under Fénelon's patronage Ramsay studied religion. So impressed was he with the Archbishop's liberal Catholicism he converted to the Roman Catholic faith in order to further understand the Quietest philosophy. He remained with Fénelon until his death early in 1715, moving then to Paris to become tutor to the young Duc de Chateau-Thierry (1719–1732). In this post he became a friend of the Regent, Philippe d'Orléans (1674–1723), who conferred upon him the Order of St. Lazarus and by which he was entitled to use the title Chevalier (Knight). At The Hague, in 1723, Ramsay published the *Life of Fénelon*. The following year he became tutor to the two sons of the exiled James VIII and III (1688–1766), also commonly known as the Old Pretender. The eldest son was Charles Edward Stuart (1720–1788) or the Young Pretender, and also known as 'Bonnie Prince Charlie'. The younger son was Henry Stuart (1725–1807) who later was to become Cardinal of York with whose death the Stuart line came to an end. In Rome, Ramsay was tutor to the Stuarts for 15 months. This connection, and the fact that he was a Catholic, was later used to suggest that Ramsay was intimately involved in plans to restore the Stuart monarchy in Great Britain. An offer of employment came from an unlikely source. He was invited to become tutor to William Augustus, Duke of Cumberland (1721–1765), third son of George II (1727–1760, b.1683), who was then King of Britain and was the very person who would have to be deposed if the Stuart monarchy was to be restored. Ramsay declined the offer because he did not think it proper for a Roman Catholic to take such a position in a Protestant household. This indicates high ethical standards on Ramsay's part, a stance which had a part to play in subsequent events. By 1727 he had returned to Paris where he published the very successful *Travels of Cyrus*, a work which attracted a great deal of literary acclaim. It appeared in several languages and was still in print in 1816. Following this success he returned to Britain and his work ensured that he was well received wherever he travelled including Scotland where he stayed with John Campbell, 2nd Duke of Argyll (1678–1743) at Inveraray, Argyll had led government forces at the Battle of Sheriffmuir (13 November) and although the outcome was inconclusive the forces of the Old Pretender were so demoralised that the Jacobite Rising of 1715 was effectively ended. On 12 March 1730 Ramsay was in Oxford where was elected to the Gentleman's Literary Society many members of which were Freemasons. On 16 March he was Initiated into Freemasonry in the Horn Lodge, London, now The Royal Somerset and Inverness Lodge, No.4. A report appeared in the London Evening Post for 17 March as follows:

> '*On Monday night last at the Horn Lodge in the Palace Yard, Westminster (whereof his Grace the Duke of Richmond* [? — 1750 *is Master] there was a numerous appearance of persons of distinction; at which time the Marquis of Beaumont, eldest son and heir apparent to his Grace the Duke of Roxburghe, Earl Kerr of Wakefield, a Peer of Great Britain; Sir Francis Henry Drake, Bart., the Marquis de Quesne; Thomas Powell of Nanteos, Esq., the Chevalier Ramsay; and Dr. Misanbin, were admitted members of the Ancient Society of Free and Accepted Masons.*'[22]

Ramsay does not appear to have taken any interest in Freemasonry in Scotland and all his subsequent Masonic experiences were in England and France. It should be noted that the Horn Lodge was also the Lodge of which James Anderson was a member, being recorded as such in 1723.[23] Whether or not he met Ramsay in that Lodge is not known.

Later in 1729 he was elected a Fellow of the Royal Society and the following year was awarded the degree Doctor of Civil Law although there was opposition to the award because he was a Roman Catholic and had served James III, the Old Pretender. When put to a vote he was accepted by 85 to 17. He became the first Roman Catholic since the English Reformation (1535) to receive a degree at Oxford. On his return to France he took up a position as intendent of the Prince of Turenne at Pointise.[24]

Thus far nothing in Ramsay's life was sufficiently remarkable to merit his present Masonic reputation. His fame, or infamy, depending on one's point of view, is due to what is now commonly referred to as '*Ramsay's Oration*'.

This was allegedly given at a meeting of the Grand Lodge of France in 1737 although many now consider this to be unlikely.[25, 26] However, the *Oration* still exists in two forms and the fact that it was intended to be given, if not actually given, before that Grand Lodge, has ensured its importance in Masonic history.[27] In his *Oration* Ramsay seems to be trying to improve Freemasonry's appeal to the upper strata of French society who would have found the idea of being involved in a lowly workingman's (that is a stonemason's) pastime difficult to accept, i.e.:

> '*The word Freemason must therefore not be taken in a literal, gross and material sense, as if our founders had been simple workers in stone, or merely curious geniuses who wished to perfect the arts.*'[28]

By suggesting that Freemasonry was ultimately chivalric and Christian in origin and nature it became much more acceptable to such people. Yet Ramsay too did not mention the KT. He mentions Crusaders and the Order of St. John (once). Freemasonry, according to Ramsay, existed prior to the Crusades. In this he agrees with Anderson that Freemasonry pre-existed the medieval Order of KT.

> '*Our ancestors, the crusaders, gathered together from all parts of Christendom in the Holy Land, desired thus to reunite into one sole Fraternity the individuals of all nations.*'[29]

> '*Our order, therefore, must not be considered a revival of the Bacchanals, but as an Order founded in remote antiquity, renewed in the Holy Land by our ancestors...*'[30]

> '*Our Order formed an intimate union with the Knights of St. John of Jerusalem. From that time our lodge took the name of Lodges of St. John.*

This union was made after the example set by the Israelites when they erected the second Temple who, whilst they handled the trowel and mortar with one hand, in the other held the sword and buckler.'[31]

Some have suggested that Ramsay *meant* to say KT and not Crusaders and Hospitallers (the Order of St. John). The interpretation of his words in that way seems to be due to the fact that it was in France that, within a relatively few years, the Masonic Order of KT (and some other *hauts* [high] *grades*) was born and that the romantic ideas attributed to their deeds, wealth (which was 'lost') and unfair abolition made them the natural choice for a new Masonic ceremonial. However, attempting to interpret what someone *meant* to say, i.e.: *'Ramsay made a point of stressing to the brotherhood that they were descended from the Crusader knights, which was a thinly veiled reference to the Templars'*, can be no more than speculation.[32] Even the respected and much used Masonic Encyclopaedia by Henry W. Coil perpetuates the error: ' *...the earliest known exposition of the alleged connection between Freemasonry and the Knight Templar or other Crusaders'*.[33] If Ramsay was alluding to a specific group of Crusaders one would have thought it was more likely to have been the Order of St. Lazarus of which he was a knight. Even this suggestion must be mere conjecture. The fact remains that the only reference he made was between Freemasonry and the Knights of St. John of Jerusalem — not the KT.

Ramsay also provides a Franco-Scottish connection and it too continues to be used:

' *...in Scotland, because of the close alliance between the French and the Scotch. James, Lord Stewart of Scotland,* [?–1309] *was Grand Master of a lodge established at Kilwinning, in the West of Scotland, MCCLXXXVI* [1286] *shortly after the death of Alexander III, King of Scotland,* [1249–1286, b. 1241] *and one year before John Balliol mounted the throne. This Lord received as Freemasons into his Lodge the Earls of Gloucester and Ulster, the one English, the other Irish.'*[34]

He has, in this passage, introduced one of the central elements of the myth as used by later exponents — that Kilwinning was, in the 13th century, a centre of Freemasonry. He states that Scottish, Irish and English members of the nobility were involved in Freemasonry from the outset. The flaws here are numerous and have been perpetuated to this day. The alliance with France did not exist until

1296 and up to 1286 Scotland was at relative peace, Alexander III having married the daughter of Henry III (1216–1272, b.1207) of England. The facts however were irrelevant. Ramsay was creating an antiquity of Freemasonry that, although it did not exist, appealed greatly to the aristocracy of France.

Anderson Again

In 1738 Anderson published his *New Constitutions*. Whether he had any knowledge of Ramsay's *Oration* of the previous year is unknown. In Chapter 6 he details '*Masonry in Scotland till the Union of the Crowns*' (1707) and he provides a great deal more information relating to the history of Freemasonry in Scotland than in the 1723 *Constitutions*.[35, 36] He begins by making passing reference to the Picts and Scots before beginning a specific history commencing with Fergus II in A.D. 403.[37] He then lists monarchs of Scotland, occasionally mentioning individuals who were noted for their building activities, the first being Malcolm III (*c*.1031–1093) who is mentioned thus:

> '*He built the old Church of Dunfermline, a Royal Sepulchre, and levell'd the Footstone of the old cathedral of Durham, which he richly endow'd. He fortified his Borders, Castles and seaports, as the Royal Grand Master and Patron of Arts and Sciences, till he died, A.D. 1093.*'[38]

Although Malcolm III is stated to be the first Grand Master of Scotland at least one other was stated to have 'patronised' the Craft. Anderson's use of this word is perhaps indicative of knowledge of the content of the St. Clair 'Charters'. For the purpose of clarity it is considered worth listing those named by Anderson who filled these positions.

Name	Birth–Death	Position
Malcom III	1031–1093	Grand Master
Alexander I	*c*. 1078–1124	Patron
David I	1084–1153	Grand Master
William the Lion	1143–1214	Grand Master
Henry Wardlaw, Bishop of St. Andrews	?–1440	Grand Master
James I	1394–1437	Grand Master
William Sinclair, Earl of Orkney	*c*. 1404–*c*.1484	Grand Master
William Turnbull, Bishop of Glasgow	?–1454	Grand Master
Sir Robert Cockeran	?–1482	Grand Master

Alexander, Lord Forbes	?–1491	Grand Master
William Elphinston, Bishop of Aberdeen	1431–1514	Grand Master
Gavin Dunbar, Bishop of Aberdeen	?1455–1532	Grand Master
Gavin Douglas, Bishop of Dunkeld	?1474–1522	Grand Master
George Creighton, Abbot of Holyrood House	?	Grand Master
Patrick, Earl of Lindsay (?)	?–1526	Grand Master
Sir David Lindsay	?1551–1610	Grand Master
Andrew Stewart, Lord Ochiltree	*fl.* 1548–1593	Grand Master
Sir James Sandilands, Knight of Malta	?–1579	Grand Master
Claud Hamilton, Lord Paisley	?1543–1622	Grand Master
James VI & I	1566–1625	Freemason

According to Anderson the first Grand Master of Scottish 'masons' lived in the early 11th century, almost a hundred years before the institution of the medieval Order of KT.

Robert I (1274–1329) has been used as a major figure in the Popular Approach to the history of Scottish Freemasonry. His involvement will be discussed in more detail later. However, as Anderson was the first to provide a 'history' of Freemasonry it is appropriate to repeat here what he has to say about this Scottish monarch:

> '*Robert I. Bruce fled to Scotland. And was crown'd 1306 And after many sore Conflicts, he totally routed King Edward II.* [1307–1327, b.1284] *of England at Bannockburn, A.D. 1314. obtain'd a honourable Peace, and died illustrious, A.D. 1329.*'[39]

> '*During the Competition,* [for the crown] *Masonry was neglected; but after the Wars, King Robert I. Bruce, having settled his Kingdom, forthwith employ'd the Craft in repairing the castles, Palaces and Houses; and the Nobility and Clergy follow'd his Example till he died, A.D. 1329.*'[40]

Also important is the reference to William Sinclair (*c.*1404–*c.*1480), Earl of Orkney:

> '*In this reign James II* [1430–1460)] *William Sinclair the great earl of Orkney and Caithness was Grand Master, and built Roslin Chapel near*

> *Edinburgh, a Master Piece of the best Gothic, A.D. 1441. next Bishop*
> *Turnbull of Glasgow, who founded the University there, A.D. 1454.*'[41]

However, note should be taken that Anderson refers only to Sinclair as one in a succession of Grand Masters and who only served in this mythical capacity for a few years.

The *Constitutions* of 1723 and 1738 are the first printed 'histories' of Freemasonry and although both contain large amounts of fiction the different treatment of the history of Scottish 'Masonry' in the two editions is striking. The 1723 edition is a generalised account, e.g. *'The Kings of Scotland very much encouraged the Royal Art . . .'* and does not provide the name of any individual king. William Sinclair, Earl of Orkney, is not mentioned. It does, however, contain the seed of part of the future myth in stating that the 'Masons' of Scotland had a *'fix'd Grand Master and Grand Warden who had a Salary from the Crown'*. This is the earliest suggestion that there was a Grand Master of Scottish Freemasons and that he was an 'employee' of the monarch. The 1738 *New Constitutions* provides more detailed information, even although almost all is again imaginative. The detailed, chronological, account of 'Masonry' in Scotland beginning with Fergus II, maintains that 'Masonry' pre-dated the establishment of the medieval Order of KT, and for the first time gives a list of Grand Masters of Scottish Freemasonry one of whom was William Sinclair, seventh in the list of twenty. It is difficult to ignore the fact that, in 1736, the Grand Lodge of Scotland had William St. Clair of Rosslyn as its first Grand Master something of which Anderson would have been aware. A more detailed discussion of the role of the Sinclair family and Rosslyn Chapel is provided in chapters 4 and 6.

Early Royal Order

The origins of the Royal Order of Scotland are obscure and have been explored and discussed in detail elsewhere.[42] It is appropriate here to mention briefly that part of the Order's traditional history as it has relevance to the myth presently under examination. The late Brother Robert S. Lindsay in his history *The Royal Order of Scotland* points out that for the first 26 years of its life, the Order (1741–1767) made no reference to Robert I or the Battle of Bannockburn.[43] The King of Scots was recognised as being the hereditary Grand Master of the Order but no particular monarch was named. Laws drawn up on the 5 January 1767 changed this position:

*'The Election of these Officers shall be annually upon the fourth day of
July being the Anniversary of the Battle of Bannockburn, fought anno
1314, after which King Robert Bruce held a Grand Lodge of this Order
and created several Knights upon or near the Field of Battle as he did
afterwards many more at Kilwinning. This was the beginning of the Bruce
tradition . . .'*[44]

At this time the Jacobite rising of 1745 was still fresh in the memory of many and
the choice of Bruce as one of the individuals most associated with Scotland's
independence (seen by many as having been lost at the Union of Parliaments in
1707) might be considered to be 'cocking a snook' at the authorities that
vigorously enforced laws which sought to eliminate some of Scotland's more
obvious cultural differences (e.g. the wearing of tartan, the playing of bagpipes,
etc.).[45] The Order appears to have had a fairly healthy and active life until *c*.1788
when the first signs of decline are noted. The Order was virtually moribund
between 1794 and 1839.[46]

Pocket Companions and other Publications

Pirated copies of Anderson's 1723 *Constitutions* were in circulation from at least
1735, beginning with Smith's *Pocket Companion*, London (1735). At the
formation of the Grand Lodge of Scotland Office-bearers were supplied with
copies of this for their guidance. The same work was published in Dublin, also in
1735, and there was a re-issue of Smith's book by Torbuck, London (1736). A
second edition was published in 1738. These pirated copies may have been one of
the reasons for Anderson's production of the 1738 edition. This also reproduced
the pamphlet *'Defence of Masonry, published A.D.1730. occasioned by a
Pamphlet call'd Masonry Dissected'*, in response to the exposure by Samuel
Pritchard (1730) suggesting that Anderson had another motive for the new edition
of his *Constitutions*. Such pirated copies, or *'Pocket Companions'*, were common
during the 18th century. It was obviously a lucrative market and anything to do
with Freemasonry easily sold.

In 1752 the first 'Scottish' *Pocket Companion* was published by W. Cheyne
(Edinburgh).[47] (Plate 4). This is nothing other than a copy of Anderson's
Constitutions but at least the printer is unashamed and 'up front' about it for in the
Preface he states:

'At the Desire of a great many of the Brethren this History was comprised,

(which, for the most Part, is extracted from Dr. Anderson's Constitution-Book).'

What is surprising is that Cheyne makes no mention of Scottish Masonic history and omits even Anderson's original limited references. The only concession to Scotland is the inclusion of '*An alphabetical list of the Lodges that are in the Roll of the Grand Lodge of Scotland.*'[48] This again suggests that the accepted view of the history of Freemasonry in Britain and Ireland was so widely understood that Cheyne had no need to create a distinctively Scottish version of Masonic history.

As late as 1759 a *Pocket Companion* published in England by J. Scott (a third edition) makes no reference to Scotland, which, together with Cheyne's similar omission, suggests that a Scottish Masonic history had not yet been established although was probably in the process of being created. (Plate 5)

It is not until 1761 that we find the first reference, in Scotland, to Scotland and its Masonic history. Ruddiman, Auld and Company (Edinburgh), initially follows Anderson's 1738 version of Scottish history beginning with the Picts (AD 297–AD 840) but the writer quickly moves on to a more detailed history. The author states: '*The Fraternity of Free-Masons in Scotland always owned their King and Sovereign as their Grand Master.*'[49] The writer then claims that, prior to 1441, kings of Scotland were Grand Masters of the Craft.[50] When they were not, they appointed one of the Brethren as a Deputy. He states that James I (1406–1437, b.1394) was a '*Royal Grand Master*'. The narrative then proceeds:

1441. '*William St. Clair Earl of Orkney and Caithness, Baron of Roslin, etc, etc, got a grant of this office* [Grand Master] *from King James II.* [1437–1460, b.1430].'

'*By another deed of the said King James II this office was made hereditary to the said William St. Clair, and his heirs and successors in the Barony of Roslin; in which noble family, it has continued without any interruption till of late years.*'

'*They* [the Sinclair family] *held their head court (or in Mason style) assembled their Grand Lodge at Kilwinning in the West Country where it is presumed Masons first began in Scotland to hold regular and stated Lodges.*'[51]

Although Ramsay was the first to mention Kilwinning by stating that '*James, Lord Steward of Scotland, was Grand Master of a Lodge established there . . .*' in 1286, Ruddiman and Auld use Kilwinning but elevate the Sinclair family by describing them as presiding over the Grand Lodge there (e.g. they were Grand Masters) and that they had so presided since *c*.1286. The myth then is at an elementary stage of creation but even at this early stage contradictions are apparent. In this instance how could the Sinclairs be Grand Masters in 1286 if they were first appointed to this position in 1441?

Following Ruddiman and Auld's *Pocket Companion* a second edition by them was published in 1763. The same publication was printed for Alexander Donaldson of Edinburgh also in that year. Neither added anything new. Interestingly, Donaldson's book states that it was sold in his shops in London and Edinburgh. In 1765, a further edition was published by Auld and Smellie (Edinburgh). This too had nothing new to add. In 1765, an almost exact copy was published by Galbraith of Glasgow and in 1771, Peter Tait (Glasgow) published a very similar *Pocket Companion*, which repeated, with some minor variations, the same chapter on the 'history' of Scottish Freemasonry. It is clear that there was at this time a considerable demand for such works. Given the repetition of the same 'history' contained in each it might be argued that this version of the past had gained wide circulation and acceptance.

In 1769 Wellins Calcott published '*A Candid Disquisition of the Principles and Practices of the most Ancient and Honourable Society of Free and Accepted Masons;...*' (London). It contained verbatim reproduction of the chapter headed '*An Account of the Establishment of the Present Grand Lodge of Scotland from Ruddiman and Auld*'. This demonstrates that by 1769, not only in Scotland, but also in England this version of Scottish Masonic history was being disseminated. Although Donaldson's *Pocket Companion* was being sold in London by this time, Calcott may have been the first entirely English source to give a Scottish version of Masonic history.

In 1774 a small booklet entitled *An Account of the Chapel of Roslin* was published in Edinburgh by James Murray, and whilst not a '*Pocket Companion*', it demonstrates that at this time the chapel had no Masonic connotations. Only when reprinted in 1778 did the printer make a direct appeal to Freemasons although the booklet contained no Masonic references other than the dedication.[52] Written by the Episcopalian Bishop, Dr Robert Forbes (1708–1775), it provides an early description and history of the chapel. Bishop Forbes does not refer to Anderson's *Constitutions*, or any of the numerous *Pocket Companions* nor does he mention Freemasonry or KT. It was no coincidence that this second, pirated, copy was published in 1778 in order to take advantage of the market created by the death of William St. Clair of Roslin in that year. The booklet bore the dedication: *'Humbly inscribed to the Ancient Fraternity of FREE AND ACCEPTED MASONS'*. Given the large amount of material relating to the history of Scottish Freemasonry in circulation, in Scotland, at this time, the conclusion that a connection between Scottish Freemasonry, the KT and Rosslyn Chapel had yet to be invented is almost unavoidable.

William Preston (1742–1818)

Preston was born in Edinburgh and is best remembered for his *Illustrations of Masonry* (1772). So popular was this work that a total of 17 editions were published (not including modern reproductions). Although Preston was a Scot and although the first edition of *Illustrations* was published eleven years after the first Scottish 'history' of Scottish Freemasonry, he made no reference to that history. His account of the origins of Freemasonry generally follows Anderson (whom he quotes) although he begins with the Druids, rather than Adam, and charts the Grand Masters (of England) from St Alban (AD *c*.264–AD 304) to the then Grand Master (of the Premier GL of England), Robert Edward, 9th Lord Petre (1742–1801). Of interest here is the following passage:

> *'During the reign of Henry II the grand master of the Knights Templars superintended the masons, and employed them in building their Temple in Fleet Street, AD 1155. Masonry continued under the patronage of this Order till the year 1199.'*[53]

He describes the relationship between the Knights Templar and 'the masons' as that of employer and employee and nothing more. He, like many writers before and after him even to this day, confuses 'masons' (stonemasons) with 'Masonry' (Freemasonry) but importantly we can see from this reference that Preston places Masonry (Freemasonry) before the formation of the Knights Templar (*c*.1118). In this instance, their only connection with 'Masonry' was for a period of 44 years — presumably when the church was built. According to this account the employer–employee relationship was a contractual one only and ceased a long time before the medieval KT were suppressed.

William Hutchinson FSA (1732–1814)

The other author of the period that requires to be mentioned is William Hutchinson. His book *Spirit of Masonry* first published in 1775, like Preston's and Anderson's work, was officially sanctioned by the Grand Lodge of England. (Fig. 14) There are a number of references in his work that are of significance to the present discussion:

> '... all Europe was influenced with the cry and madness of an enthusiastic monk, who prompted the zealots in religion to the holy war; in which for the purpose of recovering the holy city and Judea out of the hands of the infidels, armed legions...in tens of thousands [they] poured forth from every state of Europe, to waste their blood . . .' p.180

> 'It was deemed necessary that those who took up the ensign of the cross in this enterprise, should form themselves into such societies as might secure them from spies and treacheries: and that each might know his companion . . . as well in dark as by day.' p.180

THE

SPIRIT

of

MASONRY

in

MORAL and *ELUCIDATORY*
LECTURES.

by Wm Hutchinson

The Second Edition

CARLISLE

Printed by F. Jollie

MDCCXCV.

Figs. 3 and 4: *An early Masonic use of the 'All Seeing Eye' - 1778.*

'. . . *the priests projecting the Crusades, being possessed of the mysteries of masonry, the knowledge of the ancients, and of the universal language which survived the confusion of Shinar, revived the orders and regulations of Solomon and initiated the legions therein who followed them to the Holy Land:— hence that secrecy which attended the crusaders...*' p.184

'*Amongst other evidence which authorizes me to conjecture that masons went to the holy wars, is the doctrine of that order of masons, caller the HIGHER ORDER. I am induced to believe that order was of Scottish extraction; separate nations might be distinguished by some separate order: but be that as it may, it fully proves to me that masons were crusaders.*' p.184

'*We may conjecture that these religious campaigns* [i.e., the Crusades] *being over, that men initiated in the mysteries of masonry, and engaged and inrolled under those rules and orders, which were established for the conduct of the nations in the holy war, would form themselves into Lodges, and keep up their social meetings when returned home, in commemoration of their adventures and mutual good offices in Palestine and for the propagation of that knowledge into which they had been initiated.*' p.213

By way of summation Hutchinson's main points are:

• Participants in the Crusades were formed into 'societies' protecting them from spies and to be able to identify each other by night as well as by day.
• These 'secret societies' were condoned and encouraged by the Roman church.
Priests were 'masons' and they possessed the mysteries of masonry, the knowledge of the ancients, and of the universal language.
• It was these Priests who initiated and organised those going to the Crusades.
• Some Scottish masons were part of a Higher Order of 'masons'.
• Freemasons, especially Scottish 'masons', were Crusaders.
• Once these Initiates returned home they wished to maintain contact with each other for the propagation of '*initiated knowledge*' as well as for social and personal reasons. The most obvious method was to perpetuate their Lodges.

Although Hutchinson was not a Scot (he hailed from Barnard Castle, Co. Durham) he clearly had some thoughts as to how, and where, the Scots fitted into the origin and development of Freemasonry and particularly in relation to the Crusades. He suggests that a 'Higher Order' of 'mason' was of Scottish origin and that 'masons' were crusaders. He, in common with all previous authors of Masonic history until that time, has a clear belief that Freemasonry pre-dated the Crusades. The medieval Order of the KT, which he never mentions, must have come into being after Freemasonry. This demonstrates that another prominent Masonic author, in common with those other earlier and contemporaneous authors, from Anderson to Preston, considered 'masonry' to pre-date the medieval Order of the KT.

Hutchinson's book became very popular in Scotland and is important because soon after its publication Alexander Deuchar (1777–1844) established the modern Scottish Masonic Order of the Knights Templar (the Edinburgh Encampment of Knights Templar, later the Royal Grand Conclave) in 1808. The first edition of *Spirit of Masonry* published in Scotland was produced by McEwan (Edinburgh) in 1813. Another, second edition of the book was published, again by McEwan, in the same year. A third edition, published by Dick (Edinburgh), appeared in 1815. Three editions in two years indicates a very strong interest in this publication and, therefore, in Hutchinson's ideas regarding early Freemasonry. All these editions were produced very soon after Deuchar had begun to take charge of 'foreign' ceremonials practised earlier by some Scottish Craft Lodges. It is not unreasonable to suggest that those Scottish Freemasons interested in those ceremonials, and declared by the Grand Lodge of Scotland not to be Masonic, eagerly purchased Hutchinson's work. The material from which to create the myth was now readily available and widely read including members of the new Masonic Knights Templar Order.

Father Hay's work on the St. Clair muniments brought to the attention of Freemasons the existence of documents (principally two letters) that might suggest a long lineage for Scottish 'masonry'. Those involved in the formation of the Grand Lodge of Scotland interpreted these documents as being evidence of the existence of even earlier Royal Charters which granted the Sinclair family unspecified hereditary rights and privileges over the stonemasons of Scotland. All the flaws, errors and ambiguities in the 'charters' were ignored. By having a descendant of the Sinclairs (also William, 1700–1778) (Plate 6), to whom the 'Charters' had originally been addressed, resign these alleged hereditary rights and electing him the first Grand Master of the new Grand Lodge, the first steps were taken in the creation of a 'Traditional History'.

In 1723 Anderson issued, under the authority of the Grand Lodge of England, his brief and fantastic history of Freemasonry in which he claimed that kings of Scotland had been Grand Masters and one, at least, had '*Patronised*' the Craft. By 1738 he had compiled a list of the Grand Masters of the Scottish Craft beginning with Fergus II. Included in the list, during the reign of James II, was William Sinclair, Earl of Orkney, who was stated to be a Grand Master. From then until the Union of the Crowns (1603) Anderson lists 12 subsequent Grand Masters of Scotland.

Ramsay's *'Oration'* introduced the concept of a tenuous connection between Freemasonry and the Holy Land and mentioned Crusaders. He specifically linked Freemasonry with the Knights of St. John of Jerusalem. In common with all histories of Freemasonry at this time he made no mention of the medieval Order of KT. In 1761, Ruddiman and Auld's *Pocket Companion* elaborates on Anderson's, unsubstantiated, statement that William Sinclair was a Grand Master by stating:

> '*By another deed of the said King James II this office was made hereditary to the said William St. Clair, and his heirs and successors in the Barony of Roslin; in which noble family, it has continued without interruption till of late years.*'[54]

This is a major advance in the development of the myth. Until this time (1761) St. Clair had been but one fictional Grand Master out of a total of 20 Scottish Grand Masters.[55] The list, together with the rest of Anderson's 'history', was (and is) obviously, from a modern perspective, fantasy and no one sought to disprove Sinclair's (or anyone else's) alleged position as 'Grand Master'. Elevating St. Clair to the position of hereditary Grand Master meant that all twelve Grand Masters listed by Anderson, in 1738, succeeding St. Clair were erased from Scottish Masonic history as if they had never existed. This did not appear to have caused a problem for the Freemasons of the time. This raises a question; if all 12 Grand Masters following St. Clair were not, in fact, Grand Masters of Scottish masons (stonemasons or otherwise) what credence can be placed on Anderson's assertion that the five preceding St. Clair were Grand Masters (six if we include the *'Patron'* Alexander I)? As a consequence the suggestion that St. Clair was a Grand Master is also doubtful. Indeed, Ruddiman and Auld eliminate five of the six pre-St Clair Royal Grand Masters — the exception being James I. The embryonic myth, therefore, had already begun to develop and 'facts' previously accepted as being accurate were suddenly ignored, or changed, in favour of new 'facts' which enhanced a particular view of the history of Scottish Freemasonry. Describing St Clair as a hereditary Grand Master in a published history was almost inevitable as at the formation of the Grand Lodge of Scotland, in 1736, William St Clair of Roslin (1700–1778) (Plate 6) signed a *'Deed of Resignation of the Office of Hereditary Grand Master'*. (Appendix VI) The KT still are not mentioned at this time.

Ruddiman and Auld appear to have had knowledge of the embryonic, and mythical, history of the Grand Lodge of Scotland, the current Scottish Masonic 'scene', as well as Anderson's history for they create a blend of various elements to embellish the myth. They leave intact Anderson's assertion that the Romans introduced 'Masonry' into Scotland but subtly change his claim that six kings, before St. Clair, had been Grand Masters to the assertion that it was the Freemasons themselves who recognised the king to be their Grand Master (e.g. *'The Fraternity of Free-Masons in Scotland always owned their King and Sovereign as their Grand Master.'*). They were aware also of St. Clair's 'Deed of Resignation' and gave an explanation why it had been required:

> *'William Sinclair of Roslin Esq: (a real Mason, and a gentleman of the greatest candour and benevolence, inheriting his predecessors virtues without their fortune) was obliged to dispose the estate: and, having no children of his own, was loth that the office of Grand Master, now vested in his person, should become vacant at his death: more especially, as there was but small prospect of the Brethren of the country receiving any countenance or protection from the crown (whom the office naturally reverted, at the failure of the Roslin family), as in ancient days, our Kings and Princes continually residing in England.'*[56]

This Deed was necessary, it is argued in the Deed itself, because if Sinclair died childless the office of hereditary Grand Master would revert to the Crown and, presumably the soon to be created Grand Lodge of Scotland could not countenance the monarch imposing a Grand Master (hereditary or not) upon them. However, the Deed, and the need for it, is no more than part of the creation of a 'Traditional History' for the new body comparable with that created by James Anderson for the Grand Lodge of England. This can be demonstrated by an examination of the Deed and the circumstances surrounding its creation. In the first place it is a myth that Sinclair died childless. He had several children:

> *'The male representation of the family of Rosslyn terminated in William Saintclair, who married Cordellia, daughter of Sir George Wishart of Cliftonhall, by whom he had three sons and five daughters, who all died young, except his daughter Sarah.'*[57]

Sinclair signed the 'Deed of Resignation' on 24 November 1736, when he was 36 years of age and it is almost inconceivable that he willingly signed away rights that could, by hereditability, be passed to his daughter, Sarah, or any of her children. It would be unnatural that he would sign away such rights at the early age of 36 when it was not impossible for him to marry again and have more children. This, and the fact that he lived for another 42 years, suggests that the 'Deed' was created for the benefit of one party only — the Grand Lodge of Scotland. The sole beneficiary of the alleged and unspecified 'rights', the Grand Lodge, enhanced its antiquity, and therefore its legitimacy, especially in comparison to the fantastic and mythological 'history' of the Grand Lodge of England created by Anderson. Ruddiman and Auld, who reproduce the 'Deed of Resignation' in full, make complimentary remarks about St. Clair of Rosslyn who was still alive in 1761 when their *Pocket Companion* was published. This then is a contemporary source that reveals the perceptions of the history of Scottish Freemasonry at that time.

However, it can now be seen that this view of the past is seriously flawed. This 'history', or at least parts of it, is repeated uncritically today. The claim that 'Masons', '... *always owned their King and Sovereign as their Grand Master'*, neatly sidesteps the problems created by stating that certain kings of Scotland were Grand Masters. In 1761 it was Freemasons themselves who claimed them all to be Grand Masters (according to Ruddiman and Auld). This is a meaningless claim but it still manages to convey the impression that over many centuries monarchs were involved with 'Masons'.

In this way the 'historical' emphasis of Scottish 'Masonry' began to become focused on the Sinclairs of Rosslyn and two monarchs, James I and James II. In modifying the myth Ruddiman and Auld had James I establishing a system of governance for the Masons of Scotland, which was then adapted by his son, James II:

'Accordingly we find James I. That patron of learning, countenancing the Lodges with his presence, "as the Royal Grand Master; till he settled an yearly revenue of four pounds Scots, to be paid by every Master-Mason in Scotland, to a Grand-Master chosen by the Brethren, and approved of by the crown, one nobly born…'[58]

This crucial element of the myth is still repeated today, i.e.:

'By the time of James II Stewart, the St Clairs had changed their name to Sinclair and William Sinclair, Earl of Caithness, Grand Admiral of Scotland, was appointed Hereditary Patron and Protector of the Scottish Masons by King James II in 1441. The document of appointment, is held by the Grand Masonic Order, of Scotland, and is Lodged [sic] at Freemasons' Hall in Edinburgh.'[59]

James I having created this system for the benefit of 'masons', it was James II who, in 1441, made William St. Clair, the builder of Rosslyn Chapel, Grand Master of masons and thereafter by another, separate, 'Deed' created him and his heirs and successors hereditary Grand Masters.[60] There is no evidence connecting James I to Masonic Lodges of any kind, that he ever visited such Lodges or that he was Grand Master of 'masons' of Scotland. Central to the myth are the activities of his son, James II. It is alleged that, in 1441, he appointed St. Clair the Grand Master [of masons] and also made that position hereditary. James was born in 1430 and would, therefore, have been eleven years of age when he allegedly made St. Clair a Grand Master. It is known that James II took no part in government until 1449 when he was 19 and so could not have conferred that title on anyone.[61]

More to the point, however, is that this position of Grand Master simply did not exist. The offices of the Scottish Crown (for example Chancellor, Chamberlain, Comptroller, Justiciar of Scotland, Custodian of the King's Person, etc.) are known — the post of Grand Master is not one of them. The term Grand Master first appears in the 18th century, used in a Masonic context by Anderson in 1723, when he claims that the Patriarch, Moses, was the first Grand Master.[62] The title was applied, retrospectively, by subsequent writers on Freemasonry. Father Hay found no trace of deeds from James I or James II when he examined the Sinclair muniments *c*.1700. In the absence of such proof later authors accepted the claim in the second St, Clair 'Charter' (*c*.1628) that there had previously been such deeds and that they had been lost in a fire. This means that the Charters allegedly issued by James II were lost by fire sometime after 1441 but before 1601. There is a report in Hay's *Genealogie of the Sainteclaires of Rosslyn* that such a fire took place in 1447 but that reference states that Sinclair's Chaplain rescued all the documents: '. . . *declared how his charters and writts were all saved*'.[63] This being so, the charters allegedly granted by James II must have been destroyed in another fire sometime after 1447 but before 1601. Another fire at Rosslyn Castle occurred in 1722.[64] There appear, therefore, to have been a total of three major fires at Rosslyn Castle but fortunately the two St. Clair 'Charters' survived on each occasion. Unfortunately, the Deeds allegedly issued by James II, one appointing Sinclair Grand Master and the other making that position hereditary did not survive — assuming of course that they ever actually existed.

This was with all its flaws, the generally accepted version of Scottish Masonic history, with minor variations and elaborations from time to time, that prevailed until the end of the 18th century.

[1] Slezer, John. *Theatrum Scotiæ*. 1693.

[2] The common mistake of using the date 1441 appears to originate from James Anderson's use of that date in his '*Constitutions*' of 1738.

[3] A second, revised, edition was published by the Grand Lodge of Scotland in 2002.

[4] *Hay's Antiquities,* Hay, Father Richard, A., MSS. 34.1.8-9. The National Library of Scotland.

[5] *Account of the Templars together with an Account of the Joannites or Knights of St. John,* Hay, Father Richard, A., (Ed. James Maidment), (Edinburgh, 1828).

[6] *Genealogie of the Sainteclaires of Rosslyn* Hay, Father Richard. A., (Ed. James Maidment), (Edinburgh, 1835).

[7] Hay performed the same service for his own family; *Genealogie of the Hayes of Tweeddale, The* (Edinburgh, 1835).

[8] My thanks are due to John Wade, PM, for his translation of this Charter a full translation of which, together with many others (also translated by Brother Wade), is to be found in *Genealogie of the Sainteclaires of Rosslyn,* Second Edition (Grand Lodge of Scotland, 2002).

[9] These MSS are the property of the Grand Lodge of Scotland.

[10] For a more extensive background to these documents see Stevenson, David, *The First Freemasons*. 2nd edn. (Grand Lodge of Scotland, 2001) and *The Origins of Freemasonry* (Cambridge University Press, 1988).

[11] *Historical Sketch* (Grand Lodge of Scotland), App III, p. 34. Both 'charters'

are reproduced (although not translated) in this publication.

[12] *Op. cit.*, p. 36.

[13] *Ibid.*

[14] These were Canongate Kilwinning, The Lodge of Edinburgh, Kilwinning Scots Arms and Leith Kilwinning. The latter two are now dormant.

[15] Whether or not this was a 'revival' as claimed by Anderson is not for debate here.

[16] Only a few stonemasons were members of this Lodge and it cannot, therefore, be considered to be an entirely operative lodge.

[17] As previously noted, the St. Clair 'Charters' relate to stonemasons. Anderson, in his *Constitutions,* does not distinguish between stonemasons and Freemasons, using the terms Mason and Masonry to describe both. This may have been due to the lack of differentiation between members of his father's Lodge with which Anderson was familiar. The fact remains that ever since Anderson the difference between 'mason' (stonemason) and 'Mason' (Freemason) is rarely made or considered. Whilst this may cause little difficulty elsewhere, when transferred to the Scottish context, where most of the early records relating to stonemasons and their lodges exist, confusion is very easily the result. Those who adopt the Popular Approach rarely make such a distinction and this ensures that whenever 'masons' and 'masonry' are discussed the assumption is that the writer is referring to Freemasons, and Freemasonry, in the modern sense.

[18] Desaguliers was probably responsible for the *Charges of a Freemason* and Anderson the *History* contained within the *Constitutions.* See, for example, *Mackey's Revised Encyclopedia.* Vol. 1. p. 277).

[19] *Constitutions of the Free-Masons, The,* Anderson, Revd. Dr. James, (London, 1723), pp. 37-38.

[20] *Op. cit.*, pp. 38-39.

[21] *Op. cit.*, p. 46.

[22] *An Introduction to the History of the Royal Somerset and Inverness Lodge.* London. 1928. p.16.

[23] *Constitutions of the Free-Masons The,* Vibert, Lionel, Facsimile Edition, (London, 1923), Introduction. p. x.

[24] He subsequently wrote a book: *History of the Viscount Turenne.*

[25] *Andrew Michael Ramsay and his Masonic Oration,* Kahler, Lisa (in *Heredom*, Scottish Rite Research Society), Vol. 1. pp. 19-47.

[26] *Gould's History . . .* Vol. 5. p. 79.

[27] *Op. cit.*, p. 20.

[28] *Ramsay's Oration: the Épernay and Grand Lodge Versions,* Batham, Cyril N. (in *Heredom*, Scottish Rite Research Society), Vol. 1. pp. 49-59. This is a most useful comparison of the two known versions of the *Oration.*

[29] *Op. cit.*, p. 50.

[30] *Op. cit.*, p. 57.

[31] *Ibid.*

[32] *Templar Revelation, The,* by Lynn Picknett and Clive Prince. p. 131.

[33] *Coil's Masonic Encyclopedia*, by Henry W. Coil. p. 500.

[34] *Batham, op. cit.*, *Vol. 1. pp. 57-58.* The James referred to is the 5th High

Steward of Scotland and died 1309. His son, Walter, was knighted on the field
of Bannockburn by Robert I.

[35] *New Constitutions, The,* Anderson, Revd. Dr. James, (London, 1738), pp.
82–91.

[36] The additional information suggests that he may have had a source in
Scotland. The Grand Lodge of Scotland was founded in 1736 and it too,
apparently, was engaged in creating its own 'Traditional History'.

[37] Most historians now agree that Fergus II died *c.*501.

[38] Anderson, *op. cit.,* p. 84.

[39] *Op. cit.,* p. 86.

[40] *Op. cit.,* p. 7.

[41] *Op. cit.,* p. 89.

[42] See, for example *The Royal Order of Scotland,* Lindsay, Robert S., 2nd edn
(Edinburgh, 1972).

[43] 36 years if one accepts the claim that the Order was founded in 1731.

[44] The battle was fought 23-24 June. The use of 4 July may be due to the author
using the Julian calendar which was replaced, in England, in 1752 by the
Gregorian calendar.

[45] The 1747 *Act of Proscription* was repealed in 1782.

[46] There were sporadic and poorly attended meetings between those two dates.
See *The Royal Order of Scotland,* Lindsay Robert S., 2nd edn (Edinburgh,
1972), pp. 101-104.

[47] James Reid of Edinburgh copied Cheyne's edition in 1754 also citing
Anderson as the source.

[48] *Pocket Companion,* Cheyne, W. (Edinburgh, 1752), pp. 111-114.

[49] *Pocket Companion,* Ruddiman, Auld and Company (Edinburgh, 1761), p. 111.

[50] If this is taken at face value the monarch would have had a say as to 'his'
deputy.

[51] *Op. cit.,* p. 112.

[52] Re-printed by the Grand Lodge of Scotland, 2000.

[53] *Preston's Illustrations of Masonry,* Prescott, Andrew, (Academy Electronic
Publications Ltd, 2001), 2nd edn (1775), p. 205. This CD-ROM contains the nine
editions published during Preston's lifetime.

[54] *Pocket Companion,* (Ruddiman, Auld & Co.), *op. cit.,* p. 112.

[55] Anderson, *op. cit.*

[56] *Pocket Companion,* (Ruddiman, Auld & Co.), *op. cit.,* pp. 113-114.

[57] Maidment in *Genealogie of the Sainteclaires of Rosslyn,* (Edinburgh, 1835),
p.ii, quoting *The Baronage of Scotland,* p. 249 by Sir Robert Douglas of
Glenbervie Bt. (Edinburgh, 1798).

[58] *Pocket Companion,* (Ruddiman, Auld & Co.), *op. cit.,* p. 111. Modern
examples of the uncritical repetition of such material include, for example:
Sword and the Grail, The, Sinclair, A., p. 167. *Templar Legacy and the Masonic
Inheritance within Rosslyn Chapel, The,* Wallace-Murphy, T., p. 23.

[59] *Forgotten Monarchy of Scotland, The,* Stewart, Michael, J. A., H.R.H. Prince
Michael of Albany, pp. 101-102. Despite the author's assertion that the
'*...document of appointment, signed by James . . .*' is in Freemasons' Hall, I can

confirm that it is not.

[60] *Pocket Companion,* (Ruddiman, Auld & Co.), *op. cit.,* p. 112.

[61] McGladdery, Christine, *James II*, p. 49, makes it clear that James II did not take up royal authority until 1449.

[62] *Constitutions*, Anderson, Revd. Dr. James, (London, 1723), p. 8.

[63] *Genealogiie of the Sainteclaires of Rosslyn*, Hay, Father Richard A., (Ed. James Maidment), (Edinburgh, 1835), p. 28.

[64] *Temple and the Lodge, The*, Baigent, Michael, & Leigh, Richard, 1989 p. 116.

Chapter 3
The 19th Century

The Romantic Age

In 1804 Brother Alexander Lawrie (also spelt Laurie) (1768–1831) published a book that offered an alternative origin of Freemasonry, challenging the 18th century prevailing view of events. It had the wordy title:

> '*The History of Free Masonry drawn from authentic sources of information with an account of the Grand Lodge of Scotland, from its institution in 1736, to the present time, compiled from the records; and An Appendix of original papers.*'

Lawrie was Bookseller and Stationer to the Grand Lodge of Scotland. The dedication suggests that he had an eye on his future as it was dedicated to George, 9th Earl of Dalhousie (1770–1838) who was, at the time the book was published, Depute (Deputy) Grand Master. Lawrie describes Dalhousie as Grand Master Elect and he did become Grand Master Mason on 30 November 1804, serving in that capacity for two years.

The minute of a meeting of Grand Lodge on 3 August 1801 reveals that he was appointed Bookseller and Stationer to the Grand Lodge in recognition of years of service to that body. The minute of the next meeting of Grand Lodge on 2 November 1801, includes the following:

> '*The Substitute Grand Master* [John Clark] *stated that he had received a letter from Brother Lawrie bookseller and Stationer to the Grand Lodge inclosing a prospectus of a History of Freemasonry that Brother Lawrie proposed to publish which letter being read it is as follows:*
>
> *Parliament Square No.24 - 2nd November 1801*
> *Right Worshipful Sir,*
> *I take the liberty of sending you a prospectus of a work which I intend to publish, I shall esteem it a particular favour if you will communicate the same to the Grand Lodge of Scotland for the honour which the Grand Lodge conferred on me last Quarterly communication to be their Bookseller and Stationer I shall always be grateful and if I should be*

fortunate enough to obtain their sanction to the above work it will add another favour which will be highly gratifying to your most obedient and humble servant... Alex Lawrie.

The above mentioned prospectus having been read the Substitute Grand Master proposed that the above work should be sanctioned by the Grand Lodge which was unanimously agreed to and the Grand Lodge further authorised the Grand Secretary and Grand Clerk to furnish Brother Lawrie with the records and other writings belonging to the Grand Lodge and with every material within their power which may in any degree lend to the advancement of the work.'

Here then is another possible motive — that of a devoted servant seeking to promote the body that had recently recognised his services. If Lawrie hoped for promotion as a consequence (and such a motive is by no means obvious) he must have been disappointed for he had to wait until 1810. Even then his promotion was to that of Joint Grand Secretary, with William Guthrie (?–1812), who had served as Grand Secretary since 1797. In 1812, Lawrie became Grand Secretary in his own right, probably on the death of Guthrie. Lawrie remained Grand Secretary until 1826 when he again became Joint Grand Secretary, this time with his son William Alexander (1799–1870). He continued in that joint position until 1831 when his son became sole Grand Secretary — a position he held until 1870. While Grand Secretary, William A. Lawrie reproduced the book bearing his father's name, in 1859. This book did not introduce any fundamental changes to his father's work but re-worked each chapter, making them fuller and using more factual information. It also included considerable new additions, which were principally the activities of Grand Lodge up to 1859 (up to 1804 in his father's edition) together with an account of Mark, Royal Arch and Ark Masonry and other Orders including the modern Masonic KT. His 'history' of the KT from their inception follows that published by the Grand Conclave in 1843. He takes the opportunity to mount a more vigorous attack of Barruel's opinion of the KT (see below), utilising more historical evidence than was used in his father's book.

The preface to the work suggests additional motives. The author alludes to the events in Europe and Freemasonry's possible part in those events, specifically mentioning the French Revolution. The allegations that Freemasonry played a part in the original revolutionary 'conspiracy' probably puzzled Scottish Freemasons especially as the British Government had exempted Lodges from the strictures of the Unlawful Oaths Act (1797) and the Unlawful Societies Act (1799) designed to eliminate, or at least control, organisations thought to be potentially subversive or revolutionary. In that sense the difference between Freemasonry in Scotland and Europe is demonstrated. But Lawrie's avowed motive for publishing the *History* was stated to be:

> '*The best way of refuting those calumnies which have been brought against the fraternity of Free Masons, is to lay before the public a correct and rational account of the nature, origin, and progress of the institution; that they may be enabled to determine, whether or not its principles are in any shape, connected with the principles of revolutionary anarchy.*'[1]

This laudable aim, reinforced by the view that previous histories of Freemasonry were '. . . *of such a repulsive nature . . . that a new and accurate work was necessary'* suggests that the book was anticipated.[2] It is divided into two parts, the first being a fantastic 'history' of Freemasonry from pre-historic times. The second part is an annual summary of the activities of the Grand Lodge of Scotland, from its foundation in 1736 to the date of the book's publication. Interestingly the previously mentioned two manuscripts transcribed by Father Richard A. Hay known, as the 'St. Clair Charters' are reproduced as Appendices where they are again described as 'charters'. This, again, demonstrates the importance placed on these documents even if their original purpose was not understood as, whilst in the text of the book they are described as being Charters granted by James II, the Appendix describes them as being Charters granted by the 'Masons' of Scotland.[3]

It is ironic that this book, which Lawrie apparently put so much effort into producing, was not even written by him — but by a 'ghost-writer', who received no credit. Once the official sanction of Grand Lodge to produce the book was given, he appears never to have denied being the author. In fact Lawrie seems to have allowed himself to be identified as the author, if not actively promoting himself to be the writer. The Minutes of Grand Lodge dated 6 February 1804 contain the following:

> '*Br. Carphin stated that he had read with great satisfaction a late publication upon Masonry under authority of the Grand Lodge. He considered that the book in question would prove of good utility to Masonry in general and most useful to the Grand Lodge and the Lodges holding under her when this was considered, he was satisfied that every*

*member present would heartily join him in moving the thanks of the Grand Lodge to Brother Alex. Lawrie **author** of the publication alluded to — this motion having being seconded the thanks of the Grand Lodge was unanimously voted to Br. Lawrie.*'[4]

Who then was the un-named author? Most authorities agree that Sir David Brewster (1781–1868) penned the material and this view is confirmed by the following undated entry in a copy of the book that belonged to Dr David Irving (1778–1860), Librarian to the Faculty of Advocates:

'*The history of this book is somewhat curious, and perhaps there are only two individuals now living by whom it could be divulged, The late Alexander Lawrie, Grand Stationer, wished to recommend himself to the Fraternity by the publication of such a work. Through Doctor Anderson, he requested me to undertake its compilation, and offered a suitable remuneration. As I did not relish the task, he made a similar offer to my old acquaintance David Brewster, by whom it was readily undertaken, and I can say was executed to the entire satisfaction of his employers. The title page does not exhibit the name of the author, but the dedication bears the signature of Alexander Lawrie, and the volume is commonly described as Lawrie's History of Freemasonry.*'[5]

While Sir David Brewster made a huge, albeit anonymous, contribution to the history of Scottish Freemasonry, he was also an important figure in Scottish society and academia. At the time of the publication of the book Brewster was a young man and had not yet determined a course in life. No doubt he found the monetary reward most useful. His involvement in Scottish Freemasonry appears to have been limited to the production of the book for Lawrie.

L'Abbé Augustin Barruel (1741–1820)

The book by Lawrie/Brewster was published partly in response to Barruel's *Memoirs, illustrating the history of Jacobinism* (1797) which claimed:

'*Your whole school and all your Lodges are derived from the Templars after the extinction of their Order, a certain number of guilty knights, having escaped the proscription, united for the preservation of their horrid mysteries. To their impious code they added the vow of vengeance against the kings and priests who destroyed their Order, and against all religion which anathematised their dogmas. They made adepts, who should transmit from generation to generation the same hatred of the God of the Christians, and of Kings, and of Priests. These mysteries have descended to you, and you continue to perpetuate their impiety, their vows, and their oaths. Such is your origin. The lapse of time and the change of manners have varied a part of your symbols and your frightful systems; but the essence of them remains, the vows, the oaths, the hatred, and the conspiracies are the same.'*[6]

This attack is one of the earliest non-Masonic sources that explicitly claims that Freemasonry is a perpetuation of the medieval Order of KT. The reversal of the previously accepted chronology had consequences within Freemasonry within a matter of a few years. This appears to be the first suggestion that Freemasonry came into being *after* the medieval Order of KT. The fact that a member of the church which had suppressed the medieval KT claimed that Freemasonry was a direct descendant of that Order augmented the belief that a direct link existed between the two and immediately added some legitimacy in support of that idea. Brewster, the son of a Presbyterian, had trained for the Presbyterian Church of Scotland. It is possible that, because of his antipathy towards the Roman Church, he defended the reputation of the KT, and therefore that of Freemasonry, not because he had researched the alleged link between them but because it afforded him an opportunity to attack a religious enemy. That Barruel specifically excludes 'English' Freemasons (probably meaning to include also Scottish, Irish and Welsh Freemasons) from his attack was not sufficient to deflect Brewster. Up to this point the link with Freemasonry and the KT was a notion within Freemasonry although *not* in Scotland. Brewster's response to Barruel's attack on Freemasonry in Europe, incorporated in his *History...* ensured that the imagined connection between the KT of the Middle Ages and Freemasonry in the 18th century gained additional credence. In fact Brewster's discussion of Freemasonry and the KT in a Scottish Masonic publication served to reinforce the notion that there was a link between the medieval Order and modern Freemasonry within Scotland. Even at this stage, 1804, the KT are not seen as the originators of Freemasonry, quite the reverse: '... *the order of the Knights Templars was a branch of Free Masonry*.'[7,8]

John Robison (1739–1805)

Lawrie/Brewster quotes another anti-Masonic work, by John Robison, '*Proofs of a Conspiracy against all the Religions and Governments of Europe, carried on in the secret Meetings of Freemasons, Illuminati, and Reading Societies. Collected from good authorities*' (1797). Robison states that he was Initiated in a Lodge at Liège. He was probably an Écossais mason given that he comments that he witnessed ceremonies (and which to a certain extent he describes) that did not exist in his native land, i.e. '*I was importuned by persons of the first rank to pursue my Masonic career through many degrees unknown in this country.*'[9] A review of the book states: '*It betrays a degree of credulity extremely remarkable in a person used to calm reason and philosophical demonstration.*'[10] The book was intended to prove that the Illuminati, alleged to be an Order of Freemasonry, was involved in a plot to overthrow Christianity and civil government throughout Europe.[11]

It appears that Robison explained the ideas for his book to Barruel when he met him in London during 1795/6. Barruel was at that time a refugee of the French Revolution and he promptly trumped Robison by publishing his book first.[12] Like Barruel, Robison is at great pains to exempt British Freemasonry from his criticism of European Freemasonry and begins to do so as early as page 1:

'. . . *in my early life, I had taken some part in the occupations of (shall I call them) of Free Masonry; and, having chiefly frequented the Lodges on the continent, I had learned many doctrines, and seen many ceremonials which have no place in the simple system of Free Masonry which obtains in this country.*' [Britain]

Robison was a prominent figure in Edinburgh and Scottish society. In 1773 he became Professor of Natural Philosophy at Edinburgh University. '*The sciences of mechanics,*' wrote Professor John Playfair (1748–1819), his successor, '*hydrodynamics, astronomy, and optics, together with electricity and magnetism, were the subjects which his lectures embraced*'. In 1783, when the Royal Society of Edinburgh was founded and incorporated by Royal Charter, Robison was elected the General Secretary and he served in that capacity until 1798. David Brewster became a member of the Society in 1807. Robison's *A System of Mechanical Philosophy with Notes by David Brewster, LL.D.* was published posthumously in 1822.

Like Barruel, Robison's motives are complex, although profit cannot be dismissed as a major factor. For a respected academic this work is a puzzle. Compared to his other published work, the *'Proofs...'* is little more that a long rant against Freemasonry and other so-called secret societies such as the Illuminati. His lack of supporting evidence, quoting un-named individuals, the absence of logical argument together with his frequent claims that his book is not an attack on 'English' Freemasonry suggests that he did not, like Barruel, wish to antagonize those whom he expected to purchase his work. However, he cannot be dismissed as a mere writer of fiction for he reveals a detailed knowledge of the work of, for example, Anderson and Ramsay. Robison was apparently initiated in Lodge La Parfaite Intelligence at Liège in March 1770 and his book demonstrates the value he placed on his Masonic obligations.

Lawrie/Brewster provided a fairly standard history of the KT from the inception of the Order, and takes its links with Freemasonry for granted, without investigation:

> '*It would be needless labour to enter into any investigation in order to prove that the order of the Knights Templar was a branch of Freemasonry. This fact has been invariably acknowledged by Free Masons themselves; and none have been more zealous to establish it than the enemies of the order* [i.e. Barruel]. *The former have admitted the fact, not because it was creditable to them, but because it was true; and the latter have supported it, because by the aid of a little sophistry, it might be employed to disgrace their opponents.*'[13]

In other words, because some Freemasons claim that there is a connection between the two Orders that is sufficient proof of the connection! It is significant that, without any attempt to prove the alleged link, Lawrie/Brewster state that the 'public' reason for the formation of the KT was to protect pilgrims visiting the Holy Land but the real reason for their existence was to preserve, and practise, 'Free Masonry', the implication being that they intended to re-introduce it into the Holy Land where, presumably, it had ceased to exist or had become badly corrupted. Thus Lawrie/Brewster argue that the Order of Knights Templar perpetuated Freemasonry and not the other way around. Brewster, and those around him (including his presumed paymaster, Lawrie) believed, and sought to confirm, that the medieval Order of Knights Templar had descended from the original Freemasons.

Barruel claimed that the allegations against the medieval KT were true and that some members of the Order had escaped the general suppression to metamorphose into the Order of Freemasonry. That Order was merely a perpetuation of the medieval KT, the members of which continued to practise their sinful, evil and heretical practices within Masonic Lodges. Freemasons plotted to extract revenge for the treatment of their precursors, the medieval Order of the KT, by overthrowing civil government and Christianity throughout Europe. The most dramatic manifestations of that alleged malevolent intent was the French Revolution, which was instigated by Freemasons. This is very reminiscent of later claims that there was a Jewish/Masonic conspiracy to create a 'New World Order'.

Such attacks by two authors, one of whom was a Scot, within a very short period of time ensured widespread discussion. It seems that the idea of a connection between Scottish Freemasonry and the medieval Order of the KT entered Scottish Masonic mythology not because of any rational or methodical debate. Simply because 'someone' had said at this time that Freemasons and the KT were one and the same, and that they were automatically both BAD, Scottish Freemasons rushed to defend the KT on the basis that one's enemy's enemy is one's friend!

It is almost exactly 500 years (i.e. after the suppression of the medieval Order of the KT) that the KT first enter Scottish Masonic mythology, with the publication of Lawrie/Brewster's book, and it is not until more than 200 years after the first Masonic records begin (i.e. 1599–1804) that the KT are first mentioned in Scottish Masonic history. Since the myth began to achieve its modern form it has remained part of Scottish Masonic mythology for almost 200 years (i.e. from 1804 to the present time). This is an indication of the tenacity and romance of this particular myth.

After Lawrie/Brewster's book, endorsed as it was by the Grand Lodge of Scotland, the myth of a connection between the medieval KT became an accepted part of Scottish Masonic history.[14] Throughout the 19th and 20th centuries numerous authors enunciated the myth, refining and elaborating it in the process, but never discussing its validity. It is curious that the writings of so many non-Masons have had such a dramatic impact upon Freemasons' own perception of the history of their organisation.

Reaction of the Grand Lodge of Scotland

Thus far the origin and development of the myth had been relatively straightforward. There is, however, one event that sheds light on the attitudes of Scottish Freemasons of this period and which demonstrates that this process was not as straightforward as the simple chronology above delineated might suggest.

In repeating, and elaborating, the accepted mythological history of Scottish Freemasonry Lawrie/Brewster's book represented a contradiction at the heart of Scottish Freemasonry then and now. Since at least 1792 the Grand Lodge of Scotland had railed against the introduction of non-Masonic ceremonies.[15, 16] The Minutes of Grand Lodge dated 19 May 1800 contain the following entry:

'Before closing the Lodge R. W. Bro. Lawrie of Canongate and Leith, Leith and Canongate said he had a motion to make which from what had passed tonight he hoped would meet with the approbation of the Grand Lodge he therefore stated "that the Grand Lodge of Scotland sanction the three orders of Masonry and these alone of Apprentice, Fellow Craft and Master Mason being the ancient Order of St John but understanding that other descriptions of Masons under various titles had crept into this country borrowed from other nations which he conceived to be inconsistent with the purity and true principles of the order. He therefore moved that the Grand Lodge of Scotland should expressly prohibit and discharge all Lodges from holding any other meetings than that of the three orders above described under this certification that their charters shall be forfeited ipso facto in case of transgression.'[17]

Lawrie's motion was remitted to a later meeting of the Grand Lodge, which was held on 26 May 1800. Its deliberations are recorded as follows:

'Right Worshipful Bro. Lawrie's motion respecting Royal Arch Masonry and Knights Templars was then taken under consideration... Hereby resolve that none may pretend ignorance expressly to prohibit and discharge all Lodges having Charters from the Grand Lodge from holding any other meetings than those of the three orders above described under this certification that the Grand Lodge will most positively proceed, on information of an infringement of this express prohibition to censure or to the forfeiture of the Charters of the offending Lodges according to the circumstances of any particular case, which may be brought before them.

The Grand Lodge appoint the above resolution to be printed and a copy of it sent to every Lodge in Scotland holding under her, and the Substitute Grand Masters Committee are appointed to meet for the purpose of drawing up a circular letter to be transmitted along with the above resolution.'[18]

The wording of the circular letter was approved at a meeting held on 9 June 1800 and was then sent to every Scottish Lodge that was a Daughter Lodge of the Grand Lodge.[19]

What is to be made of this? These Minutes reveal that the Grand Lodge of Scotland was gravely concerned about the introduction of 'foreign' ceremonials that were not part of the pure Scottish form of St. John's Freemasonry. The new and contaminating elements had '. . . *crept into this country borrowed from other nations...*', indicating that these had been introduced by stealth and without the sanction of Grand Lodge. Could this have been because the practitioners of those ceremonies were aware of the attitude of the Grand Lodge? The use of terms such as *'purity'*, *'true principles'* and *'ancient'* in describing Scottish Freemasonry suggests that members of Grand Lodge were worried that Freemasonry as it had existed until then, in Scotland, was now being challenged by the introduction of non-Scottish practices.[20] This attitude is similar to the position adopted by Barruel and Robison who argued that continental Freemasonry was a corrupt form of Freemasonry. The Grand Lodge of Scotland identified these 'corruptions' as the ceremonies of the Royal Arch and the Knights Templar.[21]

The Masonic degrees that could be conferred by Daughter Lodge are specified in the Charters granted to them by Grand Lodge:

'Hereby giving granting and Committing to them and their successors full and ample power to meet and convene as a regular Lodge and to receive and enter Apprentices pass fellow Crafts and raise Master Masons.'
[Extract from a Grand Lodge of Scotland Charter dated 1741][22]

There was, however, another situation that had a major impact at this time and that was the enactment of the Unlawful Oaths Act (1797) and the Unlawful Societies Act (1799). Both were introduced as a response to the Revolution in France, general political unrest, and the perception that private meetings of 'secret' organisations such as The Society of Friends of the People, and Masonic Lodges, were a guise for the gathering of radicals and revolutionaries. It was also thought that some of these had a role in the events of the 1789 Revolution in France and in subsequent events in that country. Robison devoted a chapter of his book to this subject and this no doubt added to the concerns of the establishment regarding Freemasonry. The legislation was designed to eliminate so-called 'secret societies' that might pose a threat to the British State. Freemasonry would, under the original terms of these Acts, have had great difficulty in surviving but last minute amendments ensured the continued existence of Freemasonry on the basis that the Grand Lodge stood as guarantors for the good behaviour of 'regular' Daughter Lodges. An administrative system was put in place whereby the Grand Lodge of Scotland had to 'vouch' for each of its Lodges by issuing certificates stating that the lodges concerned were Masonic Lodges and that they existed within, and abided by, the terms of the Acts. Each Lodge was required to register its members with the local judicial authorities (a J.P. or other Magistrate) on an annual basis. If these conditions were not met, Lodges could be forced to close. This presented the Grand Lodge of Scotland with more power than it had had previously. The Grand Lodge suddenly had the ability to determine which Lodges were true Daughter Lodges and those which were not. Those not so designated could be forced to close. Previously throughout the 18th century, the Minutes of Grand Lodge regularly record its inability to control its Daughter Lodges, as it would have wished and, more particularly, the recurrent difficulty in obtaining monies due from them.

On 11 February 1800 Lawrie proposed that all Lodges in Scotland, holding of Grand Lodge, be identified and the amount of the arrears due from each be established. Nowhere is it plainly stated that the Grand Lodge of Scotland would use its new, and unexpected, powers to have Lodges comply with its need for finance and its desire to purge Scottish Lodges of exotic and foreign ceremonials which could not be described as indigenous Scottish Masonic practice, that is, those of the Royal Arch and Knights Templar.

The Grand Lodge of Scotland understood that Freemasonry consisted of three degrees, and that these were the oldest and purest form of Freemasonry. The introduction of other, spurious ceremonials alien to Scotland contaminated true Freemasonry. The Grand Lodge of Scotland could do little to stop the performance of these importations until presented with the legal obligation to vouch for the regularity of the activities of its Daughter Lodges. That opportunity meant that it could ensure its Lodges acted as it directed. Lodges began to pay their arrears to Grand Lodge and most appear to have ceased to work the 'impure' continental ceremonies.

Here we can see the major dichotomy of Scottish Freemasonry. The Grand Lodge of Scotland had tried for a number of years to have its Lodges dispense with alien ceremonies. It did not have the means to do so until the Government required it to be guarantor for the conduct of all of its Lodges. The Grand Lodge of Scotland could therefore ensure that its Daughter Lodges behaved as it wished — sending monies due and working only the three, pure and original degrees of Scottish Freemasonry. Two years later the proposer of the motions against Royal Arch and Knights Templar ceremonials, Alexander Lawrie, published the book that specifically linked Freemasonry with the medieval Order of KT!

How can such opposite views be accommodated within the same organisation? This most difficult of questions cannot be answered in an entirely satisfactory manner. The nature of Scottish culture and idiosyncratic Scottish Masonic practice has a part to play. It is a little difficult to explain to Freemasons who are not Scottish and even more difficult to try to explain to people who are not members of the Craft (whether or not they are Scottish). It is suggested that the book by Lawrie/Brewster was created as a response to a variety of motives. Some of these concerned financial gain, religious prejudice and opportunism, a defence of Freemasonry and self-aggrandisement. But it was also created from a desire that Scottish Freemasonry should not to be left behind in the whirlwind debate as to where Freemasonry originated, which country had the oldest Masonic pedigree and which country practised the purest and original Masonic degrees.

Lawrie's motion to the Grand Lodge of Scotland in May 1800 to separate 'inconsistent' ceremonies, specifically those of the Royal Arch and Knight Templar, from pure St. John's Freemasonry appears to have upset more than a few. The popularity of these ceremonials is indicated by the explosion in the number of Encampments (now known as Preceptories) chartered, in Scotland, by the Early Grand Encampment of Ireland after 1804.[23] The publicity created by the book may have also helped to popularise these ceremonies.[24] The book may well have been an attempt, by him, to rehabilitate himself with those disaffected Freemasons. He also appears to have had a general desire to impress those of influence within the world of Scottish Freemasonry but his lack of formal education meant that he did not have the ability to write such a book. By having Brewster do so, on his behalf, he did the next best thing and produced a 'history' of Scottish Freemasonry at his own expense. Brewster almost certainly required the income and the fact that his name does not appear as the author suggests that he was anxious to protect his anonymity. The fantastic nature of some of the contents, the uncritical repetition of myth and legend and the attitude towards the

Roman Church would have been detrimental to his reputation. From a personal point of view this anonymity would have suited Brewster as much as it did Lawrie.

19th Century Developments of the Myth

The Grand Lodge of Scotland was the only active Masonic body in Scotland when it prohibited its Daughter Lodges from working non-Masonic ceremonials.[25] That, however, did not lead to the disappearance of those ceremonials. Some Freemasons who enjoyed them may have continued to confer them clandestinely within Lodges. There were also several Encampments which existed separately from any other body.[26] The Grand Lodge's stated reason for outlawing its Lodges from working these ceremonials was because they were not Masonic and not Scottish. However, the decision may also have been partly a reaction to the activities of Lodge Mother Kilwinning, No.0 that, between 1743 and 1808, was independent of Grand Lodge. The late Brother George Draffen of Newington states:

> '*In the middle and latter half of the eighteenth century, it was the commonly held, but quite erroneous, opinion that Lodge Mother Kilwinning was the repository of all sorts and conditions of High Masonic Degrees. One of the results of this was that, in 1779, when Lodge Mother Kilwinning was independent of the Grand Lodge of Scotland certain Irish masons sought from her, and were granted a Charter under the title of The High Knight Templars of Ireland Kilwinning Lodge. This was purely a Craft Charter, but, as mentioned above, there was at that time an erroneous idea that a charter from Lodge Kilwinning granted authority to confer all manner of High Degrees. As far as can be ascertained, this lodge confined itself to the working of the Knight Templar Degree.*'[27]

Lodge Mother Kilwinning did not work any degrees other than the three Craft degrees and the idea that they did probably came from the fact that it did grant a Charter to an Irish Lodge with the title: 'The High Knight Templars of Ireland Kilwinning Lodge'. Freemasons in Dublin were granted a *Craft Lodge* charter but that Lodge also worked the Knight Templar ceremony thereby reinforcing the notion that Craft Freemasonry and the non-Masonic, imported, Knight Templar ceremonial were somehow linked. Although this Irish Lodge granted charters to other Lodges in Ireland, no Lodges of this 'type' were created in Scotland.

At about the same time there was another body apparently claiming jurisdiction over the KT ceremony by the title of *The Early Grand Encampment of Ireland*, which claimed to have existed since 1705.[28] Prior to 1800 this body had granted two charters to modern KT encampments at Aberdeen and Kilmarnock. Once the Grand Lodge of Scotland prohibited the imported KT ceremonial in its Daughter Lodges, devotees of the ceremonial sought legitimacy by obtaining charters from elsewhere. After 1800 the *Early Grand Encampment of Ireland* granted a further 17 KT charters in Scotland.[29] One of these Encampments subsequently formed the *Royal Grand Conclave* of Scotland and another, the *Early Grand Encampment of Scotland*.[30] These bodies passed through a number changes and reorganisations the details of which need not detain us here other than to note that ultimately they came together, in 1907, to form the present *Great Priory of Scotland*. Unfortunately, most of the early records of these bodies are missing but the way they viewed their origins can be discerned by examining other sources and are discussed below.

Although the Grand Lodge of Scotland's decision to compel its Daughter Lodges to cease conducting the non-Masonic ceremonies of Royal Arch and Knight Templar they did not disappear from the Masonic landscape of Scotland. These ceremonials might have died out had some Freemasons not decided to maintain them by creating bodies to act as 'Grand Lodges'. One individual in particular should be mentioned — Alexander Deuchar (1777–1844).[31] In 1809 Deuchar, who was then Commander of the Edinburgh Encampment No.51 (Chartered by the Early Grand Encampment of Ireland) convened a meeting of *The Grand Assembly of Knights Templar in Edinburgh*.[32] He announced that Prince Edward, the Duke of Kent (1767–1820), who was Grand Master of the Order in England (1804–1807) and Grand Patron of the Order (1807–1820), had accepted the position of *Royal Grand Patron of the Order for Scotland* and that he, Deuchar, had been appointed *Provisional Grand Master*. In 1812 the Duke of Kent's brother, Augustus Frederic, Duke of Sussex (1773–1843) became Grand Master of the Order in England. The Duke of Kent provided a Charter of Dispensation for the new Scottish body known as the Royal Grand Conclave. The Duke granted a 'full' charter in 1815 which named Deuchar Grand Master for life.[33] The Charter is headed:

HIS ROYAL HIGHNESS PRINCE EDWARD DUKE OF KENT
Knight of the Most Honourable and Illustrious Orders of the Garter, St. Patrick, etc. etc. etc.
To the Knights Companions of the Exalted Religious and Military Orders of the Temple and Sepulchre, and of Saint John of Jerusalem.
H.R.D.M. K.D.S.H.
HEALTH - PEACE - GOODWILL.[34]

The Royal Grand Conclave then tried to bring all the existing KT encampments in Scotland under its jurisdiction by having them surrender their Irish Charters and issuing replacements. Independent encampments were encouraged to seek Charters from the new body. The Royal Grand Conclave was, initially, only partly successful and some encampments preferred to continue as before.

Deuchar had, apparently, planned to have all the Christian ceremonials brought under the control of the Royal Grand Conclave and all those which were not Christian were to be governed by another body — the Supreme Grand Royal Arch Chapter for Scotland (S.G.R.A.C.) which was founded in 1817 with Deuchar as one of its leading lights.[35] The history of these Masonic bodies has been adequately described elsewhere, particularly by authors such as Draffen, Lindsay, etc. and whilst there is much of interest, need not detain us here.

The early years of the two bodies fall into the period during which the fascination for the myth that the medieval Order of KT had a connection with modern Scottish Freemasonry first had a wide circulation. This coincides almost precisely with the era of Romanticism, that intellectual view of the world which was characterised, in many western artistic and literary works of the late 18th to the mid-19th century, by a rejection of the precepts of order, calm, harmony, balance, idealisation, and rationality that typified Classicism in general and late 18th-century Neo-classicism in particular.[36] It was also a reaction, by some, to the Enlightenment and against 18th-century rationalism and physical materialism in general. Romanticism emphasised the individual and the subjective, the irrational and the imaginative, the personal and the spontaneous, the emotional, the visionary and the transcendental. This period was characterised by two opposing views of the world: the calculating rationality of the Enlightenment (with particular emphasis for the purposes of this book on the Scottish Enlightenment $c.1730–c.1790$) and the Romantic or mythological vision. It is tempting to suggest that the Grand Lodge of Scotland held to the former and those who advocated that the Royal Arch and Knight Templar were legitimate components of Freemasonry held to the latter.

In Scotland, the beginning of Romanticism can be traced to the work of James 'Ossian' Macpherson (1736–1796). His epic Gaelic poetry caught the imagination of many and the second edition of his major work: *Fingal, an Ancient Epic Poem, composed by Ossian the son of Fingal* (1773) was translated into seven European languages. These translations inspired men such as Franz P. Schubert (1797–1828) and Felix Mendelssohn (1809–1847) to interpret the author's romantic writings as romantic music. Schubert specifically set to music parts of Macpherson's work (i.e. *Ossian's Song after the Death of Nathos*). Other examples of the 'romanticising' of Scotland appear in the work of Mendelssohn's *Overture: The Hebrides (Fingal's Cave), Opus 26* (1829). *Ivanhoe* (1819) was made into an opera by Gioacchino Rossini (1792–1868) and Scott attended its premier in Paris. At the same time the widely reported gallant and heroic activities of a variety of Scottish Regiments added to the romantic image of the kingdom. Sir Walter Scott's (1771–1832) historical novels, the first of their type, did much to promote the romantic Scottish myth so well known to us today. Scott typified the Romantic Movement and fully understood the mood of the country. His earlier historical novels were set in Scotland and dealt with Scottish subjects, e.g. *Rob Roy* (1817). These appealed to his country people but when he extended his work to encompass England, his work gained a national, and international, appeal. The first of these 'English' novels was *Ivanhoe* and was also interpreted, musically, by Schubert (i.e. *Romance of Richard the Lionheart*, from *Ivanhoe — The Crusader's Return*). *Ivanhoe* has Sir Brian de Bois-Guilbert, a Knight Templar, as a central character. Scott portrays him as sinister, manipulative and violent.[37] The character of de Bois-Guilbert whilst important does not convey the dominant theme of the novel. The concepts of chivalry, honour, martial prowess, secret quests, glory, defending the weak and courtly love are paramount. Although Scott casts de Bois-Guilbert in an entirely negative manner that did not stop the Grand Conclave, no doubt swept along by the romantic tide, from inviting him, in 1823, to be Grand Master of the Scottish Knights Templar![38] He declined, he said, for reasons of health.

This era of romanticism is amply demonstrated by two events: the visit to Edinburgh in 1822 by George Augustus Frederick, George IV (1820–1830, b.1762) and the Eglinton Tournament. The king's visit was orchestrated by Scott and led directly to the popularisation of 'romantic Scotland' throughout the 19th century and which still colours the perception of the country to this day. George was Initiated in 1787, when Prince of Wales, and served as Grand Master (of the premier GL) 1790–1813.[39] He was an elder brother of Prince Edward, Duke of Kent, who had granted Charters to the Scottish KT in 1813 and 1815. The Coronation of George IV in 1821 was conducted according to ancient feudalistic and chivalric codes from the medieval period. The Coronation service took place in Westminster Abbey followed by a variety of ceremonies in Westminster Hall including a public state banquet for the Peers of the Realm. The Earl Marshal, the Lord High Constable and the Lord High Steward escorted the first course into the royal presence whilst on horseback. The food having been delivered, the three had then to retire, backwards, for a considerable distance — no mean feat of horsemanship in the confines of the hall. The king was presented with tokens of loyalty and fealty; the Archbishop of Canterbury presented a bowl of dilligrout.[40] The Duke of Atholl, as Lord of Man, presented two falcons and the Lord of the Manor of Nether Blissington gave three maple cups. The king's hereditary champion, in full armour, and caparisoned on a charger, preceded by two trumpeters, two esquires carrying his lance and shield, and escorted by the Earl Marshal and Lord High Constable, issued a general challenge to all comers to fight if they disputed the new sovereign's right to the throne. He did so by throwing down his gauntlet three times. He too had to retreat from the royal presence by backing his horse away for a considerable distance. This was especially difficult, mounted, and in full armour. Although intelligent and cultured, George IV was self-indulgent and prone to excess — his Coronation cost over £25,000 and the subsequent state banquet degenerated into an orgy. However, he set the taste in fashion for many years and his appearance in Edinburgh, wearing a kilt, made Scotland and all things Scottish, fashionable.

For the Coronation of Queen Victoria (1819–1901), in 1838, the Whig government led by the Prime Minister, William Lamb, 2nd Viscount Melbourne (1779–1848) decided to sweep away these medieval ceremonies and replace them with a comparatively simple procession from Buckingham Palace to Westminster Abbey.[41] The Government cited the excesses of the Coronation of George IV and that the economy was in a dire situation. There was, for instance, a huge number of unemployed and it was estimated that many thousands of weavers were starving. Despite the economic argument of 'we can't afford it', the decision was taken at a time when interest in all things medieval was high. Scott's books about knights in armour, the quests of knights and the saving of damsels in distress were best sellers. Inevitably there was a reaction, at least from those who most identified with the social continuity such ceremonies represented — the nobility (mainly Tory supporters) and many 'country' Whigs. Others, who could trace their ancestry to the time of the origins of chivalry and royal service, even if no longer in positions of power and influence, also found such a wholesale reform distasteful. Despite all the questions in the House and all the letters to *The Times*, Queen Victoria's Coronation followed the new Whig format.

Archibald William Montgomerie, the 13th Earl of Eglinton (1812–1861), who would have been involved in Queen Victoria's Coronation had it been conducted in its original form, decided to stage a medieval tournament at the family estate near Kilwinning. Eglinton, egged on, bullied, encouraged and applauded by friends, family and all who detested the Whig evisceration of one of the most powerful ceremonies demonstrating 'their' place and station in the country, poured huge sums into the project. The Eglinton Tournament took place on 28 and 29 August 1839. Watched by an estimated 80,000 spectators, knights in armour jousted for the favours of maidens. Lavish banquets were held and entertainment was supplied. Chivalry was once again on display in all its glory. Unfortunately the weather was unkind as it rained heavily and although the tournament was held it was a damp and uncomfortable affair for most of the participants as well as the spectators.

The motives for Eglinton's decision are simple and straightforward. As a child he was brought up on a diet of the honour and antiquity of his ancestry and the family's chivalric role in Scottish society throughout the medieval period. This view of the past was reinforced by his childhood pastimes of reading the works of the likes of Walter Scott, role playing and dreaming of knights in armour and their 'derring-do'. There was a political element but this was secondary to his desire to display to the world that chivalry, and all that it inculcated, had relevance in the modern world. The political dimension was the motivating force of many of those who encouraged him in this endeavour.

Had Walter Scott accepted the offer to become Grand Master of the Masonic Knights Templar in 1823 the Order may well have taken a quite different course. After Scott declined the position the Order experienced a severe decline to the point that it almost ceased to exist:

> *'The Society of Templars he revived from a profound slumber, which had well nigh passed into the sleep that knows no waking and the few hours of leisure he could command during the closing months of absence from Bombay, he dedicated to a 'Memoir of the Order of the Temple'.*[42]

The individual who revived the Order was James Burnes (1801–1862) whose Great Grandfather was the brother of William Burnes — father of Caledonia's Bard, Robert Burnes (later Burns) (1759–1796). The life and Masonic career of Burnes have been described elsewhere.[43] Of great importance here, however, is his publication of '*A Sketch of the History of the Knights Templars*' in 1837 — a year after a large number entered the Order.[44] (Plate 7) The book was dedicated to '*His Royal Highness, Prince Augustus Frederic, Duke of Sussex, K.G. &c., P.R.S., Grand Prior of England*'.

Burnes had gone to India in 1821 to serve in the army as a medical officer with the artillery and infantry. He was appointed Surgeon to the Residency of Cutch in 1825. Becoming ill he left India for Scotland in 1834. In August of that year he was made a Freemason in Lodge St. Peter, No.120, along with his brothers Charles and David.[45] Also in attendance on that occasion were his father, also named James, and his two other brothers, Alexander and Adam, who had been initiated in that Lodge in 1830.

For the first time the origin of the alleged Scottish connection between the medieval Order of the KT and modern Freemasonry can be pinpointed with accuracy. Burnes' book consists of 61 pages:

- Introduction
- Chapter 1 — The Hospitallers [*sic*]
- Chapter 2 — The Knights Templars
- Chapter 3 — The Persecution of the Templars
- Chapter 4 — The Continuation of the Order
- Chapter 5 — The Knights Templars in Scotland, and
- Appendix — containing the Bull of Pope Clement V and the Obligation of the Scottish Masonic KT (both in Latin)

In the Introduction Burnes explains that following a handsome gift presented to him by the Freemasons of Scotland in advance of his return to India he can think of no better way to repay their generosity than leaving with them '. . . *some Memoir of the Order of the Temple*, . . .'[46] He readily admits that much is taken from other publications. In relation to the history of the medieval Order he presents a standard view. Thus chapters 1 and 2 contain nothing out of the ordinary. In Chapter 3 Burnes becomes an apologist of the Order describing Philip the Fair as '*tyrannical and rapacious*' and he describes Pope Clement V as a '*creature of Philip*'. Here Burnes provides information not generally found elsewhere. Clement V invited the Knights of St. John and the Knights Templar to come to discuss '. . .the best mode of supporting the kings of Armenia and Cyprus'. Jacques de Molay, Grand Master of the Templars, obeys the Pope and departs from Cyprus — ' ...with a train of 60 knights and a treasure of 150,000 florins of gold, and a great quality of silver money'. The Hospitallers do not attend the meeting. Subsequent events described by Burnes regarding the arrest of the KT, their imprisonment, torture, confession and details etc. of their alleged crimes are unsurprising.

Chapters 4 and 5 are of great importance as this is the original source of the myth of the connection between the KT and modern Freemasonry in its Scottish guise. Chapter 5 is reproduced as appendix XI. The importance of Chapter 4 lies in the plan that Burnes sets out for the new, revived, Order in Scotland:

'... the Order of the Temple, being exclusively devoted to the Christian religion, cannot be considered in the slightest degree connected with Free Masonry, which, it is well known, welcomes equally to its bosom the Jew and the Gentile, the Christian and the Mahommedan, requiring from each only a belief in a Divine Being, with a just sense of moral rectitude and conscientious obligation.'[47]

The revived Order of Masonic Knights Templar was not initially considered to be Masonic in the same way as Craft Freemasonry. This is an extremely important point and is one that has been glossed over by modern writers who have assumed that because the Order was created by Scottish Freemasons it was Masonic. Certainly the Order subsequently came to be accepted as Masonic but that lay some years in the future. Another ancillary point is Burnes' emphatic statement that the Order was Christian — not Roman Catholic. This was necessary because the new Order was to be open to all Christians and was not to be a part, as originally, of the Roman Church. Having 'adjusted' the religious basis of the Order it was now necessary to amend the vows to be taken by the candidates on admission to the Order. Burnes explains the need for this in the following manner: '. . . the [original] vow contains many dispositions which, misconstrued, might appear incompatible with the advance of knowledge and manners of the age'. In other words, the vows taken by the Medieval Order of the Knights Templar were no longer suitable for the new Order. Burnes re-interpreted the four vows of the Medieval Order: Poverty, Chastity, Obedience and the (re) Conquest of the Holy Land.

In relation to poverty the vow was no longer to reduce the members to '*absolute poverty*' and was changed to merely remind the candidates that they '. . . *ought always be ready to share their fortune with the unfortunate*'. The vow of chastity became the '*obligation that society imposes on all men to labour to overcome their vicious propensities, in order not to outrage either decency or morality*'. The obedience due to the Grand Master (of the Order) has been adjusted to also include the duty to obey '*as a citizen, the government of his country*'. The re-interpretation of the last vow was explained at greater length:

'. . . *their principal aim is not to recover the dominions of which the Order was despoiled, or the earth which received the body of Jesus the Christ but to reconquer to the doctrine for which was precipitated into the tomb that divine preceptor of men . . .*', and to emphasise the point: '— *in a word, that the Templars are not ambitious of subduing the physical universe to their domination, but the nations that cover it to Christian morality*'.[48]

The differences between the Medieval Order and that which was created, supposedly in its image, in the late 18th century and formalised in the 19th, are enormous. It behoves us all, always to bear in mind what *kind* of Knight Templar is being discussed at any given time in any particular publication. Failure to do so leads to exactly the same kind of confusion as to what kind of 'masonry' — Masonry (Freemasonry) or masonry (stonemasonry) — is being discussed.

This activity took place after Burnes arrived back in Scotland. As has been seen, the precursor of the modern Masonic KT underwent a revival when, in 1836 and later, a number of influential Freemasons joined the Grand Conclave. Between January and May 1836, 72 new members were admitted.[49] However, it was not only the Masonic KT that was revived at this time. In 1839 the Royal Order of Scotland underwent a revival also due to an influx of new members. Deuchar had continued to be very involved with the Grand Conclave and S.G.R.A.C. and had yet more ideas for the development of Freemasonry in Scotland. There were, at that time, three 'Masonic' systems that were not under the control of any single body and he had plans to create the equivalent of a Grand Lodge for:

- The Rite of Perfection.
- The Rite of Mizraim.
- The Ancient and Accepted Scottish Rite.[50]

However, he was over-burdened by his existing duties and sought the assistance of George A. Walker Arnott of Arlary (1799–1868) and requested that he form a Grand Council of Rites to control these three systems within Scotland. Walker Arnott accordingly formed this body and that eventually led to a conflict with Dr Charles Morison of Greenfield (1780–1849) who, in 1846, set up the Supreme Council for Scotland and claimed jurisdiction over the above-mentioned Ancient and Accepted Scottish Rite.[51] Although this is another interesting aspect of Scottish Masonic history it is not essential to the subject presently under discussion. What is important here is that all this activity, during the first half of the 18th century, demonstrates one thing — no one and no body (apart from the Grand Lodge of Scotland) was quite sure what non-Craft Masonic ceremonies there were, who should have control of them and, most importantly, of what the ceremonials consisted. This latter point is demonstrated by the fact that at a meeting of the Grand Conclave on 11 March 1842 a letter was read from Frater. G. A. Walker Arnott enquiring about the degrees of H.R.D.M. + K.D.S.H. which belonged to the Grand Conclave by virtue of the Charters granted by the Grand Master of the KT of England, the Duke of Kent, in 1813 and 1815. Although Walker Arnott apparently wrote the letter in his capacity as a Knight Templar he was then making vigorous attempts to revive the Royal Order of Scotland.[52] His enquiry was probably an attempt to clarify the situation in respect of the 'unallocated' ceremonials to assist in his work of setting up the Grand Council of Rites. Those present at that meeting of Grand Conclave apparently had no knowledge of the ceremonies of H.R.D.M. + K.D.S.H. thereby indicating that the KT were unaware of, and did not practise, those ceremonies. The meeting of 11 March was important for another reason in that it authorised the production of the Statutes of the Order which contained the first Scottish history of the Masonic KT. Moreover, the existence of evidence of the continuation of the Order of the KT since the official dissolution in 1312 to the present day is claimed. One Dom Augustin Calmet is specifically mentioned in this respect. No further information is provided as to a source for the involvement of this individual until almost 150 years later and so will be considered in more detail in the next chapter.

The Grand Secretary (1842–1856) of the Grand Conclave, John Linning Woodman (1811–1856), wrote to the Grand Conclave of England seeking clarification regarding the degrees of H.R.D.M. + K.D.S.H. included in their Charter. The answer received was '...*several of the Masonic degrees mentioned in their Charter from the Duke of Kent, are practised either by the Order of Mizraim or the Royal Order of Scotland*'. This is a significant revelation. The

Duke of Kent's Charters of 1813 and 1815 apparently granted the Scottish KT jurisdiction over the Royal Order of Scotland's ceremonies! Grand Conclave thereupon in January 1843 remitted the whole matter to a committee consisting of Fraters. G. A. Walker Arnott, John L. Woodman and Alexander Deuchar, PGM, but it does not appear ever to have reported officially.[53]

The formation of such a Committee shows that it was considered necessary to determine what non-Craft ceremonies there were, and which body should have jurisdiction over them. Walker Arnott's seemingly innocent question is therefore of great importance. By asking the question in the first place — the question as to 'who governed what' had to be debated. Walker Arnott was the leading light of the ROS ('...*it is not until February 1843 that meetings become regular with Dr Walker Arnott, though only a member of the Order for two years, generally in the Chair and taking the leading part...*') a member of the Grand Conclave, and someone who has agreed to set up a Grand Council of Rites to govern a large number of 'Masonic' ceremonies was obviously seeking information which would clarify the position of these ceremonies in Scotland and allow *him* to arrange and 'allocate' these non-Craft ceremonials according to his remit from Deuchar.[54] The absence of any records as to the outcome of any discussion regarding jurisdiction over the non-Craft ceremonies suggests that this very small group of prominent Freemasons simply decided among themselves how to organise non-Craft Freemasonry in Scotland.

The significance of the 'shared membership' of the Orders is revealed further when the Grand Conclave published its second *Statutes* in 1843, which included, for the first time, an *'Historical Notice of the Order'*.[55] The account gives a brief, but standard, version of the history of the medieval Order and its suppression. Thereafter in the *'Historical Notice'* the legitimacy of the French Masonic KT is questioned because of its claimed descent from the medieval Order based on the forged Charter of Larmenius.[56] The account then provides, for the first time, a reasonably comprehensive Scottish KT history:

'*It is agreed by all hands, even the French, that the Templars joined the standard of Robert the Bruce, and fought in his cause, until the issue of the Battle of Bannockburn in 1314, securely placed him on the throne. That Monarch was not ungrateful.*'[57]

It is alleged that the KT joined Bruce before the Battle of Bannockburn, but as with the suggestion that they were present at that battle, there is no evidence that they did so. However, it shows that Robert the Bruce is seen as central to their 'Traditional History'. Interestingly they distance themselves from the Royal Order of Scotland:

'The institution of the "Royal Order" by King Robert after the battle of Bannockburn, has led some historians to suppose that the Templars were identified with that body, and when we consider that for centuries that Order was connected with the higher grades of Masonry, which in our own day have been recognized by the Templars, it is not surprising to find that this error has been very prevalent. M. Thory in his "Acta Latomorum," gives an account of the Royal Order, otherwise called the Orders of H. D. M. of Kilwinning, but does not attempt in any way to combine it with the Temple. Indeed, as will subsequently appear, no such amalgamation ever took place.'[58]

The need to mention the Royal Order of Scotland appears to have been due to a desire to keep the two Orders separate despite common elements in their 'Traditional Histories' then being created. This is probably a manifestation of the influence of the 'shared membership'. The Grand Conclave claimed, therefore, to be older than the Royal Order, by a few years at least, and this required them to assert that they, the KT, had joined Bruce *before* the Battle of Bannockburn took place. We are confronted, therefore, with the situation that Robert the Bruce was allegedly responsible for the establishment of two Scottish Masonic bodies — the KT and the Royal Order immediately after Bannockburn, both of which continue to exist today. As a further conundrum we are presented with the sight of one Masonic body, the Grand Conclave, using part of the traditional, that is mythological, history of another Masonic Order to support its own mythological past. Those who wrote the 'Traditional Histories' of these two Orders at least attempted to keep their mythological histories separate and distinct, even though they were members of both. The conflation of the two (and other) mythical histories is a more modern construct of authors who were not members of either Order. Bruce's place in the myth has been developed almost beyond recognition since Anderson made the simple statement, in 1738, that following the Battle of Bannockburn, Bruce *'employ'd the Craft* [stonemasons] *in repairing the castles, Palaces and Houses'*.

The main elements of the myth, which are still in general circulation today, were created, therefore, by the KT themselves as a 'Traditional History' between 1842 and 1843 (based on Burnes Sketch of the Order) and is confirmed by internal evidence from the *'Historical Notice of the Order'* (1843). Part of this evidence is the incorporation of Latin Charters, which are reproduced in full in the *'Historical Notice . . .'*. These deal with the transfer of land which once belonged to the medieval Order of KT and are dated *c*.1340 and *c*.1440. These Charters were transcribed by Father Hay *c*.1700 and made available in print for the first time by James Maidment in *The Genealogie of the Sainteclaires of Rosslyn*, published in 1835. The text of the Charters as used by the Grand Conclave in its *'Historical Notice'* are almost certainly copies of Maidment's printed versions of the Charters. This can be said with certainty because the KT version contains the same Latin errors, in translation, as those of Maidment. This being so, the modern myth can be now seen in the process of creation. The modern KT were well acquainted with Maidment's work for their *'Historical Notice . . .'* quotes from his *Templaria* (1828) which was also taken, and edited by him, from Hay's MSS.

The creative process is further revealed by the use of other, more recent, material. The *'Historical Notice . . .'* quotes from Walter Scott's poem, *Halidon Hill* (1822). The *'Historical Notice . . .'* states that this battle took place in 1402 and claims that because Scott uses as characters: a Scottish KT by the name of Adam de Vipont and the Prior of Maison-Dieu (a Preceptory of the Knights Hospitaller), this was proof that the two Orders had continued to exist, separately, until the early 15th century. That Scott made it clear that his poem was fiction, although based on the events at the Battle of Homildon Hill (1402), which he transferred to the Battle of Halidon Hill (1333), entirely escaped those who wrote the *'Historical Notice . . .'*.

Here then is reached a pivotal point in the myth-making process — it, the myth, was published in 1843 for, and by, the modern Scottish KT. It had not then yet attained its present, full, form and therefore the main elements of the 1843 myth might usefully be tabulated for comparative purposes.

- Everywhere except Scotland the KT were tried and condemned and their lands confiscated.
- The medieval Order of the KT *'survived rather than flourished'* in Scotland.
- The claim of the French KT to have descended directly from the medieval Order is false, being based on the forged Charter of Transmission of Larmenius.
- Walter de Clifton was Grand Preceptor of Scotland in 1309 and later became Grand Master.

- In 1309 Robert the Bruce was a proscribed fugitive.
- In 1309 two KT, Walter de Clifton, Preceptor, and William de Middleton, were interrogated by a Papal Legate, John de Soleure, and William Lamberton, Bishop of St Andrews (?–1328).[59]
- The Preceptor, Walter de Clifton, admitted that the rest of his Scottish Brethren had fled and joined Robert the Bruce.
- Clifton and Middleton were imprisoned for a short time.
- The fugitive KT fought at the Battle of Bannockburn and as a reward Robert the Bruce confirmed their former 'grants.'
- Robert the Bruce established the Royal Order of Scotland, otherwise known as the 'Order of H.D.M. of Kilwinning', immediately after the battle but this new Order had nothing to do with the KT.
- Proof of the continued, separate, existence of the KT in Scotland is confirmed by the fact that they held land as demonstrated by Latin charters owned by the Grand Conclave and Scott's poem *Halidon Hill*.
- In the reign of James IV (1488–1513, b.1473) the Order of St. John and the KT, together with their lands, were finally amalgamated.
- In 1560 Sir James Sandilands, Preceptor of Torphichen, resigned the lands of the amalgamated Order to the State in return for a temporal Lordship and 10,000 crowns.
- The Knights '...*thus deprived of their patrimonial interest drew off in a body, with David Seton, Grand Prior of Scotland, at their head*'.
- After vanishing for 200 years the Order re-appeared.
- The suggestion that the Order then came under the control of the leaders of the Jacobite party and that this began the Order's association with Masonic bodies is a '*gross error*' created by those who wished to '*escape the labour of investigation*'.
- John Graham, Viscount Dundee (?1649–1689) died at the Battle of Killiecrankie wearing a Grand Cross of the KT.
- John Erskine, 6th or 11th Earl of Mar, (1675–1732) succeeded Dundee as Grand Master of the KT and he was succeeded by the Duke of Atholl.
- The Duke of Atholl was succeeded by Charles Edward Stuart (the Young Pretender) at a KT ceremony held at Holyrood Palace in 1745. This is supported by the existence of a letter '*in the archives of an old and distinguished Scottish family*', describing the ceremony.
- After the failure of the Jacobite rising most of the Scottish KT went into exile

with their Grand Master. Those that remained hid within the ranks of Freemasons.

- After the death of Charles Edward Stuart, John Oliphant, of Bachilton, became Grand Master and that after his demise in 1795 no Grand Master was elected until after the death of the last of the Stuart line, Henry Benedict Maria Stuart (1725–1807) the Cardinal of York. Thereafter, the history continues with details of Alexander Deuchar's 'reign'.

The small group who were responsible for the creation of the myth were largely those who, in 1836, were instrumental in re-invigorating the Order.

'The compiler of this Historical Note is unknown, but it is generally believed to have been J. Linning Woodman, who was Grand Secretary and Registrar of the Order from 1842-1854. He seems to have been assisted by Walter Arnott, Murray Pringle, W.S., and W.E. Aytoun, Professor of Belles Lettres at Edinburgh University. The Note is a mixture of fact and what may be fiction, so ingeniously interwoven as to produce a fabric which is very difficult to subject to accurate tests as to genuineness.'[60]

This shows that the myth by this time was becoming similar to the modern version. The missing elements are the notion that French KT fled from France to the west of Scotland together with 'treasure', it was they who assisted Bruce at Bannockburn, that the St. Clairs of Rosslyn were KT and that Rosslyn Chapel was some kind of repository for a variety of artefacts.

Not until after Charles Darwin (1809–1882) published his *'On the Origin of Species . . .'* (1859) would the study of the past gain a more rigorous and 'scientific' methodology. Even then, this way of examining the past began to be used to study the creation and development of the nation state rather than the experience of individuals and/or groups. The myth has never, therefore, been seriously challenged since its creation and it has become so entrenched within the mythology of Freemasonry that any challenges, especially from within Freemasonry itself, are ineffectual and frequently are ridiculed.

In 1859 Lawrie's son, William Alexander Laurie, (1799–1870) Grand Secretary of the Grand Lodge of Scotland, published a second edition of his father's work and he provides a chapter on the history of the KT in Scotland which repeats and elaborates the earlier work. The book is well written, is more comprehensible, and is a more detailed account of the history of Scottish Freemasonry. The amount of space devoted to the 'history' of the KT is perhaps an indication, by then, of the widespread acceptance of the myth as fact. Laurie reproduces a letter from J. Linning Woodman, Registrar of Grand Conclave, dated 22 March 1844, to the effect that henceforth membership of the KT will no longer be restricted to Freemasons. The letter was sent to him as Grand Secretary so that the decision might:

'...be generally communicated to the Free Masons belonging to Scotland'.

The letter also includes the assertion:

'...the Knights of the Temple — who's Scottish descent from the Ancient [Medieval] Order is unquestioned — that although the connection which has for a considerable period of time subsisted between them and Masonic Associations is now in some measure severed...'[61]

According to the new history of the KT the medieval Order had pre-existed Freemasonry and it had created Freemasonry. Logically, therefore, it was not necessary to first become a Freemason. It is surely ironic that a 'history' so recently created from other Masonic traditions, so quickly had the effect of making a Masonic body, founded by Freemasons for Freemasons, into a non-Masonic body! Grand Conclave did not go so far as to demand that individuals become KT before becoming Freemasons! There are indications that some genuinely believed in the superiority of the KT over Freemasonry, given that, for example, some Lodges demanded that only KT could be Lodge Office-bearers and that KT encampments demanded pride of place in Masonic processions.[62] It is perhaps fortunate that Grand Conclave did not allow its encampments to admit non-Masons, preserving that privilege for itself; one which it never, apparently, exercised. In 1856 Grand Conclave reversed the earlier decision and once again became an entirely Masonic body.[63]

Laurie provides no new evidence in support of the claimed link between the medieval Order of the Knights Templar and Scottish Freemasonry. He does however give a clear insight to the thoughts of Freemasons of the mid-19th century on that subject:

'It will be necessary to give some account of the Knight Templars, the *fraternity of Freemasons, whose affluence and virtues aroused the envy of contemporaries, and whose unmerited and unhappy end must have frequently excited the compassion of posterity. To prove that the order of the Knight Templars was a branch of Free Masonry would be a useless Labour, as the fact has been invariably acknowledged by Free Masons themselves, and none have been more zealous to establish it than the enemies of their order.'[64]*

This statement shows how deeply rooted the belief in a connection between the two groups had become within only 60 years of the connection first being claimed by Barruel. What is more, there is no need, according to Laurie, to prove the connection because not only do Freemasons know the link exists but also the enemies of Freemasonry know the link exists! Laurie's book was published after the Masonic KT (based on Burnes' 1837 work) published its 'Traditional History' which disavowed any connection with Freemasonry and yet Laurie was a member of the KT! The above quotation provides one more point worthy of consideration. Laurie is following the 19th century Masonic belief that Freemasonry existed before the Crusades (see Ramsay's *Oration*, 1737, etc.) — '*the Knight Templars was a branch of Free Masonry*'. Having dispensed with the need to prove the existence of a link between the Scottish Freemason and the KT, Laurie goes on to provide a lengthy, sympathetic and fairly standard history of the medieval Order which by its very inclusion in a book on the history of Scottish Freemasonry tends to lend credence to the claim that there was a link between the KT and Freemasonry. But Laurie seems to be trying to keep everyone happy. As a member of the Masonic Knights Templar he promotes their pretensions but supplies no supportive evidence, merely relying on the argument: '*the fact has been invariably acknowledged by Free Masons themselves*' but at the same time placating Craft Freemasons by stating that the KT are a branch of Freemasonry.

D. Murray Lyon (1830–1903) in his book '*History of the Lodge of Edinburgh Mary's Chapel No.1, embracing an account of the rise and progress of freemasonry in Scotland*' (1873) made a valiant attempt to set the record straight. At the commencement of the chapter dealing with Knights Templar he states:

'*In their ardent desire to associate ideas of antiquity with the "High Degrees," some writers have not hesitated to identify the Masonic Templars now existing as the rightful representatives of the Knight*

Templars of the middle ages. In this they are altogether mistaken. Masonic Templarism does not in any respect bear relationship to the Templars of the Crusades, but is a branch of the system of Masonic Knighthood which had its origin on the Continent some hundred and thirty years ago.[65] [That is, soon after Ramsay's *Oration* of 1737]

D. Murray Lyon became a Freemason in 1856 in Ayr which is the heartland associated with the myth of the Knights Templar and the Lodge at Kilwinning.[66] He was ideally placed to examine the various theories and debates then taking place. The tale of the alleged connection between the KT and Freemasonry attracted his attention and he published a short tract on the subject which he later expanded upon in his 1873 publication mentioned above.[67] Lyon became Grand Secretary of the Grand Lodge of Scotland in 1877. He was, therefore, able to examine all the relevant documents and other material relating to the alleged connection between the Knights Templar and Freemasonry. Note that he had no axe to grind in this respect, having made his initial investigation a few years before becoming Grand Secretary. He was well acquainted with the details of the myth and the work of two of his predecessors in office, Alexander Lawrie and his son W. Alexander Laurie, who had published their histories of Freemasonry in 1804 and 1859. Lyon's examination of documents and other material was accelerated when he was invited to write the history of the Lodge of Edinburgh known as the '*Tercentenary Edition*.'[68] He re-visits his earlier work but evidently during his later research he found nothing to change his original position. He repeats his criticism of both Laurie's work, specifically referring to the major flaws regarding the claimed existence of a hereditary Grand Master. He does so by again quoting, at length, the critical analysis of that claim by James Maidment.[69]

When he discusses the Masonic Knights Templar of Scotland he is able to cite sources and individuals with precision.[70] That is an indication of his intimate knowledge of the subject. He identifies Alexander Deuchar as being '*chiefly instrumental in instituting the Grand Conclave of Knight Templars*'.[71] As has been shown above, it was this body which adapted and used the Traditional History provided by James Burnes which was the basis of the modern myth regarding Freemasonry and the Knights Templar so popular today.

There is one glaring inconsistency that few have noticed. Why did those involved in 'reviving' the KT as a Masonic Order early in the 19th century, one which they claimed had a direct lineal descent from the medieval Order officially suppressed in 1312, and had a continuous existence which was well known to everyone, need a charter from the modern English Order of KT?

Into the 20th century

The Modern Era

The 'history' provided by Burnes, elaborated by Woodman, and perpetuated by numerous others was continued into the 20th century. For many the argument that there was a link between the medieval Order of the Knights Templar and modern Freemasonry had been won — the debate had begun to become repetitive. Attention therefore shifted to finding evidence — the search for a 'missing link', one which would prove the myth to be true. The search for a 'missing link' led to the discovery of several — Rosslyn Chapel, the Kirkwall Scroll and the Battle of Bannockburn. Others do not attract the same level of attention but are nevertheless significant, more particularly because of their cumulative effect. One such example concerns the Battle of Killiecrankie which is often cited as an example of the proof which exists to confirm the continued existence of the KT hundreds of years after it had been suppressed. An author writing in 1921 examined this story:

'*It has been said that* . . . [the well-known French historian and theologian] *Dom Calmet has lent the authority of his name to three important statements: (1) that John Claverhouse, Viscount Dundee, was Grand Master of the Order of Templars in Scotland; (2) that when he fell at Killiecrankie on July 27, 1689, he wore the Grand Cross of the Order; (3) that this Cross was given to Calmet by his brother.*[72] *If this story be true we are brought at once into the presence of a Templar survival or restoration which owes nothing to the dream or realities of Chevalier Ramsay* . . . [nothing to the passion for the High Grades of Masonry,] *and nothing* . . . [so far as can be told] *to masonry itself* . . . [, whether Operative or Speculative.] *We know that evidence is wanting at every point for the alleged perpetuation of the old Templar Order in connection with Masonry and the legends of such perpetuation bear all the traces of manufacture... But if a Grand Cross of the Temple was actually and provably found on the body of Viscount Dundee, it is certain that the Order of the Temple had survived or revived in 1689.*'[73]

This quote, as reproduced in 1989, is flawed as some important points are missing. For the sake of clarity the omissions (contained within [ ] — see above) from this quote have been restored. The omission of the statement: ' …*whether Operative or Speculative*'. is extremely important because it completely changes the emphasis of what is being said. The publication promotes the claim that there is a direct connection between modern Scottish Freemasonry and the medieval Order of Knights Templar. Up to this point in the discussion Waite is explaining that even if the KT had continued to exist in Scotland after 1312, it did so without any connection whatsoever with any form of 'masonry'.[74] The omission of four words '. . . *whether Operative or Speculative*' gives the appearance that this historian is saying something that he was not. This may be an example of misquoting or simple error as discussed in the first chapter.

However, even more important is another omission. Waite detailed the legend of the alleged continued existence of the Order of Knights Templar in Scotland for 377 years not to support it but to oppose it. At the end of his discussion (above) Waite makes the following statement:

> '*As regards the secret continuation of the Order of the Temple and its reappearance in the eighteenth century under the guise of Templar Masonry, in one or other of its several forms, an almost irresistible conclusion is negative to all such claims, though the soul of the Order may have survived . . .*'

Waite is making an extremely important point here — that the actual, physical continuation of the Order, in the sense of generation after generation of KT continuing to exist, in secret, for almost 400 years is virtually impossible. However, the continued existence of the ideals of the Order may well have come down to the present (he was writing in 1921). Even here Waite remains to be convinced of that notion. However, the point here is that the actual physical continuation of the Order from 1312 to 1689 is not supported by this Masonic historian, notwithstanding his quote as detailed above. The authors of the Popular School seem to be more concerned with proving a continuous, lineal, descent from those KT who allegedly fled to Scotland in 1307 rather than the possibility that a small group of people, all of whom were Freemasons, were attracted by the ideals of the medieval Order and sought to reinstate those ideals in the (then) modern era by creating a completely new and unconnected group who merely acknowledged a romantic attachment to the original Order.[75]

Waite, and the authors quoting him, provide another useful avenue of research and that is an attempt to track down the origin of this particular story. Waite states: '*It has been said that the well-known French historian and theologian Dom Calmet has lent the authority of his name to three important statements . . .*'. It is important to note that he states '*It has been said that . . .*', that is, Waite is reporting hearsay not fact.

The person cited by Waite as being the source of the story that '. . . *John* [Graham of] *Claverhouse*, [1st] *Viscount Dundee, was Grand Master of the Order of Templars in Scotland*' is Dom Augustin Calmet (1672–1757). Calmet is first mentioned in the 19th century when he is cited as being able to prove that the medieval Order of KT had a continuous existence until the present.

The 'Traditional History' created by Chevalier James Burnes for his fellow Scottish Freemasons in 1837 has been discussed earlier. Burnes' traditional history does not mention Calmet. In 1843 the Masonic KT published an 'official history' of the '*new Masonic Order*' contained within the Statutes of the Order. This history used Burnes' 'history' but introduced Calmet as proof regarding John Graham, Killiecrankie, etc. Burnes had returned to India in December 1837. What he thought of the Order's adaptation of his history, assuming that he knew of it, is unknown. A crucial point is that it was the new, emergent, Scottish Masonic Knights Templar who first claimed, in 1843, that Calmet was the source of the story:

'*We find from the testimony of Abbé Calmet, that he had received from David Graham, titular Viscount of Dundee, the Grand Cross of the Order worn by his gallant and ill-fated brother at the Battle of Killiecrankie. "Il etoit," says, the Abbé, "Grand Maitre de l'order des Templiers en Ecosse."*'[76]

This embroidery gives the appearance of supplying supporting evidence but it is important to appreciate that in fact no evidence whatsoever is given. All that is offered is a statement allegedly made by Calmet.[77]

All subsequent commentators on the story that John Graham of Claverhouse wore, and died wearing, the 'Grand Cross of the Order of Knights Templar' at Killiecrankie have accepted that claim uncritically.[78] Yet no one appears to have gone to the source of the story — '*Mémoire sur la correspondence inédite de dom Calmet*' in order to check the accuracy, or otherwise, of what it is claimed (by the Masonic Knights Templar) Calmet said. As has been expressed several times in this book, it is the duty of an historian to check and recheck the sources and material used as 'historical evidence'.[79] In the case under discussion here, the 'paper chase of evidence' can be brought to a conclusion.

As one popular book states: '*If the story outlined above is true, it constitutes the most important evidence of a Templar survival in Scotland since the late sixteenth century . . .*'[80] The opposite of that observation might also be considered. If the sources used to claim that the story is true can be demonstrated to be fictitious then 'evidence' of a Templar survival does not exist.

Fortunately the exact source of the story has now been provided — Maggiolo, '*Mémoire sur la correspondence inédite de dom Calmet . . .*'.[81] However, the claimed source of the story regarding Viscount Dundee at the Battle of Killiecrankie is simply fiction. The *Mémoire* contains no reference whatsoever to John Graham of Claverhouse, the Battle of Killiecrankie, or the Grand Cross of the Order of the Knights Templar in Scotland. The piece was written by the '*modest Vicar of Ménil-le-Horgue*' who '. . . *gladly makes himself a beggar for the glory of Father Calmet*', and which contains a brief biography of Calmet together with extracts from a number of his letters. In total the piece reveals Calmet's observations on the ecclesiastical news, political and other events of the time as well as details regarding his private life. Given the total absence of any reference in this publication to the Battle of Killiecrankie, John Graham of Claverhouse or the 'Grand Cross of the Order', etc. it is not possible to explain why it was used to support the claim that the KT were still in existence in Scotland in the late 17th century. By the time Calmet is first mentioned in support of a KT survival in Scotland he had by then been dead for 85 years. Despite Lyon's and Waite's criticisms, people continued to accept that the myth was fact.

For example, the 1933 '*Statutes of the Great Priory of Scotland*' includes a '*Historical Notice of the Order of the Temple*' (in other words the Traditional History of the Order) repeating that history provided by Burnes (but not repeating any of his doubts and caveats) 100 years earlier. The principal points of the modern day myth are present:

- Knights Templar were at the Battle of Bannockburn
- Robert the Bruce rewarded the Templars
- Bruce established the Royal Order
- Templars were allowed by Bruce to continue to exist
- The Royal Order and Templars were separate organisations

- The continued existence of the Templars is proved by documents dated after 1314
- Latin texts (not translated) are reproduced as proof
- John Graham, 'Bonnie Dundee', died wearing the 'Grand Cross' of the Order
- Charles Edward Stuart (Bonnie Prince Charlie) was the Grand Master of the KT

This then, more or less, was the situation regarding the myth at the close of the 19th century and which continued well into the 20th. The debate was expressed in a variety of Masonic publications, particularly in articles published in the annual journal of the oldest Lodge of Research in the world — Quatuor Coronati Lodge, No.2076 (London, England). The point is that the debate was essentially a Masonic debate and one which largely took place within Freemasonry and not in the public arena. It was not until 1982 with the publication of '*The Holy Blood and the Holy Grail*' (referred to in Chapter 6 — Rosslyn Chapel) that the debate began to take on a public dimension.

This brief survey of some of the material relating to the Scottish aspects of the myth demonstrates a process of addition, embellishment and adaptation of a fictional story which was begun as early as 1628 by stonemasons seeking the sure foundation of a distinctive Scottish history. The blend of myths and legends with half remembered truths was used to create a rich romantic 'Traditional History' which continues to grow and develop.

[1] *History of Freemasonry…* etc., Lawrie, Alexander (Edinburgh, 1804), p. vii.

[2] *Op. cit.,* p. viii

[3] *Op. cit.,* p. 100 and Appendix I & II, pp. 297-304.

[4] *Minute Book No.1.* (Grand Lodge of Scotland), p. 227.

[5] That it was common knowledge that it was the work of Brewster is affirmed by Maidment's reference to '*Brewster's Encyclopædia*' in *the Genealogie of the Saintclaires of Rosslyn.* 1835. p. v.

[6] *Memoirs, Illustrating the history of Jacobinism.* Barruel, Abbé Augustin, (English edn.). (London, 1797), 4 Vols. p. 381. Vol. II. Also quoted in *Mackay's Revised Encyclopedia*, Vol. 2. p. 568. (Chicago, 1958).

[7] *History of Freemasonry…* etc. Lawrie/Brewster (Edinburgh, 1804), p. 58.

[8] Augustin Barruel's motives are unclear but as Norman Cohn notes in *Warrant*

for Genocide — The myth of the Jewish world-conspiracy and the Protocols of the Elders of Zion: 'Barruel's book made him a rich man.' p. 27. I am grateful to Prof. Dr. Jan A. M. Snoek, of Heidelberg University, for bringing this reference to my attention.

[9] *Proofs of a Conspiracy...* etc. Robison, John, 4th edn. (London, 1798), p. 3.

[10] *Encyclopaedia Britannica.* Quoted in *Mackay's Revised Encyclopedia,* Vol. 2. p. 863. Chicago. 1958.

[11] Robison, *op. cit.,* p. 105.

[12] Norman Cohn. *Warrant for Genocide — The myth of the Jewish world-conspiracy and the Protocols of the Elders of Zion.* p. 25-26.

[13] Lawrie/Brewster, *op. cit.,* p. 58.

[14] Grand Lodge endorsed the book before it was published.

[15] *Historical Sketch* (Grand Lodge of Scotland, 1986), p. 21.

[16] The position of the Masonic KT in England was quite different. As early as 1791 the Order had been reorganised under Thomas Dunckerley. The hiatus following his death in 1795 was overcome and the Duke of Kent had control (at least nominally) over the Order from 1804. The involvement of senior and respected Freemasons in England ensured that the Order was accepted there. *'Early Statutes of the Knights Templar'* by A. C. F. Jackson. AQC. 89 p. 214 *et seq.*

[17] *Minute Book No.1.* (Grand Lodge of Scotland), p. 50.

[18] *Op. cit.,* p. 53.

[19] At that time there were a number of Lodges that were independent of Grand Lodge and this regulation did not, therefore, apply to them. There is no evidence, however, that they had practised, or continued to, practise the ceremonies in question. The Lodges concerned were, for example The Lodge of Glasgow St. John, No. 3*biz*; founded 1628 and remained independent until 1850. Lodge Melrose St. John, No. 1[2]; known to be in existence in 1599 and which remained independent until 1891. There are other early Lodges of which nothing is known except from their location or a reference to them in the records of another Lodge.

[20] The arrival in Scotland of the RAC and KT ceremonials appears to be generally later than elsewhere. Why Grand Lodge simply did not adopt these ceremonials as their own (and consequently gain the control and revenue therefrom) is not known but that they were not so 'absorbed' suggests that Grand Lodge could simply not bring itself to consider them, despite all the obvious advantages, to be in any way Masonic and they had therefore to be rejected.

[21] These terms covered, and continue to cover, more than just the two ceremonies named.

The Royal Arch series cover:

1. Master Passed the Chair
2. Mark Mason
3. Mark Master Mason

4. Excellent Master
5. Super Excellent Master
6. Arch Degree
7. Royal Arch Degree
8. Ark Mason
9. Link and Wrestle
10. Babylonian Pass or Red Cross of Daniel
11. Jordan Pass
12. Royal Order or Prussian Blue
13. High Priest

The Knight Templar series cover:

1. Black Mark
2. Mediterranean Pass
3. Knight of Malta
4. Knight of the Holy Grave
5. Knight of Patmos
6. Knight of the Red Cross of Constantine
7. Knight Templar

Exactly which ceremonies were being practised at any specific time, and by which Lodges, is difficult to determine. The above list gives the ceremonies under the jurisdiction of the Supreme Grand Royal Arch Chapter of Scotland and the Great Priory of Scotland respectively. Several of these ceremonials are no longer conferred in Scotland. Readers should be aware also that the Royal Arch ceremonies have never been part of the Craft degrees. The Mark ceremony is unusual in that it can be conferred either in a Craft Lodge (as an extension of the Second Degree) or in a Chapter as the first ceremony of the Royal Arch series.

[22] The Chartulary of the Grand Lodge of Scotland.

[23] *Pour La Foy,* Draffen, George, CD-ROM (Grand Lodge of Scotland, 2000), p. 15.

[24] Eight Royal Arch Chapters were Chartered in Scotland by the Supreme Grand Chapter of England 1787–1817. All were near the border of the two kingdoms. All but one was founded after 1792 — when the Grand Lodge of Scotland first expressed its concern regarding foreign ceremonials.

[25] The Royal Order of Scotland was virtually moribund from 1794–1839. Lindsay, pp.101-104.

[26] Draffen, *op. cit.,* p. 7.

[27] *Op. cit.,* p. 14.

[28] *Op. cit.,* p. 15.

[29] Only three were not in the west of Scotland, indicating the preferred superior body of Freemasons in that part of the country.

[30] Draffen, *ibid.*

[31] What little is known of his life and Masonic career has been gleaned from a

variety of sources, i.e. Lindsay, Draffen, etc.

[32] Draffen, op. cit., p. 16.

[33] The Charters are reproduced in full in Appendix IV and VI, pp. 145-147 and pp. 151-152 of Draffen's Pour La Foy.

[34] The addition of 'Holy' [Temple] in the 1815 Charter is the only difference in the headings of the two.

[35] Scottish Rite for Scotland, The, Lindsay, Robert S. (Edinburgh, 1958), p. 71.

[36] Classicism and Neoclassicism: in the arts, historical tradition or aesthetic attitudes based on the art of Greece and Rome in antiquity. In the context of the tradition, Classicism refers either to the art produced in antiquity or to later art inspired by that of antiquity; Neoclassicism always refers to the art produced later but inspired by antiquity. Thus the terms Classicism and Neoclassicism are often used interchangeably.

[37] In two other novels by Scott, Tales of the Crusades; The Betrothed and The Talisman (1825), the KT are portrayed in an equally negative light.

[38] Draffen, op. cit., p. 49. Scott had joined his father's Lodge, Lodge St. David, No. 36, in 1801.

[39] The Craft: A History of English Freemasonry, Hamill, John, (1986), p. 55.

[40] A thin gruel with prunes.

[41] The pomp and ceremony for the 1831 Coronation of William IV (1765–1837) had been somewhat reduced, thereby partly creating a precedent.

[42] 'Masonic Celebrities: No.VIII — The Chevalier Burnes.' Robert F. Gould. AQC. Vol. XX. p. 47.

[43] 'Masonic Celebrities: No.VIII — The Chevalier Burnes.' Robert F. Gould. AQC. Vol. XX. pp. 44–53.

[44] There is no proof that Burnes became a Masonic KT but he certainly wrote his history of the Order for those responsible for its revival.

[45] The Lodge was founded in 1769 and continues to meet in Montrose.

[46] A Sketch of the History of the Knights Templars. James Burnes. Edinburgh. 1837. p. i.

[47] A Sketch of the History of the Knights Templars. James Burnes. Edinburgh. 1837. p. 36.

[48] A Sketch of the History of the Knights Templars. James Burnes. Edinburgh. 1837. p. 37.

[49] Petition Book of the Grand Conclave.

[50] Lindsay, op. cit., p. 72.

[51] Op. cit., p. 75.

[52] Royal Order of Scotland, The, Lindsay, Robert S., Vol. 1. p. 105.

[53] Draffen, op. cit., p. 81. Deuchar died in August 1844 and this may be the reason why the Committee never reported. See p. 85.

[54] Royal Order of Scotland, The, Lindsay, Robert S., Vol. 1. p. 107.

[55] The Grand Conclave issued a set of statutes in 1837 but this contained no history of the Order. See George Draffen, Pour La Foy. p. 80.

[56] ' "Charta Transmission" of Larmenius, The', Crowe, Fred J. W., AQC. Vol. XXIV. (1911) pp. 185-198.

[57] Grand Conclave. Statutes of the Religious and Military Order of the Temple,

as established in Scotland with an Historical Notice of the Order (Edinburgh, 1843), p. viii.

[58] *Ibid.*

[59] Bishop of St Andrews from 1298. He was one of only three bishops that presided at the Coronation of Robert I in 1306.

[60] *Pour La Foy,* Draffen, George (Dundee, 1949), p. 9. I suggest that the late Brother Draffen is being diplomatic here. It is clear that Walker Arnott was a significant contributor to the creation of the 'Traditional History' of the Scottish Masonic KT. In 1845 he tabled *'...some further points of history...'* for consideration by Grand Conclave. *See* Draffen p. 86. Draffen appears to be unaware of the significance of Burnes' 1837 history.

[61] *History of Freemasonry...* etc., Laurie, William A. (Edinburgh, 1859), p. 252.

[62] Lodge Lindores, No. 106, (Newburgh, Fife) formally invited the KT encampments at Perth and Cupar to attend the laying of the foundation stone of their new Lodge building in 1815. The encampments demanded to lead the procession on the basis that they were the most senior Masonic body present. The Lodges refused to acknowledge the alleged seniority of the KT and the encampments refused to participate further. Grand Conclave subsequently complimented them on their principled stand. Draffen, George, *Pour La Foy*. p. 12 and p. 33.

[63] *Op. cit.*, p. 99.

[64] Laurie cites Barruel as one of those enemies.

[65] *History of...* etc., Murray Lyon, D. Edinburgh, 1873. p. 286.

[66] Lodge Ayr St. Paul, No.204.

[67] The publication was entitled: the *'High Knight's Templar Lodge'* [of Ireland]. nd.

[68] The full title is: *'History of The Lodge of Edinburgh (Mary's Chapel), No.1. embracing an account of the rise and progress of freemasonry in Scotland.* London. 1900.

[69] Lyon quotes the whole argument as presented by Maidment in *Genealogie of the Sainteclaires of Rosslyn*. James Maidment. Edinburgh. 1835. pp. xxxix — xxxvii.

[70] He even quotes the date of death of Deuchar's last surviving daughter in 1892!

[71] *'History of The Lodge of Edinburgh (Mary's Chapel), No.1. embracing an account of the rise and progress of freemasonry in Scotland.'* pp. 310–311.

[72] John Claverhouse's name should be correctly given as John Graham of Claverhouse, Viscount Dundee.

[73] Arthur E. Waite (1857–1942) *A New Encyclopaedia of Freemasonry*. London. 1921. Quoted in *The Temple and The Lodge*. p. 165.

[74] It is important, again, to point out the need for clarity when dealing with 'masonry' (stonemasonry) and 'Masonry' (Freemasonry).

[75] Even the normally insightful Waite could miss the obvious — simply owning an antique piece of jewellery (in this instance allegedly the 'Grand Cross of the Order') does not mean one is a member of the organisation for which the piece was originally made!

[76] Grand Conclave. *Statutes of the Religious and Military Order of the Temple, as established in Scotland with an Historical Notice of the Order* (Edinburgh, 1843), p. viii. No source for this statement is provided in this or any subsequent publications of the Grand Priory.

[77] This cannot be taken as an independent source and nor is it contemporary evidence given the date that Calmet is first cited.

[78] The so-called Grand Cross appears also to be an embellishment, it being unknown before this reference.

[79] This is probably one of the reasons why the critical analysis of the work of popular writers lags a considerable time behind the publication of their work.

[80] *The Temple and The Lodge.*

Chapter 4
The St. Clair Family

Comit thy Werk to God

Father Richard Augustine Hay (1661–*c*.1736)

It is fortunate indeed that Father Richard A. Hay transcribed the documents of the St. Clair family. These had been kept in Rosslyn Castle but are now lost. Hay's work provides a great deal of information about the St. Clair family and their activities since their arrival in Scotland in the 11th century.

Richard A. Hay was the second son of Captain George Hay and was born in Edinburgh on 16 August 1661. His early years were spent with cousins at Dysart, Innerleithen and Foord and he attended schools at Edinburgh, Dalkeith and Traquair. When he was about five years old his father died. His mother, Jean Spottiswood (daughter of Sir Henry Spottiswood, High Sheriff of Dublin) married Sir James St. Clair of Rosslyn soon after and Hay entered a turbulent period until, at the age of about 13, he was sent to France where he entered the Catholic Scots College in Paris. He also took a course in grammar at the college of Navarre. He moved to Chartres after four years and became a pensioner at St. Chéron's abbey of Canons Regular and completed his education in rhetoric. He became a Canon Regular at Sainte-Geniève's in Paris in 1678 and took his vows in 1679. From there he went to the abbey of Saint-Jacques de Provins, remaining for two years during which time he received the tonsure and the four minor orders during October 1680. He studied philosophy and divinity at the abbey of Saint-Pierre de Rillé at Fougères, Brittany and, in September 1683, he was ordained sub-deacon and deacon. Appointed to teach the third school, he returned to Chartres and was there ordained priest on 22 September 1685. Exactly two years later he was commissioned to establish the Order of Canons Regular in Scotland and England, and left Paris expressing the wish '*to sie the smoak of his own country*'.

After reaching England he kissed the hand of James VII at Windsor and from there travelled to Leith but his plans to establish his order in Scotland came to naught due to the 'Glorious Revolution' of 1688. He was ordered to leave the country and returned to France in June 1689. He became sub-prior of Hérivaux in November of that year and transferred to Essomes also as sub-prior. He became prior of Bernicourt, Champagne, in August 1694 and in January 1695 was appointed prior of St.-Pierremont-en-Argonne but appears to have been in Scotland before *c*.1718. He returned to live permanently in Edinburgh *c*.1718 and in 1719 proposed a scheme to print John de Fordun's (*c*.1320–*c*.1387) '*Scotichronicon*'. He died in poverty in Edinburgh's Cowgate *c*.1736.[1]

James Maidment (*c*.1795–1879)

The *Genealogie of the Sainteclaires of Rosslyn* was first published in 1835 by James Maidment and was limited to 120 copies only. It is a work that is often quoted as a source, either directly or within bibliographies, but so few copies were produced that they are extremely difficult to find. Even when a copy is located the reader is often further handicapped by the fact that large portions of the text are in Latin[2]

Like his father, Maidment took the law as a profession. He was born in London *c*.1795. He was called to the Scottish bar in 1817 and soon earned a reputation, as an advocate, for his expertise in cases that required genealogical investigation and, as such, was often consulted in disputed peerage cases.

He enjoyed antiquarian and historical research and that brought him into contact with men of letters such as Sir Walter Scott. He edited material for the Abbotsford, Bannatyne, Hunterian and Maitland Clubs as well as the Spottiswoode Society.[3] He was the principal editor of '*Kay's Portraits*' (1837). One of his most important works is the '*Dramatists of the Restoration*' (14 vols., Edinburgh, 1877). He was a great collector of books and following his death the sale of his library took 15 days.

Most of his writings, of which there were a large number, were published anonymously and a number privately printed. His legal mind and genealogical expertise are demonstrated in his introduction to his 1835 edition of the St. Clair '*Genealogie*'.

Hay and Maidment's contribution

Hay examined all the documents then owned by the St. Clair family. His transcriptions and comments on these are contained in three manuscript volumes, now in the National Library of Scotland (catalogued as *Hay's Antiquities*, 34. 1. 8. and 34. 1. 9, (i and ii)). It was those volumes that Maidment edited to produce his book in 1835. On page 175 (of Maidment) Hay states:

> '*Those* [charters] *of any consequence I have insert att length, and I have copied them off the originals; what is of lesser value I have only taken an abridgement thereof, and I scarce think to have omitted any charter in the cartulary, . . .'*.

Hay explains therefore that he has transcribed *all* the charters, the important ones in full and those of *'lesser value'* he abbreviated. This is significant in that we can be certain that Hay provides details of all the charters, deeds, etc. then in possession of the St. Clair family but which have subsequently been lost. Hay tried to present his work in chronological order and, in the main, he succeeded — a method to which Maidment also tried to be faithful. The first 34 pages of the *'Genealogie'* consist of Hay's history of the St. Clair family based not only on the family's papers but also on oral accounts — that is, the family's traditions. The documents transcribed by Hay provide an insight to the activities of a Scottish noble family from before 1061 until *c*.1690 and as such are an important source of information on a variety of subjects including land transactions, religious matters before, during and after the Reformation, the St. Clair family and Rosslyn Chapel.

The present purpose is, however, to comment on those aspects which are alleged to have some bearing on Scottish Freemasonry. Maidment's publication is often cited as a source by some writers to support the contention that some members of the medieval Order of the Knights Templar, having been forewarned of the impending mass arrest of members of the Order in France on 13 October 1307 escaped via the port of La Rochelle in a fleet of Templar ships harboured there and made their way to Scotland. Robert I (1274–1329), who had been excommunicated for his murder of John 'the Red' Comyn on 10th February 1306, gave them shelter. Scotland was chosen because it was the only place where papal law could not be applied. The fugitive KT hid in Argyll for seven years until re-appearing at the Battle of Bannockburn (23–24 June 1314) in time to turn the battle in favour of the Scots army. Bruce could not expect Scotland to be re-admitted to western Christendom whilst there were heretic KT at large. He also wished to reward the fugitive KT for their part in winning independence for Scotland, but could not do so openly. He therefore created the Order of Freemasonry and the fugitive KT were admitted as members. In this way Bruce could claim that there were no KT in Scotland. This is a popular hypothesis for the origin of Freemasonry and one which claims that modern Scottish Freemasonry is merely a perpetuation of the medieval Order of KT. This notion, briefly outlined above, has been examined in detail elsewhere. The elements of the hypothesis that are, allegedly, supported by evidence produced by Hay shall be briefly discussed.

There are a number of charters that record land transactions involving the St. Clair family. Because the land concerned is described as *'Temple Land'* or *'of the*

Temple' some have claimed this to be proof that the St. Clair family was intimately involved with the KT. This is reading too much into what these charters represent. The first of these charters records the transfer of land (at Gourton) from William of Lisours, Laird of Gourton, to Adam son of the late Waltar.[4] The charter shows that William of Lisours obtained the land only after it had been previously owned by at least two others. It is not until the sixth charter, dated 1317, that the land is transferred to a member of the St. Clair family. This shows that the St. Clair family did not receive the land directly from the KT as it was previously owned by a number of other families.[5] It also demonstrates that the KT had disposed of this land a long time prior to the dissolution of the Order in 1312. Charters such as these were handed over at each transfer of land in order that the new owner could provide a continuous record of land transfers thereby proving present ownership. Such charters were therefore very important, as they were the ultimate proof of ownership. This situation prevails to this day in Scotland although it is no longer the responsibility of an owner of property to have the details of all previous transactions — such records are now held by a government department. Some writers have deduced that because land, referred to as '*Temple Land*' etc., was recorded in similar charters dating from after the dissolution of the KT, the Order continued to exist in Scotland. This fails to recognise the simple fact that a great deal of property once owned by the KT continued, and continues to this day, to be described as '*Temple Land*' etc.

As might be expected there is a considerable amount of material regarding Rosslyn Chapel. Hay explains the reason why the chapel was built:

'*Therfor, to the end he* [William St. Clair, Earl of Orkney, (*c*.1404–*c*.1484)] *might not seem altogether unthankfull to God for the benefices he receaved from him. It came to his mind to build a house for God's service, of a most curious worke…*'

Rosslyn Chapel therefore represented one man's thanks to God — expressed in a '*curious manner*', that is, of a special and unique design. Hay provides an interesting and useful description of the building process used at the building of the chapel.[6] A multitude of tradesmen were employed who '. . . *were brought from other regions and forraigne kingdoms*'. This suggests that local tradesman did not possess the level of skill that St. Clair required. The foundations of the chapel were laid in 1446. St. Clair had designs drawn on boards and carpenters carved those designs in wood that were in turn carved by masons in stone. He was kind to all his tenants and turned no poor person away. He was generous to stonemasons:

> '. . . *because he thought the massones, had not a convenient place to lodge . . ., he made them to build the towne of Rosline . . ., and gave every one of them a house and lands . . .'.*[7]

His generosity did not stop there:

> '*He rewarded the massones according to their degree* [i.e. their level of skill], *as to the master massone he gave 40 pounds yearly, and to every one of the rest 10 pounds and accordingly did he reward the others, as the smiths and the carpenters with others.*'[8]

All this information is not taken from documents but is family lore handed down from generation to generation and no doubt eagerly listened to, and recorded, by Hay. Unfortunately the gift of houses and land to '*massones*' is not confirmed by charter. It is obvious that he was familiar with the chapel as it was prior to 1688. He took particular note of the heraldic devices within the chapel, which, as the genealogist of the family, were of special interest to him.[9] Given his apparent interest in Latin, it is unsurprising that he should quote the only Latin text contained within the fabric of the chapel:

> '*The only monuments undefaced att present in the chapel are ane inscription in Gothick lettres on a pend before that you goe doun to the vestrie, where you see visibly the following words: "Forte est vinum, fortior est Rex, fortiores sunt mulieres super omnia vincit veritas*" ['Wine is strong, the king is stronger, women are stronger, truth conquers all.' Esdras I. Chapter 3. Verses 10–12].[10] (pp. 107-108 of Maidment). (Plate 8)

The use to which this has been put by authors of the Popular Approach is discussed in Chapter 6. The only other undamaged 'monument' within the chapel is described thus:

> '... *is att the back of the Earle of Cathnes* [Caithness] *tombe; theron is a man in armour graven on a flat stone; at his head two scuctcheons having*

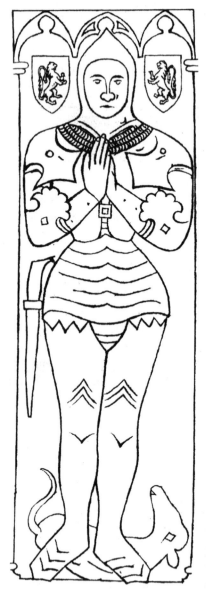

Fig. 5: *Floor slab between pillars 15 and 16 in Rosslyn Chapel*

each a lyon contoured; no supporters nor ornaments (Fig. 5).'

Hay's familiarity with the chapel is further confirmed by his comments regarding the damage done to the chapel on the night of 11 December 1688 by a rable [*sic*]. He comments:

> '*Those monuments, with some other part of the Chapell, as a Queue de Lampe, some statues yet remaining, a pend goeing from east to west att the first pillar, the Earle of Cathness his tomb, were a little defaced the rable ... after the castle had been spoiled where I lost severall books of note . . .*'[11]

There is, and has been, a great deal of speculation as to the purpose of Rosslyn Chapel, notwithstanding the observations of Hay as to the motives of the builder, as mentioned above. It has been suggested that it is an unfinished copy of a Jewish Temple, a pagan place of worship or a Masonic building. Hay provides unambiguous evidence that it was a Christian church, more precisely, a collegiate church. William St. Clair, Earl of Orkney, was not exceptional in building such an edifice. Many members of the nobility built, and endowed, such establishments. Edinburgh and the Lothians of Scotland have a number of such ecclesiastical buildings, 15 of which were erected during the period 1342–1540. Almost exactly contemporary with the foundation of Rosslyn Collegiate Church (1446), and in close proximity to it, are the collegiate churches of Crichton, Midlothian (1449); Dirleton, East Lothian (1444); Dunglass, East Lothian (1448) and Markle, East Lothian (1450). Interestingly, in the years immediately following the death of the builder of Rosslyn Collegiate Church, *c*.1484 (according to Hay, page 107 of Maidment), the building of two other collegiate churches commenced: Restalrig in Leith, Edinburgh (1487) and Seton, East Lothian (1488). It can be only speculation that those tradesmen who no longer had employment after the death of St. Clair found alternative work on these new collegiate churches.

If Rosslyn Collegiate Church is not unique, merely being one of many in the immediate area, why the hyperbole? A clue might lie in Hay's explanation that the builder decided that the church must be '*a most curious worke*'. Given the number of other collegiate churches nearby it may be that although St. Clair could match them in size (as attested by the existence of the unused foundations — Plate 10) he planned to surpass them all with his interior design and decoration — the profusion of which remains visible today.

One of the charters transcribed by Hay is dated 1523 and makes it clear that Rosslyn was already a collegiate church. It had been so created as early as the mid 1450's.[12] The purpose of this charter was to make provision for church officers, Prebendaries, who would officiate during various church rituals. Each Prebendary was allocated an altar to maintain and at which prayers were to be said for the souls of the benefactor, his family and ancestors in perpetuity. William St. Clair, grandson of the builder of the collegiate church, formalised by this charter the position of the Predendaries. His instructions are quite precise. The Prebendaries were to have a house built for them, and land allocated to each. The produce of this land would supply a living for each Prebendary, allowing him to live locally and be 'on hand' for regular prayers for the souls of the St. Clair family. According to this charter there were four altars within Rosslyn Collegiate Church:

- The altar of St. Matthew was in the care of the Provost who is named as being Lord John Dickson.
- The altar of the Virgin Mary was in the care of the Sacrist.
- The altar of St. Andrew was in the care of the third Prebendary
- The altar of St. Peter was in the charge of the fourth Prebendary.

In 1527 James V (1512–1542) confirmed by charter the lands of Roslin and made specific mention of the collegiate church.[13] It can be seen that the chapel was built as, and was always intended to be, a Christian building and that it was actively promoted as such by successive generations of the St. Clair family.

John Slezer (?–1714), a contemporary of Hay's, published, in 1693, his *'Theatrum Scotiae'* containing views of towns and castles.[14] He included a view of Rosslyn Chapel and described one of the internal pillars which he called the Prince's Pillar, probably after John St. Clair (*c*.1630–1690) a 'prince among men' who had died shortly before Slezer visited the chapel. In all his comments and observations regarding the chapel Hay makes no mention of what is now known as the Apprentice Pillar (Plate 13) or the legend now associated with that pillar. It is said that:

> '. . . *a model of this pillar had been sent from Rome, or some foreign place, the master-mason upon viewing it, would by no means consent to work off such a pillar, till he should go to Rome, or some foreign part, to take exact inspection of the pillar from which the model had been taken; that, in his absence, whatever might be the occasion of it, an Apprentice finished the pillar as it now stands: and that the master upon his return, seeing the pillar so exquisitely well finished made enquiry who had done it; and being stung with envy, slew the apprentice.*'[15]

In light of Hay's propensity to record the oral traditions of the St. Clair family, his failure to record this dramatic legend is surprising.

Of all the information regarding Rosslyn Chapel provided by Hay what he has to say about the vault beneath the chapel is arguably the most interesting. He states that his step-father (?–*c*.1688) was the first to be buried in a coffin. Ten previous heads of the family had been interred in the vault below the chapel dressed in their armour.[16] During his step-father's funeral it was observed that William St. Clair's (?–1650) body was clothed in armour and appeared to be '*intire*' but when touched crumbled to dust. Hay, and others, therefore had access to the vaults and were inquisitive enough to examine the bodies of the deceased. Hay makes no mention of anything unusual, nor the discovery of any 'treasure' in the vaults.

Most important, in respect of the history of Scottish Freemasonry, are two manuscripts transcribed by Hay which he terms '*Charter*[s] *Granted by the Masons to Sir William Saintclair*.[17, 18] Hay does not date these manuscripts but it is now known that they are dated *c*.1601 and *c*.1628 respectively.[19] (Plates 1 and 2) (Appendices IV and V) Hay makes no comment regarding the importance, or otherwise, of these documents. Hay's description of these documents as 'charters' is unfortunate as this suggests that they are similar to the other charters also transcribed by him. They are, in fact, not charters but letters and have been more correctly described as '*Letters of Jurisdiction granted by the Freemen Masons in Scotland to Sir William St. Clair of Rosslyn*'.[20] Even this description suggests, inaccurately, that some kind of official authority resided with William St. Clair, probably because the first letter was signed by the king's Master of Work, William Schaw (*c*.1550–1602). The first of these letters commences by stating that the masons (that is, stonemasons) have always considered the St. Clair family to be their '*Patrons and Protectors*' and, through the stonemasons' negligence, the association has been allowed to lapse. The letter is an attempt to re-establish that relationship. From the outset it is the stonemasons, not the St. Clair family, who claim the family to be hereditary patrons. The fact that this patronage had been allowed to lapse, assuming that it ever existed, demonstrates just how important it was considered to be by both parties. However, the letter reveals the true motives of the stonemasons in approaching the St. Clair family — they are so poor that they cannot afford to go to court to have their disputes resolved and even if they could, the legal system is too slow for their needs. In other words the stonemasons are asking William St. Clair to become the arbitrator of their internal disputes and *nothing else*.

Unfortunately for the stonemasons their choice of who should be approached to become their patron was not a good one. Hay describes him as a '*leud*' [lewd] man who was forced to run away to Ireland although he is of the opinion that this was more to do with trouble with the Presbyterian Church (St. Clair was a Roman Catholic) than his adulterous affair with a miller's daughter!

The second St. Clair 'Charter' or letter has already been discussed and analysed elsewhere but the involvement of Sir William St. Clair with the stonemasons of Scotland is worth some discussion here.[21] The second 'Charter', *c*.1628, is addressed to the son, also William, of the St. Clair addressed in the first 'charter'. This is essentially the same as the first document, although longer. The central theme remains that the stonemasons consider the Sinclair family to be their '*Patrons and Protectors*'. The stonemasons once again assert that the break between them and the family was due to their (the stonemasons') negligence and that the letter is an appeal to re-establish the connection. This demonstrates that the first attempt had been a failure. The second letter makes two 'new' claims:

'Like our predecessors we obeyed, revered and acknowledged them [the Sinclair family] *as patrons and protectors thereof* [who] *had letters of protection and other rights granted by his Majesty's most noble progenitors of worthy memory together with sundry others of the Lairds of Roslin his writings were burnt in a flame of fire within the Castle of Roslin in an* [sic] .....[blank]'.[22]

Here and for the first time, the Scottish monarchy, stonemasons and the Sinclair family are linked together. Most significantly, however, it is claimed that the king granted rights to the St. Clair family. But once again it is stonemasons, *and no one else*, who allege such an association and who claim the monarch was involved. More specifically this second letter claims that an un-named king issued letters of *'protection and other rights'* to the Sinclair family over Scottish stonemasons. It is in this document that these letters of protection are first mentioned — the same document that goes on to claim that they were lost in a fire at Roslin Castle. The monarch is not named, the nature of the 'rights' over stonemasons are not specified and the space for the date of the fire at Roslin Castle has been left blank. Hay reports that such a fire took place in Roslin Castle in 1447 but also states that the family chaplain saved all the manuscripts.[23, 24]

The prime mover behind the first letter or charter, William Schaw, the King's Master of Work, had died in 1602. The character of William St. Clair of Rosslyn doomed the stonemasons' attempt to have him as their *'Patron and Protector.'* The matter was not left to rest however as shown by the second 'charter' of 1627 or 1628. Sir William St. Clair, unlike his father, took an active interest in the stonemasons' activities probably from coming into contact with them whilst they were building living accommodation at Roslin Castle during the early part of the 1620's. Where Schaw, as the King's Master of Works, had promoted the involvement of the St. Clairs in the affairs of the stonemasons, some of his successors did not. The second 'charter' had been sent to London and Charles I (1625–1649, b. 1600) was inclined to grant royal approval of the charter but before doing so asked the authorities in Edinburgh to confirm that this would not disturb the system of government already in place. There was an almost immediate reaction. The Kings Master(s) of Works, Sir James Murray (?–1634) and Sir Anthony Alexander (?–1637) objected.[25] After almost a decade of wrangling over who had jurisdiction over the stonemasons of Scotland Alexander was victorious. Although the matter had not been entirely resolved and St. Clair was apparently still willing to fight, the whole affair was dropped as the country slid towards civil war. However, the fact remains that St. Clair did *not* become 'Patron and Protector' despite his willingness and the stonemasons' desire for him to do so. The government appointee, the Master of Works was confirmed as having jurisdiction over the stonemasons, not St. Clair. As has been pointed out, this seems to be a very trivial matter to have involved the king and numerous officials over such a long period of time. However, it was not the issue of jurisdiction that was important but had more to do with a power struggle in the royal court. St. Clair had married the daughter of John Spottiswoode (1565–1639), the Archbishop of St. Andrews, who was the king's Chancellor. Sir Anthony Alexander's father was the Earl of Stirling — the king's Secretary. It has been adroitly put:

> 'The chancellor controlled the seals through which Alexander's grant had to pass, but the secretary controlled the king's correspondence which gave orders as to what should pass the seals!' [26]

Most important of all perhaps is that Sinclair's claim of hereditary rights over the stonemasons was noted but not granted. Charles, angry at St. Clair's interference in Alexander's application, wrote of St. Clair:

> '. . . pretending ane heritable charge of the Maissones of our said kingdome, though we have nevir gevin warrant for strengthning of aney heritable right.' [27]

This document dated 27 February 1635 is of crucial importance for it reveals that the king denied that the Crown had ever granted the St. Clairs any hereditary rights. In any event, what the king's statement would mean, assuming that hereditary rights had previously been granted, was that he now had removed them. Sir William died in 1650 having never obtained the official sanction for the second St. Clair 'Charter' but this shows that not only did he want these vague hereditary rights but also probably believed that his family had actually possessed them. In this sense at least the stonemasons of Scotland succeeded in creating a 'history' for themselves which continues to have repercussions for Freemasonry to the present time.

It is on this document, *c*.1628, that much subsequent speculative writing on the origin, and development, of Scottish Freemasonry together with even earlier alleged connections with the St. Clair family, is based. This inaccurate interpretation of these documents continues to be repeated today:

> '*To his son William were granted the charters of 1630 from the Masons of Scotland, recognising that the position of Grand Master Mason of Scotland had been hereditary in the St. Clair family since it was granted by James II 1441.*'[28]

From reading the actual document (Appendix V) it can be seen that this is simply wrong. James II is not mentioned, there is no date (1441) given and the term Grand Master Mason is not used. The date of 1441 was first used by Anderson in his '*New Constitutions*' of 1738 in relation to the building of Rosslyn Chapel. Lawrie, in his history of 1804 states:

> '*The office of Grand Master was granted by the crown to William St Clair, Earl of Orkney and Caithness, Baron of Roslin, and founder of the much admired chapel of Roslin. On account of the attention which this nobleman paid to the interests of the order, and the rapid propagation of the royal art under his administration, King James II. made the office of Grand Master hereditary to his heirs and successors*'[29] and:

> '*In Hay's Manuscript in the Advocates' Library, there are two charters granted by the Scottish Masons, appointing the Sinclairs of Roslin their hereditary Grand Masters.*'[30] and:

> '*It deserves also to be remarked, that in both these deeds* [the St. Clair 'Charters'], *the appointment of William Sinclair, Earl of Orkney and Caithness, to the office Grand Master, by James II. of Scotland, is spoken of as a fact well known and universally admitted.*'[31]

The modern quote (1997) given above is merely a repetition of Lawrie's (and others) grossly inaccurate reading of the St. Clair 'Charters' — the very same 'Charters' which he reproduces in his book! Why Lawrie offered such an inaccurate interpretation can be suggested. Building Rosslyn Chapel commenced, according to Anderson, in 1441 when James II was king and that made it clear, to Lawrie, that it must have been James II who made William St. Clair Earl of Orkney and Caithness hereditary Grand Master because the '*Deed of Resignation*' signed in 1736 by William St. Clair (see the discussion below) 'proved', to

Lawrie at least, that the family were hereditary Grand Masters. Lawrie however, makes some elementary mistakes. The St. Clair 'Charters' make no mention of the Earl of Orkney and Caithness, a Grand Master (hereditary or otherwise) or James II. The alleged involvement of the St. Clair family with Freemasonry is therefore based not on the actual documents, charters etc. but on grossly inaccurate interpretations of them — Lawrie's being the prime example. It is this error which is being perpetuated today.[32] Given the use made of these manuscripts at the formation of the Grand Lodge of Scotland (1736), of which more below, it is important to appreciate that there is nothing within them to suggest a connection between the Sinclair family and Scottish Freemasonry. Nor is there any suggestion that any Sinclair was a Grand Master or that he was associated with any stonemasons' lodges. The documents were written by stonemasons for stonemasons and cannot be interpreted as if they have reference to modern Scottish Freemasonry.

When, in 1736, four Lodges in Edinburgh decided to form a Grand Lodge and to seek a Grand Master they not unreasonably sought relevant documents that might have some bearing on 'masonry' in Scotland just as had been done at the formation of the Grand Lodge of England in 1717. The machinations of the formation of the Grand Lodge of Scotland have been amply examined elsewhere.[33] The 'Letters of Jurisdiction' became an important part of that process.

Those who began the process, initially members of Lodge Canongate Kilwinning, which led to the creation of the Grand Lodge, followed the methods employed at the formation of the Grand Lodge of England. Elements of Lodge Canongate Kilwinning formed a new Lodge, Lodge Leith Kilwinning, as part of the plans for the formation of the Grand Lodge of Scotland. Such a Lodge was necessary because the English model dictated that only four Lodges could be 'founding' Lodges.[34] The Lodges instrumental in this process were Lodge Canongate Kilwinning, The Lodge of Edinburgh and Kilwinning Scots Arms together with the newly created Leith Kilwinning. Surprisingly these Lodges did not officially meet until 15 October 1736 to decide on the procedure for the election of a Grand Master and the first regulations of the new Grand Lodge. William St. Clair of Rosslyn (1700–1778), even at this late stage, was not seen as the automatic choice for Grand Master (Plate 6). This position was to be filled by election rather than appointment. It was not until 2 November 1736 that the members of Canongate Kilwinning recorded their desire to have St. Clair as Grand Master. In other words they left it late to 'go public' as to their preferred candidate by which time they would have had a fair idea of what opposition there was to their preferred choice.

William St. Clair was Initiated into Freemasonry in Lodge Canongate Kilwinning on 18 May 1736 and became a Fellow of Craft on 2 June 1736. On 22 November, Lodge Canongate Kilwinning met and St. Clair became, in succession, a Master Mason, Junior Warden, Senior Warden and then Master of the Lodge. This curious procedure was necessary so that St. Clair could attend the inaugural meeting of Grand Lodge as only the Master and Wardens of invited Lodges could attend. Given what occurred subsequently it is clear why he required to be present. Other Lodges across Scotland were made aware of the intention to form a Grand Lodge, and to elect a Grand Master, by the issue, on 20 October 1736, of a circular letter from the four 'organising' Lodges. No mention is made in this letter of St. Clair's candidature but the election of a Grand Master is mentioned no fewer than three times. The Lodge of Edinburgh met on 25 November 1736 to discuss, for the first time, the creation of a Grand Lodge and instructed its representatives to vote for William, 8th Earl of Home (?–1761), as Grand Master. Home was then Master of Lodge Kilwinning Scots Arms and, in addition, had the support of at least four other Lodges (Glasgow, Hamilton, Falkirk and Dunfermline) and probably several more.[35] There was a third candidate, John, 20th Earl of Crawford (1702–1749), who was an honorary member of The Lodge of Edinburgh and who had also been Grand Master of the Grand Lodge of England in 1734. How widespread support was for Crawford is unknown. Only one lodge, the Lodge of Inverness, is known to have intended to vote for him but there may well have been others.

On 30 November 1736, in Mary's Chapel (the meeting place of The Lodge of Edinburgh) representatives of 33 lodges attended in order to elect the first Grand Master. Just before the election took place William St. Clair of Rosslyn rose and read '*a renounciation and discharge*' (Appendix VI) of his alleged hereditary rights over the 'masons' of Scotland. He had signed this document on 24 November. This had a dramatic impact on the meeting and the effect is recorded in the Grand Lodge Minutes:

> '*by ane unanimous vote of the whole Society the said William St. Clare of Rosline Esquire was elected and chosen Grand Master.*' (Plate 6)

This apparently magnanimous gesture ensured St. Clair's unanimous election as the first Grand Master of the Grand Lodge of Scotland. The work of Hay, particularly his transcription of the *Letters of Jurisdiction*, thus played a major role in the formation of the new Grand Lodge and subsequently on the perceived history of Scottish Freemasonry. The full title of the '. . . *renounciation and discharge*' is: '*Deed of Resignation of the Office of Hereditary Grand Master by William St. Clair of Rosslyn*'. Despite the contents of the '*Letters of Jurisdiction*' (the St. Clair 'Charters'), which made *no* reference to a Grand Master, the Freemasons of 1736 had St. Clair resign the 'office' anyway![36] We can see that this was a 'put up job' from the simple fact that only one Lodge was aware of St. Clair of Rosslyn's alleged status as hereditary Grand Master — the Lodge which was orchestrating the foundation of the new Grand Lodge, Lodge Canongate Kilwinning, the Lodge in which St. Clair had become a member and which promoted him as the first Grand Master. Other Lodges were preparing to vote for different candidates, something they would not have done had they known that a Grand Master, and a hereditary one at that, already existed. Needless to say, there was no time to consider the accuracy of the '*Deed of Resignation*' as read by St. Clair but it too contained several flaws. Firstly, if James II had granted the title Hereditary Grand Master to the St. Clair family then St. Clair could only have resigned it back to the Crown, not to the Grand Lodge of Scotland. The '*Deed of Resignation*' does not claim that the builder of the chapel, William St. Clair, Earl of Orkney and Caithness, was granted any right. Instead it states that:

'... *any grant or charter made by any of the Kings of Scotland, to and in favour of the said William and Sir William St Clairs of Roslin, my predecessors...*'[37]

The St. Clairs who were allegedly granted hereditary rights where the father and son to whom the *Letters of Jurisdiction* (the St. Clair 'Charters') were addressed in 1601 and 1628. Those involved in drawing up the '*Deed of Resignation*' (Appendix VI) were confused as to which St. Clair allegedly was granted hereditary rights, and when. It also shows that in 1736 those forming the Grand Lodge of Scotland and their Grand Master 'in waiting' were not prepared to state which king allegedly made the St. Clairs hereditary Grand Masters of the Scottish 'masons'. It is known when the two William St. Clairs (father and son) named in the '*Deed of Resignation*' were alive and as the documents can be dated fairly accurately (*c*.1601 and *c*.1628) only two kings could be involved — James VI of

Scotland and I of Great Britain and his son Charles I. According to the '*Deed of Resignation*' those founding the Grand Lodge and William St. Clair of Rosslyn thought that the first hereditary Grand Masters were the two individuals named in the 'Charters' of *c*.1601 and *c*.1628 *not* the St. Clair who built Rosslyn Chapel. It was Charles I who wrote in 1635 denying that the St. Clairs had any heritable rights over the stonemasons of Scotland (see above).

The St. Clair 'Charters' were signed by the following stonemasons' lodges:

c.1601   Edinburgh
                 Dunfermline
                 St Andrews
                 Haddington
                 Aitcheson's Haven

c.1628   Dundee
                 Edinburgh
                 Glasgow
                 Ayr (not described as a lodge)
                 Stirling
                 Dunfermline
                 St Andrews

The membership of these lodges was comprised of stonemasons. The first admissions of non-stonemasons did not take place until 1634. A little more than 100 years later these stonemasons' lodges had apparently forgotten that they had a hereditary Grand Master and that they had signed the St. Clair 'Charters'. The only lodge which possessed that knowledge was not a stonemasons' lodge at all but one that was recognisably a modern Masonic Lodge! At least one of the lodges which signed the first 'charter' was unimpressed. The Lodge at Aitchison's Haven, at the first meeting (January 1737) after the foundation of the Grand Lodge of Scotland, decided:

> '*not to trouble the Grand Lodge nor themselves farther, they choosing to stand on their own footing and rights as they have done these many years and ages past.*'[38]

As has been discussed elsewhere, Aitchison's Haven was not alone — many other lodges, nearly all of them stonemasons' lodges, decided not to participate in the new Grand Lodge 'system'. This is hardly a ringing endorsement by lodges over which the St. Clairs were alleged hereditary Grand Masters!

Maidment too saw many flaws in the suggestion that William St. Clair was a hereditary Grand Master of Scottish 'masons' and explained these in his '*Introductory Notice*' to the 1835 edition.[39] They remain valid today. There are a few observations regarding the *Letters of Jurisdiction* or 'Charters' that require to be made for the purpose of clarification.

Throughout the history of Scottish Freemasonry there has been no attempt to differentiate between masons (stonemasons) and Masons (Freemasons) and this has led to a belief that the two terms are interchangeable. Stonemasons wrote the *Letters of Jurisdiction*. Yet it was *Freemasons* who induced William St. Clair to resign the alleged and unspecified 'rights' granted to him by *stonemasons*. In doing this Freemasons were improving the antiquity, and therefore the legitimacy, of the new Grand Lodge, even though it had very little to do with the craft of stonemasonry. This confusion of the terms (masons and Masons etc.) was, and is, common and appears to have originated in the erroneous belief that there was essentially no difference between the two. In any event this confusion suited those intent on forming a new body, the Grand Lodge of Scotland, and such niceties were unimportant for them. Today that dichotomy remains unresolved in the writings of many who comment upon Scottish Freemasonry.

Maidment considered Hay to be a propagandist: '*Father Hay, in his anxiety to blazon forth the honours of the Saintclairs …*'. In seeking to promote the St. Clair family and the activities of its members Hay uncovered a huge range of material. When one turns to Hay for information regarding the hypothesis mentioned earlier in the Introduction there is little or nothing in its' support. When one realises that Hay had nothing whatsoever to say about the Knights Templar, Scottish Freemasonry and the St. Clair family's alleged involvement with either of those bodies then it seems obvious that he found nothing, either in the family's written history or oral traditions, to substantiate such a connection. This is all the more significant when one is aware that Hay wrote a very brief, but sympathetic, history of the Knights Templar which was also edited and published by Maidment.[40] He does mention Robert I and the Battle of Bannockburn in relation to the St. Clair family where he states that a William St. Clair was rewarded for fighting at Bannockburn by being made Bishop of Dunkeld.[41] That this William St. Clair was a bishop of Dunkeld is correct but he was not made a bishop as a reward for fighting at Bannockburn. He had been elected to that position in 1311 and was consecrated as such the following year.[42] This is one of several oral traditions of the family recorded by Hay and demonstrates that oral accounts of this kind can be unreliable. This inaccurate claim is also repeated by modern authors who have accepted Hay's statement without checking its accuracy.[43]

From a Masonic point of view Hay's reproduction of the *Letters of Jurisdiction* was very important because they provide some information regarding the connection of the St. Clair family not with Freemasons, but with stonemasons. The subsequent use to which these documents were put, at the founding of the Grand Lodge of Scotland, gives an insight to the desires and aspirations of those instrumental in establishing one of the oldest existing Scottish institutions. Whilst their actions are understandable, and many would argue laudable, the consequences for Scottish Masonic history are more problematic given that subsequent writers have failed consistently to understand that those Freemasons in 1736 were intent on creating a suitable pedigree and were not concerned with historical accuracy.

Gypsies and the St. Clairs

Why did Maidment describe Father Hay as the 'arch propagandist' of the St. Clair family? One further subject will perhaps serve to illustrate his opinion. Hay is the source of a story regarding the St. Clair family and their involvement with gypsies who like many other minority groups were misunderstood, mistrusted and therefore frequently persecuted. There is one story that has been repeated many times:

> '*He* [Sir William St. Clair (?–c.1602)] *delivered once ane Egyptian* [gypsy] *from the gibbet in the Burrow Moore,* (Burgh Muir) *ready to be strangled, returning from Edinburgh to Roslin, upon which acoumpt the whole body of gypsies were, of old, accustomed to gather in the stanks* [marshes] *of Roslin every year, where they acted severall plays, dureing the months of May and June. There are two towers which were allowed them for their residence, the one called Robin Hood and the other Little John.*'[44]

The two towers were outworks of Roslin Castle and are almost certainly named after the play '*Robin Hood and Little John*' performed by gypsies. This play was one of the best known of the May Day events (another was the Abbot and the

Prior) which were held to welcome the coming of summer. Such festivities were not restricted to one day, as is now often the case but were spread over a considerable period — the gypsies at Roslin were resident there for two months. The play was one of a number of a cycle enacted during this festival but other activities and events also took place: dancing round a May Pole; electing a May Queen and King; choosing the Abbot of Unreason; Morris Dancing and the celebration of the Green Man. The latter is discussed more fully in Chapter VI in relation to Rosslyn Chapel. The cult of Robin Hood and his associates (Little John; Friar Tuck and Maid Marian, etc.) was ancient and it must be borne in mind that this play was about *a* Robin Hood not *the* Robin Hood.

> '*On the first Sunday in May, the citizens of Edinburgh foregathered at the Greenside, under the patronage of the magistrates, to witness the frolics of the famous outlaw and his band. Robin Hood and Little John robbed bishops, fought with pinners, and contended in archery; Maid Marian disported herself in a flower-sprinkled kirtle, with bow and arrows in here hand; the Abbot of Narent kicked up his heels and played antics like a pantaloon; and the Morris dancers, with their fantastic dresses and jingling bells, added to the gaiety of the scene.*[45]*

That these anti-church and pagan-based festivities were tolerated by church and civil authorities across Europe suggests that they were considered a 'safety valve' which allowed the common people to let off steam. In 1555 the excesses during the festivities led to the Scottish Parliament to pass an Act abolishing the May Games. That Act was followed by riots and numerous prosecutions but it was several decades before the festival finally disappeared. The report by Father Hay regarding the gypsies at Roslin Castle and their enactment of the Robin Hood play followed a brief biography of Sir William St. Clair who died about 1602 and suggests that the events took place after 1555. The gypsies appeared to have visited Roslin annually but by 1623 things had changed:

> '*The Privy Council had their attention drawn to this Patmos* [place of exile] *of the outlawed race. They remark that, while the laws enjoined all persons in authority 'to execute to the deid* [death] *the counterfeit thieves and limmers* [robbers], *the Egyptians,' it was nevertheless reported that a number of them were now within the bounds of Roslin, 'where they have a peaceable receipt and abode as if they were lawful subjects, committing*

stowths [thefts] *and reifs* [plundering] *in all parts where they may find the occasion.' The Council therefore issued an order to the sheriff of the district who happened to be Sinclair, younger of Roslin, himself commanding him 'to pass, search, seek hunt, follow and pursue the said vagabond thieves and limmers,' and bring them to the Tolbooth* [prison] *of Edinburgh for due punishment.'*[46]

William St. Clair complied and men, women and children were taken prisoner and delivered to Edinburgh Tolbooth. In January 1624 eight gypsy leaders were tried and sentenced to death. Within the week all eight had been executed by hanging at the Burgh Muir.[47] The women and children were found guilty also and sentenced to death by drowning. Their fate was deferred pending a decision of the king (James VI of Scotland, I of Great Britain) who commuted the sentences to branding and deportation. It was this St. Clair to whom the second St. Clairs 'Charters' had been addressed. Maidment, as librarian of the legal library of Scotland, had access to reports such as this and this may well explain the reason for his antipathy towards the 'arch propagandist' Hay.

Hay can be seen from this to be biased in favour of his new family, omitting the bad, and promoting the good. He contributes little to the history of Scottish Freemasonry. It was rather the use to which his material was put by subsequent writers that had an impact on that history. Maidment attempted, in vain, to point out the major flaws and inconsistencies of later writers. His comments and observations remain valid today. The absence of any comment by Hay on matters such as the so-called 'St. Clair Charters' reveals just how important this 'arch propagandist' for the family thought those documents were. That is because they were *not* important until 1736 when they were used to ensure that William St. Clair of Rosslyn was elected as the Grand Master of the Grand Lodge of Scotland.[48]

It is not the purpose in this brief chapter to detail the entire history of the St. Clair family. The intention has been, in accordance with the hypothesis, to examine the connection the family had with Scottish Freemasonry. From the foregoing it now seems clear, perhaps for the first time, that no such connection ever existed until 1736 and that even then it was an entirely artificial creation based on error and the desire to create a non-existent pedigree. The St. Clair family did have a connection with the *stonemasons* of Scotland but initially that was merely an employer/employee relationship necessary in order to build Rosslyn Chapel and parts of the castle. Later, as evidenced by the St. Clair

'Charters', William Schaw attempted to build another kind relationship between stonemasons and the family — one which allowed the stonemasons of Scotland to call on the services of William St. Clair as an arbitrator of their disputes and nothing else. The first attempt apparently failed because of the character of the St. Clair chosen to be the '*Patron and Protector*' of Scottish stonemasons. The second attempt was, initially, more successful. Times had changed however, and those in supreme authority denied that any such relationship had previously existed nor did they wish such a relationship to be created.

[1] Hay's legacy of eight diverse works on matters of genealogy and history were obtained by the Advocate's Library, now the National Library of Scotland. Exactly when he transcribed the St. Clair documents is unlikely to be known with any certainty but it is likely to have been during 1690–1700.

[2] The Grand Lodge of Scotland in publishing a second edition (2002) and did so with two principal aims: firstly, to make the work more widely available and secondly, to make the book useful to more people by having the Latin text translated into English.

[3] Societies which published material of literary and antiquarian interest. They were, respectively: Abbotsford Club
Founded in Edinburgh, 1833. Published more than 30 volumes of historical source material. The Bannatyne Club
Founded 1823. Published material relating to the history and literature of Scotland the Huntarian Club
Founded in Glasgow, 1871, to reproduce '*works of Scottish writers of Elizabethan times*'. The Maitland Club
Founded in Glasgow, 1828, '*to print works illustrative of the antiquities, history and literature of Scotland*'. The Spottiswoode Society
Founded in Edinburgh, 1843. Published works by members of the Episcopal Church and material relating to Scottish history.

[4] See the '*Genealogie*' p. 37.

[5] See the '*Genealogie*' p. 49.

[6] See the '*Genealogie*' p. 27.

[7] See the '*Genealogie*' p. 27.

[8] See the '*Genealogie*' p. 27.

[9] See the '*Genealogie*' p. 107.

[10] *The Apocrypha According to the Authorized Version*. Oxford University Press. nd.

[11] See the '*Genealogie*' pp. 107–108.

[12] *Medieval Religious Houses of Scotland*. Cowan, Ian B. and Easson, David E.

2nd edn. 1976. p. 225.

[13] See the 'Genealogie'. pp. 127–129.

[14] It is not impossible that Slezer and Hay met when Slezer visited Rosslyn Chapel in order to have it engraved for his book.

[15] An Account of the Chapel of Roslin 1778. Ed. Cooper, Robert L. D. The Grand Lodge of Scotland. 2000. p. 29

[16] Ibid. p. 22

[17] These manuscripts are the property of The Grand Lodge of Scotland.

[18] See the 'Genealogie'. pp. 157–163.

[19] The First Freemasons. Stevenson, David. 2nd edn. p.187. The Grand Lodge of Scotland. Edinburgh. 2001.

[20] Rosslyn — Country of Painter and Poet. Rosslyn, Helen and Maggi, Angelo. National Gallery of Scotland. Edinburgh. 2002

[21] See: The Origins of Freemasonry — Scotland's Century 1590–1710 by David Stevenson. pp. 57–67

[22] See the 'Genealogie' p. 159.

[23] See the 'Genealogie' p. 28.

[24] The castle was again set on fire in 1544 by the Earl of Hertford during the so-called 'rough wooing' of Mary Queen of Scots and these charters again survived.

[25] Both jointly held the post although Murray was senior; on his death Alexander became the sole Master of Works.

[26] For a detailed analysis and discussion of the rather complex issues surrounding the second 'charter' see: The Origins of Freemasonry — Scotland's Century 1590–1710, by David Stevenson.

[27] The Origins of Freemasonry — Scotland's Century 1590–1710 by David Stevenson. p. 64.

[28] 'Rosslyn Chapel' by the Earl of Rosslyn. 1997. p.46.

[29] The History of Free Masonry by Alexander Lawrie. 1804. p. 100.

[30] The History of Free Masonry by Alexander Lawrie. 1804. p. 102.

[31] The History of Free Masonry by Alexander Lawrie. 1804. p. 103.

[32] This is not surprising given that no popular author has been to Freemasons' Hall to read the original documents.

[33] For example: Freemasonry in Edinburgh 1721–1746 (Institutions and Context). Kahler, Dr. Lisa. Unpublished thesis. University of St. Andrews. 1998

[34] Ibid. p. 219.

[35] Ibid. p. 228.

[36] Modern publications continue to repeat the error: 'The Lodges then appointed him the first non-hereditary Grand Master Mason of Scotland.' See for example: 'Rosslyn Chapel' by the Earl of Rosslyn. 1997. p. 47.

[37] The History of Free Masonry by Alexander Lawrie. 1804. p. 149.

[38] The Grand Lodge of Scotland — Historical Sketch 1736–1986. The Grand Lodge of Scotland Year Book 1986. p. 73.

[39] See the 'Genealogie' pp. i–xx.

[40] Account of the Templars together with an Account of the Joannites or Knights of St. John. Hay, Father Richard, A., (Ed. James Maidment) Edinburgh. 1828.

[41] See the 'Genealogie' p. 12.

[42] *Robert Bruce and the Community of the Realm of Scotland.* Barrow, Geoffrey W. S. Edinburgh. 1996.

[43] See for example: *The Sword and the Grail.* London. 1993. p. 47.

[44] See the 'Genealogie' p. 136.

[45] *The Silver Bough — Scottish folk-lore and folk-belief,* by Marian F. McNeill, pp. 78–79.

[46] *Domestic Annals of Scotland* by Robert Chambers. Quoted in *Scottish Gypsies under the Stewarts* by David MacRitchie. p. 98.

[47] Those executed were Capitane Johnne Faa, Robert Faa, Samuell Faa, Johnne Faa, younger, Andro Faa, Williame Faa, Robert Broun and Gawin Trotter.

[48] Hay was almost certainly dead by this time and not around to comment on the way these documents were used. It would be idle speculation to suggest that those intent on creating a Grand Lodge took advantage of Hay's demise. The methods they used to provide St. Clair with the necessary Masonic qualifications demonstrate that they were not averse to bending the rules.

Chapter 5
A Description of Rosslyn Chapel

'An altogether unique architectural monstrosity'[1]

Before discussing Rosslyn Chapel a comprehensive description of it, its architecture, principal carvings and symbolism is thought necessary in order that the scale and detail might be appreciated — especially to be able to understand the more detailed discussion which follows. The description, here, has been drawn from a variety of sources in order to make it as full as possible (including some historical details) and even those familiar with the chapel may find information here previously unknown to them. One of the main sources is the original guidebook first issued in 1892 and written by the chaplain to the 4th Earl of Rosslyn, Francis Robert (1833–1890) the Rev. John Thompson.[2] This has the benefit of describing a great many of the details (carvings etc.) of the chapel which have subsequently deteriorated to the point where the eye can no longer interpret what it sees. In that sense this chapter could be used as a guide to the chapel (before or during a visit) although that is not its main purpose. In order to assist identifying where in the chapel certain piers (or pillars), carvings etc. are located a ground plan, which has been marked and numbered to match the item in the text below, has been provided.

The chapel is located on the left bank of the North Esk south-south-west of the present village of Roslin and overlooks Rosslyn Glen and Roslin Castle on what is called College Hill. Rosslyn or Roslin is a Gaelic word of two parts meaning *'Point of the Waterfall'* — 'Ros' meaning the head or point of a promontory (near to which the chapel stands) and 'Lynn' meaning waterfall. There have been a variety of spellings in the past (Roskelyn, Rosslin, etc.) Multiple spellings of words were normal throughout the medieval period (and later) but the meaning of the name has remained the same.

Although the exterior of the chapel has some interesting features it is the interior for which the chapel is renowned. Even as long ago as 1696 the chapel and particularly the interior was considered worthy of comment. This small space is packed with a superabundance of carvings and on a first visit can be almost overwhelming. One must wonder if this is not exactly the effect that the builder, and those who subsequently completed it, had intended? As has been seen elsewhere, Rosslyn Chapel cannot be considered to be unusual, certainly not in terms of form and function, as other family owned collegiate churches in Scotland which were built for exactly the same reasons. However, no other collegiate church can compete with the sheer number and types of carvings at Rosslyn Chapel. Was William St. Clair's purpose *not* to compete at all with other families in the size of his church but instead did he deliberately choose to outdo them all when it came to decoration? A clue might be found in the comments of Father Richard Augustine Hay:

> '*Therfor, to the end he* [William St. Clair, Earl of Orkney, (c.1404–c.1484)] *might not seem altogether unthankfull to God for the benefices he receaved from him. It came to his mind to build a house for God's service, of a most curious worke* . . .'[3]

Rosslyn Chapel as it presently stands is simply the choir of what was intended to be a cruciform church. The chapel is oblong in shape and in common with the majority of medieval churches the building is on an east–west axis. It consists of a choir of five bays, with north, south and east aisles, and a retro-choir, or Lady Chapel, the former meaning a last or separate choir and the latter meaning a chapel dedicated to the Blessed Virgin and which was often placed to the east of the main altar. The side aisles (north, south and east) are divided into bays with seven at the north and south and four at the east. The divisions are created by buttresses which project from the main wall by 3 feet 8 inches (1.12 metres.) The north and south walls of the aisles are strengthened at each bay by substantial buttresses, topped by pinnacles of various designs; from the buttresses rise rudimentary flying buttress, which are required to take the downward thrust of the roof vault at the clerestory walls. The walls are 2¼ feet (0.66 metres) thick. In 1892 it was noted that on the gable of the unfinished west wall was a square bell-cot for two bells. This was included in the engravings made by Father Hay about 1690. It is not known whether it was ever used in that capacity, though the broken stonework suggests that bells were forcibly removed.

Each bay on the north and south sides has lights (windows) of stained glass.[4] Each consists of two lights in the form of a pointed arch. There are niches in the jambs, one of which bears a corbel in the left jamb of the window of the extreme west bay on the south side, which is of special interest, and which shall be discussed later. Below the sills there is a sill course which runs around the building. There is, at ground level, a heavy base course. This is relevant to the discussion, below, especially regarding the west wall.

There are two bays which do not have windows as described above. In the fifth bay, from the east, in the north and south walls, doors are to be found opposite each other which lead into the chapel. Above each is a triangular window (a curved equilateral triangle) with a curved sill. The north door has an external lintel whereas that in the south has an arched entryway. The differences appears to be due to the north doorway having been designed to be opened outwards suggesting that another, projecting, structure, perhaps a sacristy, had been planned but not built.[5]

There are a variety of dates given for the commencement of the building of the chapel. Anderson gives the date 1441. But the most commonly quoted is 1446. Externally the top of the north wall terminates in a cavetto cornice with projecting heads between which there are a series of shields. Some bear the engrailed cross of the St. Clair family. Engrailing is a heraldic term and has nothing to do with the Holy Grail! Others sport single letters in the following sequence: W. L. S. F. Y. C. Y. Z. O. G. M. C. C. C. C. L. This translates as follows: '*William Lord Sinclair Fundit* [founded] *Yis* [This] *College* [Collegiate Church] *Ye* [The] *Zeir* [Year] *of God 1450*.'[6] The discrepancy between the dates is due to the fact that the building was commenced in 1446 when the foundations were laid. As can be seen from the ground plan these were quite extensive. The foundations complete, a start could be made on the walls and by 1450 William St. Clair was confident enough to declare that was the year of foundation of the collegiate church although it would be some time before Papal approval was sought and granted. The use of the date 1441 for the date of the foundation of the chapel is a repetition of the error made by James Anderson in his '*New Constitutions*' (of which more below).[7]

The roof is of stone and is 9 inches thick and is covered on the outside by a thick coating of asphalt which, in 1894, according to the Rev. Thompson '*gives it an unsightly appearance*'. The Rev. further states:

'*There seems never to have been any independent roof as one would naturally expect, though Bishop Robert Forbes, in his tract on Roslin Chapel about the middle of the last century* [1774] *affirms that it was well covered with flagstones but there is no trace of this*' [now].

Forbes may have been commenting on the roofs of the Lady Chapel and side aisles which were so covered. There are traces of another roof over the side aisles which were probably temporary and there are raglet marks cut in the east transept walls, the splays of the clerestory windows and the pinnacles.[8] The effect was of covering the clerestory windows up to two thirds of their height. This roof was continued over the east aisle and Lady Chapel which in section would appear thus: M. This design ensured that the large east window was not obscured by the roof. This roof was apparently put in place in an effort to shed rainwater more effectively.[9] That roof must have been quite old as Forbes mentions it in 1774 but Hay did not include it in his engraving of c.1690. When the roof was removed is not known.

On the north side door (commonly referred to as the Bachelor's door) there are gargoyles over the porch and on the right is a man with pointed ears tied up with ropes. There is also a man with a stick between his arms and legs — another method of binding someone — and a warrior on horseback. These carvings show some wear. On the left of the door is a representation of the ancient nursery rhyme — a fox running away with a goose, with a farmer (or perhaps his wife!) in pursuit. There are a number of heads and hands holding foliage.

On the west wall (No.17 in plate 11) was a representation of St Christopher with the Infant Saviour in his arms although this is now badly weathered. On the north side (No. 18 in plate 11) is St. Sebastian being tied to a tree by two men, with arrows sticking in his left side. This too is now worn. Above these and forming capitals to shafts, on the north side, the crucifixion is depicted. On the south side is a carving said to represent Elijah being taken up to heaven in a chariot of fire — also an allusion to the ascension of Christ. This too is so worn that it is now very difficult to make out clearly although 100 years ago it was clear enough to be identifiable.

Entering through the north door there is no doubt that this is a special place. The lighting effect of the stained-glass windows and the sheer amount of carving rarely fails to impress the first time visitor.

Internally the chapel consists of a central aisle with additional aisles to the north, south and east (the retro-choir) complete with the bays described above. Piers or pillars divide the central aisle from the other three and also support the clerestory, or upper, level above the central aisle. The piers number 14 in total, six dividing the central aisle from the north side aisle, and another six serving the same purpose for the south aisle. An additional pier is centred between the two most easterly piers and these three have been described as being the Master Mason, Fellow Craft and Apprentice Pillars. These piers also serve to mark the division between the east aisle, or retro-choir, from the central aisle. (ground plan Plate 11) A further, central, pillar is positioned to the west of the 'Fellow Craft' pillar and supports the east wall of the clerestory. The piers are eight feet in height.

The internal dimensions are: choir 48 feet 4 inches (14.73 metres) x 17 feet 10½ inches (5.45 metres); height: 33 feet 6 inches to the highest point of the arched roof. The total dimensions (including aisles and Lady Chapel) are: length (east–west): 69 feet 8 inches (20.95 metres); breadth (north-south): 35 feet (10.67 metres); height: 41 feet 9 inches to the apex of the roof. The sacristy (occasionally referred to as the vestry) is attached to the main structure at the south east corner of the building and lies about 17 feet (5.18 metres) lower. It is reached, internally, by a stair at the north east corner of the chapel. The sacristy measures 36 feet 2 inches (11.02 metres) from west to east and 14 feet (4.27 metres) from north to south. (Plate 11).

As the aisles and Lady Chapel have flat roofs reaching to just above the arches, there is no triforium. One peculiarity of Rosslyn Chapel is the use of so-called 'straight arches' in the aisles rather than ordinary arches or lintels. The straight arches are hollow internally and carry no more than their own weight as they disguise the existence of 'saving arches' beneath them. (Plate 9) In some instances these are quite visible; others are hidden by the hollow lintels. Each bay of the aisles is vaulted from east to west, thus giving height to the windows on the north and south.

The retro-choir or Lady Chapel extends the full width of the chapel. It is 7 feet 6 inches wide and 15 feet high and the floor is one step higher than the rest of the choir. The roof is groined (the angle formed by the intersection of vaults) in the simplest way although there is a huge amount of detail in the roof's ornamentation. The diagonal ribs join to form a keystone which has been developed into a pendant of approximately 2 feet in length. All the lower windows in the retro-choir have two lights which are separated by shafted mullions, the tops and bottoms of which are carved. The splays are fitted with curiously carved brackets to support figures.[10]

The roof of the choir is of stone and is barrel vaulted. There are five sections divided by four carved ribs, each of which is profusely decorated and of different design. Each section is dotted with stars, roses, squares and paterae decorations.[11]

In the wall space between each of the clerestory windows are a double row of brackets for statues, 12 on each side. The canopies of the lower brackets form the bases of the brackets above. Above the central pillar under the east window is a niche of more elaborate design in which stands a modern figure of the Blessed Virgin with the infant Jesus in her arms. Figures of the Apostles and Saints also probably occupied the other brackets but they were removed at the Reformation (1559).

There were four altars in the Lady Chapel each dedicated to a particular saint. Beginning at the north end of the retro-choir these were: St. Matthew; the Virgin Mary; St. Andrew and St. Peter.[12] This last named altar is sometimes called the 'high altar' because it was placed on a platform making higher than the others but this was necessary to make headroom for the stairway leading down to the sacristy. The main altar of the chapel stood in front of the central pillar under the figure of the Madonna and Child where the present altar stands.

In the south-east corner of the chapel are the stairs leading to the sacristy or crypt. This is claimed to have been built by Lady Margaret Douglas, first wife of Sir William Sinclair, as suggested by the 'coat of arms' found on the south side of the only window in the east wall. This structure has puzzled many as to its purpose. It was used as a sacristy until the latter part of the 19th century and soon after became the vestry. It is unlikely that this was its original purpose. It seems that it is of a somewhat older date than the chapel and it has been suggested that it had been attached to an earlier building, some believing that to have been the first castle but this is considered unlikely. The unknown purpose of the structure is probably due to writers attempting to attribute one purpose to the sacristy. However, it seems likely that over the course of the centuries it had a variety of uses. Initially it may have been a charnel house (or mortuary) used until the chapel was built. Later it was converted to a dwelling for use by officiating priests. It certainly appears to have been used as a drawing-room during the building of the main chapel as there are drawings on the internal north and south walls. On the north wall are incised drawings of window arches and the arched ribs of the main chapel. The south wall bears the incised drawing of a buttress finial. The sacristy was probably used by Father Hay in the late 17th century. He mentioned that he lost several books of note here after the castle had been spoiled by the mob but it is likely that these books were in his library in the castle and not in the sacristy.[13]

Another suggestion has been that it was the burial place of junior members of the St. Clair family — the vaults under the main chapel being reserved for the head of the family. However, there is little evidence to support this especially as it has a fireplace and what may have been presses in the walls and two doors (in the north and south walls), the latter indicating that access was required to other building, which no longer exists.[14] The other elements suggest that it was at one time intended to be the dwelling place of the priestly custodian. The crypt contains an altar (under the east window), a piscina and an aumbry.[15] The altar, piscinæ and aumbry would have been used during divine services and it may be that this was its function during the period when the upper chapel was being built. Thereafter, the crypt may have reverted to a dwelling place once the chapel was complete enough for divine services to be held there.

A shield bearing the Rosslyn arms (an engrailed cross) is located on a corbel to the north of the window. Another is found to the south of the window, described in heraldic terms:

> '*Couped Orkney and Rosslyn; and the second part couped of three, Douglas and Touraine; in the first, three stars; in the second, three fleurs-de-lis; in the third, a heart, being the arms of Lady Margaret (or Elizabeth) Douglas, first wife of the founder.*'

The sacristy roof is a round stone vault bearing a band and four ribs which, where they intersect, form engrailed crosses, the arms of which rest on carved corbels. Unlike the main chapel the sacristy has no ornamentation other than that described above. One wonders if this was intentional on the part of the builder. To enter the main chapel one would be moving from a bare, dark, place to a lively, colourful, place.

It is worth stopping (please do be careful though as the stairs are quite steep; extra care is needed when the chapel is busy) at the last few steps, before returning to the upper chapel, as this is one of the best views of the straight arches in the south aisle mentioned previously. In addition there is a good view of the roof of the Lady Chapel from this position.

In addition to the 'coats of arms' in the sacristy or crypt another is to be found over the capital of the central pillar in the east gable. This is a shield bearing Orkney, Caithness, and Roslin. These arms are helpful in confirming dates. They must date from the period 1455, when the founder was granted the Earldom of Caithness by James II and 1476 when he resigned it in favour of his third son, William (second son of the second marriage), and progenitor of the Caithness family.[16]

Another 'coat of arms' is to be found on the north wall pillar opposite the pillar No.16. (Plate 11.) This is another example of the engrailed cross of the St. Clair family. The arms feature frequently in the chapel not only as 'coats of arms' but also in ceilings of the side aisles, window tracery and, as previously mentioned, the crypt and other places.

The vaults below the choir are constructed from polished ashlar and are divided into compartments which are arched from east to west with a wall running down the centre of the chapel. The entrance to the vaults is under a large slab between Pillar No.14 and 15 (Plate 11). When stamped on, it gives a deep hollow sound. Between Pillar Nos.15 and 16 (Plate 11) is an incised slab with the representation of a knight in armour and in an attitude of prayer thereon (see page 106). On each side of his head are small shields on each of which is a lion rampant. A dog lies at his feet (a common image on such graveslabs.) In the 19th century it was popularly believed that this graveslab designated the burial place of Sir William St. Clair (?–1330) who fought at Bannockburn. This romantic belief, however, cannot be true as he died in Spain as part of the expedition, led by James 'the Black' Douglas (c.1276–1330), to take Bruce's heart to the Holy Land — more than a century before the building of Rosslyn Chapel commenced.

More credible is the suggestion that it marks the tomb of William St. Clair, the founder of the chapel, especially as a shield bearing his 'coat of arms' together with those of his first wife are to be found on the north wall opposite Pillar No.16. (Plate 11) Equally credible is the claim that this marks the last resting place of Alexander Sutherland of Dunbeath, father of the founder's second wife, Marjory Sutherland. In his will, dated 15 November 1456, he states his desire for his body to be buried in the collegiate church.

The last potential candidate is the second son of William St. Clair (c.1424–c.1484), the builder of the chapel, and Marjory Sutherland, also named William who died at the Battle of Flodden in 1513. This suggestion has been made because of the fact that he died in battle and is shown wearing armour.

There is one other monument to another member of the family within the chapel that is worth mentioning and that is to George, 4th Earl of Caithness (?–1582) who was the great grandson of the chapel's founder. The monument is testimony to the transition from the Gothic to the Renaissance style. It is designed as an arched opening resting on a pedestal. On each side of the recess is an enriched pilaster with a moulded base and capital from which the arch springs. In heraldic terms the monument is described as follows: the intrados is semicircular and the extrados is orival and terminates in a globular finial imbricated. The topmost course within the recess bears a shield supported by dragons and charged quarterly, first and fourth, a lymphad, second and third, a lion rampant. The quartering is engrailed and the lymphad in the first quarter is placed within a tressure flory-counter flory. Above is a coronet surmounted by an eagle. On a label is carved, in raised lettering: 'commit thy verk to God'. On the next course under the shield is the inscription also in carved raised letters:

JACET NOBILIS AC POTENS DOMENVS [*sic*]
GEORGIVS QVONDAM [CO]MES CATHANENSIS
DOMINVS SINCLAR IVSTICIARIVS [HER]EDITARIV[s]
DIOCESIS CATHANENSIS QVI OBIIT
EDINBVRGI 9 DIE MEMSIS SEPT
MBRIS ANNO DOMINI 1582

This monument was originally situated to the north of the graveslab mentioned above but was moved to its present position in the north west corner by General St. Clair who acquired the chapel in 1736.

Carvings

Although unfinished, Rosslyn Chapel still presents a wonderful array of carvings to tempt and intrigue all who see them. The temptation to guess as to the exact nature of some of the carvings has led to numerous speculative re-interpretations of them but the discussion of that is for the next chapter. Here the concern is to describe the internal carvings in order that the arguments contained in the next chapter might be a little easier to follow.

Rosslyn Chapel might be truly described as being William St. Clair of Rosslyn's 'unfinished thoughts in stone'. The sheer amount of intricate carving of a variety of subjects means that it is somewhat difficult to describe briefly in words and therefore I hope that I shall be excused of being more exhaustive than might normally be expected. The extent and variety can be daunting and the lack of a complete 'stone by stone, carving by carving' catalogue means that much can be, and has been, interpreted and re-interpreted when otherwise there would have been no necessity to do so. The subjects which the stonemasons carved include Jesus Christ, angels; heraldic devices and coats of arms, musicians, saints, sinners, apostles, green men, animals, fantastic beasts, warriors, numerous biblical characters, 'ordinary' people and even God himself.[17] Foliage in particular abounds and includes the rose, sunflower, ferns, kale, oak and cactus leaves as well as stylised versions such as fleurs-de-lis, trefoils, etc. and these are only those which can be positively identified! Unlike any other church in Scotland (some of which do have carvings of such subjects albeit in much smaller quantities) Rosslyn Chapel crams all these into a small space covering much of the interior surfaces. Even architectural features which tend, elsewhere, to receive more standard treatment, such as pinnacles, ceiling, ribs and windows are all interpreted differently — as if the designer was determined to also make their decoration as diverse as the rest of the chapel.

Because of the number of carvings it is quite easy to miss many, even when looking straight at them. Some are also difficult to interpret because they are defaced to some extent or other. The interior is a uniform grey colour (which varies according to the internal and external lighting) and this was the result of the application of a limewash to the whole interior between 1954 and 1957.[18] The collegiate church of St. Matthew, Rosslyn Chapel, has quite rightly been described as a 'Bible in Stone' and for this reason the description of the carvings will commence at the west, that is, the baptistery, entrance. The first feature to consider is the roof. This is divided into five sections. The first section, on entering from the west, contains a profusion of stars and the right side contains what has been described as four angels. Three, including one bearing a sword (representing the power and authority of God), are angels, but the fourth figure of a bearded man, whose head is surrounded by a halo, with both hands uplifted represents God in the act of creation. On the left side of this section of the roof, in addition to numerous stars, are the sun, moon and the head of a man. The man's head is also surrounded by a halo (the symbol of divinity) and he has his right hand raised in blessing. This is Jesus Christ. The dove in flight represents the Holy Ghost.

'*And Jesus, when he was baptized, went up straightway out of the water: and, lo, the heavens were opened unto him, and he saw the Spirit of God descending like a dove, and lighting upon him.*
And lo, a voice from heaven, saying, This is my beloved Son, in whom I am well pleased.' (St. Matthew 3:16-17)

This roof section therefore not only shows the Holy Trinity (Father, Son and Holy Spirit) but also shows the Heavens (and perhaps Heaven itself) as created by God. (See: Gen. 1:1-18.)

The next section of the roof contains a profusion of roses. These relate to the Virgin Mary — The Mystic Rose, the Rose of Sharon and the Rose without a Thorn (sin). '*I am the rose of Shâr-on, and the lily of the valleys* (Song of Solomon 2:1). A red rose reputedly sprang from drops of Christ's blood shed on Mt. Calvary represents principally martyrdom but also love.[19] The rose here therefore represents a number of dualities: the Virgin Mary and Jesus Christ, mother and son, masculine/feminine and perhaps the dual nature of Christ (human and divine).

The next roof section is in the middle and contains open flowers, that is; flowers open to the sun. Flowers in general refer to the Virgin Mary but there is also a duality here as in the previous roof section. The flower is the beginning and end in that it grows, dies and provides the seeds for its own re-birth. This is reminiscent of Revelation 22:13: '*I am Alpha and Omega, the first and the last, the beginning and the end.*' The open flowers also indicate adoration of God the creator.[20]

The fourth section from the west is decorated with lilies. The lily is white and symbolises purity and here again the symbolism relates to the Virgin Mary: *I am the rose of Shâr-on, and the lily of the valleys. As the lily among thorns, so is my love among the daughters* (The Song of Solomon 2:1-2). When the lily is stylised it becomes a *fleur-de-lis* and the three prongs refer to the Holy Trinity.

The last section and that furthest away from the west entrance consists of daisies. Daisies are white and represent innocence. But because they are common and prolific are also taken to indicate all of humankind as created in the image of God. Humanity is hardly 'innocent' but the daisy here symbolises humankind before the Fall — prefect and innocent. The daisy therefore is a symbolic reminder of what human beings once were and what, through Jesus Christ, they could be again. It is significant that this is above the high altar.

The roof then represents the Holy Trinity (Father, Son and Holy Ghost — separately and collectively), heaven, the Virgin Mary, mother of Jesus and, coming last on the list, humankind, not as it is today but as when it was first created. The symbolism of the roof is, as a unit, important symbolically because it reveals the overriding concerns of the builder. Although Rosslyn Chapel is dedicated to St. Matthew, he is not represented in the roof symbolism, nor are a whole host of other biblical figures and symbols. The Holy Trinity etc. is therefore above (literally and metaphorically) and over all else.

At the very apex of the roof in the west corner of the first panel is a head with a scar on the right temple perhaps to represent the unfortunate apprentice. About halfway up the west wall of the choir on the south side (under the pedestal of a niche which once held a statue of St. Paul (the Rev. Thompson writing in 1892) is another head of the apprentice likewise with a deep scar on the right temple, while in the opposite corner is that of the master who is said to have killed him. On the east of the apprentice under the next niche is another head, said to represent the sorrowful and widowed mother of the apprentice. These heads are said to have been carved by his fellow workmen when the walls had reached that height in order to commemorate the feat of the apprentice.

The carvings will now be described beginning with the central pillar (No.1 in Plate 11) under the east window. Above this pillar is a modern figure of the Madonna and Child. It is no mistake that on this pillar scriptural subjects commence with the Fall of Man and the Expulsion from Eden given the contents of the roof section above. A carving shows a tree with two figures approaching and two figures moving away from it. This is related in Genesis chapters 3–5. On the north side of this pillar is a huge beast being restrained by a collar and chain with a chord in its mouth. A man lies on the beast's back representing the never-ending struggle of man to control sin (the beast.) On the opposite, south, side are palm leaves symbolising victory over sin. The palm also represents victory over death. Both of these are achieved through the martyrdom of Christ and so this symbol has another third meaning — Christ's entry into Jerusalem (St. Matthew 21:1-11).

The retro-choir is next considered. This part of the chapel is the most richly carved — particularly the groined roof and capitals of pillars. There is a suspicion that the retro-choir is incomplete. Where one would expect to find detailed carvings simple foliage that exists elsewhere in the chapel has been inserted.

In the most northerly (first) compartment of the Lady Chapel on the ribs of the groined roof there is a column of figures stretching up the rib. Each figure is approximately 8 inches long.

Beginning at a corbel (A in plate 11) and on the south east side of the rib (a in plate 11) the column of figures rises towards the pendant capital (P in plate 11) and they can be identified as:

1. An abbott
2. An abbess
3. A man of learning (a doctor? - the head is missing and is badly damaged)
4. A lady looking into a mirror
5. Completely defaced
6. A bishop
7. A cardinal
8. A courtier
9. A king

On the rib rising from pillar 2 (No.2 in Plate 11) also on the south east side (b in plate 11) and rising to the pendant capital (P in Plate 11) are another seven figures. These are:

1. A ploughman
2. A carpenter
3. A gardener (with a spade)
4. A sportsman
5. A child
6. A husband and wife
7. A farmer

Carvings of people from all sections of medieval society were not unusual in churches of the period but what makes these carvings unique are the skeletons which accompany each figure.

It has been said that these carvings *represent the Resurrection, by people rising out of the graves like skeletons and improving into proper forms placed close to the skeletons*.[21] Although it is not impossible that these have a dual symbolism, it is much more likely that this is a representation of the Dance of Death or *Danse Macabre*. It is a reminder that no position of rank, class or wealth can prevent one's ultimate fate — a lesson well known to the Freemason. It certainly reminds us: 'In the midst of life we are in death.'[22]

On the opposite sides of these ribs (c and d in Plate 11) are doves carrying olive leaves in their beaks. At the time of the flood, sent by God to purge the world of evil, Noah twice sent a dove to determine if the waters had receded. On the second occasion: '. . . *the dove came to him in the evening; and lo, in her mouth was an olive leaf* . . .' (Gen. 8:11.) In addition to heralding the end of the flood the olive branch represents peace. In Genesis this represents God's covenant with Noah. Scenes depicting the Annunciation occasionally show Gabriel, the Archangel, carrying an olive branch as a symbolic announcement of the coming of Jesus Christ and in anticipation of a new covenant between God and humankind.[23] Because the olive leaf is an emblem of peace and as it is so close to the Star of Bethlehem, some have suggested that it relates to the Fall of Man and the Redemption and refers to the angelic song 'peace on earth'.

In the fourth (south) compartment of the retro-choir (above the stairs leading to the crypt or sacristy) a rib springs from a corbel in the south east wall (marked e in Plate 11) bears four figures:

1. A warrior wearing a helmet and bearing a sword and a spear
2. A monk and drinking
3. Death apparently crouched waiting to pounce

4.   A man in a robe with very wide sleeves

Opposite this, on the rib rising from a corbel on the east wall (marked f in Plate 11), are a further four figures:

1. A queen
2. A lady seated in a chair
3. Another lady kneeling in prayer
4. A warrior

These eight figures also have skeletons accompanying them and it seems that the original intention was to 'mirror' the *Danse Macabre* in the north compartment. However, this Dance of Death is incomplete, especially when compared with that in the north compartment, because it extends over only half the rib. The remaining space is filled with foliage and this is an important indication that the work was finished hurriedly. The ribs of the two middle compartments are also filled with foliage and again support the view that these were carvings which were quickly and easily available. There remains one feature worthy of mention here.

In the second compartment from the north side the pendant (marked S in Plate 11) bears a large eight pointed star. Known as the Star of Bethlehem it is surrounded by eight figures some of which are unfortunately too indistinct to be identified with any certainty. In the south the Virgin and Child can be identified and to their right is the manger, then the three Kings (Magi) — identifiable by their staffs. Next appears to be the Angel of Death included here, no doubt, to represent the fear experienced by sinners caused by the arrival of Jesus Christ.

On the capitals of the third pillar, parts of which face this pendant, bearing the Star of Bethlehem, (Plate 12) there are 12 angels, all of them singing or playing musical instruments (including one playing a bagpipe), and the 'Host of Heaven' rejoicing in the birth of the Saviour.

> '*And suddenly there was with the angel a multitude of the heavenly host praising God and saying,*
> *Glory to God in the highest, and on earth peace, goodwill towards all men.*' (Luke 2:13-14)

The other pillar, adjacent to the pendant bearing the Star of Bethlehem, (No.2 in Plate 11) has on the side facing the star, a carving of an angel holding an open book.

It is also here in the retro-choir or Lady Chapel that there are a few faces discreetly placed amongst the other carvings and decoration. One of these is claimed to be that of Robert I (commonly called Robert the Bruce). Other carvings of winged figures are stated as being in 'postures of significance to Freemasons' — claims which are discussed further in the following chapter.

In the other compartments of the groined roofs, the ribs are covered with foliage. But the pendant S (Plate 11) is very interesting having a large star on the lower surface with eight points. This is called the Star of Bethlehem. Around it are eight figures. On the south point is the Virgin and Child; on her right is the manger, the three Kings (Magi), each with a long staff or sceptre in his hand, the Angel of Death, and other figures, all doubtless connected with the birth of the Saviour; while on the capitals of the pillars facing the star are 12 or 13 figures of angels, singing and playing upon instruments of music (amongst them the bagpipes — demonstrating that this is truly a Scottish chapel!), representing the heavenly host, who rejoiced and praised God at the birth of Christ (Luke 2:13.)

On pillar No.2 (Plate 11) there is an angel with a book open before him — proclaiming the gospel (Good News) which was announced by the 'Angel of the Lord' at the time of Christ's birth.

The pillar in the south of the Lady Chapel (No.4 in Plate 11) next to the entrance to the crypt is the famous 'Apprentice Pillar', or as it was called by Slezer, the Prince's Pillar. The legend concerning this pillar is briefly discussed:

The 'Apprentice Pillar' is unique even in this unique place. It is different in design and workmanship from any other pillar in the chapel. At the base are eight dragons intertwined. In Christian symbolism the dragon represents 'dark forces', evil, in other words — Satan.

'And there was war in heaven; Michael and his angels fought against the dragon; and the dragon fought and his angels,
And prevailed not; neither was their place found any more in heaven.
And the great dragon was cast out, that old serpent, called the Devil, and Satan, which deceiveth the whole world: he was cast out into the earth and his angels were cast out with him.' (Rev. 12:7-9)

Tendrils from the dragons mouths lead into four double spirals of foliage in 'basso-relievo'.[24] The spirals of foliage are 'bound' to the pillar by ropes which are positioned centrally on the foliage. Each of the spirals of foliage is separated from its neighbour by 18 inches. The spirals consist of nothing but leaves and the securing rope, and this has led to speculation that because the foliage has no fruit of any kind this is indicative of the dragons (evil, Satan, etc.) sucking the life blood from the world.

The capital of the Apprentice Pillar consists principally of foliage but on the south side there is a carving of the sacrifice of Isaac — including the ram caught in a thicket by the horns:

'And Abraham lifted up his eyes and looked, and behold behind him a ram caught in a thicket by his horns: and Abraham went and took the ram, and offered him up for a burnt offering in the stead of his son.' (Gen. 22:13)

Bishop Forbes describes the capital of the Apprentice Pillar as also having (on the east side) in his time a carving of Abraham 'with his hands lifted up prayer' in the centre of this group but this has since disappeared.[25] On each capital of the three pillars in the Lady Choir there are a number of angels playing a variety of musical instruments and which again represent the heavenly choir.

The south side of the architrave (lintel) that connects pillars four (the Apprentice Pillar) and five (No. 4 & 5 in Plate 11) has at the east corner a king wearing a crown. This is thought to be Darius. In the west is a carving of a man playing bagpipes and below is a man lying asleep; this too represents Darius. These figures are believed to refer to the inscription, in Lombardic letters, on the architrave which connects pillar number four with the south wall: (Plate 8)

'Forte est vinū [vinum]: fortior est Rex: Fortiores sunt mulieres: sup̄ [super] om̄ [omnia] vincit veritas'

'Wine is strong: the King is stronger: Woman are stronger: but above all Truth conquers.' (Trans.)[26]

These words and the carvings previously mentioned are about the 'test of wisdom' described in I Esdras, Chapters 3–4. Briefly, this relates the story of how three bodyguards of King Darius each wrote a 'sentence of wisdom' which were then placed under the king's pillow whist he slept. After rising the next morning the three sentences were presented to him and he; *'called all the princes of Persia and Media, and the governors, and the captains, and the lieutenants, and the chief offices'* (I Esdras 3:14–15) to judge the writings. Each of the three explained their writings before this council. Zerubbabel won with acclamation: *'. . . all the people*

then shouted, and said, Great is Truth, and mighty above all things'. I Esdras
4:41). Darius asked what Zerubbabel would like as a reward and was reminded of
his promise to fulfil the decree of Cyrus allowing the Jews to return to Jerusalem
and rebuild the temple. Thus ended the 70 years' captivity and, as the *subsequent*
events form the basis of the Masonic Royal Arch ceremonies, some have claimed
that this inscription means that the builders of Rosslyn Chapel had knowledge of
the Royal Arch and, therefore, that the chapel has a Masonic 'connection'. This is
a subject which will be considered in more detail in the following chapter.

The architrave which links pillar five (No.5 in Plate 11) to the south wall
presents medieval depictions of vice and virtue — on the east side (a in Plate 11)
are the corporeal acts of mercy. At the left is a cardinal bishop, a crozier in his left
hand and a book with two clasps in his right. The acts of mercy are then shown in
the following order:

1. Helping the needy — a lame man on crutches leading the blind
2. Clothing the naked
3. Visiting the sick
4. Visiting the imprisoned
5. Comforting the fatherless (the figure with a child under each arm)
6. Feeding the hungry
7. Burying the dead

At the end of the sequence is St. Peter standing at the entrance to heaven,
holding a key in his hand, waiting to admit those who have practised the works
of mercy.

On the west side of the architrave (b in Plate 11) are the vices. At the beginning
of the sequence stands a bishop, pastoral staff in his left hand with his right arm
bent and the index finger of his right hand raised — making the sign of the cross
in Anathema. The seven capital vices (sometimes called the seven deadly sins) are
depicted as follows:

1. Pride: A young man dressed in rich clothes. Sometimes said to be a
   Pharisee
2. Gluttony: a man with a large pitcher up to his mouth
3. Anger: two men drinking; one with a hand raised as if to strike the other
4. Sloth: a careless warrior, with a child clinging to his left side. (See Tim.
   2:4)

5. Luxury: a man with hands across his breast surrounded by clusters of
   grapes
6. Avarice: a miser with a long purse in his hand
7. Lust: the sinful lovers

Luxury is incorrect here. Envy is one of the seven vices but has been omitted and
'luxury' included in its place. It may be that the carving depicting envy had to be
replaced for some reason and this inaccurate carving substituted.[27]

The last part of the sequence shows the Jaws of Hell with the Devil standing
between them and in his hands a three pronged rake which he is stretching out to
rake in the sinners.

The next pillar, (No.6 in Plate 11) has a head and two birds on the capital but
the import is not clear. The capital of pillar seven has been quite badly damaged
and only a group of people and animals can be discerned.

Opposite pillar seven, to the east (left) of the south door, on a 'wall pillar'
(known as a respond) there is a group representing Christ (the head is missing)
before Pilate. Christ is the central figure with arms folded across his breast. Pilate
is shown at the right of the group and is washing his hands in a bowl of water. A
figure between Christ and Pilate is pouring water over Pilate's hands. There are
two headless figures to the left of Christ who appear to be intended to represent
armed Roman soldiers.

Pillar eight bears the figure of a female kneeling and has been claimed to show
Anna the Prophetess. (St. Luke 2:36-38) On the other side (north) of the pillar a
lion and a horse can be seen but the rest is too degraded to be clear. Pillar nine
although also damaged retains detail which is sufficient to identify the carvings.
There is a group of carpenters: the central one has a nimbus (halo) and can only
refer to Jesus as the Carpenter of Nazareth. On the east side of this pillar are two
men on their knees struggling and represent Jacob wrestling with the Angel. (Gen.
32: 24-29) On that the westside there is a man fighting with a lion, probably
Samson:

'*Then went Samson down, and his father and his mother, to Tîm-nâth: and
behold a young lion roared against him.*
*And the Spirit of the Lord came mightily upon him, and he rent him as he
would have rent a kid, and he had nothing in his hand...*' (Judges 14:5-6)[28]

On the respond opposite pillar eight and to the west (right) of the south entrance is a group of five or six figures. Christ is again central and is shown bearing the cross on which he was crucified. To his left a figure carries the crown of thorns (John 19:2) and next to him is a soldier carrying the scourge (John 19:1). To his left is Veronica holding up the veil which bears the impression of the facial features of Christ.

It is obviously intentional that these groups relating to the Passion of Christ are placed either side of the south entrance and on one (west) side of the north entrance. In order to be coherent a fourth carving would, logically, be found on the respond opposite pillar 14, that is, to the east of the north entrance but there is only foliage. The fourth part is located on the west side of the first pier on the south side (No.9 Plate 11). This carving shows the Resurrection, with Christ, in a shroud, stepping out of the sarcophagus with his right leg (which is now missing) and at either side are soldiers sleeping. Whether this carving was displaced from the north door or was placed there by mistake cannot now be determined.

Between pillars eight and nine, above the arch, and facing north are 17 figures — Apostles and martyrs. These can be identified by the items associated with each figure. From the lowest figure on the right of the arch these are:

1. James the Greater	pilgrim's staff	
2. James the Less	club	
3. Jude	carpenter's square	
4. Philip	cross	
5. John the Baptist	open book displaying a paschal lamb	
6. John the Evangelist	chalice	
7. Matthias	battle axe	
8. Matthew	book	
9. Foliage	apparently inserted to fill a space	
10. Peter	keys	
11. Thomas	spear	
12. St. Roche (Roque)	with plague spot on his leg	
13. Tree with a figure in front	This may refer to the lesson of the withered fig tree (Matthew 21:18–22)	
14. Paul	sword and book	
15. Andrew	cross	
16. Simon	saw	
17. Bartholomew	flaying knife	

These carvings bear a resemblance to the carvings in one of the windows in the south aisle — see below.

The next pillar is not a free-standing pillar but is on the west wall at the south side of the baptistery entrance. (No.10 - Plate 11) On the capital of this pillar is a bearded figure wearing a crown, holding a sword in his right hand and looking east. This is said to be a representation of the builder of the chapel, William St. Clair of Rosslyn, but as he was never a king it would be quite inaccurate.[29] The crown has a dual symbolism, one indicating the King of the Jews and the other the crown of thorns — both representing Jesus Christ. The figure is looking east — towards Jerusalem. The sword reinforces this interpretation representing power and authority — God's power and authority in earth through his only son. On pillar 11, also on the west wall to the north of the baptistery entrance, there are intertwined dragons and underneath an angel looking east and holding a scroll.

The next true, that is free-standing, pillar is No.12 and here is said to be depicted the prodigal feeding swine (representing the degradation of sin). On the other side are two doves and foliage and a man struggling with the boar. Also on this capital is a dove and one bird, perhaps a pelican, feeding another.

Pillar No.13 here has three figures looking across to the scene on the opposite wall pillar — the crucifixion (see below). Bishop Forbes suggested that this is the Mater Dolorosa and the beloved disciple looking on the crucifixion opposite. But there are three (not two) figures and it may be asked whether they stood that far off; was it not close 'beneath the Cross of Jesus'? It may be that they refer to the three women mentioned in St. Matthew 27:56 and St. Mark 15:40, namely Mary Magdalene, Mary the mother of James and Joses, and Salome the wife of Zebedee and mother of Zebedee's children. Alternatively, as one might be taken for a man, the group may be intended to represent the three great divisions of the human family which took part in and witnessed the crucifixion, viz., 'Hebrew, Greek and Latin' as was set forth in the 'superscription of his accusation'. (St. John 19:20)

On one side of this pillar are two animals: one chained, the other held by a man; and on the other side two animals are struggling, bound by cords. This may be an attempt to depict 'the lesser of two evils' — the 'greater' evil being permanently chained and the 'lesser' evil is controllable by man if he has the will to do so. On the opposite side of the pillar are two animals which are bound and struggling to get free. This perhaps demonstrates that the will to control even lesser evil failed and man is doomed never to completely control evil.

On the wall pillar opposite No.13 (to the left of the north door) is a representation of the crucifixion which consists of nine figures in total. The focus here is entirely on the crucifixion of Jesus. There are ladders to each arm of the cross and there is a figure each with a hammer on each ladder. Behind the right arm is a figure holding a spear (or perhaps a sword). His wrist is being grasped by a soldier as if to restrain him. On the opposite side is another figure holding something that is too worn to identify. The two thieves crucified with Christ are missing.

On the capital of pillar No.14 (facing north) are two figures which are unfortunately quite badly damaged but sufficient remained in 1894 to see that they were angels rolling away the stone from the door of the sepulchre (Luke 24:4 and John 20:12).[30] On the other side of this capital are two monstrous beasts to represent Death and Hades which were subjugated by the resurrection of Christ. (Rev. 1:18)

On the opposite wall, on a respond, is a plaited crown of thorns — a standard symbol of the crucified Christ. There is on the capital of pillar 15, facing north, an enormous lion's head with hands as if rending its jaws (Samson rending the lion). There are also a plaited crown, an elephant and a group which is too difficult to describe with any certainty. At one time the head of a serpent was here also but by 1894 it had disappeared.

On the respond opposite pillar No. 15 is the shield '*which has been absurdly described as an ensign armorial having a cross arising from the backward beast like a dog and a billowing flag on top of the cross*'. This Christian emblem of the lamb and pennon of a double tressure symbolises victory through the blood of the lamb. It is frequently referred to as the *Agnus Dei*, an emblem which was used by the Knights Templar and is a carving which shall be discussed in the next chapter.

Above this in the end of the architrave and close to the north wall is a crowned figure playing upon a harp. This is King David and beside him is a demon using its right hand to pull the king's arm to prevent him from playing and with its left to try to snatch the crown from David's head. This relates to King David and the temptations to which he was subjected from time to time (Rev. 3:11).

On the east end of this architrave there is a dog leading a blind man and at the other end on the east and west sides are dragons' mouths. The space between these figures is filled with foliage but it seems clear that the full length of these architraves was to be filled with other imagery similar to that in the south aisle. This opinion is reinforced by the existence of the dragons' mouths which have no obvious relationship to anything else on these architraves. If correct this means that the final designs for this aisle were never completed.

The capital of the last free-standing pillar to be mentioned here, pillar 16 (Plate

11), bears a group of figures which is now completely destroyed but as there is a plaited crown here also there can be little doubt that this would originally have been a scene from the life of Christ.

On the wall pillar, respond, opposite pillar 16 is a shield supported by two men kneeling. The first quarter of the shield contains a ship within a double tressure flory-counter-flory (for Orkney); the second quarter a lion passant; the third quarter an engrailed cross (for Rosslyn) and in the fourth quarter a heart on a quarre, with tears on each side. These are the arms of Sir William St. Clair as a widower, impaled with those of his first wife, Lady Margaret (or Elizabeth) Douglas who died *c*.1452.

The slab marking the burial place of Sir William and his wife is opposite the shield between pillars Nos.15 and 16 (Plate 11.)

On the east side of the architrave from pillar 16 to the north wall there are eight figures. A central figure can be seen sitting upright with hands upraised in blessing and is very reminiscent of the figure in the first roof section mentioned earlier which also has both hands raised in this manner. The seven other figures have crowns on their heads (one has a harp) and are lying horizontally. These have been claimed to be the Philistines lying dead, opposite to what is said to have been Samson pulling down the house of Dagon. But this is surely a mistake. It is either our Lord seated in glory and addressing the angels (i.e. bishops) of the seven churches in Asia (as in Rev. 1:11) or, what is far more probable, it is the consummation of what was intended to be a complete series of religious subjects, that is — our blessed Lord seated in glory while the seven Kings are lying prostrate before him. (Psalm 72:11)

On the architrave which links pillar No.16 and pillar No.2 is a figure pushing through foliage using both hands and this has been claimed to be Samson pulling down the pillars of the house of Dagon. However, although difficult to see, it may be meant to be a Green Man of which there are about 100 within the chapel.

There can be little doubt that the designer(s) of the carvings had an overall vision of what it was they were attempting to create. A resume of the above would assist in illuminating that 'vision'. Commencing from the central pillar (No.1 - Plate 11) and passing through the retro-choir and keeping to the right is (probably based, initially at least, on the religious ideals of the founder — William St. Clair) represented in stone, the Fall and Expulsion from Eden (the 'beginning' of the story); the Dance of Death (Death being a constant presence especially in the mediaeval period when the chapel building was commenced); the birth of Christ etc.; the Sacrifice of Isaac; the Victory of Truth; the contrast between Virtue and

Vice; the Conception or Annunciation; the Presentation of Christ in the Temple; Jesus working as a humble Carpenter; the Prodigal feeding swine; the Crucifixion and Descent from the Cross; the Resurrection and rolling away of the stone from the Sepulchre; the Conquest of Death and Hades; and lastly, the Lord seated in Glory, with kings lying prostrate before Him. From this can been seen a rough sequence of events from the Bible. The events, people and symbols carved in stone were apparently the choice of the founder and those who followed him. The sequence is certainly incomplete but if time is taken to consider the chapel's carving in their totality one can clearly discern that a story was intended to be told by the carvings.

Carvings in the Windows etc.

The carved corbels (supports or brackets) of niches in the windows also merit description and discussion here. In the windows of the Lady Chapel there are several angels in postures said to be of 'significance to Freemasons'.[31] These carvings, because of the Masonic attributes assigned to them, will be discussed in the following chapter. In Plate 11 the windows in the south aisle are indicated by the letters A–E (A being in the east and E in the west) and those in the north aisle by the letters F–L (F being in the east and L in the west). The corbels bearing the carvings are indicated by the letter *a* or *b* — *a* being the corbel on the left of the window concerned and *b* that on the right. Beginning on the south-side windows:

A *a* An angel with a scroll. This is a common carving symbolising the angel as a 'messenger of God'. There are a large number of carvings of angels within Rosslyn Chapel this being but one. The significance of these is discussed more fully in the next chapter.

A *b* An angel with hands clasped and in an attitude of prayer.

B *a* Priest wearing a cloak and holding a chalice.

B *b* Here is an angel is holding a scroll but it is too damaged to be certain.

The north side of the arch of the second window from the east:

The arch of this window has a series of figures — six on each side of the arch. These are:

1. James the Less	club
2. Andrew	cross
3. John the Evangelist	chalice
4. Paul	sword and book
5. Bartholomew	knife
6. Peter	keys
7. Too worn to be identified	
8. Matthias	battle axe
9. Thomas	spear
10. Jude	cross with trefoil terminals
11. Philip	cross
12. Matthew	scroll

On the south side round the second window from the east are twelve figures of which six are holding books and round the third window are nine angelic figures.

C *a* Angel holding before him a heart on a cushion. The symbolism of the heart is important here and is discussed further in the following chapter.

C *b* A figure with horns holding a tablet in his right hand and in his left a scribe? This is said to be the Devil making a record of the souls he has managed to ensnare. The symbolism of this carving is, like several of the others mentioned above, important not only for individual analysis but also for the overall understanding of the chapel itself. This carving is also discussed further in Chapter 6.

In common with the window previously described, this window (C) has figures on the arch with nine figures depicting the Angelic Hierarchy:

First Hierarchy: The angels of the first sphere act as heavenly counsellors: Seraphim, Cherubim, Thrones (or Ophanim)

Second Hierarchy: Angels of the second sphere work as heavenly governors: Dominions, Principalities, Powers

Third Hierarchy: Angels who function as heavenly messengers: Virtues, Angels and Archangels.

D *a* Angel holding a scroll.

D *b* Another, similar, angel also holding a scroll.

E *a* This figure, mounted on horseback, is a warrior clad in chain mail and holds a spear in his right hand. Behind him stands an angel holding before him a cross. This was said to be a carving of the seal of the Knights Templar and is another carving which will be discussed in more detail in the next chapter.

E *b* The figure of a man with a scroll which he appears to be in the process of unrolling. In addition there is the figure of a female in the attitude of prayer with an open book in her lap.

F *a* On the right hand side there is an angel holding a cross.

F *b* Opposite the angel is a couple who are kneeling and looking towards the cross. Watching them is a carving of the Devil, suggesting that this pious couple have escaped his clutches. The message here is clearly to turn away from evil.

G *a* An angel holding a cross and a scroll.

G *b* An angel with a scroll.

H *a* An angel with an open book

H *b* An angel holding a shield on which is the engrailed cross of the St. Clair family.

K a Another angel holding only a scroll.

K *b* An angel with his arms folded over a closed book.

Over this window are carvings of the 12 Apostles — identified by the nimbus over the head of each. These carvings correspond to those over the opposite window (B in the groundplan) in the south aisle.

L *a* An angel with a scroll.

L *b* An angel with his hands crossed over his breast.

The difference between the north and south windows is marked. The windows of the north wall, apart from window F, contain much that is similar — the use of angels holding scrolls etc. is very repetitive and is in marked contrast to the variety of carvings in the windows of the south wall. This suggests that the north was dealt with much more quickly than the south. Making similar carvings would take much less time than commissioning new and different ones for each window. The chaplain and guide of Rosslyn Chapel, the Rev. John Thompson, stated that these carvings were replacements, for damaged and defaced ones, put in place during the 18th century restorations. They may even have been entirely new carvings placed where none had ever existed. In any event it is important to bear in mind that the north windows in particular do not contain original carvings.

Stained Glass Windows

There is no evidence that Rosslyn Chapel had stained glass windows before the first Victorian glass was put in place in 1867 by Francis Robert, 4th Earl of Rosslyn (1833-1890). Prior to that plain glass had been installed by General St. Clair, in 1736, soon after he purchased the chapel from William St. Clair of Rosslyn. Between 1446 and 1736 the windows were almost certainly unglazed; metal hinges for exterior shutters are still be seen.

The stained glass in the Lady Chapel is the work of Clayton and Bell, London. The brass plates located on the window sills of the Lady Chapel read:

> '*Ac majorem Dei gloriam: In memory of dear parents, by whom the Chapel was restored to the service of God A.D. 1862, the stained-glass windows in this Lady Chapel were placed by Francis Robert, fourth Earl of Rosslyn, A.D. 1867.*'

All the other stained glass windows were inserted after that date. The six windows, each of double lights, in the Lady Chapel are filled with figures of the Apostles.

Beginning on the left (L – Plate 11) these are as follows:

1. St. Peter and St. James the Greater
2. St. John and St. Andrew

   3. St. Philip and St. Bartholomew
   4. St. Matthew and St. Thomas
   5. St. James the Less and St. Thaddeus
   6. St. Simon and St. Matthias

In the east aisle; north window:

   1. St. John the Baptist, with a lamb standing on a book
   2. St. Paul with sword

South window:

   1. St. Mark and St. Luke

In the north aisle, commencing at the west end:

   1. The Annunciation and the Nativity
   2. Presentation at the Temple and the Baptism of Jesus
   3. The Sermon on the Mount and the Miraculous draught of fishes

In the south aisle:

   1. The miracle at the Marriage Feast of Cana and the Raising of Jairus's
      daughter
   2. Christ blessing little children and the Last Supper
   3. The Crucifixion of Christ and his Resurrection

The east window, of two lights, shows the Resurrection of Jesus Christ and the three women arriving at the sepulchre. Seated are two angels, one of whom is holding a scroll which bears the words: '*he is not here, but he has risen*'. This window is dedicated:

   '*to the glory of God. In most affectionate remembrance of his only sister,*
   Harriet Elizabeth St. Clair, daughter of James Alexander, third Earl of
   Rosslyn, and wife of George Herbert, Count Münster of Dernburg in
   Hanover. This window was entirely restored and filled with stained glass
   in November 1869, by Francis Robert Earl of Rosslyn. She was born,

June 26, 1851; married, August 22, 1865; and died at Dernburg,
November 29, 1867 where by her own request she was buried.'

The west window over the organ gallery represents the Lord in Glory. His right hand is raised in blessing whilst in his left hand he holds a sceptre. He is supported on the left by an angel holding a book with the Greek letters: A (alpha) Ω (omega), representing the law of God where all things begin and end. On the right is another angel holding a cup representing the sacrament or gospel.

By 1894 only two clerestory windows held stained-glass. These were added in 1887. That on the north represents George and the Dragon, and was inserted by Robert Francis, 4th Earl in memory of Mr Andrew Kerr, architect, who superintended the building of the baptistery, and other work connected with Roslin Castle. That on the south, representing St. Michael, was inserted at the same time by Mr W. Mitchell SSC as a 'thankoffering 1887, W. and H. A. Mitchell, Rosebank'. It was intended to fill all clerestory windows on the south side with Old Testament warriors, and on the north with Christian soldiers, according to designs by Clayton and Bell.[32]

Besides numerous small niches for statues in the window jambs etc. there are double rows of niches between the clerestory windows, 12 on each side and one over the east central pillar for figures of about four feet in height. The Rev. Thompson noted that:

'five of these have of late years been filled with statues the work of Mr
Williamson of Esher. At the east end, the Blessed Virgin and Child are
over the altar, with Mary of Bethany on the left, and Mary Magdalene on
the right. At the west end are St Peter on the right and Saint Paul on the
left.'

But now only that of the Virgin and Child remain in place. I have been unable to establish what happened to the missing statutes.

As suggested earlier, the above description could be used as a guide when visiting the chapel but that is not the principal purpose for including the chapter. Many publications presently available do not provide comprehensive details, for example, of the carvings, their location and condition. Supplying that kind of detail is important for the discussion in the next chapter which goes into considerable detail regarding the chapel, its carvings and the various theories which link it to the Knight's Templar, Freemasonry and associated subjects.

[1] *Memorials of Edinburgh in the Olden Time*. Sir David Wilson. Edinburgh. 1848.

[2] This guidebook was again published by the Masonic Publishing Co. in 2003.

[3] *The Genealogie of the Sainteclaires of Rosslyn*. Ed. Cooper, Robert L. D. The Grand Lodge of Scotland. 2002. pp. 26-27.

[4] Except the bays in the extreme west which are screened by transept buttresses.

[5] Such additions were common and that one was apparently planned for Rosslyn Chapel suggests that the building was not completed as originally intended.

[6] The translation was made by Dr. Thomas Dickson of Edinburgh Register House.

[7] *The New Constitutions*, 1738. p. 89. Slezer gives the date as 1440.

[8] Raglet, raggle. A Scottish building term: a groove cut in stone (or wood) to receive another stone etc. e.g., in the steps of a staircase, the edge of a roof.

[9] It is ironic that the present steel canopy was put in place to try and solve the same problem.

[10] Splay — the expansion given to doorways, windows etc. by slanting the sides.

[11] Paterae — circular ornaments resembling dishes, often worked in relief on friezes etc.

[12] See: Charter of William Sinclair of Roslin made for the Prebendaries — 1523. *Genealogie of the Sainteclaires of Rosslyn*. pp. 124-127.

[13] *Genealogie of the Sainteclaires of Rosslyn*. p. 107.

[14] Presses — cupboards or box-beds built into a wall.

[15] Piscinae — a water-drain situated near to an altar, often a shallow stone basin with a hole in the bottom to carry away whatever was poured into it. The priest would wash his hands in the piscinae as well as rinse the chalice at the time of the celebration of the mass. Aumbry — a cupboard where sacred vessels and church plate were kept; also came to be used for a cupboard where books were kept.

[16] The relevant charters have recently been published by the Grand Lodge of Scotland. See: Charter of King James the Second of the Earldom of Caithness, 1455. *Genealogie of the Sainteclaires of Rosslyn*. pp. 73-76, and see: Charta Whillielmi Comitis Orcadiae Baroniae de Roslin Facta Olivero de Sancto Claro, MCCCCLXXVI (1476) *Genealogie of the Sainteclaires of Rosslyn*. pp. 82-87.

[17] This short list is by no means comprehensive.

[18] The work was carried out by the Ancient Monuments Branch of the Ministry of Public Buildings and Works in an attempt to preserve the decaying stonework.

[19] There are 160 roses in total — 80 in each half of the roof section.

[20] There are 80 flowers in total — 40 in each half.

[21] *An Account of the Chapel of Roslin — 1778* by Bishop Robert Forbes. p. 17.

[22] *Scottish Book of Common Prayer*. Edinburgh, 1929.

[23] The Annunciation is the point at which Jesus Christ commences His human aspect.

[24] Sculptured work the subject of which projects less than half of its true proportions from the surface on which it is carved.

[25] *An Account of the Chapel of Roslin — 1778* by Bishop Robert Forbes. p. 23.

[26] This translation is from: The Illustrated Guide to Rosslyn Chapel. P. 63.

[27] Modern guidebooks of the chapel describe this carving as envy but this is incorrect as the carving is not appropriate — something recognised more than 100 years ago.

[28] It may also refer to David's claim to have killed a lion with his bare hands. (I Samuel 17:34–35)

[29] Even the description 'Prince of Orkney' is inaccurate and was never used in his lifetime.

[30] St. Matthew 28:2 mentions only one angel.

[31] *An Illustrated Guide Book — Rosslyn Chapel.* Plates pp. 28–29.

[32] Stained glass depicting St. Maurice and St. Longinus have been added.

Chapter 6
Rosslyn Chapel

A 'Glorious Freak'[1]

Like the graveslabs at Kilmartin, Argyllshire, which will be discussed later, Rosslyn Chapel has been cited as physical evidence for the alleged connection between the KT, Freemasonry and the St. Clair family, which is the principal focus of this chapter. The carvings within the chapel have been described in detail in the previous chapter. The need here is to provide general details before discussing (below) specific examples which have been re-interpreted by some modern authors.

Rosslyn Chapel is first mentioned in a Masonic connection in Anderson's *New Constitutions* of 1738. It has previously been shown that this second publication was an elaboration on the 1723 *Constitutions*. William, Earl of Orkney and Caithness, is specifically mentioned, and for the first time, as having been a Grand Master of 'Masonry.'[2] In the *New Constitutions* Anderson created an elaborate history: Anderson is therefore repeating the suggestion in the original *Constitutions* (1723) that 'Masonry' began shortly after the creation of the world and that Adam *'retain'd great Knowledge, especially Geometry'*.[3] It is worth outlining Anderson's history of 'Masonry' as this will allow William St. Clair and Rosslyn Chapel to be clearly seen in Anderson's scheme of things.

'The History of Masonry from the Creation throughout the known earth; till true Architecture was demolish'd by the Goths and at last Revived in Italy'

Chapter I	From the Creation to the Grand Master Nimrod
Chapter II	From Nimrod to Grand Master Solomon
Chapter III	From Solomon to Grand Master Cyrus
Chapter IV	From Cyrus to Grand Master Seleucus Nicator
Chapter V	From Seleucus Nicator to Grand Master Augustus Caesar
Chapter VI	From Augustus till the Havock of the Goths
Chapter VII	The Revival of Old Architecture, or the Augustan Stile.'

Anderson then charts the history of Masonry in Britain:

'The History of Masonry in Britain, from Julius Caesar, till the Union of the Crowns, 1603.

Anderson then completes his history in Part III: *'The History of Masonry in Britain, from the Union of the Crowns to these Times (1738).'* He creates a history of 'Masonry' in Scotland beginning with Fergus II (403) and a false lineage of Grand Masters of Scotland beginning with Malcolm III (1031–1093). It is worth noting that this first Grand Master of 'Masonry' died years before the formation of the medieval Order of KT.

No apology is made for detailing the context in which William St. Clair and Rosslyn Chapel is referred to and which is as follows:

'James I. Stewart, tho' unjustly captivated, ruled by his Regent the said Robert Duke of Albany.

Henrry Wardlaw, Bishop of St. Andrews, was now Grand Master, and founded the University there, A.D. 1411. tho' it was long before a Place of Education.

Robert Duke of Albany died A.D. 1420. and his Son Duke Murdoch was Regent till the King was ransom'd, restor'd and crown'd, A.D. 1424.

King James I. prov'd the best King of Scotland, the Patron of the Learned, and countenanced the Lodges with his Presence as the Royal Grand Master; till he settled an Yearly Revenue of 4 Pounds Scots (an English Noble) to be paid by every Master Mason in Scotland, to a Grand Master chosen by the Grand Lodge, and approv'd by the crown, one nobly born, or an eminent Clergyman, who had his deputies in Cities and Countries: and every new Brother at Entrance paid him also a Fee. His Office impower'd to regulate in the Fraternity what could not come under the

Cognizance of Law-Courts: to him appeal'd both Mason and Lord, or the
Builder and Founder, when at Variance, in order to prevent Law-Pleas;
and in his Absence, they appeal'd to his Deputy or Grand Warden that
resided next to the Premisses.

... he was basely murder'd in the Dominican Abby at Perth, by his Uncle
Walter Stewart Earl of Atholl, A.D. 1437. and being justly lamented by All,
his Murderers were severely punish'd... he had [a son]

James II. Stewart, a Minor of 7 Years, under the Regency of Lord
Calendar.

In this reign William Sinclair the great Earl of Orkney and Caitness was
Grand Master, and built Roslin Chapel near Edinburgh, a Master Piece of
the best Gothic, A.D. 1441. next

Bishop Turnbull of Glasgow, who founded the University there, A.D.
1454'.[4]

What then had occurred since 1723 and what may have induced Anderson to
include William St. Clair in his fictitious list of Grand Masters? Three major
events had occurred during this time: the publication of Smith's *Pocket*
Companion (1736); the founding of the Grand Lodge of Scotland (1736) with
William St. Clair of Rosslyn as its first Grand Master; and Ramsay's '*Oration*'
(1737).[5] Smith's book uses Anderson's *Constitutions* of 1723 for the history of
Freemasonry and, like Anderson, Smith says nothing about Rosslyn Chapel. The
only building in Scotland that he mentions is Holyrood Palace. Anderson's *New*
Constitutions (1738) may have been a reaction to any, or all, of these events. It is
of paramount importance to appreciate that Anderson would have been well
aware that a Grand Lodge had been established in his native country and that
William St. Clair was its first Grand Master. The inclusion of the builder of
Rosslyn Chapel (which Anderson describes as being "*Master Piece of the best*
Gothic) in the list of Grand Masters would have been irresistible — just as it was
irresistible not to have included, for example, Sir Robert Thomas Cockeran
(?–1482), allegedly a humble mason who built the Great Hall for James III
(1452–1488) within Stirling Castle.[6] St. Clair is placed in the chronology of the
list of Grand Masters so as to make him Grand Master *at the time he commenced*
the building of Rosslyn Chapel.[7] In other words he began building Rosslyn Chapel
when he was Grand Master. Like other figures in Anderson's list of fictitious
Grand Masters, St. Clair is identified with a particular building, Rosslyn Chapel,
not because the building was necessarily important but because it reinforced the

claimed association of 'Masonry' with aristocratic building and architecture.

Here then is the first occasion that St. Clair is described as being a Grand Master, in a Masonic or any other sense. Not only that but Rosslyn Chapel is begun during his tenure of Grand Master and all this in a book about Freemasonry written by a Freemason who was Scottish! From this important, and apparently legitimate source, the story of the involvement of the St. Clair family with Freemasonry would develop.

The various *Pocket Companions* published during the 18th century repeat Anderson's list of fictitious Grand Masters, albeit with numerous changes, but none make reference to Rosslyn Chapel. Even the first guide book, *An Account of the Chapel of Roslin — 1778*, which describes the chapel and the St. Clair family, makes no mention of it having a connection with Freemasonry or the KT.[8] The guide book does state, quoting Father Hay: '*These Barons . . . were successively, by charter, the patrone and protectors of masonry in Scotlan'* — a matter which has previously been fully discussed.[9] It would be a century before Anderson's claims would be developed further.

Even Sir Walter Scott, the 'inventor' of the historical novel and a Scottish Freemason steeped in Scottish Masonic lore and Scottish history, never linked Rosslyn Chapel with Freemasonry or the KT for, although he wrote about all three, he did not associate any of them with each other. References to the chapel by Scott are found in his *Lay of the Last Minstrel* (1805) where he mentions the building six times.[10] It is a lengthy poem said, by Scott, to have been recited by an old minstrel to the Duchess of Buccleuch and her attendant ladies at Newark Castle. However, the scope of the poem is much larger than the repeatedly published few lines which mention Rosslyn.[11] That selectivity has served to give the impression that Rosslyn is the dominant theme in the work and that Scott considered Rosslyn in isolation. Nothing could be further from the truth. Rosslyn is but one small part of Scott's work. The poem is much too long to be reproduced here but in order to demonstrate the above point, lines before and following those about Rosslyn Chapel are reproduced at Appendix X.[12]

Scott was not aware of any claims of a link between the KT and Scottish Freemasonry and nor could he because it was not invented until seven years after his death.

The addition of Rosslyn Chapel, as opposed to the St. Clair family, to the collection of myths, begun by Anderson, is therefore a very recent elaboration. There is a huge gap of more than 500 years (1446–1982) when no one suggested that such a connection had ever existed. Up to the late 1970's Rosslyn Chapel was selling a guide book, originally written by the Rev. Thompson in 1892 which, although making passing references to Freemasonry and the alleged connection with the St. Clair family, never even hinted at the elaborate myth as we now know it. It is surely significant that for almost 100 years (200 if you include Bishop Forbes' publication) the official guide book of Rosslyn Chapel did not contain any of the intricate and detailed story of Scottish Freemasonry, the Knights Templar, the St. Clair family and the chapel. It is almost as if there was some catalyst towards the end of the 1970's that caused a major change in the way the history of the chapel was perceived. In 1982 a book: *'The Holy Blood and the Holy Grail'*, took the world by storm. In the chapter entitled 'Conspiracy through the Centuries' a sub-section, 'Rosslyn Chapel and Shugborough Hall' relates some of the earliest known reference to Rosslyn Chapel as part of the modern myth. It is worth providing the details in full here:

'. . . *we encountered repeated references to the Sinclair family — Scottish branch of the Norman Saint-Clair-Gisors family. Their domain at Rosslyn was only a few miles from the former Scottish headquarters of the Knights Templar, and the chapel at Rosslyn — built between 1446 and 1486 — has long been associated with both Freemasonry and the Rose-Croix. In a charter* [the first St. Clair 'Charter'] *believed to date from 1601, moreover, the Sinclairs are recognised as 'hereditary Grand Masters of Scottish Masonry'[13] This is the oldest specifically Masonic document on record. According to Masonic sources, however, the hereditary Grand Mastership was conferred on the Sinclairs by James II who ruled between 1437 and 1460.'[14]*

Shugborough Hall has more or less disappeared from the repertoire of the Popular Approach in sharp contrast to the now central position occupied by Rosslyn Chapel. This is one of the earliest references of Rosslyn Chapel being included in the modern myth but even this recent mention states only that the chapel had '*long been associated with both Freemasonry and the Rose-Croix*' and is still not yet central to the myth.

In order for the building to be added to the myth and to accord it a central position in the modern version of the myth, it became necessary for it to undergo a radical reinterpretation. Before *c*.1979 guide books, commentaries on, and other descriptions of, the chapel remained firmly rooted in the western Christian tradition although the elementary forms of the myth, e.g. those which accepted

Anderson's fiction regarding Grand Masters etc. but not the chapel itself, were also in circulation and some had even been repeated in the official guidebook.[15] This reinterpretation centred on the need to show that the chapel was *not* a Christian building, or at least contained a substantial amount of non-Christian material. Once the chapel had effectively been 'de-Christianised' it could then be claimed to be, according to the opinion of the author, a pagan place of worship; an unfinished Jewish Temple or some kind of Masonic building.[16]

This attempt to redefine the chapel is bound to fail if for no other reason than the amount of information that proves otherwise. Before proceeding to discuss specific examples of this process of 'de-Christianisation' the opportunity is taken to discuss Rosslyn Chapel in a religious context.

It has been seen that Rosslyn Chapel is, today, almost always considered and discussed in isolation as if it has no relationship to Scottish ecclesiastical history.[17] By adopting an holistic approach one can see that Rosslyn Chapel fits into a pattern, but that pattern, whilst clear to academic historians and others, has become obscured by attempts to 'reinterpret' the building.

There were a total of 42 collegiate churches in Scotland.[18] The earliest was founded *c*.1248 and the last *c*.1546.[19] There were 16 established before Rosslyn Chapel and 24 after, with one the foundation date of which cannot be provided with any certainty.[20] Rosslyn Chapel can, therefore, be compared to other Scottish collegiate churches so that its status etc. might be assessed.[21] In the first instance, that Rosslyn Chapel was part of a common pattern cannot be doubted — 52% of all Scottish collegiate churches were founded in the same century as Rosslyn Chapel and 50% of all Scottish collegiate churches are to be found in Midlothian and the counties surrounding it (East Lothian, Berwickshire, Lanarkshire and Peeblesshire). These figures demonstrate that Rosslyn Chapel was part of the area of Scotland where the most vigorous and sustained building of collegiate churches took place. To write about the chapel whilst ignoring this fact is to suggest that it has nothing in common with these other collegiate churches when nothing could be further from the truth. Secular collegiate churches, of which Rosslyn Chapel is an example, were part of a system of worship widely practised in Europe and Scottish collegiate churches were merely emulating the same pattern established elsewhere.[22]

If Rosslyn Chapel is merely an example of an existing pattern, what were such churches actually for? Collegiate churches were established for one primary purpose — the saying of prayers for the dead, especially in respect of a particular group or family.[23] Prior to the Reformation the prevailing view was that the dead were people who were simply no longer with the living. That meant that they still had needs and some of those needs could only be fulfilled by those who were alive. The principal need of the dead was to move out of a place known as Purgatory and into Heaven as soon as possible. The church taught that at death one's soul either went to Hell or to Purgatory. There was no hope of redemption once in Hell. Purgatory was a 'waiting room' for those on their way to Heaven. The length of time spent in Purgatory was reliant not only on the life one had lived on earth but also the amount of 'support' given by those not yet dead.[24] This support took the form of prayers for the dead, prayers which could only be offered by priests of the church. The more prayers that were said for a particular individual, family or group, the less time they spent in Purgatory. The incentive was, therefore, to ensure that in reducing the time spent in Purgatory of, say, one's father, it was hoped that one's son would do the same.

Some collegiate churches were created by groups and individuals who combined for that purpose. Merchant guilds, Incorporations and 'town councils' together with wealthy individuals would make contributions for the creation and maintenance of a collegiate church and the support of attendant priests. In return each would be allocated a particular space — normally an aisle with its own altar where prayers for deceased members of the family, Trade Incorporation, Merchant Guild etc. would be offered. St. Giles, Edinburgh, is a typical example of a larger burgh collegiate church.

Rosslyn Chapel, is of a slightly different type, one built and endowed by and for a particular family, in this case the St. Clairs. In this the family were not unusual. Other locally powerful families did exactly the same and some are in close proximity to Rosslyn Chapel. Such privately owned collegiate churches are more correctly known as secular collegiate churches because they are not owned by the church but by a secular body or person.

Father Hay, the St. Clair family priest, states that from the outset Rosslyn was a collegiate church.[25] What is known is that, by the early 1450s it was considered to be a collegiate foundation - in 1456 it was being described as a '*college kirk*'.[26] This description is found in the will (1456) of Alexander Sutherland of Dunbeath Castle. This will was written in the presence of '*William Erle of Cathness and Orkney, Lord Santcler*'. Sutherland's daughter, Marjory, was the second wife of William St. Clair (the builder of Rosslyn Chapel) and he was, therefore, St. Clair's father-in-law. In this document the chapel is described six times as being a '*college kirk*'. Confirmation that the chapel was designed for the purpose of saying prayers and masses for, and a burial place of, the St. Clair family is provided by two extracts:

'*I gif* [give] *and I lay till a priest to sing perpetually for my saul* [soul] *in the said Collegd* [college] *Kirk, 10 pounds of annualrent yearly'* and,

'*my body to be gravyt* [interred] *in the Collegd Kirk of ane* [one] *hie* [high] *and mightie Lord, Earle of Caithness and Orknay, Lord Sinclare &C. in Rosling, near quhair* [where] *he himself thinks to lye.'*[27]

The first part of this extract shows that he wanted a priest to say prayers in perpetuity for his soul and to pay for a priest to do this he donated an annual payment of £10. The extract also confirms the second, common, purpose of such secular collegiate churches — a burial place primarily for the family who built and endowed such churches. It reveals that burials in the vaults of the chapel are not restricted to immediate members of the St. Clair family. Sutherland was only connected with the family by marriage not blood. Within 10 years, therefore, the chapel vaults are being used for interments but Alexander Sutherland was not the first, as Henry, 1st Earl (succ.1358, d.1400) and Henry, 2nd Earl, (succ.1400, d.1420) were also interred in the chapel.[28] The re-burial of members of the family who had died years before the chapel was built shows that the builder of the chapel always intended it to be a family burial place. William St. Clair was himself buried below the floor of the chapel when he died *c*.1484. Burials in the vaults were not restricted to male members of the family as it is later recorded that in 1590 the Reformed Church refused permission for the wife of Oliver St. Clair to be interred in the chapel vault.[29] The previous year William Knox (brother of John Knox (*c*.1513–1572) the Scottish Protestant Reformer) had baptised '*the Laird of Rosling's bairne'* in Rosslyn Chapel — an act which led to his censure by the Presbytery. These activities show that even after the Reformation Rosslyn Chapel continued to be used for Christian purposes. The activities at the chapel attracted the attention of the Reformed Church and the Minister of Lasswade was instructed to visit the chapel and report to the Presbytery. On 24 September 1590 he reported that he had: '. . . *gone to Rosling, enterit ye Kirk and yr* [there] *fund* [found] *sax alteris* [six altars] *standing haill* [whole] *and undemolishit* . . . [undemolished]'. This quite clearly shows that the chapel remained the private property of the St. Clair family and did not pass to the Reformed Church. It was built on St. Clair land and endowed with St. Clair money.[30] The official guidebook of the chapel continued to describe it as a 'Private Chapel' until the 1970's.

Although the Reformed Church could not possess the building, it could, and did, exercise control over religion as practised in the country. It remained suspicious of Rosslyn Chapel and decided to ensure that it could not be used for 'Popish' purposes. For more than two years the Presbytery badgered St. Clair and in 1592, under threat of excommunication, he finally demolished the altars in the chapel.

That Rosslyn Chapel was private property and was not appropriated by the new Reformed Church is confirmed by the Books of Assumption:

> *'The late medieval church was, after all, the largest organisation and the wealthiest single landowner in the Scottish kingdom, with an annual income ten times that of the crown. The Books of Assumption were compiled for the crown in the expectation that a share of the church's riches might be reallocated to augment the finances of both the royal household and the reformed church which had just come into being.'*[31]

Every vicarage, priory, abbey, church etc. was identified and the income therefrom detailed in the Books of Assumption. By this means the Crown and Reformed Church were able to calculate the total income. The division of the revenue between Crown and Church could be calculated. Most, but by no means all, pre-reformation church property passed to the new church and it obtained approximately one third of the total income. A considerable amount of property and income did go to local landowners. Often those who had originally donated the land to the church were keen to have it returned but in the case of Rosslyn Chapel that did not happen because the St. Clair family, and not the church, owned the land and building. At the Reformation it was intended that priests, nuns, etc., would be permitted to continue living at their pre-Reformation location and also to continue to receive the income allocated to them. They would not, of course, be able to continue to profess the old faith nor perform the rites of the pre-Reformation church. The underlying reasoning was that these individuals would sooner or later pass away and the Reformed Church, Crown and/or local landowners would then 'inherit' the property and revenue. However, many were impatient and the income, or endowments, granted by the family for the upkeep of the Prebendaries etc. who officiated at the chapel were not paid for many years. In 1571 the legal title to the income for the Provost and Prebendaries was signed over to the St. Clair family.[32] The point highlighted here is the fact that the St. Clairs owned Rosslyn Chapel 'lock, stock and barrel' and the church was not directly involved.

It can be seen therefore that Rosslyn Chapel was always a private place and was intended to serve two principal and specific purposes for members of the St. Clair family only. Firstly, the saying of prayers for the souls of the family in Purgatory and, secondly, to serve as a family burial vault — located below the main part of the chapel. Of interest is the fact that the family adhered to the old faith and continued to use the chapel after the Reformation until being forced to destroy the altars which effectively ended the use of the chapel for one of its original purposes.

In 1523 the existing arrangements of the Collegiate Church of St. Matthew were ratified by charter, specifically those of the Prebendaries.[33] William, grandson of the builder, charges the Provost and Prebendaries with '*creating divine offices and to celebrate them for ever in the said collegiate church*'. He then grants particular parcels of land to each Prebendary for a house and garden. Also recorded are the altars and the saints to which each is dedicated where the Prebendaries are to say prayers in perpetuity for the St. Clair family. The saints and their altars are: St. Matthew the Apostle and Evangelist; the most blessed Virgin Mary; Saint Andrew the Apostle and Saint Peter the Apostle.

Many churches in western Christendom were of cruciform design, that is, in the form of the Passion Cross. Rosslyn Chapel does not appear to fit this design and this has led some to suggest that it is not Christian in design and purpose. From the previous discussion the Christian function of the chapel is beyond doubt. However, the form of the chapel as it now exists presents some difficulties which are now discussed.

Bishop Robert Forbes (1708–1775) stated, in 1774, that the chapel had been intended to be built to the common cruciform design. He explained that only the choir of the chapel had been built and that the transepts and nave had been planned, as the foundations for these had been discovered.[34] In the late 19th century these unused foundations were uncovered and accurately drawn (Plate 10.) It is unfortunate that nearly all publications which provide a ground plan do so of the chapel as it now stands, rather than as it was designed to be when completed. Doing so suggests, incorrectly, that the building was intended to be incomplete.[35] (Plates 10 and 11) The official guidebook sold at Rosslyn Chapel until about 1980 included a sketch of what it may have looked like had the unused foundations been built upon. The idea that the chapel was deliberately designed to be 'unfinished' has led to speculation as to why that should be and will be discussed later (see below).

Rosslyn Chapel carvings

Many of those offering new interpretations of Rosslyn Chapel, its carvings and symbolism etc. rely on their own particular knowledge and experience. Thus some 'see' Knight Templar, Pagan or Masonic symbolism rather than that of the Christian faith. Although it is understandable, the historian cannot disregard evidence and interpretations because they do not 'fit' a particular opinion or belief.

There is no Masonic symbolism within Rosslyn Chapel!

This statement will come as a shock, or at least a surprise, to many, especially in light of the huge amount of material in the public domain which claims that such symbolism does in fact exist. Exactly why there is no such symbolism is discussed below but equally important is the need to discuss how the process of the re-interpretation of the carvings etc. has be used to 'prove' that there is Masonic symbolism within the chapel.

Hand in hand with this decline in the understanding and use of symbols has been a decline in knowledge regarding the people and institutions that made use of them (especially in religion) in a variety of ways — in buildings, books, artefacts and in ritual. That loss of understanding means that symbolism generally is a puzzle to many and Rosslyn Chapel is an example of that process.

Before proceeding to discuss specific examples of what are today claimed to be Masonic, KT or Pagan symbols within Rosslyn Chapel, some explanation of symbolism in general is thought desirable.

Symbolism

The heyday of Christian symbolism in the western Christian faith was during the medieval period and was most frequently given expression in the numerous European Gothic churches and cathedrals of that period.

Unfortunately, few today can readily interpret those signs, and more particularly symbols, the meaning of which would have been easily understood by most people in Europe during the medieval period. At the time of the Reformation (*c*.1559) much church ornamentation was condemned as idolatrous and destroyed or removed. Symbolism was not condemned *per se* but the teaching of its meaning declined to the extent that some 450 years later few understand medieval 'Catholic' symbolism, its meaning, or how it ought to be interpreted. The recent century has seen an accelerated secularisation of society and this has contributed greatly to the inability to appreciate a true understanding of such symbolism.

In an increasingly secular, materialistic and empirical world many people no longer have the ability to understand symbols as opposed to signs. Signs are designed for a specific purpose — to impart a particular piece of information — e.g. 'road works ahead'. Such a sign does not impart any other information whereas a symbol is intended to do just that. A symbol is meant to transmit abstract concepts as well as factual information. In this way a symbol can also be a sign but a sign cannot be a symbol. No sign could show 'idea ahead' as if it referred to road works. As people have become less religious (some would say less spiritual) whilst at the same time more literate, the need for symbols has declined. Once symbols fall into disuse their meaning and purpose are easily lost to all but a few.

Recently questions have been raised as to what people in the past understood symbolism to be, what individual symbols stood for, and how they were used and appreciated. That recent re-examination of symbolism has, in the context of this discussion, emphasised Rosslyn Chapel and numerous hypotheses have been offered which attempt to link modern Scottish Freemasonry with the chapel and with the medieval Knights Templar. Such hypotheses are just that, thoughts, ideas etc., and the proof offered in support of them is often a re-interpretation of the symbolism and carvings within Rosslyn Chapel. The (re)interpretation of the carvings etc. is therefore central to the debate as to what Rosslyn Chapel is, what it represents and what is its function.

The latter point is considered first. The purpose of Rosslyn Chapel lies firmly in the Christian tradition of the late Middle Ages. It was founded, in 1446, as a collegiate church dedicated to St. Matthew. For that reason alone, Rosslyn Chapel is unremarkable as numerous collegiate churches were founded at about the same time. As has already been explained many members of the Scottish nobility built, and endowed, such establishments.

Rosslyn was to be in the form of a cruciform collegiate church but consists only of a choir, parts of the east transept walls and a sacristy. As a piece of Gothic architecture the chapel is unremarkable in its construction, having much in common with churches of the same period. What does make the chapel stand out in comparison to other similar structures of its time is the profusion of the internal carving. Although some is of comparatively poor quality, the sheer abundance of carvings is what dominates the senses at first sight. Perhaps this is exactly the effect the builder intended for a small church that he knew would not compete in terms of scale with other ecclesiastical buildings.

One way of explaining Rosslyn Chapel is as one man's 'folly', his desire to be remembered or even to be immortal. Today William St. Clair has achieved both.[36] That is not a criticism. Individuals have long sought to be remembered by their descendants by using family photographs, a family bible, an imposing graveyard monument or a legacy to a charity. Follies, in which this country is rich, have not been interpreted as anything other than a rich man's hope of being remembered. This is because their use, purpose and meaning remain clear and have not been re-interpreted. Rosslyn Chapel no longer appears to conform to this pattern simply because recent writers have chosen to re-interpret the function of the chapel. As a consequence most people are not aware of William St. Clair's intentions in building it.

Symbols have, for most modern authors at least, been interpreted as nothing other than simple signs — signs with only a single, simple and literal explanation or message. Their reinterpretation of the symbols and carvings within the chapel in this way has ensured that they are rejected as having any validity other than the reinterpreted meaning. For example, the image of an old man with a long white beard, dressed in flowing white robes, holding a crook, sitting on a floating cloud, dispensing his anger at earthly transgressors using thunder-bolts, is rejected out of hand by the modern mind as being literally impossible and therefore, misleading and inaccurate. In essence this is what Karl Marx (1818–1883) described as being '*the opium of the people*' and, whilst he was referring to organised religion, he was arguing that what could not be directly experienced by the five human senses, in this case 'religion' (of all forms, of all variants, with all its symbolism etc.) was nothing more than a confidence trick.[37]

This modern perception of symbolism is one reason why many Freemasons find ritual and symbolism difficult to understand if not meaningless — they have lost the ability to understand that, like the bearded old man, the symbol of, say, the square and compasses is much more than simply an image of measuring instruments. If Freemasons themselves no longer understand their own symbolism, what hope for the non-Masons? The reasons why there is a failure to understand symbolism, be it Masonic or that within Rosslyn Chapel, is due in part to the increasingly secular and materialistic world but blame must lie also with Freemasonry as an institution for no longer investigating, probing and researching this most important aspect. In common with much of society, Freemasonry relies on rational and logical thinking to explain things which were never meant to be subjected to that process. Today the complexity of symbolism, including Masonic symbolism, has been reduced to that of a mere sign for which there is but one simple explanation. Modern writers, in dismissing the image of the 'old grey man', fail to appreciate the deeper symbolism (believing it to be literally an old grey man) and, in that failure, go on to suggest what the symbolism 'really' means. Personal interpretations are offered as the 'real', 'true' or 'original' explanations of what is 'seen' with the eye rather than the heart. Superficial interpretations are offered and frequently accepted as being correct, because the number of people with the knowledge necessary to understand the original interpretation is now very small. Successive generations have been offered less and less in the way of explanation of the spiritual and more and more of physical tangible 'things'. The decline in the explanation of symbolism, generation after generation, has ensured that most people no longer understand symbols that once were understood by all.

Signs Versus Symbols

As has been discussed, a sign is something that is intended to convey information unambiguously, e.g. 'road works ahead'(Fig. 6). What is seen and read is 'real' — that ahead there is a hole in the road. The sign allows for no other interpretation or explanation.

A symbol on the other hand exists to convey an intangible, a concept, an idea, a belief, something spiritual, etc. Unlike a sign it is intended to work on several levels. Thus a sign can never become a symbol but symbols are constantly being reduced to the status of mere signs. Symbols are things which are loaded with symbolic meaning(s) — signs are not. Thus it can be a variety of things — visual images, written words and even actions as in ritual. Occasionally these are found in combination.

How then do symbols 'work'? One method of explaining this is by use of allegory. Imagine being in a room with a window — the window can be considered as a symbol as it can allow us to see the landscape outside the room in

Fig. 6: *A sign, not a symbol*

which we stand. In other words the symbol (the window) may be used to see beyond our present location in time and space. At a literal level the window can be considered merely as an object made of wood and glass. If one focuses entirely on the window itself (that is, not looking through it) the landscape beyond completely disappears. The 'beyond' does not exist. However, as the window is used as a symbol and one re-focuses (looks through) on the view beyond, the landscape can be seen. The symbol has helped us to see from one place — the room — into another place — the landscape. The symbol is an aid, in this instance a visual aid, but in order to be able to use it one must understand that it is more that just wood and glass. Unfortunately the modern mind 'sees' the symbol as wood and glass and not what it can be used for.

From this analogy we can see that a symbol can work on more than one level if we allow it to. Symbols generally work on at least four different levels:

1 **The obvious or literal level**
   At this level the symbol is generally understood by all — it is a window.

2 **The allegorical level**
   That not only is it a window but that it can also be considered to be 'a window on the world' etc. This too is a generally accepted interpretation which is understood in this way by most people.

3 **The personal level**
   This way of understanding a symbol is specific to an individual or particular group who, in addition to the general understanding (above) actively use the symbol: 'The window gives me the ability to glimpse another place and/or time.'

4 **The mystical level**
   The symbol, now fully operational, allows the individual (or perhaps a very small group) to experience the numinous.

Although divided into four levels, it must be made clear that these are artificial divisions made only to assist with the explanation. It is quite possible to experience some, or all, of these 'levels' at the same time.

Another way to explain how symbols work is to describe them as a junction between two realities, the conscious and unconscious, the meeting point between the microcosm and the macrocosm, man and God, etc. In describing symbols and their interpretation in this abstract manner the reader will note that there is also a 'symbolism of numbers' inherent in the discussion which is dominated by the number 2.[38]

It is this way of understanding symbols that is unknown to most people today including many Freemasons.

Freemasonry adopted much Christian symbolism and iconography.[39] However, Masonic symbols cannot be used to interpret Christian symbolism for Christianity long preceded Freemasonry. It would also be a further grave error to believe that the Christian symbols appropriated by Freemasonry can be given a Christian interpretation. In this another crucial point regarding the interpretation of symbols in general and the symbolism and carvings within Rosslyn Chapel in particular is now made — it is often the case that symbols used in different places or by different groups may be similar or identical but have very different meanings. The use of the swastika in India and in Hitler's Germany is an example.[40]

Some specific examples from Rosslyn Chapel will serve to illustrate how the process of reinterpretation and the attempts to 'discover' Masonic symbolism can lead to error and confusion.

The Initiation

The corbel on the bottom left of the external south west window of the chapel is apparently a carving of two figures (see Plate 14). This is said to represent a candidate being escorted into a Masonic Lodge.[41] The figure to the right is said to be blindfolded and is being guided by the figure to the left by the use of a rope held by the conductor and which, it is suggested, encircles the 'candidate's' neck. The corbel was probably carved about 500 years ago and comparing it with today's modern Masonic practice is dangerous as there is an implicit suggestion that not only did Freemasonry exist 500 years ago but also that Masonic ceremonial was the same then as now.

By examining the earliest known Masonic rituals it may be possible to assess whether this carving has any resemblance with Masonic ceremonial in use nearer to the time the carving was created. The study of early Masonic practice is a specialist field but recent research is timely.[42] The earliest documents which provide details of the ceremonial practices of Lodges are:

- Edinburgh Register House MS, 1696
- Airlie MS, 1705
- Chetwode Crawley MS, c.1710

None of these describe the use of a rope or a blindfold. In fact the opposite is the case. The MSS show that the candidate was *not* blindfolded as the element of intimidation within the ceremonial is entirely visual. The rope and blindfold are later innovations in Freemasonry introduced during the 18th century. Modern Masonic ritual cannot, therefore, be used to interpret a 500 year old carving. As the chapel was built for 15th century religious practice it does not seem unreasonable to turn to those practices for an explanation of its function and symbolism.

Rosslyn Chapel has a huge number of carvings, many of them representing well known biblical stories and themes. If this corbel does indeed depict a person who was blind what is the biblical story being presented? First, however, a practical problem — how would a stonemason depict a blind person? In art this typically is done by showing a figure wearing a blindfold. It does not mean, therefore, that the individual *is* wearing a blindfold; it is merely a device used to indicate blindness. In Christianity, blindness was, and is, a powerful symbol with several different levels of meaning:

- Without natural sight — physical blindness
- Ignorance
- Spiritual blindness
- 'Legal' blindness

1) Being physically blind was a common affliction until relatively recently (and is still prevalent, unfortunately, in some parts of the world) and was due, in biblical times, to several causes, the formation of cataracts being one of the principal conditions.

2) Ignorance, in the context of Christianity, generally referred to the heathen, who had no knowledge of Christ nor of his kingdom. It is significant that heathen literally means 'unenlightened' — that is, without light — those who are blind.

3) Spiritual blindness specifically referred to those within the Christian community who had no spiritual knowledge or understanding.

4) In biblical times under the law blind or lame persons were not allowed to become priests nor were lame or blind animals allowed to be sacrificed, indicating that only whole persons could carry the word of God and only whole animals

were acceptable as sacrifices.

We can begin to see here several levels of complexity within Christian symbolism and the church's attempts, with varying degrees of success, to express its principles and precepts by that means. Physical blindness was occasionally inflicted by God:

> '*And they* [two angels] *smote the men that were at the door of the house with blindness, both small and great: so that they wearied themselves to find the door.*' Genesis 19:11

The angels of the Lord did this to protect Lot and his family from the riotous residents of Sodom before angels destroyed the city. This powerful and dramatic story posed some difficulties in being depicted in Christian symbolism and the expedient of using an existing symbol but providing it with multiple meanings was used.

When some Pharisees accused the disciples of Christ of transgressing the '*tradition of the elders*' his disciples said to him: '*Knowest thou that the Pharisees were offended after they heard this . . .*'. He explains: '*Let them alone: they be blind leaders of the blind. And if the blind lead the blind, both shall fall into the ditch.*' St. Matthew 15:12–14.

Christ knows the Pharisees are blind and that those who follow them are also blind. He explains to his disciples that the blind, leading the blind, will eventually trip up or wake up (that is, falling into a ditch) and there is therefore little point in trying to make them understand before they 'see the light'.

Matthew was the saint to whom the builder, William St. Clair, chose to dedicate his collegiate church. It is more than likely that he deliberately chose this story from the gospel of his favourite saint and ensured that it was prominently displayed.

The statement 'There is no Masonic symbolism within Rosslyn Chapel' is illustrated by this carving. The corbel (Plate 14) is not a Masonic *symbol*. The carving, regardless of what it represents, is not found within the plethora of Masonic symbolism. In other words the image of two men, one possibly leading another with a rope and who is possibly wearing a blindfold, does not exist within Freemasonry as a *symbol*. It is simply a carving to which a new, spurious, interpretation has been applied.

The Apprentice Pillar

This is one of three pillars at the east end of the chapel, in the south side, in the part often described as the retro-choir or Lady-chapel. (Plate 9) In order to understand the claim that this pillar is 'Masonic' it is perhaps advisable to relate the legend associated with it.

William St. Clair, the builder of the chapel, took great personal interest in the design of his collegiate church to the extent that he allegedly drew designs on wooden boards for carpenters to carve in three dimensions which the stonemasons copied in stone.[43]

The Apprentice Pillar is an ornate carving, one which the master mason in charge of the work decided was impossible to create from a drawing and insisted that he be allowed to view the original. The pillar is said to have been in Italy, Rome or Florence being quoted as the location. The master mason therefore travelled to Italy, returning to Rosslyn Chapel a couple of months later. When he entered the chapel he was astonished to find that the pillar had been completed and was identical to the original. His astonishment soon turned to anger as he realised that his long journey was a wasted one. He demanded to know who had, in his absence, carved the pillar. A lowly apprentice stepped forward and proudly claimed the work as his. Instead of receiving praise for his beautiful work the master mason, further enraged by the fact that such beauty had been wrought by a mere apprentice, struck a blow to the apprentice's forehead which killed him instantly. Soon after, the master mason realising the enormity of his action and in deep remorse, took his own life. At the south west corner of the chapel is the carving of a head which is said to be that of the murdered apprentice complete with a deep gash in the right temple. Opposite, in the north west corner, is another carving of a head said to be that of the master mason. Eastward from the carving of the master mason is another head said to be that of the apprentice's grieving mother — a widow. The apprentice was therefore the son of a widow. The legend ensured that the pillar in question is now known as the Apprentice Pillar. (Plate 13)

This then is the commonly known legend and for those with a passing knowledge of Freemasonry the connection of the murdered apprentice with the central character of the Third Degree seems obvious. The third degree of Freemasonry is concerned with the story of how the principal architect of King Solomon's Temple was murdered, as the temple was nearing completion, when he refused to divulge certain secrets to three ruffians who were not qualified to receive them. The three murderers hid the body in a shallow grave. Search parties of the same grade (i.e. Fellows of Craft) as the murderers found the body of Hiram Abiff (hereafter referred to as HA) and another party discovered the three ruffians hiding in a cave. The body of HA was re-interred within King Solomon's Temple and the three murderers executed for their crime.

Some writers have suggested that the two stories are so similar that this proves that there is a connection between Scottish Freemasonry and Rosslyn Chapel.[44] Comparing the elements of each story ought to show how many points of similarity there are and thereby reveal the strength of the claim that they prove the existence of a connection.

As has been stated before in this publication it is no longer acceptable to refer to 'masonry' without making it clear what is meant when using that term. Here is an excellent example of why that clarity of meaning is required. The murdered apprentice was a stonemason whereas HA was not. Using the term 'mason' to describe both, especially today, suggests that both were Freemasons.[45] The murdered apprentice is claimed to have been a real person who probably lived in the 15th century. HA was not a real person but was invented in the 18th century by Freemasons for allegorical purposes. The apprentice was a young man of lowly station whereas Hiram had the status of a king. The latter was the principal architect of King Solomon's Temple whereas the apprentice was a worker of stone. The lowly apprentice was killed by another stone mason, a master mason, whereas HA was killed by three allegorical Fellows of Craft who, like HA, were not real people. A comparison chart further assists in revealing points of dissimilarity (see below).

Rosslyn Chapel Legend	Masonic Legend
Apprentice murdered by a master stonemason	Grand Master murdered by three Masonic Fellow Crafts
Apprentice killed by a blow to the head	Grand master killed by three blows to the head
Legend said to be based on fact	Masonic legend is allegorical and has no factual basis
Apprentice murdered sometime soon after 1446	The Hiram Abiff legend invented c.1723
The Apprentice killed out of envy	Hiram Abiff murdered to obtain secrets
The Apprentice Pillar still exists	No equivalent Masonic lore
Descriptions of the Apprentice, his mother and the master mason claimed to be within Rosslyn Chapel	No equivalent Masonic lore

Murderer commits suicide	Three murderers judged and executed
Victim was man of lowly station	Victim was a mature man with the status of a king
Apprentice = apprentice stonemason	Entered Apprentice = a First Degree Freemason
master mason = master stonemason	Master Mason = a third degree Freemason
Victim is the son of a widow who was alive at the death of her son	Victim is the son of a widow who was deceased at the time of his death
The legend may indicate a desire to remind people (in the medieval period) not to try to rise above their station in life	The Masonic legend was devised in order to impart lessons of virtue, honour and fidelity

The major difference between the two legends lies in the purpose of each. The HA legend is an allegorical story, invented to emphasise particular moral lessons. The legend of the murdered apprentice is said to be fact and was not deliberately created. Superficially at least the two legends appear to be similar but, as can be seen from the above, they are in fact quite different in content and more especially in purpose.

The above shows that the legend of the murdered apprentice has some superficial similarities with the murder of Hiram Abiff in Masonic lore but a more considered approach reveals that these two stories are substantially different in detail. The legend at Rosslyn Chapel cannot be taken to be Masonic in any way, not least because it is directly opposite to the lesson that is being imparted in the Third Degree.

What is known about the legend at Rosslyn Chapel and does this shed any light on when the legend was created? John Slezer (?–d.1714) decided to: 'make a book of the figures, and draughts, and frontispiece in Talyduce [Scots for *taille-douce*, the French term for copper-plate etching] of all the King's Castles, Pallaces, towns, and other notable places in the kingdom belonging to private subjects'. He travelled through Scotland, and the design ultimately resulted in the publication of Slezer's '*Theatrum Scotiæ*' of 1693. Slezer's description of Rosslyn Chapel is short but informative. It is reproduced here in full.[46]

'This Chapel lies in *Mid-Lothian*, Four Miles from Edinburgh and is one of the most curious Pieces of Workmanship in *Europe*. The Foundation of this rare Building was laid *Anno* 1440 by *William St Clair*, Prince of *Orkney*, Duke of *Holdenburgh*, &c. A Man as considerable for the publick

Works which he erected, as for the Lands which he possessed, and the Honours which were conferred upon him by several of the greatest Princes of *Europe*. It is remarkable that in all this Work there are not two Cuts of one sort. The most curious Part of the Building is the Vault of the Quire, and that which is called the Prince's Pillar so much talked of. This Chapel was posses'd by a Provost, and Seven Canons Regular, who were endued with several considerable Revenues through the Liberality of the Lairds of *Roslin*.

Here lies Buried *George* Earl of *Caithness* who lived about the Beginning of the Reformation [1559], Alexander Earl of Sutherland, great Grand-Child to King Robert de Bruce, Three Earls of *Orkney*, and Nine Barons of *Roslin*.

The last lay in a Vault, so dry that their Bodies have been found intire after Fourscore Years, and as fresh as when they were first buried. There goes a Tradition; That before the Death of any of the Family of *Roslin*, this Chapel appears all in Fire.'

Slezer's publication provides the earliest known description, and image, of Rosslyn Chapel. He visited Rosslyn Chapel in order to make his drawings and became acquainted with some of the stories associated with the building. What he has to say is very important. He makes no mention of the Apprentice Pillar so well known today but refers to a 'Prince's Pillar' which may be so named after the founder and builder of the chapel — William St. Clair, 'Prince' of Orkney. The legend associated with the since re-named 'Apprentice Pillar' did not, apparently, exist at the time of Slezer's visit. As previously suggested it is not unlikely that Father Richard A. Hay, the writer of the *Genealogie of the Sainteclaires of Rosslyn*, met Slezer. It is significant therefore that Hay, the 'arch-propagandist' of the St. Clair family, also makes no mention of the legend of the murdered apprentice. That the two earliest writers on Rosslyn Chapel were unfamiliar with an existing legend is almost impossible. On this basis it seems that the legend did not come into existence until sometime after the last decade of the 17th century but was invented sometime before Bishop Forbes first wrote of it in 1761.[47]

As has previously been discussed, the involvement of Rosslyn Chapel with Freemasonry has been part of a process of elaboration, involving many other characters and places, since Anderson's *New Constitutions* of 1738. That process appears also to apply to the legend of the murdered apprentice. Slezer and Hay did not mention the Apprentice Pillar nor did they relate the legend of an apprentice killed by an envious master mason. Neither did they describe any carvings of the murdered apprentice, the master mason or a grieving widow. It is not until we read Forbes' description of the Apprentice Pillar that there is an associated legend. His description of the carving of the murdered apprentice is of interest here:

> '. . . in the south-west corner, above half-way up to the top of the inner wall, there is exhibited a young man's head, called the Apprentice's head, with a scar above the right brow, representing a wound by a stroke;'[48]

The key word here is 'representing' — that is, the scar or wound is not incised into the stone of the carving but is a superficial indication of a scar or wound. (Plate 15) Had this been an isolated reference one may have thought that Bishop Forbes was mistaken. However, as late as 1845 the alleged carving of the murdered apprentice was being described in similar terms:

> 'Legend even gossips so lustily as to point out among the sculptures the heads of the slain, the slayer, and the former's mother weeping for his fate; and, quite in the characteristic style of monkish fiction, appeals to a daub with ochre as a memento of the apprentice's wound, and blunderingly identifies his whole figure with that of a bearded old man.'[49]

This reference is even more specific than that of Forbes. The scar, or wound, is represented by a daub of coloured pigment. Others also notice the manner in which the wound was portrayed:

> 'Among the grotesque heads in the decorations, it was not difficult to find that of the master, the apprentice's mother, and the apprentice himself: the last, for the benefit of visitors from the neighbourhood of Bow bells, was made more telling, by a streak of red chalk being drawn across the brow to represent a hatchet-cut.'[50]

All of these observations reveal something very important for the understanding of Rosslyn Chapel's place in the mythology of Scottish Freemasonry, the Knights Templar etc. Of supreme importance is the fact that the carved head of the so-called murdered apprentice was not originally carved as such. The wound on the right forehead was not part of the original carving at all. It was only later, much later, indicated by the use of ochre, chalk and paint. This confirms that the legend of the murdered apprentice was a later addition to the mythology of the chapel. That means that the legend did not exist at the time the chapel was begun (1446) and only came into being more than 250 years later, that is, sometime after 1700. How can this be, especially as the carving today bears a gash which is deeply incised into the right forehead? The conclusion is inescapable — the gash, or incision, has been added later. The implication that parts of the chapel have been deliberately tampered with is enormous.

There is one further point that reinforces the above: the present day carving which is now said to be of the murdered apprentice once sported a beard and probably a moustache. These have been rather crudely chiselled away but the damage to the chin and upper lip confirms that the author, writing in 1845, who described the head has having a beard was correct in his observation. In medieval art the convention was that a mature man was depicted sporting a beard. The longer (and whiter) it was, the older the individual. A youth was shown clean-shaven indicating that he was too young to grow facial hair. Many years after Rosslyn Chapel was built someone has deliberately made major alterations to the original carving. The implications of this will be discussed later.

There is one further point regarding the design of the Apprentice Pillar. As has been discussed elsewhere, many of the carvings within Rosslyn Chapel have been added to the basic 'skeleton' — a process known as *appliqué*. The Apprentice Pillar has also been thought worthy of non-invasive investigation and the results of that investigation revealed that the pillar was hollow or at least contained cavities.[51] The existence of spaces within the Apprentice Pillar is interesting but not unusual. Like the 'straight arches' [*sic*] within the side aisles the decoration appears to have been added later. The Apprentice Pillar can be seen to be made up of a series of rings like 'doughnuts' one on top of another and would account for the apparent cavity within.

The Three Pillars

Everyone knows that there are three degrees in Freemasonry and that simple fact has been applied by some authors to Rosslyn Chapel. Logic dictates that if the Apprentice Pillar (First Degree) relates to Freemasonry then the adjacent pillars (Plate 9) must be those of the Fellow Craft (Second Degree) and Master Mason (Third Degree).[52] The oldest known Masonic rituals, previously referred to, are:

- Edinburgh Register House MS, 1696
- Airlie MS, 1705
- Chetwode Crawley MS, c.1710

All of these rituals are unequivocally Scottish. As they are the earliest known it is to be expected that an analysis of these earliest rituals shows that prior to c.1720 there were only two degrees — those of the Entered Apprentice and Fellow of Craft. The Master Mason or Third Degree did not exist until almost 300 years after the building of Rosslyn Chapel had begun. The rituals detailed above describe only two ceremonies (or degrees in today's Masonic terminology) and some of the content of the stonemasons' Fellow Craft ceremony is now contained within the third or Master Masons' degree. The evolution of Masonic ritual, albeit obscure, has been well researched and the development from the two ceremonies of Scottish stonemasons into three Masonic degrees is clearly understood.[53] The first record of the third or Master Masons' degree being conferred in a Lodge occurs on 25 March 1726 when one Gabriel Porterfield was made a Master Mason having previous been passed to the degree of Fellow Craft on 29 January of that year. Here then is a good example of the 'retrospective application' of knowledge from today (that is, modern Masonic practice) being imposed upon the past. This is a simple example of how the process of elaboration can lead some to make elementary historical errors. This 'technique' was briefly discussed in Chapter 1. The legend of the murdered apprentice and the physical elements (now) associated with it within the chapel show a process of elaboration over a period of several hundreds of years. By considering the chapel in isolation, that is, not in its ecclesiastical and historical context, one would be forgiven for believing that this legend only exists at Rosslyn Chapel. If it did, the claim that the chapel was unique, in this respect at least, would carry much more weight. However, the legend exists in such diverse places as the cathedrals of Gloucester and Lincoln (England) and Rouen (France), the bridge at Ratisbon (Germany), Melrose Abbey, Seton Collegiate Church (Scotland) and the Great Mosque at Damietta (Egypt). The claim to uniqueness is therefore illusory.[55] None of those other places has been claimed as being associated with Freemasonry. That in itself raises an interesting question. Why alone is the legend at Rosslyn Chapel used to connect it to Freemasonry? Why not at any other place? This would appear to be another example of how, by considering Rosslyn Chapel in isolation, the erroneous impression is created that Rosslyn Chapel is unique in this respect.

Figs. 7 and 8:
Masons' marks?

Masons Marks

One of most obvious testaments to the work of the stonemasons who built a particular church etc. is that they left their 'marks', and there are quite a few within Rosslyn Chapel. Masons' marks are however problematic in that they cannot be dated and cannot be ascribed to any particular individual. All are therefore anonymous. Masons marks are a form of shorthand in place of a mason's signature. It was impractical for a mason to carve his name on a block of stone but some form of identification was required because stonemasons were paid by the number, and quality, of stones they prepared. Simple geometric marks provided the answer and every stonemason on completing his apprenticeship would take a mark which was his for the rest of his life. It was common for a son to adopt the mark of his father but to differentiate it from his father's a slight alteration or addition would be made. Many of the marks in Rosslyn Chapel have been recorded (Figs. 7 and 8) but interestingly more have recently begun to appear and clearly cannot be the work of stonemasons. There is considerable doubt as to which of the marks within Rosslyn Chapel were actually made by stonemasons. The reason for the doubt is simple. Stonemasons were employed to dress stone and the mark identifying the work or each was carved on an inside face, so when the stone was laid in its final position the mark was hidden. This was done because no one wanted the wall, statue, arch etc. to be defaced by a mason's mark. The one exception appears to have been that the master mason in charge of a particular section was permitted to place one of his marks in a discreet place (often high up and at least partially hidden) to show that he had passed the work as being of an acceptable standard — his seal of approval if you will. Some marks at Rosslyn Chapel cannot be accepted as being the marks of stonemasons for several reasons. First, many are not discreetly hidden away and many are not in a high position. These marks are a form of graffiti added over the years for the same reasons that people carve their names or initials on trees. These are fairly easy to identify because they are crudely made and are not the product of a mason's maul and chisel. Marks made in this manner are deeply incised (to stop them being erased) and are made by clean angular lines. Some in the chapel appear to have been scratched with a nail or something similar revealing that they are not genuine masons' marks.

The Holy Royal Arch

The only script which is part of the internal fabric of the chapel is that found on the lintel (or straight arches [*sic*]) which extends from the Apprentice Pillar to the south wall. The script reads: '*Wine is strong, a King is stronger, Women are stronger still but Truth conquers all.*' (Plate 8) This was taken from the Apocrypha, specifically I Esdras, Chapters 3–4, and the story related there has already been described in the previous chapter but even more briefly here it gives an account of the events leading to King Darius to fulfil the decree of Cyrus granting Zerubbabel the Priest to lead the Jews to Jerusalem to rebuild the temple. The Holy Royal Arch ceremonies of Freemasonry centre on the events once Zerubbabel had returned to Jerusalem and was preparing to rebuild the temple. The extract from I Esdras (above) describes an event which took place before those described in the Royal Arch ceremony. Some authors have linked the two and in the process suggested that the existence of the text means that the stonemasons who carved it had knowledge of the Royal Arch ceremony. Here is an example of the retrospective application technique (discussed in Chapter 1) of modern practice being applied to the past. This apparent reference to the modern Royal Arch ceremony in a building hundreds of years old obviously means that the builders had knowledge of the ceremony — or does it? In fact it suggests that I Esdras was known during the period when the chapel was being built and that coincidentally hundreds of years later when Freemasons were inventing all sorts of ceremonies they turned to I Esdras for inspiration. Even then there is no coincidence — the text in the chapel appears nowhere in the ceremony and the events it describes are not part of the Royal Arch. In other words the Freemasons when designing the ceremony did *not* use this part of I Esdras. There is therefore not even a coincidental connection between that part of the chapel and Freemasonry. It seems that the desire to make the chapel Masonic has led some to make links which on examination simply do not exist.

Like the discussion above regarding the erroneous association of three pillars within Rosslyn Chapel with the three degrees of Freemasonry here too is an example of the 'retrospective application' of what is known today (the Royal Arch ceremony) onto the past, although it is known that the Royal Arch ceremony did not come into existence until after *c*.1740.

Green Man

A further complication arises with the interpretation of other symbols such as the Green Man. (Plate 16) By claiming that Rosslyn Chapel is not a Christian edifice this has allowed some to argue that the Green Man must, therefore, be pagan or at least non-Christian. This is to misunderstand church history and its use of symbols. The Green Man was certainly a pagan symbol with several meanings: the never-ending pattern of the seasons, together with pre-Christian concepts of reproduction, fertility and the agricultural cycle. The origins of the Green Man do not, however, lie with pagans as it is found, even earlier, in classical antiquity. To the Greeks and Romans it suggested the full flowering of education (i.e. the fruits of learning) and was, therefore, an inspirational symbol. Greeks, Romans, Christians and pagans have all made use of the symbol but it is important to appreciate that each endowed it with their own, different, meaning. When the Green Man was incorporated into Christian iconography it was assigned different attributes creating several layers of meaning to the Christian. The pagan's interpretation of the Green Man — that it indicated the seasons etc. — was changed by Christians to mean the immortality of the soul and the resurrection of Jesus Christ. The symbol also demonstrated all of creation: animal (represented by the human face) vegetable (the foliage) and mineral (the stone from which the symbol was carved). There are several other Christian meanings but perhaps the most important is also simplest: the Green Man is Jesus Christ (the human face) who was sent by God from heaven into the world (represented by the foliage). The symbol, therefore, shows that heaven and earth are linked through one person only — Jesus Christ.

Moses Vs. The Devil

The understanding of carvings within Rosslyn Chapel has been hampered by ignorance of the sources from which the symbolism was originally taken. An example of this is that of the figure of a man with two horns, holding a tablet in one hand and a rod in the other which, it is claimed, depicts the Devil tallying the number of souls he has ensnared (Plate 18). However, the Rev. John Thompson, makes clear on page 70 of his guidebook that this carving is of Moses. An explanation of how and why it is known to be Moses is worth relating here. A modern Bible describes, in Exodus 34:29–30, Moses after his second descent from Mount Sinai with the tablets of the Ten Commandments in the following terms:[55]

> *29 And it came to pass, when Moses came down from mount Sinai with the two tablets of testimony in Moses' hand, when he came down from the mount, that Moses wist not that the skin of his face shone while he talked with him.*
>
> *30 And when Aaron and all the children of Israel saw Moses, behold, the skin of his face shone; and they were afraid to come nigh him.*[56] (Plate 17)

After 1560 many people had reference only to Protestant Bibles and as these do not refer to Moses with horns it is understandable that the carving has, wrongly, been interpreted as being of the Devil. However, when the chapel was being built the Bible in use was, or was based on, the Latin Vulgate which does describe Moses as having horns:

> *29 And when Moses came down from the Mount Sinai, he held the two tablets of the testimony, and he knew not that his face was horned from the conversation of the Lord.*
>
> *30 And Aaron and the children of Israel seeing the face of Moses horned, were afraid to come near.*[57]

In light of this, the intention of the carved figure becomes obvious. Because fewer people than ever before are familiar with the Bible, let alone the differences between the numerous versions, it is easy to understand how non-religious and non-Biblical interpretations of the symbolism within Rosslyn Chapel have become popular.

Lamb of God

Another problem in the interpretation of symbols in Rosslyn Chapel, and which requires a brief discussion, relates to the retrospective application of symbolic meaning. An example of this is the suggestion that some of the carvings within the chapel are those of the Knights Templar. One carving is described as 'The Templar seal of the '*Agnus Dei*'.[58] (Plate 19) This symbol is a lamb together with a Passion Cross and indeed the Knights Templar did make use of this symbol. However, they adopted an existing Christian symbol which had previously been used by the church for many centuries.[59] The symbol was not designed by the KT and its origin comes from the Gospel According to St. John 1:29:

> '*The next day John seeth Jesus coming unto him, and saith, Behold the Lamb of God, which taketh away the sin of the world.*'[60]

The first seal of the KT was that of two knights on one horse. The earliest known use of the *Agnus Dei* by the KT is in 1241 by which time the symbol had been in use by the church for over 400 years.[61]

Face of Bruce

An image of a carving within Rosslyn Chapel bears the following caption: '*The carving of the death mask of Robert the Bruce*.' Additional text expands on this:

> '*Robert the Bruce who was not only a Templar but the Sovereign Grand Master of both the Military Order and the Masonic Guilds. His death mask is carved into the stonework of the Retro-choir at Rosslyn.*'[62] (Plate 20)

Never before had it been reported that a death mask of Robert I had been made, that it survived for 117 years, from the date of his death to *c*.1446 when the building of the chapel commenced, and was copied in stone in the retro-choir. Nor had it ever been previously claimed that this Scottish monarch was 'a [Knight] *Templar and Sovereign Grand Master of The Military Order and The Masonic Guilds*' — a subject discussed below. It is not clear if the carving is claimed to be the actual death mask or if it is a carved copy of the death mask. Either way if a death mask had been made and survived to be inserted into or copied in the chapel, this would be a major historical discovery. A re-examination of information on Robert I's death and burial confirms that no one had previously mentioned the existence of a death mask. The earliest known death mask in Europe is that of Edward III (1312–1377) but death masks did not become common until the 15th century. How could the existence of such a significant artefact have remained unmentioned and unnoticed for so long? In attempting to discover when the '*carving of the death mask of Robert the Bruce . . .*' was first announced to the world a problem was immediately encountered as none of the current information regarding the chapel provided any details in support of that revelation. In this case there must, surely, be corroborative evidence for such an important claim? However, only one other reference could be found and that too was also recent (1993). In that instance, however, the caption accompanying the image stated: '*Supposed death mask of Robert the Bruce*.'[63] The writer concerned was not claiming that it *was* a carving of the death mask of Robert I but that he *supposed* it to be so. He did not offer any evidence to support his supposition. Prior to 1993 no references to such a death mask, or any connection between it and Rosslyn Chapel, could be found. Writers of the 17th, 18th, 19th and 20th centuries wrote and described the chapel but none, as far as can be ascertained, made any suggestion that Scotland's most famous monarch has been immortalised within Rosslyn Chapel. This may well be an example of how a mere speculation made in 1993 is later quoted as fact.[64]

In 1818 Robert I's grave was re-discovered within Dunfermline Abbey. William Scouler, an artist, was present when the late king's skull was revealed. He had been retained to draw the skeleton but took the opportunity to make a cast of the skull. There was great excitement and interest, especially in 'antiquarian circles', but no one mentioned the (previous) existence of a death mask. It seems, therefore, that the claim concerning the carved face in Rosslyn Chapel is of more recent origin. What evidence, if any, the claim is based on is not presently known. In June 1964, Her Majesty the Queen unveiled the equestrian statue of Bruce by Charles P. Jackson at Bannockburn. Jackson had used Scouler's cast of the skull to create the facial features of Bruce. Although everyone agrees that this is a powerful depiction of Bruce it is generally considered to be romantic rather than accurate. The art of forensic reconstruction was then in its infancy but in 1996 the dental and forensic expert Brian Hill produced a reconstruction also based on Scouler's cast of the skull. This was a 'clean' reconstruction designed to produce a youthful face unmarked by time and war.[65]

Dr. Ian MacLeod, a consultant at the Edinburgh Dental Institute, assisted by Dr. Richard Neave, one of Britain's foremost forensic medical artists, produced a 'warts an' all' reconstruction of Bruce's head at the time of his death. This took account of the obvious scarring, i.e. a sword wound to the head, a broken cheekbone, a distended eye socket and upper jaw damage. MacLeod and Neave were sure that Robert I suffered from leprosy and this too is reflected in the reconstruction. Dr. MacLeod described Bruce thus:

'*The first thing that strikes you about Robert the Bruce is that the guy has tremendous presence. There is almost a Churchillian aura about him. This was a guy you would not want to get into a fight with. He would have stood out from the crowd. What we have here is a battle-scarred old man. You don't go through wars like he did without receiving a few knocks.'*

Does the carved face in Rosslyn Chapel fit any of these reconstructions? The answer must be no. The carving is of a young face rather than that of an old man. It is supposed to be a copy of the death mask of Bruce but shows none of the marks of time, none of the scarring, none of the 'wear and tear' of 55 years. The claim that the carving in the retro-choir is that of Robert I seems to be merely opinion and without any supporting evidence. This is, perhaps, another example of 'seeing' something rather than analysing and providing supportive evidence.

The claim that Robert I was 'a [Knight] *Templar and Sovereign Grand Master of both the Military Order and the Masonic Guilds*' is worthy of further mention even if only very briefly.[66] There is no evidence at all that Robert I was a Knight Templar and is another example of a claim being made for which no supporting evidence is offered. The term Grand Master, in relation to offices of the Scottish Crown, did not exist. Guilds in Scotland did not come into being until the 15th century and so Bruce could not have been '*Sovereign Grand Master*' of any of them as he died in 1329.[67] During the reign of James I (1406–1437, b. 1394) there was a great deal of suspicion regarding craftsmen and their activities but this began to change during the latter part of the 15th century. In 1469 an Act was passed which regulated burgh elections and also recognised craft 'associations' and soon craftsmen began to seek formal recognition from burgh authorities. For the record it is worth detailing the dates the various trades that became Incorporations did receive their Seals of Cause (Charters):

Baxters (bakers)	1456
Bonnet makers	1473
Skinners	1474
Masons and wrights	1475
Wobsters (weavers)	1476
Hammermen (blacksmiths etc.)	1483
Fleshers (butchers)	1488
Coopers	1489
Cordiners (shoemakers and leather workers)	1510

Obviously Robert I, king of Scotland, could not have been '*Sovereign Grand Master of all Guilds*' as they did not exist during his reign.[68] Nor is it clear to what '*Orders in Scotland*' refers - the Order of the Thistle was not instituted until

1687 by James VII (1685–1688, b.1633, d.1701).

Heart of Bruce

Not only is the face of Robert I, at the time of his death, claimed to be in Rosslyn Chapel but there is also said to be a religious tribute to him. There is a carving of an angel holding a heart which is said to be that of Robert I. (Plate 21) This example is not a case of mere opinion, but of simple error. The angel is holding a cushion on which lies the traditional, if inaccurate, shape of a heart. In Christian symbolism the meaning is well known and clear. The heart represents Jesus Christ and the winged figure represents an angel and also Saint Matthew — to whom the chapel was dedicated. The carving, is therefore, a symbol of salvation through Jesus Christ, which is being offered, quite literally, to the viewer. There are other carvings within Rosslyn Chapel which also represent Jesus Christ. In particular an angel holding a crown of thorns and with three nails through the thorns and into the heart which represents the crucified Christ. (Plate 22) The symbol of a heart in medieval churches is a frequent occurrence (for example: at Haddington – see Plate 23) and in general symbolises the Sacred Heart of Jesus Christ and his love of humankind. The devotion to the Sacred Heart has existed since at least the 11th century.[69] Exactly why there is a desire to represent such a well known Christian symbol as something it is not suggests that this is part of the process of de-Christianising the chapel and its contents. This may have the dual symbolism in also representing Lady Margaret Douglas (see p.145

Masonic Angels

A crouching, winged figure, with both hands placed under the right knee is to be found in the retro-choir of Rosslyn Chapel. This posture is said to be '. . . *of ritual significance to Freemasons*'.[70] (Plate 24) Another winged figure has the right hand under the right knee and the left hand over the right breast. This carving is said to be '. . . *associated with Freemasonry*'.[71] (Plate 25) The claim that Rosslyn Chapel is, in some ill-defined way, 'Masonic' appears to have led some commentators to 'see' Masonic symbols and, in this instance, Masonic 'postures' where none exist. The postures that these winged figures display do not exist within Freemasonry, or more specifically, they certainly do not exist within *Scottish* Freemasonry.[72] It may be that those who have made such suggestions and indeed, statements of fact, are not Freemasons and do not, apparently, have knowledge of Scottish Masonic practice.

The statement about these winged figures, which are in fact angels, has been taken to its ultimate conclusion and these carvings are now regularly pointed out as being 'Masonic angels'! (Plates 24 and 25) This is quite preposterous. There is no such thing as a 'Masonic angel' and it is offensive to many to make such a suggestion, however playfully.

What then do the carvings represent? Having confirmed that the chapel is, and always has been, a Christian edifice and as its angels are undoubtedly also Christian, it seems reasonable that it is to that religion that one should turn in order to find an explanation. There are numerous carvings of angels within Rosslyn Chapel; why they were placed there may seem rather obvious given that they were a principal element in the theology of the medieval church. They appear frequently in the Bible doing the will of God. As his instrument they wield enormous power:

> '*So it shall it be at the end of the world: the angels shall come forth, and sever the wicked from among the just,*
> *and shall cast them into the furnace of fire: there shall be wailing and gnashing of teeth.*' (Matthew 13:49–50)

When one recalls that the collegiate church was originally dedicated to St. Matthew the chapel's Christian credentials become even more obvious.[73] St. Matthew's gospel is the first of the four gospels and the symbol of St. Matthew is that of a winged man — an angel — and is a symbolic reference to the angel who allegedly dictated to him as he wrote. These carvings have therefore a dual symbolism: that of an angel and of St. Matthew. Rosslyn Chapel is a little unusual given the large number of angels it contains but when one asks the question — 'How many angels are there?' the answer is to be found in the New Testament: '*Thinkest thou that I cannot now pray to my Father, and he shall presently give me more than twelve Legions of angels?*' A legion, in the Roman army, originally consisted of three thousand men, but by the time of Christ consisted of six thousand. The word legion is used by St. Matthew to express the number of angels which simply cannot be counted (Matthew 26:53). As the chapel was dedicated to St. Matthew who said that there were 12 legions of angels (12 x 6000) it is hardly surprising that William St. Clair decided to fill the chapel with a large number of winged men or angels.

Some of the angels have only a generalised meaning — 'Praise the Lord', 'Heed the Word of God' etc. A few have scrolls on which a few meaningful words would have been inscribed. There are many examples of this type of 'messenger' in other Scottish ecclesiastic buildings such as those at Melrose Abbey which are particularly fine.

Indian Corn (Maize)

The existence of carvings of Indian corn, maize or 'corn on the cob' within Rosslyn Chapel has been cited as proof that there were Europeans in North America before Christopher Columbus 'discovered' it in 1492.[74] Maize is a plant which requires constant cultivation, rather than growing wild, and was native to North America. The plant probably originated in what is now known as Mexico and was cultivated by Native Americans. However, the plant is 'cold-intolerant' and is not naturally adapted to the climate of the north-east of what is now known as Canada. The claim that the carvings are of maize is based on two 'facts': that they *are* of Indian corn and that Rosslyn Chapel was built in 1446. Comparing the alleged carving of corn with actual specimens of Indian corn the two appear to be

completely different. (Plate 26 and Fig. 9) If the carvings do depict Indian corn then this would be a truly momentous discovery, not least because it would mean that Scots discovered America! However, attempting to trace evidence on which this claim is based was, like the carved copy of the death mask of Robert I, inconclusive and the claim is based on little more than personal opinion.[75] The other major assumption is that the carvings were placed in the chapel *before* 1492. There is no information as to when the carvings were made but it is important to recall that the building of Rosslyn Chapel was commenced in 1446 and the building work almost certainly continued for many years after. It is now known that the carvings in

Fig. 9: *As in Rosslyn Chapel?*

the chapel were added after the building was complete. The carvings were not made from the basic fabric of the chapel but were applied later to the bare, but complete, structure — of which more later.

Aloe Vera

Of the dozens, if not hundreds, of foliage carvings in Rosslyn Chapel only two have been identified as particular plants in the context of this book. They are maize, as discussed above, and 'aloe cactus' [*sic*].[76] (Plate 27) Like maize, aloe is foreign to Europe and as carvings of it appear in Rosslyn Chapel, this was used to reinforce the suggestion that people from Europe, specifically Scotland, must have visited North America returning with specimens of that plant or, at least, with a clear recollection of what they looked like. Unfortunately, the exact species is not provided by the various authors who claim that they have identified carvings of aloe. As there are more than 250 species of aloe, the scope for personal interpretation is enormous. The most commonly known form of aloe is aloe vera and it is to this that most authors refer. As with the discussion above regarding maize, a comparison between aloe vera and the carvings reveal few similarities with images of the plant as it is cultivated. (Plates 26 and 27) More significant, however, is the fact that none of the aloe species can withstand frost. The notion that the plant came from North America is based on the story of the Venetian Brothers Nicolò and Antonio Zeno's alleged discovery of that continent in 1389, more than 100 years before Christopher Columbus in 1492.[77] The story of the Zeno brothers' discovery of North America (specifically Canada) suggests that they reached Nova Scotia via Greenland, and explored some of its coastline.[78] As aloe is a semi-tropical plant it is not possible for anyone to have seen or taken such a plant from Nova Scotia and so the claim that the carvings in Rosslyn Chapel are of that plant must be rejected.

The Seal of the Knights Templar

One of the corbels in a window in the south aisle ('E' - Plate 11) features a horse and two figures. This has been claimed to be a carving of the seal of the Knights Templar thereby linking Rosslyn Chapel to that Order. If true, the significance lies in the fact that the Order of KT was suppressed in 1312

Fig. 10:
Seal of the KT – as in Rosslyn Chapel?

and the building of the chapel did not commence until 1446. That would suggest that more than 130 years later the KT was still in existence and had some connection with the chapel. Does the carving look like the seal of the KT? (Fig. 10) The seal of the KT shows two knights astride a single horse and is said to represent the poverty of the early members of the Order.

A close examination of the carving shows that the main figure is a knight holding a lance in his right hand, wearing a helmet and coif and holds the horse's reigns in his left hand. It is clear that the knight is the only person mounted on the horse and the saddle in which he sits is very obvious. The second figure is shown standing behind the hind quarters of the horse and is bearing a Passion Cross; he is *not* mounted on the horse. (Plate 19)

If it is not the seal of the KT what then does the carving depict? The Rev. Thompson, writing in 1894, had been told that the carving was that of St. George slaying the dragon (representing evil and/or the Devil) but as he correctly points out, there is no dragon present. However, the carving is damaged and the lower limbs of the horse and feet of the knight are missing. It does not seem unreasonable to assume that, like other carvings in the chapel, parts (in this case a dragon) have been removed. Support for this comes from the presence of an angel bearing a crucifix and this combination of mounted knight with a lance and an angel is one way of referring to St. George slaying the dragon. Perhaps, like the head of the murdered apprentice, this is another instance of how the chapel has been deliberately changed to suit the myth.

A 'Knight Templar' Graveslab

Within Rosslyn Chapel there is a graveslab mounted on a modern concrete plinth. The graveslab is 3 feet 3½ inches (approximately one metre), 11¾ inches wide and 6 inches thick. The central decoration consists of a three stepped base from which rises a shaft, the top of which bears a circular, floriated, head. To the right is a

Fig. 11: *Proof that William St Clair was a Knight Templar?*

short sword and on the other side is an inscription: '✠ WILL•HMDES•HINCLER'. (Fig. 11) The letters have been re-cut, overlaying a previous inscription, a process which has led to error. There were apparently three previous 'words' subsequently over-cut to read: WILL HMDES HIN. Three other letters, LER, have been added within the base, and all the letters together, make an approximation (WILL•HMDES•HINCLER) of the name of the new 'user' of the graveslab — William Sincler.[79] The modern plinth bears the legend: 'WILLIAM DE St. CLAIR KNIGHT TEMPLAR'. This is quite different from what the graveslab itself bears (see above) and must be a modern 'interpretation'. The graveslab does not bear the words 'Knight Templar'. It cannot be stressed enough that there is no way to know, principally in the absence of a date, which of the numerous William St. Clairs this slab was re-cut for. It is equally impossible to given the name of the individual for whom the slab was originally created because the name has been obliterated by the subsequent re-cutting. Nor should the re-use of this graveslab be considered in anyway unusual — it was not. What is surprising is, especially in the light of this discussion, how anyone could know which St. Clair this graveslab commemorates let alone know that any members of the St. Clair family were Knights Templar. There is, presently, no evidence to support that contention. Only the modern plinth on which this graveslab is mounted states that a William St. Clair was a Knight Templar. No supporting evidence is provided.

There is one final observation to be made — a graveslab of this size originally marked the last resting place, not of an adult, but of a child. A child baptised and who was dear enough to the Christian parents to go to the expense of having a small graveslab made to cover the last resting place of one of their children. These small graveslabs, bearing the outline of a sword, record the last resting place of a child dearly beloved by a warrior who remains as anonymous as the child he fathered.

Masonic Symbolism?

There is none! One major anomaly regarding the claim that Rosslyn Chapel is 'Masonic' in content if not purpose lies in the fact that no Masonic symbols are to be found. There are merely a very few carvings which are claimed to be 'Masonic' and more often than not without any explanation as to *why* they are Masonic. For example, the carving of the Initiation (the blind leading the blind) discussed above, appears nowhere in Masonic imagery. Within Freemasonry such an event is represented by the ritual and symbolism of the Entered Apprentice Degree. None of the carvings claimed to be Masonic are actually Masonic symbols. There are, for instance, no representations of the 24-inch gauge, the maul, chisel, square and compasses, beehive, the all-seeing eye, etc. The absence of these easily carved, and well known symbols, is telling especially in a place with a superabundance of symbolism.

A most curious situation therefore exists. Rosslyn Chapel is claimed to be 'Masonic' (in some undefined way) but no Masonic symbolism is to be found there. Whereas within Freemasonry there are none of the symbols carved at Rosslyn Chapel which are claimed to be Masonic!

Despite the fact that the purpose for which the chapel was built is known and understood, those who have imposed their own interpretation have further speculated that, because it is not Christian, its true purpose was not the burial place of the St. Clair family and was not for the saying of prayers for their souls but was for the purpose of hiding 'something'. This 'something' has been claimed to be:

- the treasure of the Knights Templar
- the embalmed head of Jesus Christ
- the 'real' Stone of Destiny
- the Ark of the Covenant
- the Nasorean Scrolls
- the Holy Grail

These claims have led to several appeals for the chapel vault to be physically investigated in order to determine the nature of its contents. Such appeals have failed, although non-invasive methods have been tried with inconclusive results. However, it is unnecessary to undertake any form of excavation as the vaults have been previously explored. Recalling that the 1st and 3rd Earls of Orkney were re-interred there, probably soon after 1446 once the vaults had been built, and that Alexander Sutherland (father-in-law to the builder of the chapel William St. Clair) was laid to rest there in 1456, means that from the very beginning people have been going in and out of the vaults. At least seven other St. Clairs and no doubt their wives (as demonstrated by the instance of Elizabeth Kerr) and people who were not immediate family members (Alexander Sutherland being such an example) have been buried in the vault.[80] The last St. Clair to be so interred was William St. Clair of Rosslyn (1700–1778), the first Grand Master Mason of the Grand Lodge of Scotland, and he was laid to rest with elaborate Masonic burial ceremonial. Before the Reformation all who were interred in the vault would have

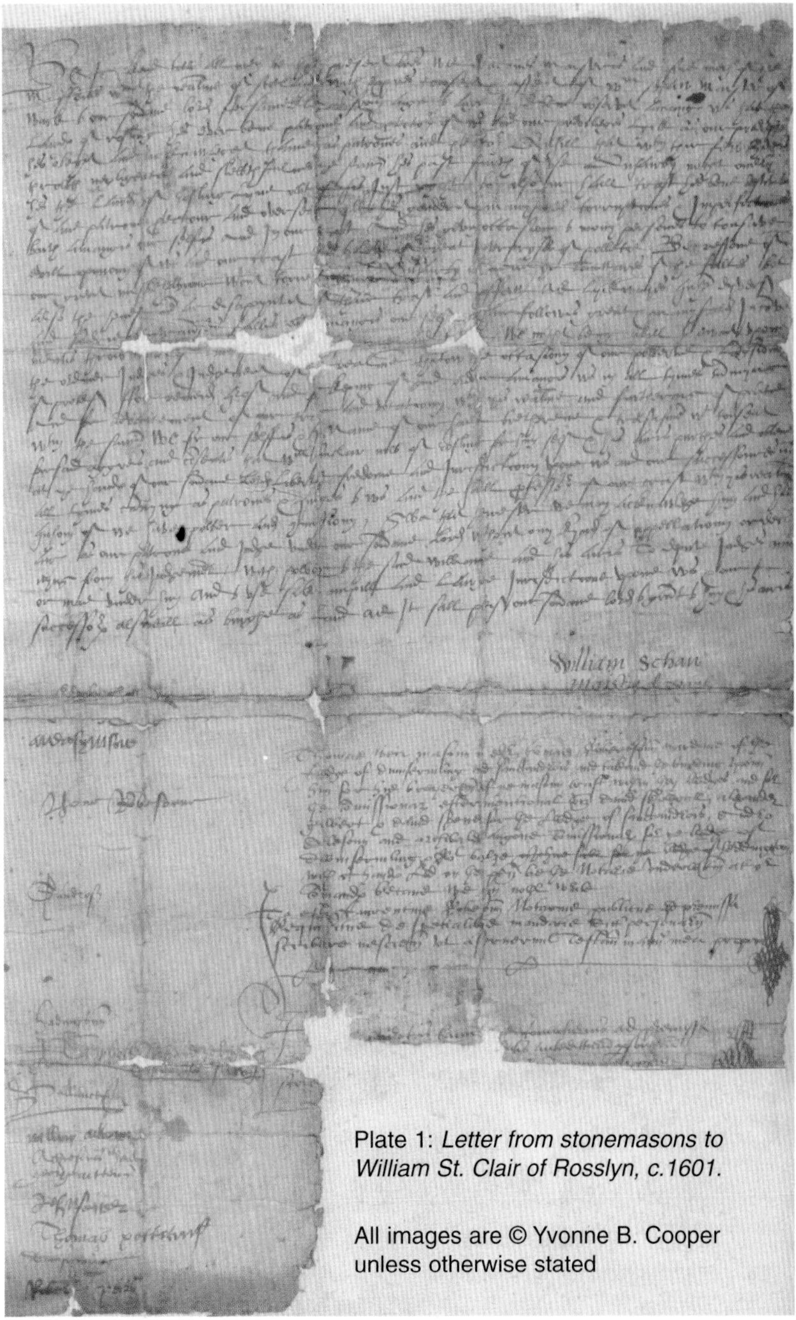

Plate 1: *Letter from stonemasons to William St. Clair of Rosslyn, c.1601.*

All images are © Yvonne B. Cooper unless otherwise stated

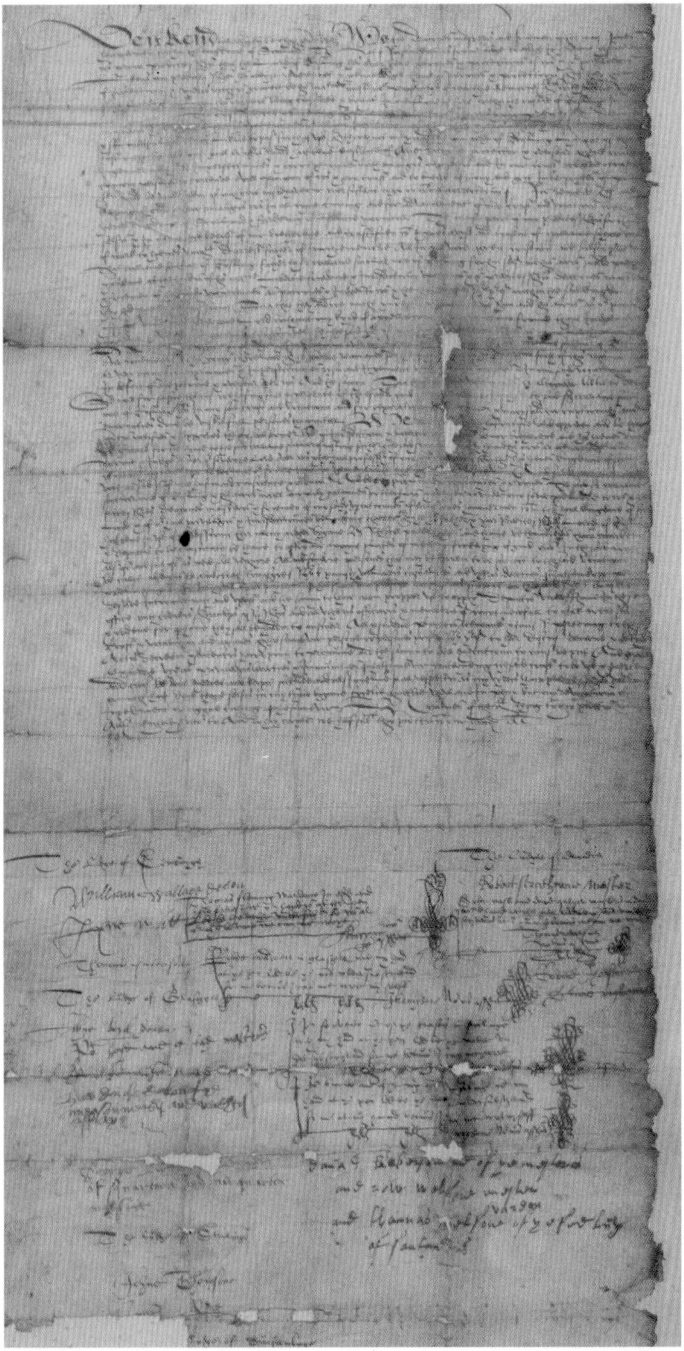

ii

Plate 2: *Letter from stonemasons to William St. Clair of Rosslyn, c.1628.*

Plate 3: *Frontispiece from The Constitutions of the Free – Masons, 1723.*
James Anderson.

Plate 4: *Engraved frontispiece from W. Cheyne's The Free-Mason's Pocket Companion, Edinburgh, 1752.*

Plate 5: *Engraved frontispiece from J. Scott's The Pocket Companion and History of Free-Masons, London, 1754.*

Plate 6 (left): *Portrait of Brother William St. Clair of Rosslyn (1700 – 1778), First Grand Master Mason 1736 – 1737.*

Plate 7 (above): *Engraved frontispiece from Burnes 'A Sketch of the History of the Knights Templars, 1837'.*

Plate 8: *Wine is strong, the king is stronger, Women are stronger, but above all truth conquers. Is this text Masonic?*

Plate 9: *The Lady-chapel or retro-choir showing the Apprentice Pillar to the left. That in the centre is described as the Fellow Craft pillar and that on the left the Master Mason's pillar.*

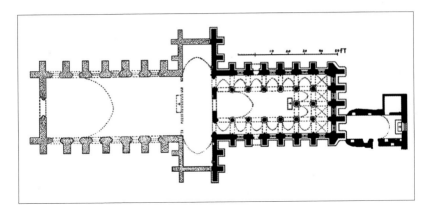

Plate 10 (above):
*Plan of the
foundations of
Rosslyn Chapel
including those
prepared for the nave
and transepts but
which were not built
upon (shaded grey)*

Plate 11 (right):
*Ground plan of
Rosslyn Chapel –
the choir.*

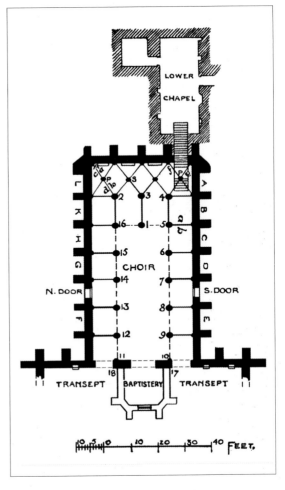

Plate 12 (above): *North aisle of Rosslyn Chapel, looking east, showing a 'straight' arch or a false lintel.*

Plate 13 (right): *The legend of the Apprentice Pillar is integral to the mythology of Rosslyn Chapel*

Plate 14: *Corbel on the west window on the south exterior of the chapel – does this show a Masonic initiation?*

Plate 15: *Carved head of the murdered apprentice – note the mark on the right temple.*

Plate 16:
A pagan symbol?

Plate 17:
18th century engraving of Moses with the 10 Commandments. Note the 'horns'

Plate 18: *The Devil counting the souls he's ensnared?*

Plate 19: *A Knight Templar symbol in Rosslyn Chapel?*

Plate 20: *The death mask of Robert I (1274 – 1329) in Rosslyn* Chapel?

Plate 21: *The heart of Robert the Bruce?*

Plate 22 (left): *Christ symbolised by a crown of thorns – Rosslyn Chapel*

Plate 23 (below): *Christ symbolised by a crown of thorns – St. Mary's, Haddington.*

Plates 24 and 25:
Figures in Masonic postures – therefore Masonic angels!

Plate 26: *Indian Corn? - proof that the Scots, not Columbus, discovered America!*

Plate 27: *Aloe – more proof America was discovered by the Scots!*

Plate 28: *St John the Evangelist - the 'patron saint' of Scottish Freemasonry.*

Plate 29: *The Kirkwall Scroll – a Masonic treasure*

Plate 30
(above): *The
west wall of
Rosslyn
Chapel. Note
the internal
features
such as the
piscina.*

Plate 31:
*The Creation
panel.*

Plate 32 (above): *The Symbolic panel.*

Plate 33 (above right): *The Halleluiah panel.*

Plate 34 (right): *18th engraving depicting Moses' brass serpent.*

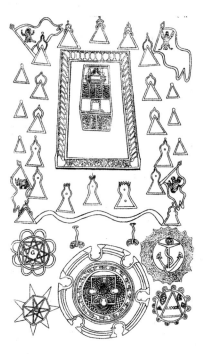

Plate 35: *The Tabernacle in the wilderness – note the tents and standards of the four principle tribes in the corners.*

Plate 36: *18th century engraving of the Tabernacle in the wilderness.*

Plate 37: *The tomb of Hiram Abiff?*

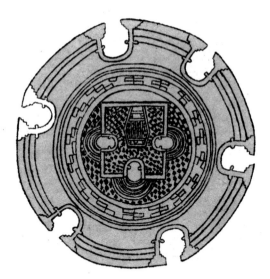

Plate 38: *Armorial bearings of the Ancient's Grand Lodge - copied from Rabbi Leon's work.*

Plate 39: *Panel showing numerous Masonic symbols.*

Plate 40: *Panel showing a multitude of symbols relating to the three Craft degrees.*

Plate 41 (above): *Armorial bearings of the Ancient's Grand Lodge from Ahiman Rezon 1754 by Lawrence Dermott.* © Reproduced by kind permission of The Museum and Library of Freemasonry (London, England)

Plate 42 (right): *Depicting Biblical journeys (Genesis, Exodus and Numbers)*

Plate 43: *Worshiping the Golden Calf.*

Plate 44: *Alleged Templar gravestone at Currie Kirk (Edinburgh).*

Plate 45: *Reverse of alleged Templar gravestone at Currie Kirk.*

Plate 46: *Alleged Templar gravestone at Corstorphine Kirk (Edinburgh).*

Plate 47 (far left): *Does anonymous = Knight Templar?*

Plate 48 (left): *A Knight Templar graveslab?*

Plate 49 (above): *Kilmory Chapel. Alleged KT graveslabs came from a variety of places.*

Plate 50 (right): *Geology of Argyll*

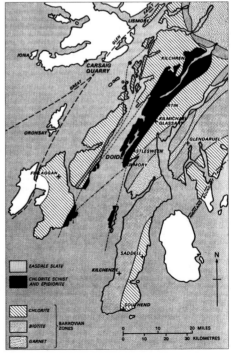

Plate 51: *Proof that Kilmory is a Templar church?*

Plate 52: *Round Church at Little Maplestead – not a Templar church.*

been buried in accordance with the rites of the Roman Church involving a large number of people. It is inconceivable that during 322 years of burials in the vault necessitating the participation of numerous people that it was never explored. Evidence of this is provided by Father Hay who gives an eyewitness account of what he saw when he attended the funeral of his step-father, Sir James St. Clair.

'He was laying in his armour, with a red velvet cap on his head, on a flat stone; nothing was spoiled, except a piece of white furring that went round the cap, and answered to the hinder part of the head. All his predecessors were buried after the same manner in their armour. Late Rosline, my gud father, was the first that was buried in a coffin, against the sentiments of King James the Seventh [of Scotland and the Second of Great Britain (1685–1688, b.1633, d.1701)], *who was then in Scotland, and several other persons well versed in antiquity, to whom my mother would not harken, thinking it beggarly to be buried after that manner. The great expense she was at in burying her husband, occasioned the sumptuary acts which were made in the following Parliament.'*[81]

These Acts of the Scottish Parliament were designed to regulate funeral expenditure and attempted to limit the number of people who could attend any particular funeral. The numbers permitted were determined by the rank of the deceased; for example, only 100 people could be present at the funeral of a nobleman. The Acts also:

'prohibits and discharges the using or carrying of any pencils, banner, and other honours at burials, except only the eight branches to be on the pale, or upon the coffin when there is no pale.'

As has been discussed earlier in this chapter Rosslyn Chapel was built by William St. Clair to fulfil two functions — the saying of prayers for the souls of the family and to serve as a burial place for the mortal remains of individual family members. In this the St. Clairs were not at all unusual as many other families of a similar status did exactly the same. Although there is documentary evidence dating from a few years after the building of the chapel commenced of the function of the chapel. There is also eyewitness testimony from later periods which confirms that, like other secular collegiate churches, the vaults below the chapel were used for the interment of people (see above). The last person to be buried in the family was, appropriately, the last 'true' Rosslyn — William St. Clair. He died on 4 January 1778 and was buried soon thereafter. The funeral was a Masonic one, attended by hundreds of Freemasons from all over Scotland and beyond. Not all could be accommodated in the small St. Clair burial vault below the chapel but the most distinguished members of the Craft were present to see him laid to rest. A special Funeral Lodge was held by the Grand Lodge of Scotland on 14 February 1778 to commemorate the life of the first Grand Master Mason of that Grand Lodge. An oration and music were prepared for that occasion. The oration is reproduced at appendix IX.

Further accounts of access to the burial vaults below the chapel are also noteworthy.

'*In 1837 the slab leading to the burial vault was removed, but as two coffins lay across the inner opening, preventing access to the vault, they were not allowed to be interfered with and the entrance was again closed. Afterwards, in the course of repairing the pavement floor, it was discovered that the arch had been broken, and one of the workmen descended and found a vault built in polished ashlar, arched from east to west, and the two coffins laying across the opening as described. The end of one was let into the side wall, and a considerable quantity of bones were piled against the wall at the back, but no remains of any kind, and no inscription or armorial bearing, could be discovered.*'[82]

Two events — the funeral of the first Grand Master Mason in the St. Clair family vault at Rosslyn Chapel in 1778, witnessed by hundreds, and the later re-opening of the vault in 1837, are extremely important for a number of reasons, especially when taken together with the documentary evidence from the 15th century about the time of the building of the chapel. First and foremost they confirm beyond any doubt that the vaults below the chapel were originally designed as the burial place for members of the St. Clair family. Not only was the vault intended to be used by immediate members of the family but others, connected only by marriage, paid for the privilege of being buried alongside St. Clairs in their family vault. There can be no doubt that the chapel was always intended to be a place of burial and that it was used as such for more than three hundred years. This shows that people regularly entered the vaults below the chapel and that it was 'tidied up' at intervals.[83] As has been detailed above, the first person to be buried in Rosslyn Chapel in a coffin was Sir James St. Clair, in 1706. The only other, and last, burial within the chapel was William St. Clair in 1778 and he too would have been placed in the vault in a coffin. It is likely therefore that these were the two coffins seen in 1837. Prior to 1706 members of the Rosslyn family were interred in the vault either in their armour or, if they had no armour, in shrouds.[84] The bones piled against a wall of the vault are almost certainly of those not buried in coffins.[85]

Given all this activity over hundreds of years it is inconceivable that this would be the location chosen to hide something as important as the Holy Grail; the Ark of the Covenant; the lost writings of Jesus Christ; the 'treasure' of the Knights Templar; the embalmed head of Jesus Christ or the real Stone of Destiny.

The Two St. Johns

The principal saint to which Rosslyn Chapel was dedicated was St. Matthew. This saint was not nearly as popular as others and had very few churches dedicated to him.[86] This may well be another example of William St. Clair making sure that his church stands out from the rest. In addition to St. Matthew, the other saints venerated at the chapel were St. Peter, St. Andrew and the Virgin Mary.[87] Many authors point out that the Battle of Bannockburn was fought on St. John the Baptist's Day, 24 June, and that as this date is important to Freemasons there must be some connection. Unfortunately, the significance of this coincidence is not explained. If, as claimed, Rosslyn Chapel is a Masonic structure then one would expect that the 'Patron Saint' of Freemasonry would be present within the chapel. St. John the Baptist has no presence within the chapel. However, even if this saint was represented in the chapel there is no connection with *Scottish* Freemasonry. St. John the Baptist is associated with the English form of Freemasonry and many Masonic events are held on or around the saint's feast day. The Scottish form of Freemasonry has St. John the Evangelist as its 'Patron Saint'. (Plate 28) The feast day of that saint is 27 December. One must suspect that when given a choice between the two saints, one whose day is in the middle of summer and the other whose day is in the depths of winter there was no doubt which was going to be selected!

In any event, the fact that there are four saints represented at Rosslyn Chapel but the one most closely associated with Scottish Freemasonry is absent does not support the claim that the chapel is in some way 'Masonic'. This point about the two St. Johns serves not only to demonstrate that there are substantial differences between Freemasonry in Scotland and that elsewhere but also to highlight the ignorance of some writers who comment on Scottish Freemasonry as if the Scottish form was the same as everywhere else.

West Wall

There is one consistent, modern, refrain regarding Rosslyn Chapel and that is that it represents something older, contains 'treasures' from earlier times, has elements from other continents, is connected with mysterious groups etc. — in other words it is a major link between modern Scottish Freemasonry and the KT etc. The chapel is cited as evidence which proves that the KT had excavated the underground part of Herod's Temple. This is proof because Rosslyn Chapel is stated to be an exact copy of part of Herod's Temple:

> '*The mission of William St Clair was to recreate the underground vaults of Herod's Temple exactly as Hugues de Payen and the other knights* [templar] *had found them over three hundred years earlier.*'[88]

Although there is no evidence that any members of the Knights Templar excavated below their quarters on the Dome of Rock, granted to them by King Baldwin II of Jerusalem in c.1118, it is not the purpose here to discuss that claim in detail as that has already been done elsewhere. However, the use of Rosslyn Chapel as evidence in support of that unsubstantiated claim is of interest here. Assuming, temporarily and for the purpose of argument only, that foundations of Herod's Temple had been explored by the Knights Templar and that Rosslyn Chapel was *not* an exact replica of that ruined temple then Rosslyn's central position in the Alternative or Popular Approach would collapse.

Whether or not the medieval Order of the Knights Templar actually mounted any excavations below the Dome of the Rock is not the issue but rather it is the belief held by some that Rosslyn Chapel is a replica of Herod's Temple [c.74–c.4 B.C.] that is of interest.[89] The west wall is claimed to be unfinished — deliberately so:

> '*The west wall is incomplete and the obvious normal conclusion is that it was never finished — but there is another reason why single walls remain; they are the remains of a ruined cathedral, or more precisely in this case a ruined temple.*'[90] (original emphasis retained) (Plate 30)

As has been seen earlier, the existence of an outward opening north door suggests that an additional structure, possibly a sacristy, was planned but never built. This is an indication that the chapel was never completed as intended.

However, there is other evidence, particularly in relation to the west wall, which confirms this. A base course, or base moulding, is found near to the bottom of the external walls of the chapel and a sill moulding is situated below the widow sills, and which returns around the building. This is a common device in medieval church architecture and was partly decorative and partly functional in that it was intended to help shed water from the walls. Such a base course is not required on internal walls and the base and sill courses do not continue where the interior wall of the incomplete transepts begin — the west wall — indicating that it was designed as an internal wall. The wall was intended to be the internal wall of the transepts and although unfinished it is part of an incomplete Christian church of a design typical of the period. (see ground plan — Plate 10) The wall also contains elements such as piscinas in which the priest would wash his hands as well as rinsing the chalice at the celebration of the mass. The existence of piscinas further shows that the wall was to be an internal wall. Piscinas are an entirely Christian feature which would not have existed in Herod's Temple. They are an internal feature. Additionally the wall has three doorways which would have given access from the transepts to the north and south side aisles as well as the central aisle via a large central door. These doorways were subsequently blocked up. Some authors have simply assumed that the chapel as it appears today was all that was built. The time taken to complete the foundations (about four years, 1446–1450) has attracted comment as that seems an inordinate length of time for such a small structure.[91] Strangely, very few modern authors appear to be aware that the foundations of the rest of the planned church exist and have on more than one occasion been uncovered and drawn.[92] However, the existence of the foundations of the remainder of the intended building explains the time taken. More importantly the existence of foundations for transepts and nave, together with other elements mentioned above, show that the building was designed as a typical medieval church. How the church would have looked had the foundations been used quite clearly show its Christian design.[93] The revelation of the existence of the un-used foundations destroys the argument that it is a deliberate copy of Herod's Jewish Temple.

Oliver Cromwell and Rosslyn Chapel

Rosslyn Chapel was not destroyed when Oliver Cromwell (1599–1658) invaded Scotland in 1650 because it is claimed, he was a Freemason, a Grand Master no less, he knew that the chapel was Masonic:

'*Scotland was a focus of Cromwell's wrath, where he destroyed Royalist*

Castles and Catholic [sic] churches wherever he found the opportunity. As
we saw earlier, the Masonic shrine at Rosslyn was known for what it was
to both Cromwell and General George Monk and therefore survived the
war intact.'[94] and,

'*When General Monk arrived with his troopers after the victory at*
Dunbar, he reduced most of Rosslyn Castle to ruins . . .[95] *General Monk*
had his horses stabled in the chapel but refrained from purging it by fire
and hammer, and made no attempt to break into the vaults. The most
convincing reason for this is that the Lords High Protector himself, Oliver
Cromwell, had studied at the Temple in London, was a Master Mason in
England, and knew that the Sinclairs were Hereditary Grand Master
Masons of Scotland and that the chapel housed Masonic mysteries.'[96, 97]

These two quotes reveal an interesting line of reasoning and one that has been
taken up by others. Because the chapel was not damaged in any way by General
George Monck (1608–1670) this must mean that Cromwell knew that it was a
Masonic building. If he knew it was a Masonic building then that could only be
because he was a Freemason. Because Rosslyn is such a special Masonic building
only a special kind of Freemason would have known this and so Cromwell must
have been a Grand Master. The first quote above would suggest that both were
Freemasons. Logically that argument in the second quote would suggest that
Monck (who went to Roslin) was a Freemason and that Cromwell (who did not
go there) was not a Freemason.[98]

It is worth examining the facts in an attempt to shed some light on this matter.
There is no evidence, other than the above assumption, that Cromwell (or Monck
for that matter) was a Freemason. There are no records of him being admitted to
a Lodge and he made no mention, at any time, of Freemasonry or of being a
Freemason. The Battle of Dunbar was fought 2–3 September 1650 and although
the capital, Edinburgh, was secured the castle held out until 24 December. The
hinterland was a major problem for Cromwell, with moss-troopers using castles
such as Dalhousie, Borthwick, Tantallon, Dirleton and Roslin from which to harry
the English forces. Cromwell did not go to Rosslyn, moving instead against the
much more important and stronger fortification at Borthwick. After taking
Dirleton on 8 November Monck and John Lambert (*c*.1619–1684) divided their
forces. The following day Lambert went on to meet Cromwell at Borthwick with
one or both of the mortars used to take Dirleton. Monck moved to attack Roslin

Castle which surrendered within a few days. The garrison consisted of 26 men. Cromwell was interested only in centres of resistance. As soon as a strongpoint was taken he moved onto another. Rosslyn Chapel like others in Mid and East Lothian were not attacked because they had no military significance. The suggestion that Cromwell did not destroy Rosslyn Chapel because it was Masonic logically means that all the other churches ('Catholic' or otherwise) in Scotland that he did not destroy were also 'Masonic'!

Seton Collegiate Church, 10 miles from Rosslyn, is an excellent example. Not only was it erected for the same purposes as Rosslyn Chapel and at almost the same time (1470) but the Countess of Winton was known to be a Roman Catholic and did not attempt to hide the fact. Her even-handed treatment of people on Scottish and English sides of the conflict gained her the admiration of Cromwell who sent her 1,000 prisoners as a present. Seton Collegiate Church was not destroyed by Cromwell.

Rosslyn Chapel is here again used out of context to support a particular claim — that Cromwell was a Freemason. When the chapel is not considered in isolation but as part of the events in Scotland at the time, other more obvious reasons why it was not damaged by Cromwell become clear.[99]

Pilgrimage

There have been claims that Rosslyn Chapel was a place of pilgrimage during the medieval period.[100] That the chapel was a place of pilgrimage is based on the observation that the steps leading to the sacristy were worn, indicating that a large number of people had used the steps over a long period of time. This suggestion was made in order to support recent claims that Rosslyn Chapel houses the Holy Grail. But worn steps can hardly be taken as proof that the chapel was a place of pilgrimage. However, as has been discussed above, Rosslyn Chapel was built by, and for, a particular family and was therefore private — for the use of the St. Clair family only. It would not have been open to ordinary people. Scottish pilgrimage routes are well known and are described in a number of places.[101] Rosslyn Chapel is not mentioned at any time as a place of pilgrimage nor is there any record of a holy relic in the chapel to which pilgrims would travel to venerate. Equally there is no contemporary evidence of any pilgrims actually visiting Rosslyn Chapel. If there was a relic of the significance of the Holy Grail at Rosslyn Chapel then pilgrims would have flocked there in their tens of thousands leaving plenty of evidence of that activity. There is no such evidence.

Design

The arrangement of the pillars in the chapel is cited as a feature which shows that it the only one of its kind — in Scotland at least. Numerous authors have speculated where and with whom the design of Rosslyn Chapel originated. Father Hay, in claiming that the builder had ' ...*caused artificers to be brought from other regions and forraigne kingdoms*' may well have led some to believe that the chapel was following a foreign design.[102] However, one does not require to look too far for the inspiration of the design of Rosslyn Chapel. St. Mungo's Cathedral, Glasgow, was begun in the late 12th century by Bishop Jocelyn and was largely completed by the end of the 13th century, although there is clear evidence of work continuing into the 14th century. The cathedral was therefore complete long before Rosslyn Chapel was begun. St. Mungo's has two levels known as the upper and lower church. The east ends of both levels have several similarities with the east end of Rosslyn Chapel not least of which is '*The ground outside falling sharply to the east...*'[103] The ground plan of the lower church also shows a number of similarities with Rosslyn Chapel. In terms of general layout both have a central aisle with side aisles to the north and south. The side aisles have access doors as at Rosslyn Chapel. It is the east end which shows the most striking similarities with Rosslyn. Both have the same arrangement of two rows of three piers. This retro-choir arrangement is identical in both churches, albeit that St. Mungo's Cathedral is on a much larger scale. The separation of the 'retro-choir' in the cathedral is marked by six steps but only one at Rosslyn. Four bays in the east wall are present in each building, although the saints to which the altars are dedicated in the cathedral are different from those at Rosslyn.[104] As has been noted above, Rosslyn Chapel was not a place of pilgrimage but St. Mungo's Cathedral was. In 1451 a few years after the building of Rosslyn Chapel had commenced, Pope Nicholas V (1447–1455, b.1397) issued a degree that a pilgrimage to the cathedral, specifically the shrine of St. Kentigern, was equal to a pilgrimage to Rome itself. There is no equivalent in respect of Rosslyn Chapel.

This brief comparison between two Scottish structures shows that Rosslyn Chapel is not unique in Scotland, certainly in terms of design, but this can only be revealed if the chapel is placed within its ecclesiastical and historical context. A comparative approach enables the chapel to be assessed holistically — something that all too often is not done.

Conclusion

Any evidence used to support a hypothesis or to prove a particular theory must be placed in context. Rosslyn Chapel is one piece of evidence that is nearly always taken out of context and considered in isolation. This has the effect of making it appear as if it is the only such building of its type in Scotland. When placed in its Scottish historical and ecclesiastical context it becomes clear that the building was a normal part of medieval church organisation. In considering Rosslyn Chapel in isolation a distorted view of Scottish history, and the chapel's place in it, is presented. This chapter and this book are an attempt to correct that distorted view.

The building of Rosslyn Chapel appears to have ceased soon after the death of William St. Clair in *c*.1484. His son, Oliver (?–*c*.1520), did not continue the work but was content simply to provide the building with a roof.[105] This means that the structure was only made weather proof sometime *after* 1484. Consequently much of the interior carving would not have been put in place until after that time as to have done otherwise would have meant that the most delicate and expensive carvings, statues, etc. would have been left open to the elements. Most, if not all, of the internal decoration, therefore, dates from after the death of the builder. The quality of carving provides some indication of this as the best are found in the east end of the choir (also known as the retro-choir or Lady Chapel), some of which is excellent. This part of the chapel was the first to be built and as, unlike the rest of the chapel, it does not bear the clerestory level and would probably have had its own roof soon after being built, it was the first part to be decorated with carvings, probably from designs made by William St. Clair. However, the quality of stonework progressively deteriorates from east to west. This supports the view that although Oliver St. Clair did not complete the building as laid out by his father, he did decorate the interior of the chapel once he had made it weather proof by adding a roof to the main structure. Oliver St. Clair may not have shared the entire vision of his father but he did at least complete the building much as it now stands.[106]

The nature of the decorative carvings reveals something very important — they were not, and are not, part of the fabric of the building. That is, the carvings are not carved from the stone which makes up the 'skeleton' of the building. The carvings have been added *after* the skeleton or basic structure was complete. It was a skeleton, or shell, to which the carvings have been 'glued'. This method of adding decoration is described as 'basso-relievo' or '*appliqué*'.[107] Because these carvings were added after the basic structure was completed there is no way of knowing exactly when any particular carving was put in place. Adding carvings did, however, continue a very long time after the shell was erected. An engraving from 1852 gives a view of the north aisle. (Plate 12) One of the so-called 'straight arches' can clearly be seen and is shown to be incomplete.[108] The 'straight arches' within Rosslyn Chapel are not load bearing and are merely a decorative device. The engraving shows that the 'straight arch' does not completely cover the load-bearing arch, although today this is now hidden. To claim, because the chapel was begun in 1446, that all its carvings also date from that year is obviously incorrect. The carvings may have been added almost anytime after the building was begun.

The myth of a Knight Templar connection with modern Scottish Freemasonry was outlined at the beginning of this book. Many popular writers use Rosslyn Chapel as a crucial piece of evidence in a vain effort to prove such a link. In attempting to do so the chapel has been 'de-Christianised' and re-interpreted as being Masonic and/or Knight Templar as well as pagan, Jewish or Celtic. However, of the thousands of carvings in the chapel only a very small percentage are used to argue that it is Masonic, or pagan or Jewish and the remainder are not discussed at all. The 'un-discussed' carvings represent 98% of the total and only 2% are used to 'de-Christianise' the chapel.[109]

It is worth again emphasising that there are no Masonic symbols to be found within Rosslyn Chapel. The origin and development of Masonic symbolism is closely allied to Masonic ritual and its origin and development. None of that symbolism is to be found within Rosslyn Chapel. Instead the Alternative or Popular school misunderstand what is symbolism and what are merely carvings. This fundamental misunderstanding means that simply decorative carvings have been reinterpreted as being Masonic but that does not *make* them Masonic. All the above examples are reinterpretations of the chapel and its carvings etc., which are based on the assumption that the building is something other than a collegiate church. From the above discussion it does seem obvious that claims that the chapel is either pagan, Masonic or Jewish are incorrect and that the symbolism in the chapel cannot be interpreted from any of these perspectives.

The most shocking thing to have been discovered is that the fabric of the building has been deliberately altered, apparently to make it 'fit' the myth. The carving of the head of what is now called the 'apprentice head' was not originally carved with a deep gash. That was added 400 years later. A beard and moustache have also been removed. This would have required someone to climb a ladder and, using a hammer and chisel, remove (none too skillfully) the beard and added a gash to the right temple. When that was done is also unknown. It is unlikely that the person or persons responsible will ever now be identified but it does indicate

the lengths to which some people will go to make sure their version of history is
the only accepted version.

[1] *'Court, Kirk and Community — Scotland 1470–1625.'* Jenny Wormald. p. 86
[2] *The New Book of Constitutions*, 1738. p. 82 *et seq.*
[3] *The New Book of Constitutions*, 1738. p. 2.
[4] *The New Constitutions*, 1738. pp. 88–89.
[5] For the circumstances surrounding the writing of the 'Oration' and a discussion
as to whether it was ever presented see: *'Andrew Michael Ramsay and his
Masonic Oration'*, by Lisa Kahler. *Heredom*. Vol. 1. Washington D.C. 1993.
[6] Cochrane (the now more common spelling of his surname) is a controversial
figure. He has been variously described as 'a mason's apprentice' and James
III's Prime Minister. He was neither but was the son of William de Cochrane of
Paisley and studied architecture in Italy. His building of the Great Hall at
Stirling Castle gained him close and influential contact with the king — much
to the annoyance of the nobility. Whether he was ever actually made Earl of
Mar is unclear but in 1482 he, along with William Rogers, a musician, and a
number of others, was lynched and hung from Lauder Bridge by a party of
nobles led by Archibald 'Bell-the-Cat' — Archibald being Douglas, Earl of
Angus, and the 'cat' being Cochrane.
[7] According to Anderson's chronology St. Clair could only have been Grand
Master from 1437 to 1453, at most, because he was succeeded by the Bishop of
Glasgow who died in 1454. This also demonstrates that St. Clair's position of
Grand Master, had it existed, was not hereditary.
[8] *An account of the chapel of Roslin – 1778.* Edited by Cooper Robert L. D.
[9] This contradicts Anderson's claim that only one St. Clair had been a Grand
Master (William, the builder of the Chapel) and that the position was not
hereditary. See: *The New Book of Constitutions*, 1738. pp. 88–89. It is important
also to note that Hay does not claim any member of the St. Clair family to have
been a Grand Master.
[10] Scott spells 'Roslin' in this way.
[11] The poem covers 150 years and concerns a border feud. Scott's description of
Melrose Abbey led to Melrose becoming a major tourist attraction. This was
also true to a lesser extent in respect of Rosslyn Chapel.
[12] Almost exactly 200 years since it was first written the *Lay of the Last Minstrel*
repays reading although the language and metre may be a little difficult to
master at first. At the time of writing there is an online version available at:
http://www.theotherpages.org/poems/minstrel.html
[13] The footnote inserted here is: Thory, *Acta Latomorum*, vol. 2, pp. 15 ff.
Gould, *History of Freemasonry*, vol. 2 p. 383.
[14] *'Holy Blood and Holy Grail'* by Baigent, Leigh and Lincoln. p. 152.
[15] e.g. *The Illustrated Guide to Rosslyn Chapel &C.* 1892 and published (2003)

as an 18th edition by Masonic Publishing Co. Ltd.

[16] For some authors none of these are mutually exclusive!

[17] This can also be considered to be part of the process of de-Christianisation — by removing the building from any other context.

[18] There were probably several more, records of which no longer exist. *Medieval Religious Houses — Scotland*. Cowan, Ian B. and Easson, David E. 2nd Edition. 1976.

[19] The former was St. Mary's on the Rock (St. Andrews) and the latter, Holy Rood (Stirling).

[20] Dunrossness (Shetland).

[21] Collegiate churches were a European phenomenon throughout the medieval period but here I am only concerned with the situation in Scotland.

[22] For example, in England and Wales there were approximately 210 secular collegiate churches which existed for a longer period than those in Scotland.

[23] This was certainly true of Scotland.

[24] Obviously if one had led a totally evil life then no amount of prayers would remove one from Hell.

[25] *Genealogie of the Sainteclaires of Rosslyn*. Ed. Cooper, Robert L. D. The Grand Lodge of Scotland. 2002. p.27.

[26] *Medieval Religious Houses — Scotland*. Cowan, Ian B. and Easson, David E. 2nd Edition. 1976.

[27] *Genealogie of the Sainteclaires of Rosslyn*. Ed. Cooper, Robert L. D. The Grand Lodge of Scotland. 2002. p. 91 *et seq*.

[28] *Theatrum Scotiæ*. Slezer, John. London. 1693.

[29] *The Illustrated Guide to Rosslyn Chapel &C*. p. 47.

[30] Some church income was diverted to the collegiate church but this does not alter the fact that the chapel was private property. *The Books of Assumption of the Thirds of Benefices — Scottish Ecclesiastical Rentals at the Reformation*. Edited by James Kirk. pp. 116–117.

[31] See the 'Charter of John Robeson, Provost of Roslin, 1571 in: *Genealogie of the Sainteclaires of Rosslyn*. Ed. Cooper, Robert L. D. The Grand Lodge of Scotland. 2002. p. 146 *et seq*.

[32] *Genealogie of the Sainteclaires of Rosslyn*. Ed. Cooper, Robert L. D. The Grand Lodge of Scotland. 2002. p.124 *et seq*.

[33] *An Account of the Chapel of Roslin — 1778*, p. 31.

[34] The chapel also conforms to other general principles for ecclesiastical buildings of the time. It is, for example, oriented east–west.

[35] Would he ever have imagined the thousands of tourists paying to see his church?

[36] *Contribution to the Critique of Hegel's Philosophy of Right*. Karl Marx. Deutsch-Französische Jahrbücher. 1844.

[37] This also implies that the original interpretation was, and remains, the correct interpretation.

[38] Symbols often have more than one meaning and use and so the 'symbolism of numbers' is not restricted to the number 2.

[39] Freemasonry doubtless used other sources and invented some but the majority

were adopted from Christianity.

40 The swastika was used by many other cultures and countries including China, Japan and Native Americans.

41 *The Second Messiah*. Knight, Christopher and Lomas, Robert. London. 1997. p. 149.

42 See *The Airlie MS* in AQC. Vol. 117. October 2005.

43 *Genealogie of the Sainteclaires of Rosslyn*. Ed. Cooper, Robert L. D. The Grand Lodge of Scotland. 2002. p. 27.

44 See, for example, *The Templar Legacy & The Masonic Inheritance within Rosslyn Chapel*. Tim Wallace-Murphy. p. 33.

45 If one was to ask the 'man in the street' what he understood the term 'the masons' to mean the answer will almost always be 'Oh, you mean the Freemasons.'

46 The capitalisation, emphasis and punctuation are reproduced as far as is possible.

47 *An Account of the Chapel of Roslin &C*. The Edinburgh Magazine. Jan. 1761. Separately printed 1774 and 1778.

48 *An Account of the Chapel of Roslin, 1778*. p. 28

49 *Scotland Illustrated in a Series of Eighty Views*. 1845

50 *The Baronial and Ecclesiastical Antiquities of Scotland*. 1852 Rosslyn Chapel, p. 2.

51 *The Sword and the Grail*. Sinclair, Andrew. 1993. p. 86

52 The Fellow Craft Pillar is occasionally referred to as the Journeyman Pillar. See: *The Templar Legacy...* Fig. 25.

53 For an analysis and comparison of these earliest rituals see, for example, *The Airlie MS 1705*, Cooper, Robert L. D. and Kahler, Dr. Lisa. *Ars Quatuor Coronatorum*, Vol. 117 (2004) pub. October 2005. pp. 83–102.

54 One must suspect that the legend of the murdered apprentice also exists in association with other buildings of which I am unaware.

55 These were the second set of Commandments, the first set having been broken by Moses in anger at the people's worship of the Golden Calf.

56 The King James Authorized Version. Most Protestant Bibles do not mention Moses as having horns.

57 *The Douay-Rheims Bible* (1568) which was a translation of the Latin Vulgate of St. Jerome. The latter had been in use since it was translated by the saint during AD 382-390.

58 *The Templar Legacy & The Masonic Inheritance within Rosslyn Chapel*. Tim Wallace-Murphy. The Friends of Rosslyn. nd. Fig. 11.

59 This symbol was used by the church prior to the 9th century but it was from *c*.820 that it became a prominent and frequently used symbol.

60 Repeated in very similar terms in John 1:36.

61 The Master of the Temple, William de la More, used this seal attached to a document making a grant of land in Yorkshire.

62 *The Templar Legacy . . .* p. 22.

63 *The Sword and the Grail*. Sinclair, Andrew. 1993. Plate 10 between pp. 150–151.

[64] The speculative comment becomes fact about a year later in *The Templar Legacy & The Masonic Inheritance within Rosslyn Chapel*. The Friends of Rosslyn. No date but 1994–1995.

[65] Brian Hill's reconstruction of Robert I is now with the Scottish National Portrait Gallery.

[66] Guilds are generally referred to in Scotland as Incorporations. The first Incorporations were created, as such, in 1475. They never had officials with the title 'Grand Master'.

[67] The origins and development of the Incorporations of Scotland have been well researched and documented. What the term 'Masonic Guild' means in unknown.

[68] *Rosslyn Chapel*. Rosslyn, Earl of. 1997. p. 31.

[69] Devotion to the Sacred Heart is particularly associated with the Benedictine and mystic writer, St. Gertrude (1256–1302).

[70] *The Templar Legacy* . . . Fig. 20

[71] *Rosslyn Chapel*. Rosslyn, Earl of. 1997. p. 55.

[72] When one is aware that prior to *c*.1720 there were only two Masonic ceremonies this becomes even more apparent.

[73] The main altar in the chapel was dedicated to St. Matthew. *The Genealogie* . . . p. xvi.

[74] The proponents of this claim omit to mention that Vikings were probably the first Europeans in America.

[75] *The Hiram Key*. Knight, Christopher and Lomas, Robert. 1996. p. 302. This was one of the first claims that these carving were of maize. The authors quote a casual conversation with the wife of a botanist.

[76] Aloe is not a cactus but is, in fact, a succulent.

[77] A detailed examination of this story, intriguing as it is, is beyond the scope of this present book. The origins of this particular story have been examined in: *The Voyages of the Venetian Brothers Nicolò & Antonio Zeno to the Northern Seas in the XIVth Century*, edited by Robert L. D. Cooper.

[78] There are several authors who provide some details of this voyage. See as an example: *The Hiram Key*. Knight and Lomas. p. 302.

[79] *Inventory of Monuments and Constructions in the Counties of Midlothian and West Lothian*. RCAHMS. Edinburgh. 1929. p. 105.

[80] It is quite likely also that less important individuals, including children, would also have been interred in the vault.

[81] *Genealogie of the Sainteclaires of Rosslyn*. Ed. Cooper, Robert L. D. The Grand Lodge of Scotland. 2002. p. 154.

[82] These Acts appear to have been ineffective.

[83] *The Collegiate Church or Chapel of Rosslyn, its Builders, Architect, and Construction*. Kerr, Andrew. Proceedings of the Society of Antiquaries. Vol. XII (1877). p. 240.

[84] That bones were seen piled against a wall of the vault and that no armour was found further confirms this.

[85] Those who were not the head of the family would have no armour and would have been buried in shrouds.

[86] Out of the thousands of churches in Great Britain only a handful are dedicated

to this saint.

[87] See the *Genealogie of the Sainteclaires of Rosslyn*. p. 124, *et seq.*

[88] *The Hiram Key*. Knight and Lomas. pp. 307-8.

[89] That the Knights Templar did carry out such excavations is based on an assumption — that because they suddenly became very wealthy and powerful, during the period they were quartered on the Dome of the Rock, they must have discovered a significant treasure. See, for example, *The Hiram Key* and *The Sign and the Seal*.

[90] *The Hiram Key*. p. 310.

[91] *The Hiram Key*. p. 307.

[92] *Inventory of Monuments and Constructions in the Counties of Midlothian and West Lothian*. RCAHMS. Edinburgh. 1929. p. 100.

[93] The original guidebook of the chapel contains a drawing of what the chapel may have looked like had the foundations been used. See: *The Illustrated Guide to Rosslyn Chapel &C*. p. 6.

[94] *The Hiram Key* by Knight and Lomas. p. 345.

[95] Rosslyn Castle was not attacked until more than two months after the battle at Dunbar.

[96] *The Secret Scroll* by Andrew Sinclair. p. 172.

[97] He was not made Lord High Protector until more than two years after General Monck attacked Roslin Castle.

[98] Anderson who claimed virtually everyone important was a Freemason but does not claim Cromwell or Monck to be Freemasons.

[99] The idea that Cromwell was a Freemason originated with Abbé Larudan in his *Les Francés-Maçons Écrasés* of 1746. The claim was made almost 100 years after the event and he provides no supporting evidence. Larudan was an anti-Mason in the mould of Barruel and Robison.

[100] *An Illustrated Guide Book to Rosslyn Chapel*. Tim Wallace-Murphy. 1993. p. 21.

[101] *Pilgrimage in Medieval Scotland*. Historic Scotland. Yeoman, Peter. Edinburgh. 1998

[102] *Genealogie of the Sainteclaires of Rosslyn*. p. 27.

[103] *A Walk through Glasgow Cathedral*. Morris, William J. Glasgow. 1995. p. 27.

[104] The 'bays' in the cathedral are large enough to be small chapels containing altars. These were dedicated to St. Andrew; St. John the Evangelist; St. Nicholas and St. Peter and St. Paul. *A Walk through Glasgow Cathedral*. Morris, William J. Glasgow. 1995. p. 33.

[105] *Genealogie of the Sainteclaires of Rosslyn*. Ed. Cooper, Robert L. D. The Grand Lodge of Scotland. 2002. p. 107. Oliver St. Clair did not, therefore, use the foundations laid by his father for the remainder of the church — transepts and nave.

[106] The carvings in the retro-choir are thought to have been place there by William St, Clair. The carvings in the central and side aisles are not of the same quality and are suggestive of Oliver's lack of interest in completing his father's design.

[107] This simply means 'applied'.

[108] '*The Baronial and Ecclesiastical Antiquities of Scotland*' by Robert W, Billings. Edinburgh. 1852

[109] Some, perhaps uncharitably, call this '*cherry picking the evidence*'. That is, only using evidence that supports a particular interpretation and disregarding the rest without other material being mentioned, let alone discussed.

Chapter 7
The Kirkwall Scroll

A Masonic Treasure

The gap between the official suppression of the KT in 1312 and the first manifestation of a Scottish Masonic Order of the same name in 1787 means that 475 years between one event and the other requires to be bridged by providing evidence of a 'Templar survival.' Failure to provide such evidence would mean that the claim of such a 'survival' is unsustainable. More extreme proponents prefer to rely on the *belief* of the existence of an 'underground stream of knowledge' that links the two periods and for which evidence is not required.[1, 2] Those of the Popular, or Alternative, view do not attempt to find contemporary evidence in support of their hypothesis for two reasons: firstly, it is claimed that such evidence has been deliberately destroyed or hidden (often in some kind of 'code') and, secondly, that those who allegedly 'continued' the Order of the KT did so in secret and therefore made sure that there were no 'traces' that could be discovered by those (often described as 'enemies') attempting to acquire their 'secrets'. This is the classic 'conspiracy theory' claim in another guise as discussed in the first chapter. The Kirkwall Scroll (hereafter referred to as the 'scroll') has recently been pressed into service as one such piece of 'evidence' to aid in filling the 475-year gap.[3] This way of approaching history, as previously explained, is at odds with normal academic standards because the search is made for evidence which serves one purpose only — to promote a particular point of view to the exclusion of all others. This intent is, in itself, an attempt to restrict and divert all thought, discussion and investigation into one particular direction — that of the writer concerned. This is an example of a 'leading question' discussed in the first chapter.

There have been some unusual claims as to the origin and purpose of the scroll made, it appears, to make it fit particular ideas.[4] One of the main contentions is that the scroll is a Knight Templar 'treasure map' and which '. . . *proves how the secret wisdom of the Middle East passed through the Templar Order into all the crafts and guilds of Europe*' and '*We discover a priceless Secret Scroll and treasure map, which finally proves how the Templars entered the Masons forever*'.[5] As is often the case only small parts of the evidence (in the case the scroll) are used in support of a particular contention and no complete analysis of the scroll has been offered from a Scottish Masonic point of view. The purpose here is to do that and, in the process, explain the scroll's origin and purpose.

Physical description of the scroll:

The Kirkwall Scroll 18' 6" x 5' 6" (5.53m x 1.68m) consists of a main panel with two side panels sown onto the central panel. (see Plate 29) The material is linen and the artist(s) used oils to paint the various symbols etc. The style is most definitely naïve. The dominant colour of the central panel is blue and the only part of the scroll where there is any attempt to replicate true to life colours is in the top panel where trees are brown, the sea is green, the earth a reddish brown, the human figure and the fish are pink, and the hills or mountains are dark brown.[6]

Even a cursory examination of the scroll confirms a biblical basis for much of the scroll's content. Like those who have provided a pseudo-Masonic interpretation of a variety of documents and artefacts, the original ownership and purpose of such places or documents are often either unknown or ignored. It has been seen previously that few modern writers discuss the chapel from a Christian point of view and nor has there been an examination of the Kirkwall Scroll from a Christian and/or Masonic perspective. This chapter will therefore discuss the known history and origins of the scroll and give a Masonic interpretation of the artefact.

Previous commentators discussed the scroll's central panel from the 'top down' and I shall follow that convention. The side panels will be considered separately. Although it is not possible to discuss every one of the numerous symbols and images packed into the scroll, the most important will be examined as a means to explaining the origin and purpose of the scroll.

First or Creation Panel

In the beginning God created the heaven and the earth (Genesis 1:1) The first images in the central 'panel' of the Kirkwall Scroll consists of the Sun (left); the Name of God in Hebrew characters (הוהי) within a Glory (centre) and the Moon surrounded by seven stars.[7] (Plate 31) (Creation Panel) The remarkable similarity of the first part of the frontispiece of the KJV bible (Fig. 13) and the same elements in the Creation Panel of the scroll confirm almost beyond doubt that the artist, if he did not directly copy from the frontispiece, was familiar with this image. In the frontispiece the Sun is at the left, the Moon (surrounded by seven stars) is at the right and in the centre is the Name of God in Hebrew characters. The sequence of symbols is therefore the same in both. As one of the purposes of this chapter is to determine the date of the scroll, the use of the KJV bible of 1611 is a significant starting point.

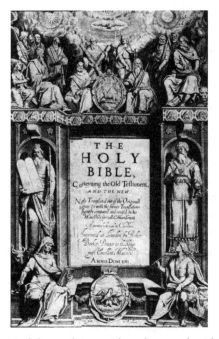

Fig. 12: *Frontispiece of the King James authorised version of the bible 1611.*

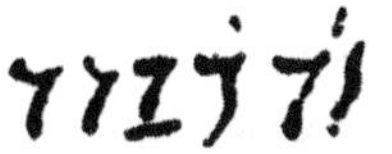

יהוה

Fig.13: *The Name of God from the Creation Panel of the Kirkwall Scroll*

And the earth was without form, and void; and darkness was upon the face of the deep. And the Spirit of God moved upon the face of the waters (Gen. 1:2). The dark, irregular mass at the left, and below the Sun etc., represents pre-creation chaos and the matter from which God created the universe and more particularly the earth which was *without form*. In representing this, the artist has succeeded rather well. Immediately below the Sun, Moon etc. are a series of wavy lines indicating the waters mentioned above:

> '*And God said, Let there be a firmament in the midst of the waters and let it divide the waters from the waters* (Gen. 1:6). *And God made the firmament, and divided the waters from the waters which were above the firmament; and it was so.*' (Gen. 1:7).

The next step, as described in Genesis, was therefore the creation of land and sea and is confirmed by Gen. 1:9: *And God said, Let the waters under the heaven be gathered together unto one place, and let the dry land appear; and it was so.* In the Kirkwall Scroll this is shown not only by the waves previously mentioned but more specifically by the range of rolling hills. Immediately below these is an area also referred to in Genesis.

> '*And God said, Let the waters bring forth abundantly the moving*
> *creatures that hath life, and fowl . . .*' (Gen. 1:20) and,
> *And God created great whales and every living thing that moveth . . . and*
> *every winged fowl...* ' (Gen. 1:21)

The artist has illustrated these verses by showing the sea as being populated by
sea creatures and the land with assorted animals. To make the division between
land and sea clear, the artist has drawn straight lines between the sea and land.

The Kirkwall Scroll does not attempt to be a comprehensive depiction of the
first chapter of Genesis but is an artist's interpretation of some of the principal
elements. The first panel does not follow the exact order of events as presented in
Genesis. For example: '*And God made two great lights; the greater light to rule*
the day, and the lesser light to rule the night: he made the stars also' (Gen. 1:16).[8]
This is represented by the first part of the panel — the Sun, Moon and (seven)
stars, and as it also referred to God (the Name of God is the central and most
prominent symbol) creating the heavens and the earth, the artist has been able to
illustrate two verses from the first chapter of Genesis with one set of images.[9] In
a similar manner the human figure is intended to represent Adam:

> '*And God said, Let us make man in our image, after our likeness: and let*
> *them have dominion over the fish of the sea, and over the fowl of the air,*
> *and over the cattle and over all the earth* (Gen. 1:26).

The posture of Adam is that of exercising dominion over the animals as indicated
by his outstretched arm. The first panel of the Kirkwall Scroll relates entirely to
the first chapter of Genesis and therefore to the six days of creation.

Second or Symbolic Panel

At first glance this panel has little to do with the preceding one which dealt
exclusively with the Old Testament book of Genesis (see Plate 32). There are 30
symbols in this panel; one 'group' of four, possibly five, symbols at the right
centre edge are considered to be one symbol or a very closely related set of
symbols. Before discussing this panel, or any other material which apparently
includes Masonic symbols, it is necessary to refer again to the origin and
development of Masonic ritual from which Masonic symbolism takes its rise. As
previously discussed with reference to Rosslyn Chapel, the earliest known
Masonic ritual is dated 1696 — the Edinburgh Register House MS. Other

closely related texts date from soon after.[10] These early rituals were simple by comparison to those in use today, and as a consequence the ceremonies were of short duration. This is a crucial point in understanding Masonic symbolism. As the first ceremonies were short and simple they could not have generated large numbers of different symbols.[11] In Scotland, lodge records exist from 1599 and none make reference to the plethora of modern Masonic symbolism until after the establishment of Grand Lodges.[12] In short, it was the transition from stonemasons lodges to modern Masonic Lodges together with the elaboration of the simple stonemasons' ceremonies that created an explosion in the creation of Masonic symbolism.[13] As this coincided with the invention of a large number of other 'Masonic' Orders and their numerous ceremonies, Masonic symbols proliferated in an often confusing manner — confusing for the Mason and non-Mason alike![14]

To suggest that there was a sophisticated and complex 'system' of Masonic symbolism in existence at a time when there were only two brief and simple ceremonies in use by Scottish lodges cannot be supported by any evidence.

On closer inspection, however, this panel does have some links to Christian symbolism and the previously discussed Creation Panel. The first three images across the top of the panel recall the three images of that panel: the Sun, Moon, seven stars and the Name of God in Glory. The first image (top left) is suggestive of the universe with the Trinity (three triangles) at its centre. The image at the top right is indicative of the Sun and Moon (our planetary system) again with the Trinity at the centre and again represented by three triangles. Between these is a single triangle in which is the word 'God' in Greek letters [ΘΕΟΣ]. This triangle may also be considered as the keystone of the arch (rainbow) immediately below.[15]

The rainbow, with each end resting on clouds, relates to a bridge between heaven and earth. This is a common Christian symbol derived from that part of Genesis which deals with the period immediately after the flood:

> '*I do set my* [rain]*bow in the cloud, and it shall be for a token of a covenant between me and the earth. And it shall come to pass, when I bring a cloud over the earth, that the* [rain]*bow shall be seen in the cloud: And I shall remember my covenant, which is between me and you and every living creature of all flesh; and the waters shall no more become a flood to destroy all flesh. And the* [rain]*bow shall be in the cloud; and I shall look upon it, that I may remember the everlasting covenant between*

God and every living creature of all flesh that is upon the earth.' (Gen.
9:13–16)

This symbol then is a reminder of the '*everlasting covenant between God and
every living creature*'. It, therefore, indicates the reconciliation between God and
man after God had cleansed the earth of all violence and corruption (Gen. 6:12-
13) by way of a flood (Gen. 6:17-24). The rainbow, together with the other
symbols below it, dominates this panel. The presence of this symbol in a Masonic
artefact is not surprising as Freemasons, like many others, merely 'recycled'
existing symbols and imbued them with a meaning particular to them — in this
instance a link between the Freemason and The Great Architect Of The Universe
(T.G.A.O.T.U.) (Fig. 14)

Immediately below the rainbow and cloud is a Passion Cross on a seven stepped
base. The cross is surmounted by the letters IHS (*Iesus Hominum Salvator*: Jesus

Saviour of Men) — a common
abbreviation of the name of Jesus Christ.
This part of the panel appears to be an
attempt to link this panel with the
previous Creation Panel and, in so doing,
linking the Old and New Testaments.

The remainder of the symbols shall be
described descending from the left, then
left to right and thereafter up the right
side of the panel.

The symbol at the centre left, below
that of the universe and Holy Trinity,
appears to be that of the Masonic Knights
Templar: cross pattée within a central
circle, the border of which contains the
words: IN HOC SIGNO VINCES — In this sign thou shalt conquer. The central
part of the circle repeats the cross pattée.[16]

Below this 'KT' cross is a hand emerging from a cloud. This is another
common, standard, symbol representing the Hand of God. This symbol indicates
that God's influence can reach anywhere. Beneath the Hand of God is a cock
representing vigilance, an entirely appropriate symbol for Freemasons who meet
in private.[17] To the immediate right of the cock is a ladder with seven steps

symbolising the seven corporal acts of mercy and is often also used to represent Jacob's ladder. Further to the right is a very common Masonic symbol — the square and compasses. Below the cock is a vessel — the pot of Manna.[18] One of the more curious symbols is shown below the vessel and, given the wavy lines, perhaps is intended to represent the sea. To the right of the 'sea' is a building intended perhaps to represent the Lodge for it is of too modest a size to refer to King Solomon's Temple (hereinafter: KST) especially when there are grander images of that building elsewhere in the scroll.

Along the bottom of the panel there are, in the bottom left corner, working tools well known to adepts of another branch of Freemasonry. Next we find a snake apparently about to bite something but unfortunately what it might be is too small to determine. Below the snake is a coiled rope which again will be familiar to those who are members of another branch of Freemasonry. To the right of the 'Lodge', snake and rope, are two object of which the upper one is the crown of thorns (Matthew 27:29 and Mark 15:17) worn by Christ at the time of his crucifixion. Below the crown of thorns is another object similar to the 'sea' mentioned above but on this occasion it is more triangular in shape and the 'waves' are not so pronounced.

To the right of the crown of thorns etc. are a hammer, tongs and three nails which are an obvious allusion to the implements with which Jesus Christ was nailed to the cross and thereafter removed therefrom. Next are found three dice and a coffin. The former are the dice which the Roman soldiers used to 'cast lots' for Christ's coat (St. John 19:23–24 and St. Matthew 27:35). The coffin represents the sepulchre in which he was placed after death (St. Matthew 27:60).[19]

In the bottom right corner in another structure altogether more imposing than the small one mentioned earlier. It has one entrance and it seems likely that this is meant to be a representation of the sepulchre in which Christ was laid after the crucifixion.[20]

Above, and to the right of, the 'sepulchre' is a hand, emerging from storm clouds, bearing a sword on which is impaled a serpent. This is a further representation of the Hand of God but in a quite different manner. The storm clouds indicate anger and in total this symbol represents God triumphing over evil (the serpent). Above the 'Hand of God Triumphant' are two triangles of lights (candles). The lower triangle again contains the Name of God in Hebrew (יהוה) and the upper triangle contains firstly a Tau Cross upside down, then what appears to be a Masonic cypher below which is another Tau Cross lying on its side. The cypher translates as R = T if the cypher is the same as that used in the lowest two panels and which shall be more fully discussed later. Around the triangles of lights are three coates or robes and three distinctive pieces of headgear. Those who are members of the Royal Arch will see a relevance to the three who preside over Royal Arch Chapters.

To the left of the two triangles of lights is a rude depiction of the 47th Problem of Euclid. In the square of the symbol are the letters RNII but reading these anti-clockwise they are: I N R I. That is *Iesus Nazarenus Rex Iudaeorum* — Jesus of Nazareth, King of the Jews. Why the 47th Problem of Euclid should be combined with a reference to Jesus Christ is not immediately clear but may indicate that to 'masons' (and therefore 'Masons') this mathematical formula was of prime importance in their working lives and that Jesus Christ held the same, prime, position in their religious lives.

This symbol is common within modern Freemasonry (if the letters INRI are omitted) and features not only in Masonic ritual but also in Masonic artefacts such as Masonic jewels and book plates as well as the Kirkwall Scroll. The symbol of the 47th problem of Euclid first appears in a Masonic context in the frontispiece of Anderson's *Constitutions* (1723) where it occupies a prominent central position. (Plate 3) Anderson refers to this in the *Constitutions*:

> '. . . *the Greater Pythagoras, prov'd the Author of the 47th Proposition of Euclid's first Book, which, if duly observ'd, is the Foundation of all Masonry, sacred, civil and military.*'[21]

The first printed Masonic ritual — '*Masonry Dissected*' was published by Samuel Prichard in 1730 in London. In the brief history of Freemasonry provided by the author he makes reference to Euclid:

> '*For at the Building of the Tower of Babel, the Art and Mystery of Masonry was first introduc'd, and from thence handed down by Euclid, a worthy and excellent mathematician of the Egyptians, and communicated it to Hiram, the Master-Mason concern'd in the Building of Solomon's Temple in Jerusalem, where was an excellent and curious Mason that was the chief under their Grand Master Hiram...*'

This first printed ritual shows, therefore, that the 47th Problem (or Proposition) of Euclid was part of the lore of the Third Degree.[22] Today the 47th Problem still plays a part in Masonic ritual confirming the continuing development of ritual throughout the 18th and 19th centuries.[23] The symbol was, and is, used on various Masonic artefacts and today frequently is incorporated in Past Masters' Jewels of English Craft Lodges.(Fig. 15)

Before leaving this panel we are required to return to the central portion where, below the stepped based of the cross, there remain three symbols to be discussed. The largest symbol in the panel is an altar of nine steps. On top left of the altar lies a skull and two crossed bones and at the top right lies an open book — probably intended to represent a bible.

This panel refers to the third, or Master Masons' degree, of Freemasonry as is evident from the theme of death. The Masonic use of Christian symbols does not mean that Freemasons are referring to that religion.[24]

Fig. 15: *Past Masters' Jewel of Lodge Cripplegate, No.1613*

Third or Halleluiah Panel

This panel returns entirely to scripture and can be considered to be a continuation of the previous two, chronologically as well as symbolically. (Plate 33) This panel refers to Christ's resurrection following his crucifixion. At the top, centre, is a representation of the Holy Trinity (Father, Son and Holy Ghost). Christ is the lower of the three figures and is wearing a crown, as King of the Jews. With hands and arms upraised in praise he is carried into Heaven on a cloud where God the Father and the Holy Ghost await him. In the centre is a snake (representing evil) entwined and fixed to a cross in a ball of fire, meaning that the Trinity has conquered and imprisoned evil. Known as the Brazen Serpent, this Christian symbol is used to link Old and New Testaments.

'And the Lord said to Moses, "Make a fiery serpent, and set it on a pole

[cross]*; and every one who is bitten, when he sees it, shall live."'*
(Numbers 21:8) (Plate 34)

The healing power of Moses' serpent is, in the words of Jesus Christ, a form of
Crucifixion and Redemption:

'And as Moses lifted up the serpent in the wilderness, so must the Son of
man be lifted up, that whosoever believes in him may have eternal life.'
(St. John 3:14–15).

The remaining symbols in this panel are, with one exception, clearly
understandable. Moving from top left down, along the bottom and up the right of
the panel these are as follows. The first at the top left of the panel shows two
clasped hands with each wrist in a cloud. This is a symbol with multiple
interpretations: God and Humankind in unity; Heaven and Earth united through
Christ and God the Father and Christ the Son etc.

Below this at the centre left is a circular device in the border of which are the
Latin words: *Nuterina et Sulterinea*. This is very poor Latin, so poor in fact that
there is considerable hesitation in suggesting a translation but it might mean: '*All*
three will advance and will never waver'. If correct, one can assume that this is
some reference to the Holy Trinity to the right and above the device.

Below this device at the bottom of the panel is a lamb with a banner. This is the
Agnus Dei or Lamb of God — Jesus Christ.[25] As the Lamb of God is standing on
what appears to be a bridge with three arches (which extends the entire width of
the panel) this symbol can be interpreted as showing Jesus Christ on earth. The
arches of the 'bridge' may well have an additional meaning — that of the rainbow.
As has been seen previously, the rainbow is a symbol indicating a link or, in this
case, links between other objects or symbols. Between the first two arches or
rainbows is a book and as the bridge and/or rainbow is an earthly phenomenon
then this means the word of God (on earth) is contained within the Bible. As this
is linked to the Lamb of God this part of the symbol is specifically with reference
to the Word of God as enunciated by Jesus Christ. Atop the middle rainbow or
arch of a bridge are two figures probably intended to represent angels which have
their arms raised in worship and adoration of what is 'above' — physically and
spiritually (see below). A serpent on a Passion Cross is placed between the middle
and the far right rainbow or arch. The link with the Lamb of God on the far left
makes the meaning clear — evil has been defeated by the crucifixion of Christ

and our sins forgiven. On top of the third arch are two tablets with Roman numerals (I to X) thereon. These clearly represent the 'two tablets of testimony' bearing the Ten Commandments which Moses received from God on Mount Sinai (Ex. 34:29).

The whole panel might loosely be interpreted in this manner: 'By abiding by the Ten Commandments, heeding the Word of God, worshipping God, understanding that the Lamb of God died to cleanse us of our sins, then all evil will be defeated and we shall attain the Kingdom of Heaven.'

Above the tablets of the Ten Commandments is what today would be described as a Papal Cross. Its purpose here is unclear.[26] At centre right above the Papal Cross is perhaps an abstract depiction of KST which, together with Noah's Ark above it, symbolises the Old Testament and links it with the New Testament symbolism found at the bottom of the panel. The Temple as a symbol has a number of interpretations including that of Heaven and earth — the Temple being God's dwelling place on earth. Noah's Ark, as a symbol, is a reminder of the Covenant between God and Humankind.

In the central part of the panel four groups of figures can be seen. The two figures at the bottom centre have previously been discussed. Above these angels there are two groups of three angels resting on clouds. In each group two are blowing trumpets and the remaining two (like the ones below) are in attitudes of worship, praise and adoration. They symbolise the acclamation of Christ's ascent to Heaven following his death and resurrection and therefore the success of his earthly ministry.

In its totality this panel is coherent in its overall message as described above. There is also a logic to the use of the symbols as the panel can be successfully 'read' anti-clockwise from top left or clockwise from top right, although I think that the latter is more successful as it has an identifiable chronological sequence (in a biblical sense). That is: Noah's Ark; KST; the Ten Commandments, the Defeat of Evil through Jesus Christ until, at the top left, the union of God and Man is shown by two clasped hands.[27] The panel is also consistent with the 'upward direction' of the symbolic content — that is, from earth to heaven. The panel contains no Masonic references and this can only be deliberate — probably in order not to obscure the panel's message.

Fourth or Tabernacle Panel

Some have argued that this panel (Plate 35) shows a ground plan of KST and that this is the same as the ground plan of Rosslyn Chapel.[28] (Plates 10 and 11) The panel is divided into two parts and the first depicts the Tabernacle in the wilderness, *not* KST. This can be stated with certainty as it is surrounded by the tents of the 12 tribes of Israel (Numbers 2). In the four corners are tents with standards depicting: a man (top left); an eagle (top right); a lion (bottom right); and an ox (bottom left). These represent the four principal tribes of Israel: Ruben; Dan; Judah and Ephraim. As is often the case with symbols they have more than one meaning. The lion represents strength and power; the ox, patience and assiduity; man, intelligence and understanding; and the eagle promptness and celerity in doing the will and pleasure of the great *I Am*.[29] In relation to the New Testament these four emblems represent the Evangelists: Saint Matthew (man); Saint Luke (ox); Saint Mark (lion); and Saint John (eagle). This is an excellent example of symbolism which was created by one group and which was later used and adapted by another — Jews and Christians respectively. The importance of these four emblems is considered more fully when discussing the next panel (see below).

There can be no doubt that the upper part of the panel is a representation of the Tabernacle in the Wilderness (see: Exodus 26-27) and which was placed in the centre of the camp of the 12 tribes during the course of their journey from Egypt to the Promised Land (Numbers 2).[30] (see Plates 35 and 36) Interestingly the artists have not followed the order of the banners as stated in Numbers 2 where the order of the four principal tribes is given as: Dan, the eagle (north); Judah, the lion (east); Ruben, the man (south) and Ephraim, the ox (west). This has a significance which will become apparent when the next panel is discussed.

The lower part of the Tabernacle Panel, separated by a 'wavy' line is distinctly Masonic. There are several Masonic symbols, two using the letter G. The line is intended to suggest that the two parts of the panel although separate have some kind of connection. The most important element in this part of the panel is the circular diagram in the centre, which like other parts of the scroll have hitherto defied interpretation but for which an explanation can now be offered. (Plate 37)

Previous writers, when viewing the Kirkwall Scroll, have not quite understood what it was they were examining in this panel — a circular construction with six arched entrances. As it looks nothing like the oblong-shaped Tabernacle illustrated above it, the circular-shaped building has, until now, defied explanation.

> '*During the Crusades, the Knights Templar, who thought the Dome of the Rock to be a remnant of the Temple of Jerusalem* [Solomon], *made their*

The site of Temple of Solomon is now covered by the Dome of the Rock. It was built in A.D.691 by Abd El Malik ibn Mirwan, the Omayad Khalif, as a place of pilgrimage. It was from the rock in the centre of the dome that Muslims believe Muhammad was brought by night and from which he ascended, accompanied by the angel Gabriel, to the presence of God.

The site has a reverence also for Jews who believe that it was here that Abraham was about to sacrifice his son Isaac, until God relented. It is here also that Jacob saw a ladder reaching to heaven. Importantly it is where the innermost chamber, the Holy of Holies, of KST was positioned.

As the first building in the Bible to be made from stone was King Solomon's Temple it was inevitable that it would assume huge importance for Scottish stonemasons — the precursors of modern Freemasons. The oldest Masonic rituals refer to KST and it occupies a central part in these. In light of this it becomes clear what the artists are attempting. KST is shown *inside* the Dome of the Rock — at the centre of the circular design.[32] Even more specifically, this way of depicting KST is Masonic — with three entrances at the east (right), west (left), and south (bottom centre) — exactly as described in modern Masonic ritual. The earliest rituals also describe three entrances but these are north east, south west and the eastern passages. The floor is made up of black and white squares. There is one further piece of conclusive proof. In this Masonic version of the Temple a coffin lies in KST. Here then is a symbolic allusion to a death in KST and, given the Masonic context, is clearly intended to refer to Hiram Abiff; this part of the panel therefore refers to the third or Master or Masons' degree.

Fifth or Armorial Panel

This is one of the most important panels in the scroll because by it the scroll can be dated with some accuracy. (Plate 38) The device which dominates this panel consists of two figures with closely associated symbols. It is fortunate indeed that there are good grounds for knowing when this device was created and by whom.

Rabbi Jacob Judah Leon (1602–1675) was by birth a Spaniard but at a young age was taken to Middleburg, The Netherlands.[33] He subsequently became Rabbi of the Jewish communities at Hamburg and Amsterdam and at the latter was appointed, in 1649, the Head Master of the Jewish schools. By 1640 be had completed his celebrated model of KST and in 1642 began publishing a variety of works on the Temple and associated subjects.[34] He obtained the patronage of

William III of Orange (1650–1702) and Mary II (1662–1694) who became King and Queen of Great Britain in 1689. His model of the Temple had been exhibited in Amsterdam and about 1674 it was brought to London together with another of the Tabernacle. There is no evidence to suggest that he accompanied the models. It has been claimed that the following year his models were exhibited to Charles II (1660–1685; b. 1630) at the Royal Palace. So closely associated was the Rabbi with KST that he is often referred to as Leon Templo. The models evidently returned to Amsterdam, as they were viewed there in 1711. In 1756 Isaac Lyon, probably the grandson of the model maker, bequeathed it in his will to his nephew, Moses de Castro. The latter exhibited the model of KST in London in 1759/60 and again in 1778. It is the exhibition of 1759/60 which is of interest here.

Before explaining the relevance of this to the panel and its connection to Leon Templo it is necessary to explain the circumstance which gave rise to the existence of two Grand Lodges in England during the last half of the 18th century. The Grand Lodge established in 1717 was, by 1750, in some disarray. This was due in part to lack of oversight by the Grand Master, 5th Lord Byron (1722–1798) (great uncle of the poet) and poor administration. Social exclusivity had begun to increase and a number of old traditions were changed or dropped altogether. Changes in the use of certain words in the 1730's may well have been the root cause of the creation of a new, rival, Grand Lodge in 1751. This new body was called the Grand Lodge of England according to the Old Institutions, or the Ancient or Atholl Grand Lodge — titles which clearly demonstrate its adherence to earlier Masonic practice.[35] Inevitably the other Grand Lodge, which was in fact older, came to be described as the 'Moderns' because of the innovations it had permitted to be introduced. The 'break-away' group was comprised almost entirely of Irish Freemasons resident in London but who apparently had no connection with existing Masonic Lodges because they had been denied admission to those Lodges. Perhaps the changes introduced by the existing Grand Lodge caused them to erect another Grand Lodge which would recognise them as Freemasons whilst at the same time allowing them to practise 'ancient' Freemasonry. Surprisingly the Moderns did not react to the creation of this new Grand Lodge and simply ignored it — at least initially. It was not until 1777 that the first official reaction is noted when in that year it was decided that 'Ancient' Masons should not be recognised. This implies that until that point both Grand Lodges had at least tolerated each other. The Grand Lodge of Scotland had maintained cordial relations with the Ancients and officially recognised that body in 1772, no doubt as a consequence of the Duke of Atholl becoming Grand Master Mason (of Scotland) in that year, having previously been Grand Master of the Ancients Grand Lodge. The Grand Lodge of Scotland, in 1782, also officially recognised the Moderns Grand Lodge. In May 1813 the Duke of Sussex (1773–1843) was elected Grand Master of the Moderns and shortly thereafter his brother, the Duke of Kent (1767–1820) was elected Grand Master of the Ancients. Through the influence of these two brothers the union of the two Grand Lodges was effected in December 1813.[36] This very brief outline of the history of the two Grand Lodges is necessary in order to explain the significance of the panel.[37]

The Ancients were a relatively small body whose members were not part of the existing Masonic 'establishment' in London and this may be one of the reasons why the Moderns were content to ignore its existence. In 1754 the Ancients, under the energetic direction of Laurence Dermott, the Grand Lodge Secretary, had garnered sufficient members and funds to publish its first 'Book of Constitutions' under the title *Ahiman Rezon*. Exactly ten years later the Ancients Grand Lodge issued a second 'Book of Constitutions' under the same title. It is the second edition which is of interest to us here because the frontispiece bears an engraving headed: '*The Arms of the most Ancient & Honorable Fraternity of Free and Accepted Masons.*' (Plate 41) The lower part of the engraving is captioned '*The Arms of the Operative Stone Masons*', Laurence Dermott provided a description and account of the engraving in *Ahiman Rezon*:

'*The free masons arms in the upper part of the frontispiece of this book was found in the collection of the famous and learned hebrewist [sic], architect and brother, Rabi Jacob Jehudah Leon. This gentleman at the request of the states of Holland, built a model of King Solomon's temple. The design of this undertaking was to build a temple in Holland, but upon surveying the model it was adjudged that the united provinces were not rich enough to pay for it; whereupon the states generously bestowed the model on the builder, not withstanding they had already paid him his demand, which was very great. This model was exhibited to public view (by authority) at Paris and Vienna, and afterwards in London, by a patent under the great seal of England, and signed Killigrew in the reign of King Charles the Second. At the same time, Jacob Judah Leon published a description of the tabernacle and the temple, and dedicated it to his Majesty, and in the years 1759 and 1760 I had the pleasure of perusing and examining both these curiosities. The arms are emblazoned thus,*

*quarterly per squares, countercharged Vert. In the first quarter Asure a
lyon rampant Or, in the second quarter Or, an ox passant sable; in the
third quarter Or, a man with hands erect, proper robed, crimson and
ermine; in the fourth quarter Asure, an eagle displayed, Or, crest the holy
ark of the covenant, proper, supported by Cherubims. Motto, Kodes la
Adonai, i.e. Holiness to the Lord...*

*As these were the arms of the masons that built the tabernacle and the
temple, there is not the least doubt of their being the proper arms of the
most ancient and honourable fraternity of free and accepted masons, and
the continued practice, formalities and tradition, in all regular lodges,
from the lowest degree to the most high, i.e. the HOLY ROYAL ARCH,
confirms the truth thereof.'*

The model which was exhibited in London during 1759 and 1760 was none other
than that of Rabbi Leon.[38] Dermott's own words confirm that he was fascinated
by KST and had in fact viewed the model. When he states: '*I had the pleasure of
perusing and examining both these curiosities...*' he was referring not only to the
model but also to various books and papers which were available at the time of
the exhibition. It is known that the Rabbi had a large number of unpublished
drawings illustrating various aspects of the Talmud and its various legends. It
seems that Dermott had access to these writings and drawings at the time of the
exhibition and simply appropriated the Rabbi's design for the use of the Ancients
Grand Lodge. Unfortunately the material which Dermott examined is no longer
extant. However, some insight can be gained from a description of the contents of
the Rabbi's published work: *De Cherubinis tractatus* (1647) contained in a letter
from him to the German scholar Johan Saubert in 1665. A. Lewis Shane is of the
firm opinion that Dermott created a heraldic interpretation of Leon's
descriptions.[39] The Ancients Grand Lodge embraced the Royal Arch Ceremonies.
Laurence Dermott himself claimed to have become a Royal Arch Masonic in
Dublin, Ireland, during 1746. The adoption of this ceremony by the Ancients
Grand Lodge is in stark contrast to the attitude of the Grand Lodge of Scotland
and which is discussed elsewhere. The earliest reference to the Royal Arch
ceremony is in Dublin in 1743: ' *...the Royal Arch carried by excellent Masons*'
during the St. John's Day parade of Youghall Lodge, No.21.[40] In 1744 another
reference is made: '*I am informed in that city is held an assembly of Master
Masons under the title of Royal Arch Masons . . .*', but as with the former
reference there is no way of knowing the nature of the ceremony itself.[41] The

Ancients Grand Lodge makes the first reference to the ceremony in a minute of 4 March 1752 which is in the nature of a complaint by Thomas Phelan and John Mackey that '*leg of mutton Masons*' had made '*Royal Archmen*' for the sake of a meal, the implication being that these '*Royal Archmen*' were not Freemasons. The first record of the ceremony of the Holy Royal Arch being conferred in a Masonic Lodge occurs in the lodge at Fredericksburg, Virginia, USA, on 22 December 1753. It was in this Lodge that George Washington (1732–1799), later the first President of the United States, had been made a Freemason the previous year. This Lodge would be considered 'irregular' today as it had no authority (that is, it had no charter from a Grand Lodge) to meet as a Masonic Lodge. This was not altogether unusual at that time given the time and distances involved in obtaining a charter. The character of the Lodge might be gleaned from the names of the members of the Lodge: Campbell, Fraser, Spottiswood, etc. — Scots. It may be thought that a national stereotype is evident here — why spend good money obtaining a charter if the Lodge might not last! As it was, the Lodge operated in this manner until 1758 when it legitimised its existence by obtaining a charter from the Grand Lodge of Scotland.[42] It is therefore ironic that the first record of the conferral of the Royal Arch ceremony in a Masonic Lodge took place not in an Ancients Lodge or an Irish Lodge but in a Scottish Lodge. As has been seen elsewhere, the Grand Lodge of Scotland had a very different attitude toward ceremonies such as the Holy Royal Arch.

The Traditional History of the Royal Arch is concerned with the release of the Jews by Cyrus, King of Persia, allowing them to return to Jerusalem to build the second Temple under the guidance of Zerubabbel. This ceremony, which is now part of mainstream Freemasonry, appeared soon after Chevalier Andrew Ramsay's *Oration* (1737), which has been discussed elsewhere in this book with particular reference to the KT. It is now conceded that Ramsay's *Oration* made no reference to the Knights Templar or the Royal Arch but it may be, and this is the subject of ongoing research, that his *Oration* was the inspiration for the creation of the so called '*Hauts Grades*' (Higher Degrees) of Freemasonry which include the KT and Royal Arch.[43] In any event it is significant that none of these '*Hauts Grades*' existed prior to the *Oration*. Those that claim that they must have so pre-existed *because* there is no evidence that they did not, are employing the technique of using a negative (the absence of any reference to these ceremonies) to 'prove' a positive — that they could (and therefore did!) exist prior to Ramsay's *Oration*. This technique is more fully discussed in Chapter 1.

What can be learned from examining the arms? Firstly the two winged figures (cherubim) which dominate this panel are described by Laurence Dermott.

> *'To this I beg to add what I have read concerning these arms.*
> *The learned Spencer says, the Cherubims had the face of a man, the wings of*
> *an eagle, the back and mane of lion, the feet of a calf. De Legib, Hebr. lib.3,*
> *diss; 5. ch.2. The Prophet Ezekiel says, they had four forms, a man, a lion, an*
> *ox and an eagle.*
> *When the Israelites were in the wilderness, and encamped in four cohorts,*
> *the standard of the tribe of Judah carried a lion, the tribe of Ephraim an*
> *ox, the tribe of Ruben a man and the tribe of Dan an eagle; those four*
> *standards composed a Cherubim; therefore God chose to sit upon*
> *Cherubims bearing the forms of those animals, to signify, that he was the*
> *leader and king of the cohorts of the Israelites. Trad of the Heb.'*

In heraldic terms Dermott is describing 'supporters' — the 'coat of arms' is the central panel containing the symbols of the four tribes.[44] The Ark of the Covenant is the crest and is above the 'coat of arms' and between the upraised wings of the supporters. The similarities between Dermott's cherubim and those in the scroll are obvious. Dermott's skill in this field has been described thus:

> *'Dermott's knowledge of heraldry was evidently of the most meagre*
> *description, and his blazon* [heraldic shield] *of the Grand Lodge Arms only*
> *serves to show that he was the veriest tryo* [novice] *in the science.'*[45]

Dermott's work is considered therefore to be that of an amateur whose knowledge of heraldry is elementary. Anyone of the same ability copying his work might be expected to produce something of even less finesse than that of Dermott. It is in that light that the supporters in the Kirkwall Scroll must be considered.

Comparing the Ancient Grand Lodge's arms with the panel reveals a number of similarities. For example the same two arms of the cherubim are raised and touch, and the other two lowered and positioned similarly. Most important of all are the constituent parts of the cherubim: *'face of a man, the wings of an eagle, the back and mane of lion, the feet of a calf'* (*Ahiman Rezon*) yet when Dermott's drawing is examined it does not exactly match his description (Plates 41). His cherubim do not have the back and mane of a lion. It seems that this defeated Dermott's skill but an examination of the panel shows that the artist has made an attempt to endow the 'face of a man' with the mane of a lion, albeit rather crudely.

One of the most significant similarities is the order in which the symbols of the four principal tribes of Israel are placed. As has been discussed in relation to the Tabernacle Panel (see above) the order in which the four tribes are placed is different from the norm. The order of the tribes is specified in Numbers:

> 'And the Lord spake unto Moses and unto Aaron, saying, Every man of the children of Israel shall pitch by his own standard, with the ensign of their father's house: far off about the tabernacle of the congregation shall they pitch.' (Numbers 2:1–2).

Tribe	Symbol	Position	Source
Judah	Lion	East	Numbers 2:3
Reuben	Man	South	Numbers 2:10
Ephraim	Ox	West	Numbers 2:18
Dan	Eagle	North	Numbers 2:25
Reuben	Man	Top left	Tabernacle Panel
Dan	Eagle	Top right	Tabernacle Panel
Judah	Lion	Bottom right	Tabernacle Panel
Ephraim	Ox	Bottom left	Tabernacle Panel
Judah	Lion	Top left	Ahiman Rezon
Ephraim	Ox	Top right	Ahiman Rezon
Dan	Eagle	Bottom right	Ahiman Rezon
Reuben	Man	Bottom left	Ahiman Rezon
Judah	Lion	Top left	Armorial Panel
Ephraim	Ox	Top right	Armorial Panel
Dan	Eagle	Bottom right	Armorial Panel
Reuben	Man	Bottom left	Armorial Panel

The designers of the Kirwall Scroll had at least three sources from which to take the order in which to place the emblems of the four tribes — the Book of Numbers in the Old Testament; the frontispiece of Laurence Dermott's *Ahiman Rezon* (1764); or the order in which they themselves had already placed them in the Tabernacle Panel. Instead of using their own design or the ultimate authoritative source, the Book of Numbers, they chose the same design used by Laurence Dermott who had based his design on the work of Rabbi Leon.

The Royal Arch, and associated ceremonies — the Mark and Excellent Masters — was a later addition to Freemasonry and was by no means universally accepted.[46] Like Craft Freemasonry, all other branches invented or developed their own Traditional History, designed to teach a particular moral story with its own esoteric aspects and symbolism. As stated and explained elsewhere in this book, the different branches were never combined into one unified whole. Over time some of these diverse elements calling themselves 'Masonic' were accepted into the Masonic 'family', others were not accepted and ceased to exist, whilst others survive independently to this day.

The panel described as the fifth or Armorial Panel contains a great deal more information than simply that relating to Rabbi Leon's drawings and Laurence Dermott's use of his work.

It should not, therefore, be assumed that this panel is merely someone else's version of Dermott's drawing. His was a design of a coat of arms for the Ancients Grand Lodge whereas the panel contains additional material which relates to the Royal Arch; the panel therefore relates to the whole 'system' of Freemasonry, with particular reference to the Royal Arch, as practised by the Ancients Grand Lodge.[47]

At top left there is a representation of the gold plate on the mitre of the High Priest and this is matched by a drawing of the High Priest's breast plate at top right. Middle left are a pick axe and crowbar and at the middle right are a rope and spade-working tools which are well known to members of Royal Arch Chapters. The panel is of course dominated by the cherubim discussed above but these are flanked by two pillars with an arch which links them together. The top centre of the arch shows a keystone. This symbol of the arch, pillars and keystone represents Royal Arch Freemasonry which has been created by adding the arch and keystone to Craft Freemasonry represented by the two pillars. This connection, it will be remembered, existed only in the Ancients Grand Lodge. The link between the Royal Arch and Craft 'branches' of Freemasonry is further emphasised by inclusion of other Craft symbols in this panel. For example, around the altar are the square, representing the Master of a Craft Lodge, the level for the Senior Warden and the plumb rule referring to the Junior Warden. These are the three who rule a Lodge. Crossed keys represent the Lodge Treasurer and the crossed quill pens together with three crowns suggest that the three who rule a Lodge do so only with the assistance of the Secretary. The panel shows therefore that, in the view of the Ancients Grand Lodge, the Royal Arch ceremony was a legitimate extension of the three Craft degrees.[48] Under the arch at the left the Sun is shown and at the right the 'All Seeing Eye'. The use of these symbols is interesting and their significance in dating the scroll will be discussed in the conclusion.

Sixth or Altar Panel

This panel (Plate 39) contains numerous standard Masonic symbols. Square and compasses (in several different configurations); a chequered carpet; a level; a plumb rule, three 'lights' (candles) and an altar. It has previously been shown that the Ancient Grand Lodge regarded the Royal Ceremony as the 'highest', or last, Masonic degree. That means that when Dermott made that specific claim, in 1764, the Knights Templar were not part of the Masonic 'family'. Whilst the Royal Arch is stated to be the 'highest' degree there were two other parts between the Craft degrees and the Royal Arch. These were the Mark and Excellent Master. The symbols on the left of the panel are from the Excellent Master and those on the right are from the Mark ceremony. At the top left is a Burning Bush with the name of God repeated three times, in cipher, below it.[49] Below the Burning Bush are a variety of working tools as well as a rather crude depiction of a withered hand. The carpet which lies before the altar consists of two parts. The black and white squares refer to the Craft Lodge and the diamond pattern on the right is appropriate to the Royal Arch Chapter. On the right of the panel there are two hands crossed at the wrist and below that what might be a level but actually is the wicket gate of the Senior Warden. Below that is the special implement used by the Junior Warden during the Mark ceremony. Also present are more common symbols such as the altar; three 'lights' (candles and candlesticks); square and compasses, plumb rule, etc. These symbols taken with those previously mentioned mean that this panel serves the same function as the previous panel — as a way to link symbolically the three Craft degrees with those of the Mark and Excellent Master and thence to the Royal Arch. There are some symbols missing that one would normally expect to be present. The reason for this will be mentioned later.

Further confirmation of the Excellent Master element of the panel is demonstrated by the cipher on the front of the altar which translates as follows:

> I AM hath sent me
> Unto you. I AM that
> I AM. I am the Rose
> Of Sharon and the Lilly

> Of the Valley. HEGEE
> ASHER HEJAH. I AM
> That I AM or I WILL
> BEE that I WILL BEE.
> JAHDADAIAH

In the scroll this is given in the form of a Masonic cipher and which will be discussed more fully, below, regarding the next panel.

Seventh or Craft Panel

The last, bottom, panel is again packed with Masonic symbolism, much of which has been mentioned above. (Plate 40) The two pillars bear a marked similarity to the two in the Armorial Panel (see above) albeit without the connecting arch. They also bear globes and this, together with all the other symbols, informs us what this panel represents — the Craft Lodge and the three degrees which are conferred therein. Some of the symbols plainly refer to the Lodge Officers — the square, level, plumb rule, crossed keys etc.[50] Other symbols are used within the Lodge. For example, the square and compasses with the points of the compasses in three different positions: both points of the compasses under the square indicating the first or Entered Apprentice Degree (at the base of the altar); one point above and one point below the square (top left of altar) referring to the second or Fellow Craft degree; and both points of the compasses above the square meaning the third of Master Masons' degree. Familiar symbols such as the chequered carpet, ladder, the letter 'G' and an altar etc. all relate to Craft Freemasonry. The panel is dedicated to that part of Freemasonry and unlike the preceding panels stands alone in what it represents except for the use of the Sun, Moon and, unusually, eight stars together with the 'All Seeing Eye' at the centre. The significance of this panel and the symbols will be discussed below.

The altar also bears an inscription which uses the same cipher as that of the previous panel. Translated it reads:

Chronikils, [*sic*] 2d Chapt'r. 48, 49.

'*Mā-ă-chäh, caleb's concubine, bare Shē-bĕr, and Tĭ-hă-n ăh.*
She bare also Shā-ăph the father of Măch-bē-năh, and the father of Gĭb-
ĕ-ă: and the daughter of Caleb was Ăch-săh.'

Judhes [*sic*] Chapt'r 12. 6, 7.

'*Then they said unto him, Say now Shĭb-bŏ-lĕth: and he said Sĭb-bŏ-lĕth;
for he could not frame to pronounce it right. They took him, and slew him
at the passages of Jordan: and there fell at that time of the E-phră-ĭm-ĭtes
forty and two thousand.
And Jĕph-thăh judged Israel six years. Then died Jĕph-thăh the Gileadite,
and was buried in one of the cities of Gilead.*'

Hensis [*sic*] Chap'r 4. 22.

'*And Zillarh, she also bare Tū-băl-cₐin, an instructer of every artificer in
brass and iron: and the sister of Tū-băl-cₐin was Nā-ă-măh.*'

I Kings, Chap'r 7. 21.

'*And he set up the pillars in the porch of the temple: and he set up the right
pillar which called the name thereafter of Jā-chĭn: and he set up the left
pillar, and called the name thereof Bō-ăz.*'

Matthew Chap'r 16. 18.

'*And I say unto thee, That thou art Peter, and upon this rock I will build
my church; and the gates of hell shall not prevail against it.*'[51]

Before the union of the two English Grand Lodges (1813) could take place,
considerable discussion between the two bodies was required. One of the major
questions was regarding the differences between the rituals used by each. In 1809
the Moderns ordered that the changes made in the ritual during the 1730s be
reversed and a special Lodge of Promulgation was created to examine in detail the
other differences between the rituals.[52] On the matter of certain words neither side
would give up the word they used and consequently two words were authorised
to be used in post-1813 rituals. The above details inform us that only one was in
use for the Master Masons' degree, by each Grand Lodge, and therefore it is
possible to state with some certainty that the Kirkwall Scroll was not
manufactured after 1813.

The inscriptions on the altars in the sixth and seventh panels are in cipher

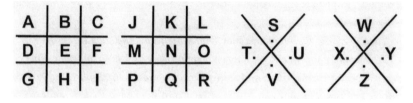

Fig. 16: *The Masonic cipher*

commonly known as a pig pen cipher similar to that shown above.

The Masonic version of the cipher first appeared in the 18th century and was apparently invented by Freemasons as a pastime. It is a very simple cipher and no one could have seriously considered using it to transmit secret messages. If that was its intended purpose it very quickly fell into disuse by reason of its very simplicity. Each letter of the alphabet has a place in the grid and it is that part of the grid which is reproduced. Thus the first nine letters of the alphabet would be given by the lines of the grid in which they were placed. For example C would be given as: ⌞ and E as ☐. The second group of nine letters would be given in the same manner but with the addition of a dot. The remaining eight letters are place in two crosses and again each letter would be signified by the line in which it was placed. The letter T would be shown thus: > and the letter X would be shown in the same way but with a dot to indicate that it came from the second group of letters.

The cipher used to inscribe the scroll is a slight variation of this and its use confirms that the scroll was created after the invention of this form of cipher.

Fittingly, the last panel provides final proof that the panel is Masonic and, together with other evidence discussed above, allows for the date of the scroll to be calculated with certainty.

The left side panel

The other parts of the Kirkwall Scroll are the two side panels. (Plate 42) These have been considered by other writers, one of whom explained that they show the wandering of the 12 tribes of Israel after their escape from Egypt as described in the Old Testament Book of Exodus. Another more recent author has suggested that these panels show the route taken by the Knights Templar to bring the Holy Grail from Jerusalem to Rosslyn Chapel.[53] This discussion of the side panels will examine these two diametrically opposed views.

The left side panel will be considered first. (Plate 42) The top part of the panel shows a coastline and is confirmed as such by the rivers flowing into a sea. Unlike the central panels, the side panels contain a great deal of writing, principally place names. Some of the rivers too are named (they are termed 'floods'). This is extremely useful in that it permits some places to be identified. Some of the writing is obscure and difficult to read but there is enough that is sufficiently legible to be analysed and discussed. The left hand panel has been ruled off to create six parts and, as previously, these will be discussed in descending order.

The first panel shows a coastline with three rivers running into it and there are towns and villages-designated by a square with a peak. Many of these bear names. Those that can be clearly read are Cisarea (Caesarea), Gilead and Hebron. The first of these, Caesarea, was also known as Palestinae, a city on the shore of the Mediterranean, on the great road from Tyre to Egypt, about 70 miles north west of Jerusalem, at the northern extremity of the plain of Sharon. Gilead is a mountainous area to the east of Jordan and because of its mountainous character is often referred to as 'the mount of Gilead' (Gen. 31:25). It was to a party of Ishmeelites from Gilead, travelling to Egypt, that Joseph was sold by his brothers (Gen. 37:25). Hebron is a city between Jerusalem and Beersheba and Sarai, wife of Abraham, died here and Abraham bought a sepulchre known as the Cave of Machpelah where Sarai was buried (Gen. 23:1-19). Abraham was himself later interred here (Gen 25:10.) From this it can be seen that the panel details places in Canaan associated with Abraham, the first Patriarch and his immediate family. Moving away from the coast the towns and rivers become fewer, with only a river and mountains being shown. However, there are the words 'Cush' and 'Rama'. In the Old Testament 'Cush' generally referred to countries to the south of the Israelites and 'Cush' in the scroll is 'south' of Gilead etc.

The next panel contains no towns, numerous mountains and one river and is described as the 'Land of Desert' and the 'Land of Lakes'. In contrast to this panel the next contains several towns, rivers and mountains, many of which are named but unfortunately are obscure. However, the name Orr (Ur) is sufficient to suggest that the area being described here is the area near the Persian Gulf occupied by the Chaldeans.

The next panel is quite different, showing a forest, mountains and a single large river. The mountains are named as the 'Mountains of Gilboa' now called Jebel Fukua, and are remembered because this was where Saul was defeated by the Philistines and his three sons killed (2 Sam. 21:12). Saul took his own life here. The mountains bound the valley of Esdraelon (Jezreel) on the east, between it and the Jordan valley. The river is named as the Tigris which is incompatible with the mountains of Gilboa.

Another horizontal line separates this panel from the one below. This panel again contains a forest, mountains and a single large river. The mountains are described as being 'mountains of Memphis', the forest as 'forest of Egypt' and the river is named the Euphrates. Whilst all these places exist, they are not placed in the correct sequence.

The final panel is by far the most cluttered, showing numerous towns and for the first time what are apparently intended to be cities together with numerous trees and rivers indicating that this is a populous and wealthy place. This panel contains, also for the first time, a human figure — a warrior on horseback, wielding a sword. This has been claimed to show a Mameluke knight at the siege of Damietta in 1219.[54] In the context here explored this must be considered unlikely. Memphis was the ancient capital of Egypt and its geographic location at the apex of the Nile delta is shown in this panel. The river flowing past Memphis is named Nillius (Nile).

How then should these side panels be interpreted? It seems that this is an account of different places, the exact locations of which are only vaguely known to the artist(s). The top part of the panel begins in Canaan and ends in Egypt at the ancient capital of that country. In between there are references to places not in either Canaan or Egypt and it cannot, therefore, show simply a journey from one to the other. It is what connects these places which will provide the answer.

Abram (later Abraham) is the most important individual in Genesis.[55] He was born in Ur near to the Persian Gulf and was therefore a Chaldee (or Babylonian.) Abraham is the ancestor of the whole Hebrew race and with him the history of the Israel begins. God chose Abraham for this purpose:

> 'Now the LORD said to Abram: 'Get out of your country [Ur], from your family And from your father's house, To a land that I will show you.
> I will make you a great nation; I will bless you And make your name great; And you shall be a blessing.
> I will bless who bless you,
> And I will curse those him who curses you;
> And in you all the families of the earth shall be blessed.' (Gen. 12:1-3)

Abram set out with his father, Terah, his wife (and half sister) Sarai (later Sarah) and his nephew, Lot. The group stopped for a time at Haran (northwest of Ur), where Terah died, before arriving in Canaan, the land promised by God to Abram. When they arrived, Canaan was suffering a famine and they continued south to Egypt. However, Sarai was a beautiful woman and Abram was frightened that the Egyptians would kill him and take his wife. After entering Egypt he referred to Sarai as his sister. However, this backfired as his sister, an unattached female, was commended to the house of the Pharaoh where the group were looked after (Gen. 12:15). God intervened and set plagues on Pharaoh until he realised that Sarai was Abram's wife. On learning this Pharaoh reproached Abram, asking why he had not told him the truth as he might have taken Sarai as a wife (Gen. 12:18-19). Pharaoh '. . . *sent him away, with his wife and all that he had*' (Gen. 12:20). By this time Abram had become very rich with livestock, gold and silver and returned to Canaan via Negev. The subsequent account of Abram's very long life need not detain us here as the details provided thus far are sufficient for the purpose of explaining the side panel.

The central panels of the scroll show that the artist(s) lacked precise knowledge in some matters and executed some of the designs crudely. This side panel reveals the same flaws but shows that the designer had some knowledge of the Old Testament. The panel is an attempt to illustrate the journey of Abram (Abraham) and his family and followers from Canaan to Egypt. However, approximately half way down the panel (at the end of the third panel) there is a sudden reference to Orr (Ur). It may be that the artist realised the omission (or had it pointed out to him) only after completing the upper portion of the panel and so inserted it in the middle. Although this meant that Abram's journey to Egypt is illustrated here, the order is incorrect when compared to that provided in Genesis. It is also incomplete. If, as has already been suggested, the Kirkwall Scroll is a visual aid or teaching tool, then this error would not have been a complete calamity because when being used, the appropriate panels would have been indicated in their correct order.

The right side panel

The right hand panel also contains much of interest. (Plate 42) Like the left hand panel this also obviously refers to the Old Testament. It also has a coastline and the place that can immediately be identified as one of the main cities is named Joppa. Previously the panel has been described and discussed from the 'top down' but on this occasion it will be considered from the 'bottom up' for reasons which shall become obvious. This side panel is divided into five panels and matches approximately the six panels on the left side. The difference in number is caused by a double sized panel (second down from the top) in the right panel.

The first place in this panel, at the bottom, is Midian — on the east side of the Gulf of Aqaba. This is the place to which Moses fled after killing an Egyptian who was attacking one of his brethren and where he was subsequently hunted by Pharaoh (Exodus 2:11-15). The panel does not therefore start at the beginning of Exodus and in so doing does not explain the plight of the children of Israel in bondage in Egypt. Also omitted is the famous story of the birth of Moses, being set adrift in a cot of bulrushes and ending up in the household of Pharaoh. The possible reason for these omissions will be discussed later. Moses spent a considerable time in Midian, married and had a son there but returned to Egypt on the death of Pharaoh. On the death of a pharaoh all pending charges were dropped by the Egyptian authorities — including those relating to capital offences. This first section of the panel includes mountains, rivers and vegetation but additionally provides details of specific events. The next illustration is described as being the 'Battle of Amalek' in which Joshua, who later succeeded Moses as leader of Israel, defeated the Amalekites at Rephidim (Ex. 17:8-16).

The panels then relate the story, although not every incident, of the wanderings of the 12 tribes of Israel as detailed in Exodus, Leviticus and Numbers. Immediately above the Battle of Amalek there is a depiction of the first camp of the Israelites (the annotation states 'Camp first') and is shown by means of four groups of tents at the foot of Mt. Sina (Sinai). (Ex. 19:2). It was here Moses received the Ten Commandments and God made the Mosaic Covenant with the nation of Israel thereby reasserting the promises made to Abraham and Sarah. Yet the panel makes no reference to these crucial events except indirectly with the Golden Calf being worshipped whilst Moses was in the presence of God on the mountain (Ex. 32:1-35). Before that event, however, the artist has attempted to show other encampments in the wilderness, one of which specifically mentions Manna from God on two occasions (Ex. 16). The tents are identical to those in the Tabernacle Panel. Three other camps are shown one bearing the legend 'Rods of the 12 Tribes' and are the last illustrations in this section which is terminated by a distinct horizontal line. The next section of the panel, in addition to mountains, vegetation and the single large river which runs the length of the panel, contains the words 'Waters of the Rock' and is

Fig. 17: *Worshipping the Golden Calf – from the Kirkwall Scroll*

illustrated by two mountains connected by a zigzag line (Ex. 17:1-7). To the right are two figures worshipping the Golden Calf on an altar (Ex. 32:1-35). (Plate 43 and Fig. 17) The sepulchre of Sarah (Gen. 23:1-19) is shown after some mountains and is a clear reference to God's original promise to Abraham and Sarah and renewed in the Mosaic Covenant, which is the central theme of this section of the panel. Close to the sepulchre of Sarah are two figures carrying between them an object on a pole. (Fig. 18) This relates to the sending of spies to Canaan. '*And Moses sent them from the wilderness of Pâr-ăn . . .*' (Num. 13:3). It is worth repeating that portion of scripture as this emphasises that this panel is based on the early books of the Old Testament.

' *...and see what kind of land it is; and the people that dwelleth therein, whether they be strong or weak, few or many;*

And what the land is that they dwell in, whether it be good or bad; and what cities they be that they dwell in, whether in tents, or in strongholds;

And what the land is, whether it be fat or lean, whether there be wood therein, or not. And be ye of good courage, and bring of the fruit of the land. Now the time was the time of the first ripe grapes.

So they went up and searched the land from the wilderness of Zin unto Rē -hŏb, as men come to Hā-măth.

And they ascended by the south, and came to Hē-brŏn; where Ă-hî-măn, Shĕ-shai and Tăl-mai, the children of the Anak, were. (Now Hē-brŏn was built seven years before Zō-ăn in Egypt.)

And they came unto the brook of Ĕsh-cŏl, and cut down from thence a branch with one cluster of grapes, and they bare it between two of them on a staff; and they brought of the pomegranates, and of the figs.

The place was called the brook of Ĕsh-cŏl, because of the cluster of grapes the children of Israel cut down from thence.

And they returned from searching the land after forty days.

And they went and came to Moses and Aaron, and all the congregation of the children of Israel, unto the wilderness of Pâr-ăn to Kā-dâsh; and brought back word unto them, and unto all the congregation, and shewed them the fruit of the land. (Num. 13:18-26)

This passage is crucial for the understanding of this panel. Representatives of each of the 12 tribes were selected to be spies who were to go into Canaan to gather intelligence for the invasion. They went as far as Hebron where, as we have seen, the sepulchre of Sarah was located. Two individuals carrying a cluster of grapes suspended between them from a single pole carried on their shoulders.[56] Showing the sepulchre of Sarah and the two men carrying the cluster of grapes confirms that, in accordance with the above passage, the spies had reached Hebron and had returned to the Wilderness of Pâr-ăn to report. However, 10 of the 12 reported that although the land flowed with milk and honey, it would be impossible to conquer because it was populated by giants — Amalekites (Num. 13:31–33). The Israelites had already defeated the Amalekites as related not only in scripture but also in the scroll. The 10 spies so influenced the people that they refused to entered the Promised Land — a direct affront to God who had made the promise (Num. 14:2-4). The two faithful spies are Joshua and Caleb. The other, cowardly, spies, (listed at Num. 13:4-15) die in a plague sent by God

Fig. 18: *The two spies returning with a cluster of grapes – from the Kirwall Scroll*

(Num. 14:26-38). Below the figure carrying the grapes back after 40 days' absence are hills named 'Phares'. This might be a corruption of Pâr-ăn but may also be that this is the location of the family of Pharez identified in the second census of the tribes of Israel taken just before they moved north into Canaan (Num. 26:20-21).

Between Pâr-ăn (where the two faithful spies are shown) and Canaan at the top of the panel a variety of places are identified. The first is appropriately described as the 'Waters of Striff'. 'Arabia' is named but should not be confused with modern Saudi Arabia. Ancient Greek and Latin sources and many later sources mean the term Arabia to include the Syrian and Jordanian deserts — areas west of Canaan. The 'Desert of Zin' is named next and was a place north of the desert of Pâr-ăn. Moses' spies passed through this area on their way to Canaan (Num.13:21).

In a mountainous area bearing the names Gosrom, Arihelneboth and Adgar, two things are depicted. Firstly, two figures apparently worshipping a snake on a cross and, secondly, a box on which are the words 'Sepulchre Aaron'.

Aaron was the brother of Moses and the first High Priest of the Israelites. He was not to see the Promised Land:

'*And Moses stripped Aaron of his garments, and put them on El-ï-zär his*

son; and Aaron died there in the top of the mount: and Moses and El-ï-zär
came down from the mount.
And when all the congregation saw that Aaron was dead, they mourned for
Aaron for thirty days, even all the house of Israel.' (Num. 20:28-29)

The scroll therefore shows the tomb of Aaron and the importance of this image
lies in that it confirms that the geographic progression of the 12 tribes as described
in the Old Testament advancing towards the Promised Land is, more or less,
accurately recounted in the scroll.

The story of the 'snake on a cross' follows closely on that of the death of Aaron:

'*And they journeyed from mount Hor* [where Aaron had died] *by the way*
of the Red sea, to compass [go around] *the land of î-dom: and the soul of*
the people was much discouraged because of the way.
And the people spake against God, and against Moses, Wherefore have ye
brought us up out of Egypt to die in the wilderness? For there is no bread,
neither is there any water; and our soul loatheth this light bread [manna].
And the LORD sent fiery serpents among the people, and they bit the
people; and the people of Israel died.
Therefore the people came to Moses, and said, We have sinned, for we
have spoken against the LORD, and against thee; pray unto the LORD,
that he take away the serpents from us. And Moses prayed for the people.
And the LORD said unto Moses, Make thee a fiery serpent, and set it upon
a pole: and it shall come to pass, that every one who is bitten, when he
looketh upon it, shall live.
And Moses made a serpent of brass, and put it upon a pole, and it came to
pass, that if a serpent had bitten any man, when he beheld the serpent of
brass, he lived.
(Num. 21:4-9) (Plate 34 and Fig. 19)

The children of Israel had once again turned on their God and on Moses, and God
punished them by sending snakes to bite and kill them. Only by looking on the
Brazen Serpent, manufactured by Moses as instructed by God, would they live.
The image of the Brazen Serpent is almost exactly the same as that contained in
the Third or Halleluiah Panel (see above). It has been claimed that these images
have a connection to the ceremonies of the Knights Templar, a matter which shall
be considered in the analysis of the scroll (see below).

After the 'Desert of Zin' the scroll comes much closer to Canaan. The first major feature encountered is a large area bounded by roads and cities and is stated to be 'Salt or Dead Sea' and 'Caspian or Gomer Sea'. This causes a problem in that the 'sea' must either be the Dead Sea or the Caspian Sea — it cannot be both.[57] The reference to the Caspian or Gomer

Fig. 19: *Moses' serpent of brass – from the Kirkwall Scroll*

Sea has intriguing connotations which are further discussed in the analysis below. Meantime the sea can be identified by some of the features which surround it. As elsewhere in the scroll there are a number of obscure words but in these last panels they are more numerous. It would not be too strong to suggest that many of them have been concocted. Whether the artist desired simply to give every place a name regardless of any kind of accuracy or whether he was indulging in school boy map making will probably now never be known.

The creator of the scroll did have enough knowledge to provide some accurate details such as the 'Jordan river' which flows into the Dead Sea and is shown in the scroll correctly flowing into it from the east. Almost as if to make the point that the artist does have geographic knowledge, just above 'Jordan river' is the word 'Mesopotamia'. Jericho is also shown but is out of position. Despite the sea being attributed with four names, it can safely be said that it is intended to be the Dead Sea.

The last, top, section of the right panel is centred on Jerusalem. It is not, however, named by the artist but its size and the named towns and places around it leave no doubt that it is Jerusalem. In this last section the artist appears to be at pains to provide accurate details even if he still cannot refrain from indulging in creating more 'school boy' names for some of the towns. Names such as Galalee [*sic*], Bethlehem, Hermon, Gilboa, Bethany and Joppa are given. The names of two of the 12 tribes are also provided — Judah and Dan.

There is one further feature in this panel which must be discussed and that is the large 'river' which runs its entire length. The 'river' begins at the lower end of the panel appearing from the left. Very shortly after it commences the following is to be found: '1 Year'. Thereafter the numbers 2–9 are inserted at fairly regular intervals with no other text to confirm that they are intended to be the years which have elapsed since the 12 tribes commenced their journey. After 9 the numbers continue, more or less evenly spaced, but in between them are now inserted a variety of words which are not recognisable e.g. 'Litum', 'Mottua' and 'Anangebit', etc.

The number '39' appears at a point in the 'river' past the 'Salt or Dead Sea'. Between that number and the next '04' some text reads 'Debiagad' (Dibon Gad) and that this refers to a place is confirmed by the next piece of writing (after '04'): 'Almondibthess' (Almon Diblathaim).[58] These are two places where the 12 tribes camped shortly before invading Canaan[59] (Num. 33:45-47). The use of '04' is an error and should be 40. This would then correctly indicate the last year of the journey of the Children of Israel to the Promised Land. In addition there are three further numbers — 14, 24 and 43. The latter repeats the same error of transposition as with '04'. Corrected, the sequence of numbers would be 39; 40; 14; 24 and 34. As the Israelites travelled overland and as the 'river' is marked with the number of years spent on the journey, together with some of the stopping places along the way, there can be only one conclusion — the 'river' is not a river at all. It represents the long and winding route followed by the 12 tribes to their final destination.[60]

This concludes the description, with some explanation, of the Kirkwall Scroll, on which the following analysis is based.

The Kirkwall Scroll — an analysis

The most provocative claim regarding the Kirkwall Scroll is that it is of medieval date, specifically from the 15th century and that this has been proved by the scientific method known as radio-carbon, or carbon-14 dating.[61] Without doubting the veracity used in obtaining a sample of the scroll, the method employed in the testing thereof, and the subsequent reporting of the results, it is difficult to accept without question the claim that the scroll has been accurately dated to the 15th century. This is especially so given the margin of error in the method used.[62] However, the total reliance on this particular scientific method in dating such an artefact is flawed for two principal reasons. Firstly, having 'proved' that the scroll dates from the 15th century, no attention whatsoever has been paid to internal evidence contained within the scroll itself. Secondly, radio-carbon dating was applied only to the material of the scroll and therefore tells us nothing about the date the images were painted.[63]

It is fortunate that the history and development of Masonic symbolism has been researched previously and this, together with recent research on the oldest rituals, means that the symbolism on the scroll can be analysed from a Masonic standpoint. In particular the analysis can be undertaken from a *Scottish* Masonic perspective for the first time.[64] To discuss the symbolism each panel (as appropriate) will be examined as previously — in 'descending' order.

Second or Symbolic Panel

The coffin shown at the bottom of the panel (Plate 32) suggests that the scroll cannot date from the medieval period because at that time the deceased were wrapped in shrouds and placed in a charnel house or buried in the ground with a graveslab (which could be entirely without decoration) to cover the corpse. The rich and/or famous may have been buried under the floor of a church and those lucky enough to own their own (like the St. Clairs at Rosslyn Chapel) were similarly interred. This means that there was no need for a coffin — something that did not make its appearance until after the Reformation, 1540 and 1559 in England and Scotland respectively. The image of a coffin in the Kirkwall Scroll means therefore that it cannot date from before 1540.[65] However, even more precise dating can be offered here due to recent research into the origins and development of Masonic ceremonies. As has been explained in more detail elsewhere, modern Freemasonry developed from lodges of stonemasons, slowly in the 17th century and at a much greater pace in the 18th. The stonemasons' lodges had a relatively simple system of two ceremonies — the prentice and fellow craft. The third or Master Masons' degree did not exist in Scotland until 1726 when it was apparently introduced from England.[66] Further confirmation of this comes from the fact that the stonemasons in Scotland who did not join the new Masonic 'system' which embodied the Third Degree, continued to work only the two degrees. Without the Third Degree (and the Masonic legend of the murder of the principal architect of KST, Hiram Abiff and his two burials) the reference to a coffin in the scroll demonstrates that it must date from sometime after c.1720.[67]

This panel provides further internal evidence which aids the dating of the scroll. The diagram of the 47th Problem of Euclid is proof not only of the scroll's date but also its place of origin. The 47th Problem of Euclid first appears in a Masonic document in 1723.[68] The 47th Problem of Euclid was not, and is not, a feature of Scottish Freemasonry. This device subsequent to 1723 came to be frequently used by English Freemasons (Plate 3) but was *not* adopted as a Masonic symbol in Scotland. This symbol does not feature, and never has featured, in Scottish Masonic practice. As it is depicted in the Kirkwall Scroll, an artefact owned and used by a Scottish Masonic Lodge, the question to be asked is why? The answer must simply be that the scroll was manufactured in England where that symbol was in Masonic use.

Fourth or Tabernacle Panel

The next panel which contains Masonic symbolism is the fourth or Tabernacle panel. (Plate 35) The part which contains the Tabernacle has been discussed and has no bearing on Freemasonry other than the fact that KST was based on its design. It is the lower part of the panel which is of interest to us here. The central, round, structure with six entrances is thought to be an attempt to depict the Dome of the Rock in Jerusalem. Contained within it is a drawing of another structure which is exactly as KST is described in modern Masonic ritual. To make the point emphatic the artist has included a coffin within the Temple. This is almost certainly a reference to Hiram Abiff, the central character of the Third Degree of Freemasonry. If this assessment is correct then it helps to confirm the date of the scroll. The Third Degree did not exist until the 1720s and there is no reference to Hiram Abiff by name within Masonic ritual until 1730 with Samuel Prichard's '*Masonry Dissected*'. In order for the artist to be able to draw KST as in the scroll he must have had knowledge of the new ritual which came into being *after* the 1720s. Lodges which existed in Scotland before the establishment of the first Grand Lodge in London (1717) were all, with one notable exception, lodges of stonemasons.[69] That does not mean to say that there were no non-stonemason members of such lodges. In fact the opposite was the case, with non-stonemasons joining stonemasons' lodges as early as 1634.[70] The point here is that they joined an existing organisation, some lodges of which were to retain their stonemasons' character and practices until the 19th century.[71] Those stonemasons' lodges which did not join the Masonic system after the creation of the Grand Lodge of Scotland in 1736 had no knowledge of the Third Degree until they came under the wing of Grand Lodge. The impact of stonemasons vs. non-stonemasons (today often referred to as 'Operative' vs. 'Speculative') lodges at the formation of the Grand Lodge of Scotland has been discussed elsewhere.[72] This ignorance of the Third Degree by stonemasons, which had long pre-existed entirely 'speculative' Lodges, confirms that only two degrees had existed prior to the 1720s. Without a ceremony, no system of associated symbolism could have existed and therefore the scroll must date from after the invention of the Third Degree.

The next panel, the fifth or Armorial Panel, has been described and discussed at length above and its importance in allowing us to date the scroll to the 18th century has been explained. However, there is one other aspect that now requires to be revealed. The Kirkwall Scroll, as the name suggests, is to be found in Kirkwall, Orkney. As the builder of Rosslyn Chapel, William St. Clair, is today frequently described as being 'Prince' of Orkney, one can see the reason for the desire to make a link between this individual and the scroll.[73] Suggesting that the scroll is medieval, had some connection to the Knights Templar and that it was subsequently 'inherited' by a Masonic Lodge means that the Popular School is able to claim it as proof of a link between the KT and modern Freemasonry. An examination of the Lodge's, and other, records might shed light on this alleged link.

Lodge Kirkwall Kilwinning, No.38[2] began its life on 1 October 1736 — that is, a few weeks before the Grand Lodge of Scotland was founded. Two Freemasons, one from Stirling and another from Dunfermline met and inducted sufficient others to form a Lodge. Meetings were not a regular occurrence, or at least were not recorded, and it was not until 2 February 1738 that notes of a second meeting were entered into the Minute Book. At a meeting in April 1739 the Lodge decided to seek a Charter from the Grand Lodge of Scotland which was granted on 1 December 1740, although it was not presented to the lodge until 1742 — probably because it awaited collection in Edinburgh. Significantly the Lodge records up to this time only mention Apprentices and Fellows of Craft but *not* Master Masons. This strongly suggests that the two who established the Lodge and who did so before the Grand Lodge of Scotland existed, had no knowledge of the 'speculative' ceremony of Master Mason. Consequently, therefore, nor did subsequent Lodge members. The charter which was granted by the Grand Lodge of Scotland in 1740 does refer to the Master Masons' degree. As charters such as this contain some interesting material, not least the reference to the Master Masons' degree, a transcription of this particular charter is provided at Appendix VII. In 1747 two men petitioned to join the Lodge in the following terms:

'Unto the Right Worshipfull the Master, Wardens and Remnant Office-bearers and Brethren of the Honourable Lodge of Kirkwall Kilwinning. The supplication of James Robertson and David Gills Operative Masons and regularly entered and Fellow of Craft in the Lodges of Aitchisonhaven and Thurso Kilwinning.[74]

Humbly Sheweth,

That we, your petitioners, having been regularly entered in the above Lodges, To witt, I James Robertson in the Lodge of Aitchisonhaven in Scotland, and I David Gills in the Lodge of Thurso Kilwinning, have resided in this county [Orkney] *for these several years at a great distance from these Lodges, whereby we cannot have communication of fellowship with them according to the Rules and orders of Masonry, and we, being fully convinced of the regular constitution of your Honrbl. Lodge, and that as visiting brethren, we have been tried by the Wardens of this Lodge and found qualified and received accordingly.*

Wee therefore humbly crave wee may be Intrat and Incorporat in your Lodge as Brethren and Fellows of Craft and be admitted to all the privileges and libertys of the same upon our becoming bound as wee hereby oblige ourselves upon the words of brethren to obey your Worships in all the rules and orders of the Lodge as we shall from time to time be desired and required.

Signed - James Robertson
Signed - David Gills'

It is again important to emphasise that this reveals that they were stonemasons, from stonemasons' lodges, who had only been initiated (made Entered Apprentices) and passed to the second or Fellow of Craft degree. They therefore had no knowledge of the third or Master Masons' degree and were applying to be admitted to a Masonic Lodge (Chartered by the Grand Lodge of Scotland) which also had no knowledge of that degree. It is not until 1754 that the conferring of a third degree is recorded in the Minutes of Lodge Kirkwall Kilwinning. This is again significant as it confirms that this Masonic degree had not attained general acceptance in Scottish Lodges — even those which were entitled, by virtue of their charter from the Grand Lodge, to confer that degree (Appendix VIII). This first record of the third degree in Orkney is 29 years after the first written reference to the Master Masons' degree being conferred in a Scottish lodge.[75] With reference to the Kirkwall Scroll this is extremely important because none of the Minute Books of Scottish lodges prior to 1726 (and which date from 1599) record anything other than two ceremonies (or degrees). This means also that they knew nothing of any of the other ceremonies alluded to in the scroll.[76] As the scroll bears numerous symbols from the third degree, and other ceremonies, of which the Lodge had no knowledge, it could not have been used for those ceremonies. It is probably only coincidence that the first Master Masons' ceremony took place in

Lodge Kirkwall Kilwinning in the same year that *Ahiman Rezon* by Laurence Dermott, Grand Secretary of the Ancients Grand Lodge, was first published.

Fifth or Armorial Panel

This panel (Plate 38) has been discussed at considerable length above and as explained there the particular and unique use of the emblems of the four tribes as designed by Rabbi Leon in the 17th century and 'appropriated' by Laurence Dermott for the Ancient Grand Lodge shows that the scroll cannot date from before the foundation of that Grand Lodge in 1751. In addition the panel contains Masonic symbolism for ceremonies which where not devised until the 18th century. In other words ceremonies such as the Royal Arch did not come into existence until the 1740's (at the earliest) and so the symbols of those ceremonies could not have existed prior to that time. Those symbols in the Kirkwall Scroll therefore strongly indicate the date after which it was made.

The 'All Seeing Eye', at the top right, below the arch, in this panel contributes to dating the scroll. The 'All Seeing Eye' does not appear in the canon of Masonic symbolism until the second half of the 18th century and it was used by the Ancients Grand Lodge.[77] However, it is not until 1772 that a written explanation of the symbol is referred to:

> *'The Sword, pointing to a Naked Heart, demonstrates that justice will sooner or later overtake us; and, although our thoughts, words and actions may be hidden from the eyes of man, yet that All-Seeing Eye, whom the Sun, Moon and Stars obey, and under whose watchful care, even the Comets perform their stupendous revolutions, pervades the inmost recesses of the human Heart, and will reward us according to our merits.'[78]*

By tracing the use and development of Masonic symbolism an approximate date of artefacts such as the Kirkwall Scroll can be offered. The 'All-Seeing Eye' is one such symbol and here the evidence again strongly points to a date of manufacture in the latter part of the 18th century.

Remaining Panels

The last two panels have been described above but the occasion is taken to highlight some other aspects which have a bearing on providing a date for the manufacture of the scroll. As has already been explained the sixth or Altar Panel

(Plate 39) contains symbols relevant to the Mark and Excellent Master's ceremonies which were practised by the Ancients Grand Lodge but not the Moderns. This confirms that the scroll is relevant to the Ancients Grand Lodge not the Moderns. The ceremonies of the Mark and Excellent Master were not created until some time after the mid 1750s. The images of three candles, in candlesticks, are intended to mean the three great though emblematic lights of Freemasonry. Here another problem is encountered because three candles used in Masonic Lodges are common in England but are not and were not, part of Scottish Masonic practice. This is another indication that the scroll was designed in accordance with English practice and therefore manufactured there.

Non-Masonic elements

There are, however, non-Masonic elements which are of assistance. Of paramount importance is that the style of writing used in the scroll can assist in its dating. The writing is most definitely not from the 15th century as it shares no similarities with writing from that period. Commonly described as 'modern cursive writing' this style did not appear until the late 17th century and did not become common until the 18th century. This style of writing appears only on the two side panels which suggests that they might have been added later to the central panel but this would rather destroy the argument that they are a treasure map of the Knights Templar. In any event there is writing in the central panel which can be considered. There are letters in the 47th Problem of Euclid in the second panel and Latin letters in the circular device at the top left of the third panel. None of this text is in a form used in the medieval period. It is capitalised cursive text from no earlier than the 17th century. Majuscules or capital letters were rarely used during the 15th and 16th centuries. Even at the commencement of a sentence or paragraph they were rarely used. When they were so employed it was nearly always to create a 'flourish' at the commencement of a document or occasionally at the start of a new page etc. It was not until after the start of the Jacobean period (c.1603–c.1625) that the use of majuscules became common and their use consistent and regular. Even then however, the use of majuscules to form complete words was unknown.[79] The Kirkwall Scroll contains capital letters for all of the proper names used and in one instance for a complete word.

In discussing the left hand panel and showing that it is an attempt to illustrate the journey of Abram (Abraham) and his family from Ur to Canaan, then to Egypt and back to Canaan there is admittedly one problem. The last part of Abraham's journey, from Egypt to Canaan, is not shown on the scroll. The reason for this has been clearly explained by Brother W. R. Day.[80] As the artist progressed with the project down the central panel he increasingly became aware that there was insufficient space for everything that had been intended. This resulted in almost half of the central panel, from the lower part of the Tabernacle panel onwards, being progressively 'squeezed' into smaller and smaller areas. By the time the end (bottom) of the scroll was reached the panels became extremely cluttered in comparison to the earlier ones. If the side panels had to be made to fit the central panel then the return of journey of Abraham to Canaan was expediently omitted.[81] However, taken together with the omission of details from the right side panel there is a more feasible explanation. The late Brother Day presented powerful arguments to suggest that what was actually missing from the scroll was a bottom panel which would have linked the stories in the two side panels into a cohesive whole. The left hand panel ends in Egypt, in the capital Memphis, and the right panel begins after the Israelites had fled Egypt. Abraham and Sarah were in the household of Pharaoh. (Num. 12:15) and as Memphis was the capital of Egypt for most of the Pharaonic period this may be why the artist has mentioned Memphis twice in the lower panel, once relating to Abraham and Sarah and second indicating the starting point for a missing, lower, panel.[82] It is not unreasonable to believe, although absolute proof is lacking, that the missing panel would have dealt with some of the major events leading up to the 12 tribes departing from Egypt.[83] Major events such as the birth of Moses and his admission to the home of Pharaoh, the Burning Bush, the Rod of Aaron, the ten plagues and the parting of the Red Sea would have been likely subjects for such a panel.

William Graeme

Masonic and church records contain references to an individual '...*who was ever in a state of trouble and unrest.*'[84] This fractious individual's name was William Graeme. He was a native of Orkney but had gone to London where he plied his trade as a house painter. After residing there for a number of years he secured the post of Keeper of Customs at Kirkwall and duly returned home. He first comes to our attention in 1785 when the records of the Lodge state that he has applied to become a member. Graeme was in London at the time, or soon after, Leon's model of KST was exhibited in 1778 — the same year the third edition of *Ahiman Rezon* was published. Although the third edition did not contain the supporters (cherubim); crest (the Ark of the Covenant) and motto (Holiness to the Lord) it does show the emblems of the four tribes in the same order as the previous edition and includes a full description of the whole design contained in the second edition. Graeme's involvement with the Lodge takes on much greater significance when it is known that he was a member of an Ancients Lodge in London (No.128) which met at a variety of taverns in London from the time of its foundation in 1767 until its disappearance in 1793.[85] That significance reaches astronomical proportions when seven months later Graeme donated to the Lodge a floor cloth. The size of the Kirkwall Scroll has led some to argue that Graeme's floor cloth could not be the scroll because it does not fit the Lodge room and has to be hung on the wall in order for it to be viewed properly. This is a disingenuous argument. Until 1890 the lodge had met in the Town Hall which was:

'...*a commodious building that at one time had stood on the Market Green, Broad Street, which was demolished in 1890. Here the brethren of Kirkwall Kilwinning meet in comfort, with ample room for Lodge expansion...*'[86]

In the light of all this evidence the argument that the Kirkwall Scroll was made by Graeme (or at least under his direction) probably early in 1786 is almost unassailable.[87] The scroll incorporates symbolism used only by the Ancients Grand Lodge and he had been made a Freemason in one of its Lodges. In addition the scroll contains material relating to Masonic ceremonies only performed in their Lodges — ceremonies which were then unknown in most of Scotland including Orkney. Ironically this might be the reason why the scroll has survived — because Lodge Kirkwall Kilwinning did not have knowledge of the ceremonies depicted in the scroll, the Lodge would have no reason to use it other than as a decorative item.

Some insight to Graeme's character might assist in shedding some further light on the scroll and its intended purpose. Graeme appears to have been an active member of the Lodge Kirkwall Kilwinning from the time he became a member (1785) but shortly before 1790 six candidates proposed by his friends were rejected. Graeme's reaction is not known but can certainly be inferred from the fact that he soon after petitioned the Grand Lodge of Scotland for a Charter to form Lodge St. Paul's which was granted on 2 December 1790.[88] He was the Founding Master and retained the chair for 14 consecutive years. In January 1791 Graeme, in his capacity of the Founding Master, cheekily wrote to Lodge Kirkwall Kilwinning asking them for their assistance in 'consecrating and erecting' Lodge St. Paul's! Needless to say the members of Lodge Kirkwall Kilwinning were not overly enthusiastic and requested proof that Grand Lodge had granted a charter. They asked that Graeme appear before the Lodge with the charter and other correspondence but as might be imagined he was not too happy with that 'request' and asked to be informed of what crime against the Lodge he had committed. Unfortunately, further details are sparse but it is known that Graeme was expelled from Lodge Kirkwall Kilwinning later in 1790.[89]

Against this background there were further problems in wider society in which Graeme was involved. Following divisions within the established church (the Church of Scotland) a number of members in Orkney formed an independent congregation as part of the dissenting Anti-Burgher faction.[90] One of the leading lights of this breakaway group was William Graeme and he was accompanied by a number of members of Lodge St. Paul's. By 1793 Graeme and the rest of the congregation had been so successful that land was purchased on which to build an Anti-Burghers' meeting house. In 1795 Lodge St. Paul's held a meeting in order to discuss how best to progress the erection of the building and within a short space of time laid the foundation stone in a Masonic ceremony. Undoubtedly the rules of the Anti-Burghers came as quite a shock — 'promiscuous' dancing and any connection with Freemasonry would not be tolerated.[91]

This very brief sketch of what is known of Graeme's life and character is provided because it shows that as well as being an ardent, if fractious, Freemason he was also deeply religious.[92] These aspects dominated his life and when one considers the Kirkwall Scroll one is struck by the fact that Freemasonry and religion are contained within a single artefact — a physical manifestation of Graeme's character perhaps?

It is timely to mention that although Freemasonry is not a religion, and never can be, examples such as the Kirkwall Scroll certainly might serve to confuse the non-Freemason on that issue. The Kirkwall Scroll is the product, probably, of one individual — not of 'Freemasonry' and it is worth emphasising that point here, with the scroll as an example. It is the manifestation of one man's opinion, attitude and ideas, not those of Freemasonry. In other words no one man, or body of men, can speak for Freemasonry. Instead individuals may only offer their opinion on Freemasonry with which other Freemasons may, or may not, concur.

What then is the Kirkwall Scroll and how was it used? The above description and analysis has followed other authors in examining the scroll from the 'top down'. This was no doubt due to the fact that when it first came to the attention of Masonic historians it was hanging on the wall of the Lodge room in Kirkwall in this manner — because it was the only means by which it could satisfactorily be displayed.[93] However, as has been mentioned previously, the Lodge originally met in the Town Hall which was very spacious and would have allowed the scroll to be laid on the floor. However, it would only be on rare occasions, if ever, that the scroll would have been revealed in its entirety. The reason is simple. The bottom panel is actually the first panel and lying on the floor only this panel would have been exposed. The candidate would have been instructed on the symbolism appropriate to whichever of the three degrees he was being admitted. This panel is therefore a composite tracing board of the three degrees. It is not impossible that the 'bottom' as well as the top of the scroll would be rolled up as necessary to expose only the required panels — something that would also have saved floor space. Brother Day has convincingly shown that the artist/designer miscalculated the size of each panel and was forced to squeeze material for all three degrees into this single panel. After the third or Master Masons', as have been discussed, the subsequent ceremonies practised by the Ancients Grand Lodge were of the Royal Arch series. The next panel, the sixth or Altar panel, contains symbolism relating to the Mark and Excellent Master's ceremonies and the next panel is explicitly devoted to the Royal Arch ceremony. It can been seen therefore that as the Freemason progressed through the various ceremonies, the scroll would have been progressively unrolled to create a continuous symbolic story or journey. The next panel (the Tabernacle panel) is the first to show scriptural elements together with Masonic symbols. This has been done deliberately in order to introduce the candidate to the central theme of King Solomon's Temple and its precursor, the Tabernacle. The next panel, discussed more fully above, is entirely Christian in character indicating links to the Old Testament, Christ's earthly mission and his resurrection. The next panel contains Masonic symbolism together with much drawn from the Christian faith and is intended to instruct the candidate on matters relating to other branches of Freemasonry which are frequently to be considered the last in a member's Masonic journey.[94] The last panel to be revealed to the Freemason was the first to be discussed above — the Creation panel. Here the Freemason would have been instructed as to the ultimate truth that, regardless of one's journey through life, one's social station, the creator of all things is God the Omnipotent.

A final point is worth making. Although the scroll, and therefore Freemasonry itself, had an overtly Jewish and Christian basis in the 18th century that was so because they were the common and dominant faiths in Great Britain at that time. That does not mean that other faiths, especially today, were or are denied a place. Rather their influence was not so obvious due to the fact that other faiths where numerically tiny in 18th century Britain.

Dating the scroll

The above shows that there is overwhelming evidence that the Kirkwall Scroll dates from the latter half of the 18th century. This is proved by the known origin and development of Masonic ceremonies, symbolism and the people who designed and used them (for example, Rabbi Leon, Laurence Dermott and William Graeme).

There is one other way to consider the scroll — to accept, but only for the sake of argument, that the scroll does date from the 15th century. Consider the implications of that — it would mean that during the 15th century, and earlier, a Masonic system with thousands of members was in existence. A multitude of ceremonies were being conferred in Lodges and Chapters throughout the country. The complex and elaborate system of symbolism would also have been in place. It also would mean that that 'system' has had a 500 year continuous history! Oddly, there are no 15th century traces whatsoever of these ceremonies and the related symbolism except on the Kirkwall Scroll itself. The fact there are no such symbols within Rosslyn Chapel, which does date from the 15th century is, to say the least, curious. Here then is an example of what is known of modern Freemasonry, its symbolism etc., and applying it retrospectively with rather ludicrous consequences.

---

[1] I, like many other historians, have no difficulty when confronted with someone who states 'I believe X, Y and Z' for I, as an historian, have no wish to debate an individual's personally held beliefs. However, when an individual states: 'I believe X. Y and Z and what's more I can prove it' then a line has been crossed and then (and only then) can I, as an historian, analyse the evidence offered.

[2] See, for example, *An Illustrated Guide Book of Rosslyn Chapel*. Tim Wallace-Murphy. 1993.

[3] The existence of the scroll has been known to Freemasons for over two hundred years.

[4] For example Andrew Sinclair in the book: *The Secret Scroll* published in 2001.

[5] 'The Secret Scroll. By Andrew Sinclair. London. 2001 – Dust Jacket'

[6] These colours are so recorded in 1905. See: *Kirkwall Kilwinning Lodge No.38[2] and its Remarkable Scroll*. Rev. J. B. Craven. AQC. Vol. 10. (1897) p. 80. The scroll has become considerably darker since Craven made his observations

[7] The Hebrew characters are corrupted as frequently is the case in Masonic documents and artefacts is the correct form of the ineffable name of God and

the generic Hebrew spelling of 'God'. It is, however, important to remember that accuracy is not the touchstone of Masonic symbolism.

[8] This terminology is well known to Freemasons.

[9] Freemasons will be familiar with this symbolism from a variety of Masonic sources.

[10] The Edinburgh Register House MS is the earliest Masonic ritual so far known, dating from 1696. Others include the Airlie MS (1705) and the Chetwode Crawley MS (1710). For detailed discussion of these MSS see various editions of AQC, the annual transactions of Quatuor Coronati Lodge, No.2076, with particular reference to: *The Airlie MS* by Robert L. D. Cooper and Dr Lisa Kahler, AQC. Vol. 117.

[11] The use of the term 'ritual' is a little misleading because these MSS are multi-functional. Although they are clearly 'ritual' in the sense that they detail a ceremony they do also include an extensive 'question and answer' section and the prominence of this means that they are often referred to as 'catechisms.' Another use was almost certainly as an *aide mémoire* to the ceremony as they were the personal property of individuals rather than a Lodge.

[12] The earliest rituals do contain some limited references to symbols but these are neither the same or as numerous as modern Masonic symbols. Masons' Marks are personal symbols and do not fall into a general Masonic category.

[13] This followed another 'explosion', a huge number of Masonic Lodges being established during the 18th century, initially in England, and then in Europe and beyond.

[14] For the sake of clarity I define Masonic Degrees as being those of Entered Apprentice (the First Degree); Fellow Craft, also known as the Fellow of Craft and occasionally Fellow of the Craft (the Second Degree) and the Master Mason Degree (the Third Degree). These were declared by the Grand Lodge of Scotland to be the only 'pure' Degrees of Freemasonry and therefore all others I describe as being ceremonies or occasionally 'grades'.

[15] From the English-Greek online dictionary at:
http://www.ectaco.co.uk/online/diction.php3?lang=5

[16] The profusion of symbols especially in the 18th and to a lesser extent the 19th century meant that some branches of Freemasonry used the same symbols albeit with different meanings. It does not follow that this particular symbol was exclusive to the KT.

[17] This is another excellent example of a symbol (a Christian one) which has been appropriated and given another meaning. This symbol was also used by other, similar, organisations, for example, the Free Gardeners and the Free Carpenters.

[18] This is a symbol which has fallen into disuse.

[19] Although inaccurate in a biblical sense it should be borne in mind that it is unlikely that the scroll was designed by someone with a detailed knowledge of the Old Testament. Other examples in the scroll suggest that the artist's knowledge was hazy at best.

[20] *Constitutions of the Freemasons 1723.* pp. 20–21.

[21] Euclid was a Greek mathematician who lived and taught in Alexandria, Egypt,

about 300 B.C. Little is known of his life but he did leave more than a dozen books which were widely translated and on which modern Geometry is based.
[22] There is a reference to the 47th problem in the English Installed Master's ceremony but not in the Scottish version of that ceremony.
[23] See endnote 16 above.
[24] This symbol was in use by the church before the 9th century but entered common use about 820AD.
[25] Even within the church '*papal crosses have for the most part only a heraldic existence*'. Online Catholic Encyclopaedia.
[26] It is acknowledged that the Ten Commandments are out of sequence here but that does not detract from the general 'direction' indicated by the symbolism.
[27] Andrew Sinclair in '*The Real Da Vinci Code*'. Channel 4 Television.
[28] *Freemasons' Guide and Compendium*. Bernard E. Jones. p. 552. Another example of the use of symbols but endowed with meaning different from the original.
[29] There is another link from the Tabernacle, and therefore Exodus, to Genesis (the first panel) in that Jabal, son of Lamech, was the inventor of tents (Genesis 4:20).
[30] From the online encyclopaedia Wikipedia — see:
http://en.wikipedia.org/wiki/Dome_of_the_Rock
[31] The Dome of the Rock is hexagonal but given imprecise rendering of other images in the scroll it is likely that the artists have only had a vague idea of the shape.
[32] For a detailed discussion and analysis of the life and work of Rabbi Leon see: *Jacob Judah Leon of Amsterdam (1602–1675) and his models of the Temple of Solomon and the Tabernacle*. By A. Lewis Shane in AQC. Vol. 96.
[33] For example:
    Retrato del templo de Salomo. 1642.
    Afbeeldinge van den Tabernakel. 1647.
    De Cherubinis tractatus. 1647.
    Libellus effigiei temple Salomonis. (Hebrew) 1650.
    Jac. Jeh. Leonis de Templo Hierosolym. 1665.
    Afbeeldinge von den Tempel Salomonis. 1669.
    Las Alabanças de Santidad. Año 5431 (1671).

[34] The title Atholl Grand Lodge is due to the fact that two Dukes of Atholl presided over the Grand Lodge for more than half of its existence.
[35] The Ancients and Moderns Grand Lodges have been discussed in a number of places. See, for example: *The Grand Lodge of England according to the Old Institutions*, by Cyril N. Batham AQC Vol. 98; *The Grand Lodge of England — History of the first 100 years*, by A. R. Hewitt. AQC Vol. 80; *The Grand Lodge of the 'Schismatics' or 'Ancients'* by Robert F. Gould. AQC Vol. 6. *The Craft: A History of English Freemasonry* by John Hamill. 1994.
[36] Because the Ancients Grand Lodge had adopted the Holy Royal Arch ceremonies there was a pre-disposition to look favourably on the so called 'Higher Degrees' including that of the Knights Templar. The Dukes of Sussex

and Kent were both Grand Masters of the Order. The situation in Scotland was quite different where as we have seen anything other than the first three degrees were considered spurious and non-Masonic foreign importations.

[37] *Rabbi Jacob Judah Leon*. By W. J. Chetwode Crawley. AQC Vol. 12, p. 150.

[38] *Jacob Judah Leon of Amsterdam (1602–1675) and his models of the Temple of Solomon and the Tabernacle*. AQC. Vol. 96 (1983). By A. Lewis Shane. p. 156.

[39] Faulkner's Dublin Journal. January 1744. This must refer to St. John the Evangelist's Day, 27 December 1743.

[40] *A Serious and Impartial Enquiry into the Cause of the Present state of Decay of Freemasonry in the Kingdom of Ireland*. Fifield Dassigny. Dublin. 1744.

[41] Because of the distinctly Scottish nature of the Lodge's membership and subsequent Charter from Scotland some claim, not without justification, that George Washington was a Scottish Freemason.

[42] For a more detailed list see Chapter 3, footnote 21. It is unlikely that a comprehensive list of Masonic and pseudo-Masonic Degrees and ceremonies will ever be compiled because of the sheer number that were invented during the 18th century.

[43] 'Coats of arms' are more correctly known as 'Armorial Bearings' but I have opted to used the more commonly used term.

[44] *Masonic Medals*. by G. L. Shackles. AQC. Vol. 10. (1897) pp. 189–193.

[45] See also chapter 3, note 20.

[46] Some Lodges of the Moderns Grand Lodge conferred the Royal Arch degrees, possibly as early as 1754, but Grand Lodge did not consider it to be the 'highest' degree of Freemasonry.

[47] The arms are mounted on an altar, the top edge of which bears an inscription which it has not, unfortunately, been possible to decipher.

[48] Members of the Royal Arch will be acquainted with the correct, or new, method of giving this.

[49] Scottish Lodges have Office-bearers not 'Officers'.

[50] The significance of these words used by the Ancients as opposed to the Moderns will be recognised by Freemasons today. There is further enlightenment as to the esoteric content of Masonic ritual, and the puzzle regarding certain words is solved here for the first time.

[52] *The Craft: A History of English Freemasonry* by John Hamill. pp. 59-62.

[52] *The Secret Scroll* by Andrew Sinclair. Chapter 14.

[53] Isaac, The second patriarch, son of Abraham and Jacob, the third patriarch, grandson of Abraham and son of Isaac, were also buried here.

[53] *The Secret Scroll* by Andrew Sinclair. Captions to plates between pp.58–59 and 154–155.

[55] Abram means 'exalted father' and Abraham 'father of many' reflecting his changed relationship with God.

[56] Given the context in which the illustration appears, how or why it could be interpreted as the Ark of the Covenant being transported is not clear. *The Secret Scroll*. Andrew Sinclair. pp. 189-190. The image in the scroll show two men carrying a pole on their shoulders suspended from which is a small 'tear'-shaped object - a cluster of grapes, whereas it is known that the Ark of the

Covenant required to be carried using two poles See Fig. 18.

[57] The Caspian Sea is to the north east of this location.

[58] The word is followed by 'well' and such a watering place would be consistent with it being chosen for a camping place.

[59] There is one other possible place marked between the years 27 and 28 — 'Thesaron' — The Saron or The Sharon which was a plain near Jerusalem, although referred to in the Old Testament, it does not appear in the books concerned with the Israelites' journey to Canaan.

[60] The suggestion that this is a river is made in *The Secret Scroll* by Andrew Sinclair, p. 190, where it is described as a '*River of Life following towards the Temple*'.

[61] *The Secret Scroll* by Andrew Sinclair. Chapter 15.

[62] Carbon-14 dating can have an error margin sufficient to cast doubt on such specific dating of the scroll.

[63] It is entirely feasible that disused sailcloth was recycled in a number of ways, this being one example.

[64] See, for example, *Sources of Masonic Symbolism* by Alex Horne and *Symbolism in Craft Freemasonry* by Colin Dyer, both of which admittedly approach the subject from a non-Scottish Masonic point of view. In respect of the earliest known rituals see endnote 9 above.

[65] There will, of course, be isolated exceptions given that many continued to adhere to the Roman Church despite strong efforts by the Reformed Church to make them desist. The point here is that the Reformed Church in Scotland *made* people change their burial methods.

[66] The first record of this ceremony being conferred in Scotland is in 1726. On 25 March 1726 Gabriel Porterfield was '*admitted and received a Master*' in Lodge Dumbarton Kilwinning, No.18 having been made a Fellow Craft in the same Lodge two months previously. Grand Lodge of Scotland Year Book. 1986, p. 68.

[67] Early Scottish Lodges performed a variety of 'services' for their members including the provision of a Mort Cloth which was used to cover a corpse (which was not in a coffin) on its way to a graveyard. This was provided free for members of the Lodge and was rented to non-members for a small fee. This shows that deceased members of early Lodges were not buried in coffins — a practice which continued until into the 18th century. See: *The Minute Book of the Lodge of Aitcheson's Haven, 1598–1764*, by R. E. Wallace-James. Grand Lodge of Scotland Year Book. 1981. pp.58–59.

[68] In the frontispiece of Anderson's *Constitutions* of that year.

[69] The exception was the Haughfoot Lodge in the Scottish borders which was founded in 1702 by local landed gentry. Other Lodges existed where the membership was 'mixed' — that is, they had non-stonemasons and stonemasons. The Lodge at Aberdeen, founded 1670, is an example, with only approximately 25% being stonemasons.

[70] *The First Freemasons* by David Stevenson. p. 26.

[71] See also: `Revenge of the operatives' in: *Marking Well*. Lewis Masonic 2006.

[72] The term 'organisation' does however imply a formality of structure which did

not exist.

[73] He was never a Prince but comments that he was 'almost a Prince' or was 'a Prince in all but name' etc. have been inaccurately truncated to 'Prince of Orkney'.

[74] The Lodge of Aitcheson's Haven is the oldest known Lodge in the world. The Minutes of the Lodge commence on 9 January 1599. The Lodge no longer exists. It was an 'operative' Lodge. There is no trace of a Lodge called Thurso Kilwinning although one was Chartered by the Grand Lodge of Scotland in Thurso in 1741 by the name Lodge St. John and it is probably of this Lodge that David Gill was a member. This too appears to have been an 'operative' Lodge. He certainly describes himself as an operative mason.

[75] See note 57 above.

[76] This may be one of the reasons that the scroll survived — because it could not be fully used.

[77] See, *Freemasonry — A Journey through Ritual and Symbol*. W. Kirk MacNulty. p. 56. This shows a painting of the Ancient Grand Lodge's 'coat of arms' as in *Ahiman Rezon* (1764) but with the addition of an 'All Seeing Eye' above.

[78] *Illustrations of Masonry*. William Preston. 1772. Quoted in: *Coil's Masonic Encyclopedia*. 1996.

[79] Handwriting has, fortunately, been extremely well researched and its origins and development are well known. In this instance see, for example, '*The Handwriting of the Renaissance: being the development and characteristics of the script of Shakspere's time*' by Samuel Aaron Tannenbaum.

[80] *The Kirkwall Scroll*. AQC. Vol. 38 (1925). p. 121.

[81] Another reason for the omission may have been that it simply was not considered important enough to include as details of the return to Canaan are very brief. (Num. 13:1-4)

[82] *British Museum Dictionary of Ancient Egypt*. Ian Shaw and Paul Nicholson. p. 180.

[83] It could be argued that the so called Knight Templar in this panel is actually intended to show Pharaoh in pursuit of the 12 tribes already amassed for departure.

[84] *Lodge Kirkwall Kilwinning, No.38² — The Story from 1736* by James Flett. Lerwick. 1976. p. 32.

[85] *Masonic Records 1717–1894* by John Lane. 1895.

[86] *Lodge Kirkwall Kilwinning, No.38² — The Story from 1736* by James Flett. Lerwick. 1976. pp 37–38.

[87] It is known that Graeme was a very enthusiastic Freemason and it is not unreasonable to think that he made, or had made, the scroll as a gift for his new Lodge.

[88] One can but wonder if the choice of name had any connection with the location of Graeme's London Lodge.

[89] When GLoS undertook a survey and renumbering of its daughter Lodges in 1809 Lodge St. Paul's was removed from the Roll — a sure indication that the Lodge had ceased to function. Within a very few years of Graeme ceasing to be

Master of the Lodge, perhaps due to his death, the Lodge ceased to function —
an indication perhaps that he was the main driving force behind the Lodge
which could not survive without him.

Chapter 8
Other 'Evidence'

Mysterious Graveslabs

Within the last 10–20 years various claims have been made for the existence of evidence, or new interpretation of events, that support the myth. Only the period *c*.1307–*c*.1329 regarding this alleged supporting evidence is examined here as that is the most crucial period for the testing of the hypothesis (that forewarned KT fled from France etc. as detailed in the first chapter) and due to the limitations of space, only the main elements of the Scottish aspects of the myth are considered.

If a number of KT ships did set sail for Scotland on or about 12 October 1307, the proponents of the myth argue that Argyll was chosen for the following reasons:

- Robert the Bruce had been excommunicated in 1306 for the murder of John 'the Red' Comyn in Greyfriars church, Dumfries, hence Papal law could not be applied in Scotland. The heretical Order of the KT was therefore beyond papal authority.
- The sea around Argyll was under the control of Robert the Bruce's allies.
- Argyll was an isolated and thinly populated part of Scotland.

Bruce's Excommunication
Bruce's excommunication is alleged to be one of the major factors in favour of the KT fleeing to Scotland.

> *'Bruce was excommunicated 10th February 1305* [sic]. *The fact that Bruce was excommunicated…was the greatest attraction of Scotland as a sanctuary — it was one of the few places on the planet where the Pope could not get at them.'*[1]

Most other popular writers also adopt this view.[2] This is a surprising contention given that the Pope was not involved at the time the KT were arrested in France on 13 October 1307. In fact the Church was not informed until *after* the arrests had been made — *'The initiative came exclusively from the King of France.'*[3] If some KT did have foreknowledge of their impending arrests and did leave the country they did so to escape Philip IV (1268–1314) and not Pope Clement V (1264–1314). The claim that fugitive KT fled to Scotland *because* Robert the Bruce was an excommunicant of the church simply does not hold water.

That the Pope excommunicated Bruce is not in question. However, the excommunication applied to an individual, not a country. There is no suggestion that the Scots generally stopped going to church or that the Church treated the people as if they had been excommunicated. Some authors have gone so far as to suggest that because of Bruce's excommunication Scotland was considered to be a pagan country and therefore liable to be the subject of a crusade![4] This is to entirely misunderstand what excommunication is and its intention — to punish a transgressor by removing him or her from the day to day activities of the Church. However, the way was always left open for reconciliation with the Church. Philip IV of France instigated the mass arrest of the KT. It was only later that Clement V added his sanction to Philip's actions. The secular authorities on behalf of the Church would have carried out any arrest of KT in Scotland, and elsewhere. Therefore, although Bruce was excommunicated he could have arrested any KT in Scotland had he so wished. That he did not do so was nothing to do with his being excommunicate but whether, or not, he felt it necessary to do so. Alternatively, there may simply have been no mass arrests because there was no mass to arrest!

In an effort to support the idea that the Church in Scotland conspired with Bruce to protect the heretical KT it has been suggested that Bruce and the Church, in Scotland, were united in their mutual aim of obtaining independence for Scotland. The clergy that supported Bruce did so in order to maintain their own clerical independence from England — independence for the Church *in* Scotland. The Scottish Church had been made, in 1192, a 'Special Daughter' of the Holy See, which meant that the bishoprics were answerable only to Rome. The members of the Church in Scotland did not want to replace that degree of independence with domination by the Church *in* England.[5, 6]

Given the extensive contacts between Scotland and France throughout this period it is not surprising that Philip wrote to Bruce requesting that he arrest any fugitive KT found in the lands under his jurisdiction.[7] Indeed, Philip wrote to all the monarchs of Europe making the same request. Scotland was not a special case in this respect.[8] What is important is that Bruce received Philip's letter and that it was discussed at the Parliament of 16–17 March 1309 held at St Andrews. That this was debated at all, although the decision, if any, of the Parliament is not known, indicates that the arrest and pursuit of all KT throughout Europe was common knowledge. The Parliament had been called for a number of reasons, one of which was that all those who had until then opposed Bruce but who wished to make amends could meet together in order to do so. This was hardly a forum into which a debate about the 'secret' existence of KT and their fate would have been introduced. In attendance at that Parliament were men who had been, until recently, Bruce's enemies — importantly Alexander of Argyll (father of John of Lorn). It is inconceivable that men from the precise area where the KT are said to have landed, and were still living as fugitives, would not have reported this to that Parliament when the matter was raised. Even had they not done so, they and others would have surely reported the existence of such 'heretic' KT in Scotland to Edward II as well as to Philip IV.[9]

There is evidence to show that members of the Church in Scotland faced a very difficult choice — to support Bruce or the Pope. Many chose to apply the sanctions demanded by the Bull of Excommunication (e.g. not celebrating Mass for Bruce etc.) and a number of priests paid with their lives for that refusal.[10] It is also known that one of his main supporters, Bishop William de Lamberton (?–1328), participated in an English trial (December 1309) of two Scottish KT.[11] This demonstrates that one of the major figures in Scotland's fight for independence was prepared to assist not only the Church but also the enemy, England, in bringing 'fugitive' KT to trial. It shows also that Bruce's excommunication meant little, or nothing, to a senior member of the Church in respect of the accusations against the KT. The result of the trial also reveals something else — that the KT were not treated at all badly by the authorities. Of the two defendants, William of Middleton was subsequently sent to the Cistercian monastery of Roche and Walter of Clifton was sent to Shelford. In 1318 John XXII (1316–1334) decreed that the ex-KT could themselves chose in which religious house they wished to live. William of Middleton choose to move from Roche to the Augustinian house at Bridlington whereas Walter of Clifton opted to remain at Shelford.[12] This treatment hardly supports the argument that the fugitive KT were in fear of their lives and that only Bruce could protect them.

The Supposed Argyll Location

It is alleged that Argyll was the ideal place for the fugitive KT to hide because access by sea was safe from those seeking them (e.g. the Pope Clement V and Philip IV) and the land was both isolated and thinly populated. The former is not that simple and the latter incorrect.[13]

It is argued that sea routes for fugitives from France, in 1307, were limited either through the Irish Sea between Ireland and England to Scotland or around the west coast of Ireland to Scotland. It is alleged that at this time the Irish Sea was dominated by English shipping and therefore the only possible sea route to Argyll was round the west coast of Ireland and up the Sound of Jura (with Islay and Jura to the west and the Kintyre peninsula to the east) into Loch Sween. The existence of this alleged 'clear channel' is based on the fact that allies of Robert the Bruce held Islay, Jura and Kintyre and that allies of Edward I and Edward II did not operate in the area.[14]

A major problem is that none of the myth's proponents define the area they describe as Argyll. Modern Argyll comprises Kintyre and Knapdale, Cowal (the area south of Loch Awe), Lorn (the area north of Loch Awe) and northern Argyll together with the islands of Islay, Jura, Mull, Tiree, Coll, Lismore, Iona, Staffa and Colonsay. All of mainland Argyll has a western coastline. By 1301 Edward I had constructed an alliance, which included the MacDonalds of Islay, and the MacDougalls of Lorn.[15] When Bruce murdered John (the Red) Comyn in 1306 the political situation in Argyll changed. The MacDougalls of Lorn were related to the Comyns by marriage as Alexander MacDougall of Argyll, father of John of Lorn, had married a daughter of John Comyn. The murder of Comyn created a blood feud between Bruce and the MacDougalls. They were primarily a land based clan but they too had sea-going warfare capability as is evidenced by a letter written to Edward II, in March 1309, in which John MacDougall mentions that he maintains galleys on Loch Etive (a sea loch) and on Loch Awe.[16] For fugitive KT to arrive, unnoticed, on the doorstep of the MacDougalls would have been most unlikely especially at the time a blood feud was underway.

The MacDonalds of Islay, led by Angus Og (*c* 1274–*c*.1320), were allies of Edward I and fought for him against the MacDougalls of Lorn.[17] The murder of Comyn by Bruce did not mean that the MacDonalds had to re-align their allegiance unlike the MacDougalls who, as mentioned above, had a marital alliance. Angus Og was in the service of Edward I in 1301 against the MacDougalls but there is no further reference to him until he is mentioned by Barbour in *The Bruce* where he is described as a supporter, *c*.1306, of Bruce.[18] Given that Barbour was writing retrospectively, albeit with the benefit of contemporary evidence, it cannot be discounted that he enhanced the role of an eventual supporter of Robert I. The weight given to this aspect of someone's work, which has otherwise been dismissed as mere legend, is indicative of the selective use of source material discussed previously in Chapter 1.[19] The point is, however, that the sea routes available to the allegedly fleeing KT were not as secure and unobserved as some writers claim. The area around Argyll was a very well used sea route and details of sea-going activities exist from the 5th century. The late 8th century saw the arrival of the Vikings for the first time, and they continued to visit and settle in Argyll over a few hundred years bringing with them all their extensive knowledge of seamanship, shipbuilding, etc.

Argyll then was far from being a quiet backwater. Not only in Argyll were events taking place that confirm this but men from Argyll were also involved in the war against Bruce elsewhere in Scotland. John MacDougall of Lorn (he was also referred to as being 'of Argyll') defeated Bruce at the Battle of Dail Righ (Dalry, near Tyndrum) in August 1306.[20] At Inverurie on 23 May 1308 Bruce defeated John Comyn, Earl of Buchan. In 1309 he clashed again with the MacDougalls at the Pass of Brander and although the MacDougalls were defeated (whilst John MacDougall of Lorn looked on from a sea galley on Loch Etive) they were not, apparently, ousted from their lands until after 1314. In 1315 Bruce deprived them of their lands and gave them to Sir Colin Campbell (the progenitor of the Dukes of Argyll) as a reward for his support at the Battle of Bannockburn.[21] The change of ownership does not mean that there was a mass exodus of people living in MacDougall territory, only that they had to change their allegiance to another clan chief.

Such activity also indicates that Argyll was not an isolated part of Scotland. In medieval Scotland the fastest and easiest way of travelling was by sea. Today we tend to think of travel in terms of time taken and miles covered over land whereas in the early 14th century safety and ease of travel were the main considerations. Because Argyll has a long coastline it was ideally placed for all types of sea-going activity: trading, fishing, boat building and repair, etc. Such activities meant that the area supported a sizeable population in comparison to other rural parts of Scotland. From the point of view of those who lived in Argyll it was a very busy place, being on or near the sea 'crossroads' for Ireland, western Scotland, the Isle of Man and northwest England. For such residents it was the rest of Scotland that was distant and isolated. The area cannot be described as isolated nor was it thinly populated. Away from the coastline the land was populated by farmers. Their homes, fields, barns and pens, and shelters for their domesticated animals have been excavated by archaeologists. In the light of all the foregoing it seems a very unlikely place for fugitives, of any kind, in which to deliberately choose to try and hide. The suggestion that fugitive KT would chose to hide there is even more curious when it is remembered that this is one part of Scotland where they owned no property or preceptories.[22]

Bannockburn

The alleged intervention of the KT at the Battle of Bannockburn is another, crucial, supporting point of the myth.[23] Thus we have, for example, the following:

> '*The battle took place near Stirling Castle on St John's Day in June, a significant date for the Military Orders [sic]. Accounts of the conflict are sparse and fragmentary. But they testify to two strange events. There was a charge by mounted soldiers against the English archers from a reserve kept back by Bruce. And when all the troops were fully engaged on both sides, a fresh force of horsemen appeared with banners flying and routed the English. While one Scottish legend claims these to have been camp-followers riding ponies and waving sheets and clubs and pitchforks, such a mob could never have put the English King and five hundred knights to immediate flight.*'[24]

This description of the battle, with minor variations, is repeated by most who hold to the Alternative, or Popular, view. However, there is a substantial body of contemporary and near contemporary evidence that is completely ignored by the myth's supporters. These sources are key to any study, and understanding, of 14th century Scotland and England. These sources are:

Author:	Title, etc.
Baker	*Chronica Galfridi le Baker de Swynebroke*, ed, E. Maunde Thompson (Oxford, 1889).
Bridlington	*Gesta Edwardi de Carnarvan auctore canonico, Bridlingtoniensi* in Stubbs Chronicles 11 (Rolls Series, 1882-3).
Brut	The Brut or The Chronicles of England ed. F W D Brie (Oxford, Early English Text Society, 1906), 1.
Brut	*Brut y Tywysogyon*, Red Book of Hergest version, ed. Thomas Jones, (UWP, Cardiff, 1941).
Brut	*Brut y Tywysogion*, ed. John Williams, (London: Longman, Green et al 1860). 1.
Flores	Flores *Historiam*, ed. H.G. Luard (Rolls Series, 1890).
Guisburg	The Chronicles of Walter of Guisburgh previously edited as the Chronicle of Walter of Hemingford or Hemingburgh,

	ed. H. Rothwell for the Royal Historical Society (Camden Series LXXXIX, London, 1957).
Higden	*Polychronicon Ranulphi Higden Monachi Cestrensis* with the English translations of John de Trevisa etc. ed. C. Babington and J.R. Lumby (Rolls Series, 1965), VII.
Holyrood	The Chronicle of Holyrood, ed. Marjorie O. Anderson, (Edinburgh, Constable for the University Press, 1938).
Knighton	*Chronicon Henrici Knighton*, ed J.R. Lumby (Rolls Series 1895). I.
Lanercost	Chronicle of Lanercost, translated by Sir Herbert Maxwell (Maclehose, Glasgow, 1913).
Lanercost	*Chronicon de Lanercost*, ed. J. Stevenson (Maitland Club, Edinburgh, 1839).
London	The Chronicles of London, ed. and trans. E. Goldsmid (Edinburgh, 1885) II.
Melrose	Chronicle of Melrose trans. by J. Stevenson, in Church Historians of England (London, 18358).
Melrose	Chronicle of Melrose, Facsimile Edition, ed. A. O. Anderson *et al* London 1936).
Melsa	*Chronica Monasterii de Melsa, auctore Thoma de Burton, Abbate*, ed. E. A. Bond (Rolls series, 1867, Longmans, Green, Reader and Dyer).
Paris	The Illustrated Chronicles of Matthew Paris, trans and ed. by Richard Vaughan, Allan Sutton, Corpus Christi, Cambridge, 1993.
Paulini	*Annales Paulini*, ed. Stubbs, (London, 1882, Rolls Series).
Rotuli Scotiae	*Rotuli Scotiae* ed. D. MacPherson, i, (Record Commission, London, 1814-19).
Rymer's *Foedera*	Syllabus of Documents Relating to England and Other Kingdoms ed. by Thomas Dufus Hardy Vol 1 .1066-1377 (London 1869).
Scalacronica	*Scalacronica* by Sir Thomas Gray of Heton, ed. and trans by Sir H. Maxwell (Glasgow, 1907).
Scalacronica	*Scalacronica* by Sir Thomas Gray of Heton, (Maitland Club, 1836)
Triveti	[Continuation of Bridlington of early years of Ed II] F.

Nicholai Triveti, *Annales*, ed. Thomas Hog for English
Historical Society, 1845.

Trokelowe   *Johannis de Trokelowe et Henrici de Blaneforde*
Chronica et Annales, ed. H.T. Riley (Rolls Series, 1865).

Vita Edwardi Secundi. ed. N. Denholm-Young (London, Nelson, 1957).

Vita Edwardi Secundi. (Rolls Series 1882).

In addition to these contemporary sources another, near contemporary, source has
been used in this book: *The Bruce*, by John Barbour. *c*.1375.[25]

Before commencing the discussion regarding Robert the Bruce, the Battle of
Bannockburn etc., there is one subsidiary point, which is specifically relevant to
Scottish Freemasonry on which comment is desirable. Almost without exception
those who hold to the Alternative view mention that the Battle of Bannockburn
was fought on 24 June and that this date is 'significant'.[26] The 24 June is the Feast
Day of St. John the Baptist, a date 'observed' by the KT. It also has significance
for Freemasons, being the day chosen for their annual celebration. But the attempt
to link Freemasonry with the KT because of an alleged co-incidence of annual
feast days and the date of a battle is doomed to failure. Firstly, most historians
concur that the Battle of Bannockburn was fought over two days (23-24 June).[27]
Secondly, the Feast Day of St. John the Baptist was but one of numerous Feast
Days which were observed by KT.[28] Indeed the medieval Order was particularly
devoted to the Virgin to whom all other saints were, of course, subordinate. The
use of this saint to link Freemasonry and KT is common: '*John the Baptist was
patron saint of both Knights Templar and Freemasons*'.[29] From this assumption it
follows, therefore, that his Feast Day, 24 June has special significance for all
Freemasons and this is probably true everywhere — except in Scotland. The
assumption that English Masonic history and practice is the same as in Scotland
is a demonstration of how some can be led into error.

Many writers do not differentiate between stonemasons and Freemasons. Links
between stonemasons and Freemasons can most easily be traced in Scotland, but
documentary traces of these connections do not exist until *c*.1599 when the first
records of a lodge of stonemasons commence.[30] Even that date has to be
considered guardedly for it is not until 1634 that the first non-stonemason is
recorded as joining a stonemason's lodge — the Lodge of Edinburgh.[31] There is,
therefore, a period of 320 years where there is no known evidence of any
connection between the two (i.e. the period between the alleged creation of
'Freemasonry' by Robert the Bruce and the earliest lodge records). More

importantly, there is no evidence whatsoever, that what 17th century Scottish stonemasons did in their lodges was what stonemasons had been doing earlier. Therefore, not only is there no contemporary evidence of a link between the medieval KT and modern Freemasonry (a period c.1314–1778) but also there is no evidence of a direct link between stonemasons and Freemasons prior to 1599.[31] The reason why 1598/9 is something of an historical turning point is amply explained elsewhere.[33]

What evidence there is relating to Scottish stonemasons prior to 1598/9 is not found in lodge Minute Books but in local and national records. These supply us with some insight as to the lives and activities of Scottish stonemasons. In 1475 the masons and wrights (carpenters) of Edinburgh were granted a Seal of Cause, which incorporated them into an officially recognised body. It granted the 'Incorporation of Wrights and Masons' certain rights and imposed certain responsibilities. The one that is of interest here is that stonemasons became responsible for the maintenance of the aisle of St John the Evangelist within St. Giles' church, Edinburgh.[34] From the time when the first lodge records begin, until relatively recently, Scottish lodges have always held their annual, Installation, meeting (often the only recorded meeting) on 27 December.[35] The emphasis on 24 June as a significant date linking Freemasons and medieval KT, in Scotland, simply does not apply.

A more important question might be: '*What contemporary evidence is there, if any, of the intervention by members of the medieval Order of KT at the Battle of Bannockburn?*'

The statement: '*Accounts of the conflict* [the Battle of Bannockburn] *are sparse and fragmentary*' demonstrates the nub of this problem.[36] No evidence is provided to support this contention. In fact, accounts of the battle are numerous and are contemporary as previously described. A few are nearly contemporaneous.

Although none of these sources provide any evidence that KT were at the Battle of Bannockburn, it can be made to look as if they were there and, what is more, that they played a crucial part in the outcome. The argument is that just when the battle hung in the balance another force appeared suddenly on the field. This fresh force caused the English knights to lose heart and they fled the field. Who else but the KT could have caused such a reaction? It is suggested that because no one mentions their sudden appearance this supports the case for their presence. The argument is presented in this manner: the Scots, it is said, could not admit that the 'heretic' KT gave them assistance in order not to antagonise the church. The English did not mention that the KT caused their defeat due to the embarrassment of that defeat.[37] The absence of any evidence of the involvement of the KT is therefore used as 'proof' that they were present![38] This is an example of the technique whereby a negative (there is no evidence that KT were at the battle) is used to create a positive (they turned the battle in favour of the Scots).

Extant evidence that is not used, or discussed, by those of the Popular Approach is worthy of brief mention. John Barbour (c.1325–1395) wrote his epic poem *The Bruce c.*1372. It recounts the life and exploits of Robert the Bruce and it is one of the key sources of information regarding him and Scotland's struggle for independence. It is particularly valuable in relation to the Battle of Bannockburn regarding the 'unknown force'. There is internal evidence to show that Barbour had access to material now lost and also to eyewitness testimony.[39] Barbour's account is nearly contemporaneous with the period and can hardly be dismissed as 'legend'.[40] As the alleged sudden appearance of the KT during the battle is pivotal to the myth it is worth repeating Barbour's description of the 'unknown force' and their part in the conflict.

'*Then he* [Bruce] *sent all the small folk and carters, with equipment and provisions in the Park a good way away from him, and had them go* [away] *from the divisions; they went the way he had ordered... The king had them all be ready for he knew that his enemies lay all night at the Falkirk ...*' (Translation)

Book 11 lines 427 to 431 and lines 441 to 444

'*At this point that I am telling you of just now, when that battle was being fought in that way, where on each side they were fighting vigorously, yeomen and boys and men on foot who had been left in the Park to guard the provisions, when they knew without doubt that their lords were fighting their enemies in desperate combat, made one of themselves,* [of those] *who were there, chieftain of them all, and fastened sheets that were fairly broad in place of banners upon long poles and spears, saying that they meant to see the fight, and help their lords to their utmost. When all had agreed to this, they gathered in one body — they were fifteen thousand or more — and then with great speed they went with their banners all in one force, as if they had been strong brave men. They came with all that gathering to just where they could see the battle, then together they gave a cry, 'Kill! Kill! On them now!' and with that they were coming, although they were still far*

*away. The Englishmen who were giving ground by force of pressure, as I
said before, when they saw coming towards them such a company, shouting
like that,* [a company] *which they thought was at least as numerous as that
fighting against them there, and which they had not seen before,* [well] *you
can believe that the best, the bravest, who were in their army that day,
wished that they were* [somewhere else] *with their honour. King Robert
saw from their pulling-back that they were close to defeat, and had his
battle cry shouted, then with those of his company pressed his enemies so
hard that they were so apprehensive that they gave ground more and more,
for all the Scotsmen who were there, when they saw them escaping from the
fighting, laid into them with all their might. They scattered in sundry
groups and were close to defeat; some of them fled openly, but those who
were brave and bold, whom shame prevented from fleeing, kept up the
struggle at great cost standing firm in the fight.'* (Translation)

Book 13 lines 225 to 281

From this it can be seen that Bruce had arranged, before the battle, that the *'small
folk and carters'* were separated from his main force because such men were
undisciplined, unreliable, and generally poorly armed. At the Battle of Loudoun
Hill (10 May 1307) he had made the same prior preparations:

*'The carriage men and poor folk who were not of value in the battle he left
behind him, standing still together on the hill.'* (Translation)

Book 8 lines 275 to 278.

This reveals significant details ignored by those who support the Alternative view.
Separating the 'small folk' from the main army was normal practice because, as
at Loudoun Hill, as Barbour puts it they *'were not of value in the battle'*. They
were *'carriage men'* (carters) and *'poor folk'* (in terms of their fighting ability). It
is known, therefore, who these extra men at Bannockburn were. They can hardly
be described as an *'unknown reserve force'*. There is no evidence to suggest that
*'The battle of Bannockburn was being won by the arrival of a Templar force led
by the Grand Master of the Scottish Templars, Sir William St Clair.'*[41] There is no
evidence whatsoever to support the contention that *'Robert the Bruce . . . was not
only a* [Knight] *Templar . . .'*[42]

Barbour's description reveals that the 'small folk' never actually took part in the fighting at Bannockburn.[43] They were so far away that by the time they arrived the English forces had already left the field. Barbour also reinforces his view of the unreliability of these men because, instead of assisting the army in pursuing the English, they stopped on the field of battle to plunder the dead and dying. '*Lads, boys and rabble, when they saw the* [English] *force defeated, ran among them and killed them like men who could put up no defiance — it was dreadful to see*.'[44] Barbour has scant regard for the fighting abilities of these '*poor folk*' and, by taking such pains to describe their unreliability, he provides a detailed understanding of the part they played before, during and after the battle. Such untrained and undisciplined men had to be included in his account of Bruce's war of independence, for political reasons, because their involvement demonstrated that the whole population supported Bruce.

Of all contemporary, or near contemporary sources, (see those previously listed) only Barbour in *The Bruce* describes the intervention of any other group in the battle. This near contemporary source, the only medieval source which mentions an intervention of another force at Bannockburn, has been dismissed as legend.[45] Yet this sole claim that there was an intervention has been presented as proof that the '*small folk*' described by Barbour were in fact KT!

General Problems

After Bruce murdered Comyn in 1306 he was a fugitive fleeing from hiding place to hiding place. When he did stand and fight he was either defeated or the outcome was inconclusive: at Methven in 1306; at Loudoun in 1307; at Inverurie in 1308; and at Brander in 1309. The period immediately following the alleged arrival of the KT in Scotland was crucial to Bruce's survival. Some writers argue that the fugitive KT came to Scotland because Bruce would welcome them and grant them sanctuary. But he was not in control, then, of any substantial part of the country. If the KT arrived in Scotland their survival would have depended upon Bruce (and Scotland) defeating the English and their Scottish allies. Only by this means would their sanctuary be secure and continue to be safe. But the KT rendered Bruce — their supposed saviour, protector, and reason for coming to Scotland — no help whatsoever during the years of his most desperate need of assistance. They ignored battles, engagements and skirmishes leaving him to win, or lose, without their assistance. Hence, according to the myth, they must have anticipated a major battle which was to take place almost seven years after their arrival in Scotland and preferred hiding for those seven years before appearing suddenly at Bannockburn.

The last major military engagement in which the KT was involved took place in 1291 at Acre when the losses of the KT were very heavy and which '. . . *led to the virtual dissipation of frontline Templar fighting forces*'.[46] To replace these losses a recruitment drive took place immediately after, which attracted few.[47] This small amount of new blood was lost when, in 1302, Mamelukes, from Tripoli, besieged and starved the island of Ruad (off the Syrian coast at Tortosa) into submission.[48] That meant that the KT had lost their *raison d'être* and became an Order without purpose. Thereafter, the Order attempted to obtain support for another crusade to re-capture the Holy Land but without success.[49] Some mythologists explain that the reason for the English rout at Bannockburn was due not only to the sudden appearance of the KT on the field but, more importantly, to their fearsome and widely known fighting prowess: '*For the charge of this new squadron struck terror in the English.*'[50] The age of those entering the Order was mid to late twenties.[51] If a fully fledged knight, capable of all the duties required, entered the Order of the Knights Templar at that age this would mean that at the fall of Acre the youngest KT present would have been born *c.*1261–1266. These KT, the last to have actual battle experience, would therefore have been 48–53 years old, or older, in 1314.[52] More than two thirds of the KT who were interrogated after 1307 were more than 40 years old.[53] At the Battle of Falkirk (1298) Sir Brian le Jay, Grand Master of the Knights Templar in Britain, was killed in combat by Sir William Wallace (*c.*1270–1305) whilst fighting for Edward I. To suggest that the fighting prowess of the KT, last tested (as a fighting force) 23 years earlier at Acre (itself a major, final, defeat), would still inspire fear among the ranks of English knights must be considered very doubtful. Not only was the effectiveness of the KT as a group after Acre in doubt but at an individual level there must have been major concerns. That no less a personage than the Grand Master of the KT fought for Edward against the Scots and was killed in battle can hardly be taken to support the idea that the KT would have '. . . *struck terror in the English*' — they had, after all, seen that prowess in action.[54]

This can be put in another way: the Knights Templar suffered a major defeat in 1291 which wiped out all of their experienced fighting men. The Order then recruited a number of knights for combat in an attempt to regain a 'toe hold' in the Holy Land. All of the new Knights Templar died at the siege of Ruad in 1302. What is being suggested by those of the Popular Approach is that in 1307 some, by then, rather elderly French KT who had not been part of the Acre *débâcle* came to Scotland late in 1307. Those KT would have had no battle experience whatsoever after 1291. They came to Scotland seeking sanctuary, landed on the coast of Argyll, remained hidden there for seven years, ignored all Bruce's desperate battles, skirmishes etc. during 1307–1314, until they decided to charge onto the field of Bannockburn. In 1314 those KT would have been elderly by any measure. Could such an ageing '*unknown force*' [*sic*] whose military prowess had been destroyed more than once in the previous 23 years, really intimidate the cream of English knighthood?

Other Physical Evidence — Graveslabs

Before discussing the graveslabs at Kilmartin it is appropriate to first discuss graveslabs in Scotland and Scottish burial custom and practice. This is necessary as many authors of the Popular Approach claim such graveslabs as 'evidence' of the anonymous burial of members of the KT in Scotland.

It is appropriate to mention, even if it is obvious, that Scottish history is different from that of England.[55] This is true not only of 'ordinary' history but also of the history of Freemasonry. All too often some writers conflate English history with British history and for that reason fall into error when dealing with Scottish history. The subject of this chapter will, in a minor way, demonstrate the persistence of that problem.[56] In other words what follows must be considered in a Scottish historical context. Where so doing creates problems these will be explained.

Whilst there are burial sites dating from the Neolithic, Bronze and Pictish periods we are here only interested in Christian burial customs. However, it should be mentioned that grave-markers for very early periods are to be found within what are now Christian burial grounds.[57] This is as a consequence of the common practice, not only in Scotland, of the church 'adopting' pre-Christian sites. These non-Christian grave-markers can be separated from Christian ones wherever they might be located.

There is strong evidence that the area immediately surrounding a church was consciously set aside for the purpose of Christian burial from a very early stage.[58] English evidence can, at this time, be accepted as demonstrating a common practice throughout what is now Britain.[59] It is recorded that '*The practice was confirmed as established by 725 AD with about thirty feet round the church being set aside for that purpose*'.[60]

As Christianity spread across Scotland more churches and other ecclesiastical establishments were created and they too began to provide space for burials.[61]

This was considered desirable as a church was, after all, the house of God on earth and having one's remains buried there meant one's physical remains were being placed as near to God as it was possible to get on this earth. There was an 'economic hierarchy' as to who was buried where. The poorest were often not buried in consecrated ground at all. Those with some money could hope to be buried in the ground surrounding a church. Cost increased the closer to the church one wished to be buried. Inhumation inside a church required substantial funds. Here too an 'economic hierarchy' applied. Those with the least money were buried below the floor of the church in unmarked plots. There was a tendency for only important people, such as kings and bishops, to be buried near to the high altar and the further away from there the cost progressively reduced. Those who could afford to do so had a graveslab made to cover their final resting place. Those who wished to spend even more money could have such graveslabs carved to indicate the identity of the deceased and perhaps with a little decoration and/or armorial bearings. Very ornate graveslabs were few due to the time and expense involved in decorating them. Very few people could afford the luxury of an ornate graveslab and those that could often had them made during their own lifetime as they could not trust their next-of-kin to be extravagant after their demise. Ornate graveslabs were always relatively few in number, which is one reason why few pre-Reformation graveslabs survive.[62]

This form of burial led to problems principally of over-crowding and the all pervasive smell of decay.[63] Church graveyards were, however, never intended to be the permanent resting place of those buried there. Once a 'respectable' period had elapsed, that is, after the flesh had cleaved from the bone, the bones were removed and stored in a charnel house.[64] It was not the 'possession' of a particular place of burial that was important, only that one had been properly interred in consecrated ground, preferably inside the church itself. Those buried within a church, either under the floor, or perhaps in specially constructed vaults, were also likely to be exhumed in order to make way for new arrivals. However, those interred inside a church were generally accorded more resting time before being 'moved on' especially if the family remained powerful and supportive of the church. The removal of graveslabs and bones caused so much upheaval that it discouraged frequent removals. Monarchs, bishops, etc. were the least disturbed for obvious reasons. The risk of having a relative removed from within a church was an added incentive to contribute to the church in order to secure a relative's, and therefore ultimately one's own, place of interment. This constant threat of removal also caused some to devise other ways of preserving, for all time, a particular, permanent, burial place. Rosslyn Chapel and other collegiate churches in Scotland are the ultimate manifestation of that desire.

The graveslabs at, for example, Kilmartin, which are used as supportive evidence that fugitive KT hid in Argyll from 1307 to 1314, are consistent with pre-Reformation burial practice. The graveslabs were certainly made to cover graves but whether they came from inside a church is unlikely. One reason is that they are too rough and large to be 'floor stones' on which people walked. Secondly, they are not carved accurately enough to fit together with other graveslabs to form a sufficiently even surface. The argument that the anonymity of these graveslabs proves that they are KT burial places is discussed under Kilmartin Graveslabs — see below.

The risk of continuous 'exhumation and re-interment' of members of a particular family was a constant worry to many. Those who could afford to do so made alternative arrangements. Rosslyn Chapel is a manifestation of this search for long term 'security'. The building of the chapel commenced in 1446 and it was designed to provide two things for the St. Clair family:

- The saying of prayers for the souls of the family (past and present)
- A permanent place of burial for members of the family

A collegiate church for the exclusive use of a particular family was an 'opt out' from existing church arrangements and the St. Clairs of Rosslyn were no different from many other locally powerful families who made the same private arrangements for their own, and their family's, future in the afterlife.[65]

However, the Reformation dramatically changed the religious landscape of Scotland. It is important to appreciate that the reasons for the English Reformation (1540), the dynastic and political demands of Henry VIII, simply did not apply in Scotland. The Reformation in Scotland was essentially a religious one which ensured that church practice was reformed *'root and branch'*.[66] The new church in Scotland immediately began to end, or substantially amend, Catholic church practice and in January 1560 it set out its main principles. One deals with idolatry.[67] This is defined as: '. . . *the Mass, invocation of saints, adoration of images and the keeping and retaining of the same . . .*'. With this one statement the Reformed Church in Scotland declared that all images, such as those of angels, saints, and the adoration thereof, were to be *'utterly suppressed in all places of this realm'*.

In the space of a few years the method of burial, the associated ceremonial, and what could be carved on a graveslab, had changed completely. After the

Reformation, the deceased could not be buried within a church.[68] No longer could carvings of saints, angels or other 'Popish', or idolatrous, images be displayed on graveslabs. More importantly, graveslabs became gravestones. This was a major change, the misunderstanding of which has led many writers into error. Graveslabs were horizontal or 'recumbent' and were used to cover the deceased who had been lucky enough to find a place below the floor of a church or church yard. At the Scottish Reformation no more burials were permitted within a church and, therefore, the need for 'graveslabs' ceased.[69] *Gravestones* replaced graveslabs and this is one simple, if approximate, method of determining whether or not a grave marker dates from before or after the Scottish Reformation. Additionally, the church's proscription of the use of 'idolatrous' images meant that, in addition to the type of burial marker (pre-Reformation graveslabs, which lay flat and 'post' Reformation gravestones, which stand upright), the images that could be shown on gravestones was quite different from pre-Reformation practice.

The pre-Reformation Church, in Scotland, in common with church practice everywhere, used many standard images and symbols.[70] This cannot be over emphasised. What is of major importance in Scotland is that after 1559 symbols of mortality were used instead of angels etc. The new church encouraged what many might consider to be non-Christian symbolism but that would be to misunderstand the theology of the Scottish Protestant church and its, ideas regarding symbols and their purpose. It was acceptable to use the skull and crossed bones because they were not 'Popish'. The symbol was intended to remind everyone of their ultimate fate. To concentrate on a few post-Reformation symbols in Scotland is misleading. There are numerous other post-Reformation symbols such as the hour glass, scythe, etc.

'After the Reformation only 'Emblems of Mortality' were allowed (skull, crossed bones, hourglass, cherubs, open book).'[71]

These were an entirely new form of abstract Christian symbolism 'designed' and sanctioned by the new church to replace those of the Roman Church because they were not idolatrous. These symbols were more abstract than the earlier Catholic symbols because they were intend to focus attention on death. Later the attitude of the church relaxed a little and other symbols such as those used by merchants or tradesmen were permitted on gravestones:[72] Because Freemasons today make use of the symbol of the skull and crossed bones in the third or Master Masons' degree this is said to be a demonstrable link between modern Freemasonry and the KT. This being true, so the argument goes, all gravestones bearing that symbol must be the burial place of either a KT or a Freemason (or both!). There are a huge number of Scottish gravestones bearing these symbols and it is now known that since these are post-Reformation gravestones they cannot be those of KT who died in Scotland after 1307. Nor can the gravestones be Masonic. The symbolism on such gravestones is claimed to relate to the third degree but this degree of Freemasonry was invented only in the 1720s in London, England. This part of Freemasonry is therefore relatively new and came into being almost 200 years after the Scottish Reformation (1559). The Third or Master Masons' degree was only slowly accepted by Lodges in Scotland. In fact a number were extremely reluctant to adopt this 'innovation' in Freemasonry and some Scottish Lodges had still not adopted this 'new' ceremony 100 years later. The oldest lodge records in the world are those of Aitcheson's Haven which commence on 9 January 1599.[73] It is not until 1814 that that lodge's records show that it began to confer the Master Masons' degree.

Two specific gravestones which are claimed to be 'Masonic' might be considered to illustrate the above point very well. Firstly, a photograph of a gravestone in the graveyard of Currie Kirk (Plate 44) is captioned as '*Masonic grave, Currie*'.[74] As can be seen from the illustration there are a number of symbols carved on the stone — bones, crossed bones, a skull, spades, an hour glass and some floral motifs. However, it is the reverse that is most revealing. (See Plate 45) The text reads:

> **'Her age 53**
> **Memento Mori**
> **Remember Death**
> **Here layes the corps of**
> **Margaret Jeffreys (?)**
> **Departed from this**
> **life in the year**
> **1723 dismber [December] 16'**

Secondly, in Corstorphine Kirk graveyard there is another gravestone which is claimed to be Masonic.[75] This also sports a skull, crossed bones and an hour glass on its side. Above is a square and compasses placed in a configuration quite different from that normally associated with Freemasonry. (See Plate 46) The reverse of this gravestone bears an inscription which, unfortunately, is now badly weathered although part of it is still legible. Fortunately the inscriptions on all the gravestones in Corstorphine Kirk's burial ground were transcribed some years ago and the full text from this gravestone is known and reads as follows:

'The corps of Janet
Muirhead Daughter to
Alexander Muirhead
Portioner [tenant] in Corsto
rophine who died
the 28th December 1751
aged 17 years'

Just why these two 18th century gravestones, in graveyards of Scottish Protestant churches, marking the last resting place of two women are claimed to mark the graves of Scottish Freemasons is a mystery. A clue, perhaps, lies in the symbolism on each of the gravestones: a skull, crossed bones, an hour glass, square and compasses, etc. Given that so many authors adopting the Alternative Approach are in no doubt that Scottish gravestones bearing the symbols of the skull and crossed bones, etc. *must* be those of a Scottish Freemason then anything which contradicts this 'fact' is disregarded. In light of the above discussion regarding the Reformed Church's burial practices and the inscriptions on these gravestones it can be said with certainty that they have no connection whatsoever with Scottish Freemasonry and certainly have no connection with the KT. In the case of the latter gravestone, the symbolism and inscription tell us more than is often the case. It was erected by Alexander Muirhead in memory of his daughter, Janet. He describes himself as a 'portioner' that is a tenant (resident) in Corstorphine. The square and compasses, which probably convinced the author that this was a Masonic grave despite the person being a woman, are not Masonic. This configuration of square and compasses is peculiar not to Freemasonry but to the trade of wrights, that is, carpenters.[76] This example shows how little is understood about Masonic and non-Masonic symbolism.

Kilmartin Graveslabs

It has been said by some that the search for documentary evidence of a connection between modern Freemasonry and the KT (in Scotland) was bound to fail as such documentary proof of the connection does not exist. However, proof is said to exist 'on the ground' and has never been examined by Masonic historians.[77]

The main physical evidence for the alleged existence of the KT in Argyll centres on the graveyard at Kilmartin. Following on from the above discussion there is little doubt that they are pre-Reformation graveslabs. They are said to prove that KT lived, and died, in Argyll and around Kilmartin in particular. They bear the simple outline of a sword (Plate 47). Such graveslabs, it is claimed, designate the last resting place of a KT because they are anonymous. Such anonymity was required due to Bruce's excommunication and the fact that he could not be embarrassed by the existence of heretic KT in Scotland as he wished the newly independent country to be re-admitted into European Christendom. But in 1307 Bruce was losing and indeed continued to be at a disadvantage for some years until unequivocal victory at Bannockburn secured his kingship. The fact he had been excommunicated in 1306 and was in imminent danger of capture and execution seems a very poor reason for fugitive KT to seek sanctuary in a Scotland then torn by civil war.

The 'physical evidence' for the alleged existence of the KT in Argyll is based on a supposed need for anonymity. It is pertinent to ask, therefore, where are the graveslabs of those KT in Scotland who died prior to 1307 and who did not require such anonymity? KT who died prior to 1307 would have had graveslabs that made it clear that those interred were KT. No such graveslabs have been identified in Scotland. It is decidedly odd, therefore, that the only graveslabs of KT which have been identified are those that are anonymous whilst graves of those KT who did not require anonymity are nowhere to be found.[78]

A similar question can be asked in respect of other military Orders, in particular that of the Order of St. John of Jerusalem (the Knights Hospitaller). In Scotland that Order owned about two thirds of the amount of land owned by the KT.[79] As the Order did not suffer the latter's fate, and had a continuous, recorded, existence until 1560, its deceased members did not need to be interred in anonymous graves. Where in Scotland are graves of Knights of the Order of St. John from the period in question to be found? There appear to be no such graveslabs. Another difficulty arises when graveslabs of the alleged anonymous KT type are found in the property of the Order of St. John. Such a stone is to be found within Torphichen Preceptory, the headquarters of the Order in Scotland, which was never the property of the KT.[80]

There is an additional problem regarding the age of the graveslabs. The earliest the KT could have arrived in Argyll — following the mass arrest of members of the Order in France — would have been within a few weeks of 13 October 1307.

The myth alleges that soon after the Battle of Bannockburn, the KT were integrated into a newly created Order — Scottish Freemasonry. This means that the need for anonymity of deceased KT did not exist in Scotland before October 1307 and ceased soon after 1314.[81] On this basis, therefore, the '*rank after strictly regimented rank*' of anonymous KT graves at Kilmartin can apply only to a period of 7 years (1307–14) because '. . . *graves with the anonymous straight sword represented a new style, a new development, in the region, which had appeared suddenly and inexplicably* . .' and coincided with the alleged arrival of the KT.[82] For such a large number of KT to die within such a short period, in such a limited geographical area, seems hardly credible.

Unfortunately, the writers who cite these graveslabs as evidence of hidden KT in Argyll do not define which graveslabs are being interpreted in this way. Vague terms are used such as: '*There were upwards of eighty of them. But what interested us were those that bore no decoration save a single simple and austere straight sword*', and '*The church at Kilmartin, near Loch Awe in Argyll, contains many examples of Templar graves and tomb carving…*' [83,84] If, for the moment, we accept that '. . . *upwards of eighty* . . .' KT died during 1307 — 1314 this has major implications regarding the number of KT who were in hiding in Argyll. If eighty KT died in that seven-year period the actual number who were alive in Argyll during those years must have been enormous.

Kilmartin graveyard contains 73 graveslabs.[85] Of these only 12 bear the simple outline of a sword. (Plate 47) If we accept that a simple outline of a sword on a graveslab *does* represent a burial place of a KT then other, similar graveslabs in the same place and of the same period must also be considered. For example — would a graveslab with the outline of a sword and with a simple, narrow, border (known as 'edge moulding') also represent a KT burial? There are 27 graveslabs with such a design at Kilmartin.[86] The addition of such a simple decorative device would do nothing to undermine the alleged need for anonymity. But if they are not considered to be KT graveslabs, there is the problem of deciding what they *do* represent. It is not sufficient to simply disregard them for they are part of the 'body of evidence' at Kilmartin. Unfortunately, none of the writers who cite such graveslabs as evidence for a KT presence provide precise descriptions of what they consider to be KT graveslabs. Some visual material has been provided by a few. From this it is possible to determine which types of graveslab decoration are claimed by those of the Popular or Alternative approach confirm that the graveslabs are those of KT. In addition to the simple outline of a sword, a number of other symbols, devices and motifs, and combinations thereof, are claimed to indicate KT graves.[87] Graveslabs carved with more than a simple sword outline are cited, or are used as illustrative material, as being KT graveslabs. This has the effect of increasing the number and variety of 'types' of graveslabs said to be KT. What then are the designs, other than the outline of a sword, which are claimed to be KT? Such designs include:

- a sword and an axe;
- a floriate cross;[88]
- a floriate cross with or without a sword;
- round headed cross and swords;
- a floriate cross and staff;
- a floriate cross, sword, intertwined foliage and a fantastic animal.[89]
- a warrior with spear and sword; a ship, foliate and cross and a 'Masonic' set square.[90]
- figures of warriors described as 'Crusaders'.[91]

All of these designs have been used, by citation, or illustration, as being examples of KT graveslabs. If these combinations of motifs on a graveslab are KT what is to be made of them in different combinations? Or of the same motifs in combination with others not mentioned above? Only some of these Kilmartin graveslabs have been used to support a particular point of view yet the remainder must be considered, as they too are part of the graveyard 'evidence'. Unfortunately such an explanation has not been forthcoming.

It is known that the parish church of St. Michael, Garway, was founded as a KT Preceptory during 1185–1188.[92] A single stone, now the lintel of a doorway, bearing the outline of a sword, is used to support the claim that similar graveslabs at Kilmartin are also KT. However, there are other stones at Garway that require to be considered. In contrast to the solitary 'sword stone' there are eight stones bearing floriate crosses.[93] These too are anonymous, that is, they bear no names. Using the same reasoning applied to the 'sword graveslabs' above, all the floriate cross decorated stones at Garway and Kilmartin must also be KT. Indeed *all* such anonymous graveslabs in Britain and Ireland must therefore be KT graveslabs. Given that the survival rate of such graveslabs over 700 years is relatively low, the implication must be that there were actually tens of thousands of KT in Britain and Ireland — something which is not sustainable.[94]

There are four identifiable 'schools' of graveslab makers in Argyll during the period in question. Each has its own distinct style. These schools are known as:

- The Iona School
- The Kintyre School
- The Loch Sween School
- The Loch Awe School

Each school worked in a specific locality and is named after each place. Because each had its own style, and had different quarries for the stone used (of which more later), its finished work can be identified wherever it appears in the West Highlands. The schools produced a variety of stonework, not only simple graveslabs, and some of this remains scattered across the West Highlands, including Argyll. This means that there was considerable trade in such stonework and that some was transported considerable distances. The sourcing of graveslabs from at least four different places together with their transportation suggests that those who employed them were not concerned with the need to preserve anonymity.[95]

The science of petrology can also assist in this discussion. It is fortunate that the western Highlands of Scotland, including Argyll, has a very distinct geology. The diversity of geological formations in a small area is reflected in the variety of the Kilmartin and other graveslabs. The different places of origin of the graveslabs shows that there was a considerable trade in the area. This is hardly indicative of a need to keep such burials secret.

Other Graveslabs Elsewhere

The alleged KT graveslabs are not all in Argyll and many writers avow that this proves that fugitive KT were present in other parts of Scotland from 1307 onwards. If it is accepted that these other slabs are KT graveslabs, similar to those at Kilmartin, then we must accept, therefore, that the same designs on graveslabs elsewhere are also KT. This has major implications for that part of the myth that argues fugitive KT sought seclusion only in Argyll. Other sites where such graveslabs have been found are:[96]

Place	County	Type
Abercorn	West Lothian	FC & Shears
Airth	Stirlingshire	FC & S
Ayr	Ayrshire	S, S & C
Balquhidder	Stirlingshire	S
Cambuskenneth	Stirlingshire	S, FC, F & S, Multiple

Corrie	Dumfriesshire	S & FC
Corstorphine	Edinburgh	S & FC
Crail	Fife	Multiple
Currie	Mid Lothian	S, FC & S, W
Dalmeny	Edinburgh	S, FC & Shears, S & C (2)
Dryburgh	Borders	S
Dunbar	East Lothian	S
Dundrennan	Galloway	S
Ettleton	Roxburgh	Multiple
Fintry	Stirlingshire	Sword, Shears & Axe.
Holyrood	Edinburgh	Sword(s)
Humbie	East Lothian	S
Inchailleach	Stirlingshire	S, FC & Shears
Linlithgow	West Lothian	S & FC
Mouswald	Dumfriesshire	S, S & FC, FC & Plough
Neidpath Castle	Peeblesshire	S
Neilston Parish Church	East Renfrewshire	FC
Ormiston	East Lothian	S
Rosslyn	Mid Lothian	FC & S
Stobo Parish Church	Peeblesshire	S
Torphichen	West Lothian	FC & S
Wauchope	Dumfriesshire	S

Key to description —

S.	Sword outline
F.C.	Floriate Cross
F.C.& S.	Floriate Cross and Sword
F. & S.	Floral motifs and Sword
W.	Warrior
Multiple	Combination of emblems

It was only in Scotland, according to the Alternative Approach, that fugitive KT needed to have anonymous burial sites — because it was only in Scotland that they were afforded sanctuary. The existence of closely similar 'anonymous' graveslabs in England, however, causes major problems for this suggestion. There are, for example, a large number of graveslabs with swords and others with swords and floriate crosses, for example, at Bellingham, Bywell, Corbridge and Newbrough (all in Northumberland, England). The existence of such graveslabs outside Scotland, let alone Argyll, creates two possiblities: either these too are KT graveslabs (in which case there are ancillary problems relating to the numbers and locations of previously unknown fugitive KT in, for example, England) or that they are not, in fact, KT graveslabs. If they are not KT graveslabs then why should it be thought that the same kind of gravelabs at Kilmartin are KT?

There are more than 300 anonymous graveslabs in and around Argyll. The number of KT indicated by these 'anonymous' graveslabs suggests that there would have been a far greater number of KT than previously imagined. No one has provided an exact figure for the number of fugitive KT who allegedly came to Scotland but the number of supposed KT graveslabs implies that there would have been many hundreds of them hiding in Argyll after 1307.

Kilmory

The name Kilmory derives from Scottish Gaelic — *Cill* meaning church and *Mhuire* (Mory) meaning Mary's. The name means therefore St. Mary's Church. The saint referred to is of course the Virgin Mary.

In addition to specific graveslabs being cited as physical proof of KT burials, several writers have suggested that there are specific structures in Argyll that can be described as KT. Kilmory, Knapdale, is one such site. (Plate 49) This is interpreted as being a Templar chapel because:

> '*Templar churches invariably had a cross either carved above the entrance or standing freely outside. The cross, whether simple or embellished, was always of a distinctive design — equal armed, with the end of each arm wider than the base. Inside the Chapel of Kilmory stood just such a cross, dating from before the fourteenth century.*'[97] (Plate 51)

The interpretation of such stones and their locations is fraught with difficulty and danger. This particular 'Templar' cross was discovered only in 1969 more than ten miles from Kilmory and it was subsequently taken to the chapel for protection. (Plate 49)[98] The cross was not originally part of Kilmory Chapel and cannot be used in support of the view that the chapel was associated with the KT. This form of cross is quite common throughout the Middle Ages and its use was not restricted to the KT. In Scotland it has a well researched and documented history which demonstrates a lineage of many centuries prior to 1307.[99]

At Kilmory Chapel there are no graveslabs bearing the simple outline of a sword as at Kilmartin. No one claims Kilmartin to be a KT chapel (or the site of one) despite large numbers of alleged KT 'sword' graveslabs. This is most odd as Kilmory Chapel *is* claimed to be a KT chapel but contains no anonymous KT 'sword' graveslabs. If this design were the principal designation of KT graves then the absence of such graveslabs at Kilmory Chapel, a supposed KT site, has to be explained.[100] An alleged KT gravestone at Kilmory Chapel has been described but not of the simple sword type. Of the 36 graveslabs now protected within the walls of the chapel there is one described as:

> '. . . *a fourteenth-century graveslab incised with a sailing galley, an armed figure, and another Templar cross, this one worked into a Floreate design. But there was more...Above the head of the armed figure with its Templar cross was carved a Masonic set square*', '. . . *Kilmory had almost certainly been a Templar Chapel* . . .'[101] (Plate 51)

As a consequence of this 'proof' — that Kilmory was a KT chapel — '*It was now safe to say that there were Templars on Loch Sween.*'[102] In 1301 John (MacDougall) of Lorn had taken Knapdale (which includes Kilmory and Castle Sween) for John Menteith. The latter had the title Earl of Lennox from Edward I but this appears to have been little more than a paper title.

By March 1309 he had joined Bruce who confirmed him in the lordship of Arran and Knapdale.[103] This area, the alleged heartland of the fugitive KT, was the homeland of the McSweens and in 1310 they received a grant of the whole of Knapdale from Edward I — provided that they could re-take it by force. That year, with the assistance of an Irish-based fleet and possibly with the assistance of John of Lorn, the McSweens lay siege to Castle Sween. They were unsuccessful. The KT did not assist in this battle even though it took place in the very area they were said to be living in and those besieged were supporters of Robert the Bruce.[104] This is a recurring problem for the idea that fugitive KT hid in Argyll doing nothing to assist Robert the Bruce in the various battles, skirmishes and rear-guard actions between 1307 and 1314.

There is no doubt, according to some, that at least one graveslab at Kilmory is that of a Knight Templar (see above). This graveslab is offered as evidence not only of a KT burial but also of a KT presence on Loch Sween (and therefore in Argyll generally), that Kilmory is a KT place of worship and that the symbolism and figures on the graveslab all relate to the Knights Templar. If this is correct then here is, for the first time, indisputable proof of what a KT graveslab is like. However, such a claim cannot be accepted without critical analysis and so here this specific graveslab is analysed in detail.

The graveslab shows a warrior holding a spear in his right hand. (Plate 48) He is wearing a helmet (a bascinet) and has a sword strapped to his left waist. He appears to be wearing gauntlets but this is not clear. Under the bascinet and over his shoulders a coif or aventail is barely discernible. On his feet are sabatons. The principal clothing is an aketon. The warrior bears a shield on his left arm. Many other graveslabs in the West Highlands show warriors in very similar garb and weapons. (Fig. 20)

When compared with carvings, drawings and other images of knights of the period, marked differences can be observed. The graveslabs of knights buried in the Temple Church, London, for example all date from the 13th century and show far superior armour and weapons than that on the Kilmory graveslab.[105] (Fig. 21) The armour and weapons used at the Battle of Bannockburn (1314) have been well researched and described elsewhere and compared with this graveslab show that knights at that battle were equipped quite differently and to a much better degree than the Kilmory 'knight'. Knights wore armour and chain mail. The figure on the graveslab has none. The warrior on the graveslab is wearing an aketon. This protective garment was made from two layers of heavy material such as

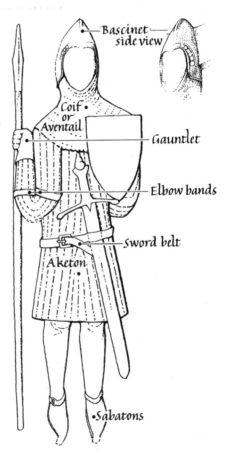

Fig. 20: *The arms and armour of a West Highland Warrior*

felt and formed into vertical 'cylinders' into which small scraps of material were tightly packed. Chain mail was occasionally worn over the garment as additional protection. The aketon was the 'armour' of a foot soldier not a knight.[106] A KT would not be depicted in this manner. One of those who fought at Bannockburn was Angus Og and as a West Highland Chief he would have been attired in the same manner as the Kilmory Knap warrior.[107] Only an eminent person, a clan chief, would have the luxury of such a graveslab. The reason for these all too obvious differences in equipment is explained by an authority on arms and armour:

Fig. 21: *The arms and armour of a 13th century knight (The Temple Church – London)*

'*Such a fashion* [as that at Kilmory Knap] *is unknown among the knightly class of England, as it probably was in the Scottish Lowlands. Yet it may result from both the isolation, poverty in iron resources, and traditional infantry and light cavalry tactics of the far west* [Argyll].'[108]

What this means is that the graveslab at Kilmory Knap is that of a West Highland Chief and not a Knight Templar. If the carving of this figure was that of a KT, another major problem must be confronted — there are many more graveslabs in the West Highlands with near identical figures. Are these also to be considered as graveslabs of the KT? In fact the problem becomes even more intractable in that in addition to the 'anonymous' graveslabs at Kilmartin with the symbol of the sword, swords and floriate cross, etc. we must now add warriors, ships, etc. and in doing so this means that virtually all the graveslabs in the West Highlands must, if this argument is pursued to its logical conclusion, be Knight Templar graveslabs.

Kilneuair

Kilneuair Church, from 'Cill an Iubhair' (Gaelic) meaning the 'church of the yew wood', is another site that is alleged to confirm a KT presence in Argyll: '. . . *there are remains of an ancient circular church and gravestone with the Templar Cross Patée.'*[109] The proponents of the myth combine what is claimed to be a circular church with a cross of Templar 'type' [*sic*] and conclude that it was a site of Templar activity. In fact this church was of a pentagonal construction.[110] However, it is now known that the construction, and use of, circular churches was not restricted to KT.[111] (Plate 52). Furthermore, the cross described as being of Templar 'type' was extensively used throughout the Middle Ages and was not used exclusively by the KT. There are, for example, a large number in Cornwall.[112] This is an example of how using incorrect assumptions to interpret evidence, a 'circular' church and cross of KT 'type', can lead to erroneous conclusions. In this particular instance it can be revealed that the church was not built by fugitive Knights Templar because archaeological evidence has shown that substantial parts were erected in the 13th century before the KT allegedly arrived from France.[113]

'Templar' Documents

There are a number of documents which are cited as proof of a connection between the KT and the St. Clair family. One of these which is frequently mentioned is that entitled 'Charter of Walter Maleville of Temple Land' and is dated sometime after 1292. What attracted attention was the use of 'Temple Land' in the charter's title and the fact that one William St. Clair purchased the said 'Temple Land'. This charter was reproduced in Maidment's version of the Genealogie of the Sainteclaires of Rosslyn in 1835. The charter was given in the original Latin. Once translated it is clear that the land in question was not owned by the KT but by one Walter Maleville [Melville] who was still calling it Temple Land even though they no longer owned it and it was he who sold it to the St. Clair family. This record of a commercial transaction reveals no link between the St. Clairs and the KT.[114]

There is a variety of other documentary 'evidence' cited as proof that the medieval Order of KT continued to exist in Scotland after its official suppression by the church in 1312. The most frequently cited document is that contained in the Register of the Great Seal of Scotland dated in the first year of the reign of James IV (1488–1513, b.1473) confirming all former grants of land made to *'Sancto Hospitali de Jerusalem, et fratribus ejusdem militia Templi Salomonis.'*[115] This has been taken to prove that the Medieval Order of the KT was in existence in Scotland more than 200 years after its suppression. This interpretation of the document is wrong. James IV confirmed the Order of St. John (the Knights Hospitaller) in its ownership of all its lands including those it obtained from the Knights Templar following the suppression of that Order. What took place can be explained as follows. The Order of St. John maintained a record of all its property in Scotland. When it received property, after 1312, once owned by the KT another record of those properties was created. A new joint record would have made a perfectly good existing record redundant. The new property continued to be referred to as Temple Land etc. This method of continuing to refer to land and other property by its original name is common and an example has already been referred to above. The fact that the Knights Hospitaller referred to farms, land and other property acquired after 1312 as Templar Land etc. does not mean that there was a body of men, Knights Templar, then in existence either separately or as part of the Order of St. John. There are a large number of places in Scotland and elsewhere in Britain that continue to bear the Templar names, such as Templeland Grove (Edinburgh) and Templeland Crescent (Dalry, Ayrshire) but no one suggests that the people who live there today are actually Knights Templar!

Leaving aside the conundrum about why they would leave such documents when they were, according to the same authors, now Freemasons. Those interested in the subject matter of this chapter cannot be anything but grateful to a number of writers for bringing to public attention the possible existence of 'hard evidence' of, for example, burials of fugitive KT in Argyll, particularly at Kilmartin. This brief examination of such material can be little other than cursory in a book of this size but it does suggest that there are some major difficulties to be resolved before it could be argued that such graveslabs etc. actually have any connection with the medieval Order of KT.

[1] *Hiram Key, The,* Knight, Christopher & Lomas, Robert. London. 1996. p. 298. As Bruce murdered Comyn on 10 February 1306 he could not have been excommunicated for that act in 1305.

[2] For example, Laidler, Keith, *The Head of God.* p. 236; Sinclair, Andrew, *The Sword and The Grail,* p. 45-49.

[3] *Supremely Abominable Crimes — The Trial of the Knights Templar* by Edward Burman. p. 3.

[4] *Temple and The Lodge, The,* Baigent, Michael & Leigh, Richard, p. 65 and *Hiram Key, The,* Knight, Christopher, & Lomas, Robert, p. 299.

[5] *Edinburgh History of Scotland — The Later Middle Ages, The,* Nicholson, Ranald, Vol. 2. p. 10.

[6] Barrow, Geoffrey W. S. in *The Scottish Historical Review:* 'The Scottish Clergy in the War of Independence', Vol. XLI. April 1963 '...*the manifesto forms part of a general rallying of clerical support after, and not before, the crucial victory of Bannockburn. During his early years, Bruce had to work as hard to gain the clergy as he had to win over the influential laymen.'*

[7] *Freedom's Sword,* Traquair, Peter, p. 163.

[8] *Trial of the Templars, The,* Barber, Malcolm, p. 65.

[9] The anti-Scottish propaganda would have been invaluable to Edward II.

[10] *Bruce, The,* Barbour, John (ed. Archibald A. M. Duncan, Canongate Classics, Edinburgh, 1997). p. 570. Throughout I have used, and quoted from, this edition of *The Bruce* as it is a relatively new edition and is readily available.

[11] Draffen, *Pour La Foy.* p. 10, states that the examination of the two KT took place at St Andrews but it is known that the examination took place in Holyrood Palace, Edinburgh, under English auspices. *See* Wilkins, David, (1685-1745), *Concilia Magnae Britanniae et Hiberniae, a synodo verolamiensi A.D.CCCCXLVI. ad londinensem A.D.MDCCXVII. Accedunt constitutiones et alia ad historiam Ecclesiae Anglicanae spectantia.* A report of the proceedings (at the time of publication), in English, is to be found at: www.rosslyntemplars.org.uk/trial_of_the_kt.htm

[12] Ex-templars in England by A.J. Forey. In: Journal of Ecclesiastical History Vol 53 (January 2002) Cambridge University Press. I am grateful to Prof. Andrew Prescott and Dianne Clements who simultaneously brought this paper to my attention.

[13] Sea routes for raiding Argyll had been established by the Vikings as early as (at least) the 8th century. The raiders were followed by settlers and traders and there were numerous Viking settlements on the coasts of Argyll — thereby belying the claim that it was unpopulated. The Western Isles off the coast of Argyll were subject to Norway until 1266. These routes continued to be used long after 1301. '*Only very gradually were these insular communities drawn into the Scottish medieval kingdom.*' See: *The Sea Road — A Viking Voyage Through Scotland* by Olwyn Owen. Historic Scotland. Edinburgh. 1999. pp. 12-13.

[14] *The Temple and The Lodge, op. cit.,* p. 106-107.

[15] *The West Highland Galley,* Rixson, Denis, (Edinburgh, 1998), p. 17.

[16] *Op. cit.,* p. 22. See also *Edinburgh History of Scotland — The Later Middle*

Ages, The, Vol. 2. pp. 77-78.

[17] *Kingdom of the Isles — Scotland's Western Seaboard, c.1100-c.1336, The,* MacDonald, R. Andrew (East Linton, 1997), p. 171.

[18] Barbour, *op. cit.,* p. 142-145.

[19] *The Sword and The Grail, op. cit.,* p. 46.

[20] *Robert Bruce and the Community of the Realm of Scotland,* Barrow, Geoffrey W. S. (Edinburgh, 1996), p. 160.

[21] Confirmed by a Charter granted by Robert I in 1315; see Donaldson, Gordon, *Scottish Historical Documents* (Glasgow, 1997), p. 51.

[22] Their land and property holdings are well documented. See *Medieval Religious Houses — Scotland.* Cowan, Ian B., and Easson, David E.

[23] Barbour, *op. cit.*

[24] *Sword and The Grail, The, op. cit.,* p. 46.

[25] *Bannockburn Revealed,* Scott, William (Rothesay, 2000). I have, for convenience, reproduced the primary sources listed in this publication. Anyone who wishes to read further regarding the various sources that provide accounts of the Battle of Bannockburn would find this publication most useful, especially for comparing major sources.

[26] *The Hiram Key, op. cit.,* p. 298. The statement that the battle was fought on 6 November 1314 is inexplicable.

[26] The events of 23 June were no mere skirmish. See the accounts in some of the sources, including *The Bruce,* listed in the main text.

[28] The medieval Order of the KT observed a large number of other feast days. The feast day of St. John the Baptist was simply one among many. See *The Rule of the Templars,* Upton-Ward, Judith M., p. 37-38.

[29] *The Templar Legacy, op. cit.,* p. 148. As with many other writers, the reason why the alleged coincidence of dates is thought to be important is not explained.

[30] Aitcheson's Haven, 9 January 1599 and The Lodge of Edinburgh, 31 July 1599.

[31] *The First Freemasons, op. cit.,* p. 26.

[32] According to Draffen the first record of a KT ceremony being conducted in Scotland occurred when members of the Lodge Scoon and Perth, No 3, visited Lodge St Stephen's No 145, (Edinburgh) in 1778. George Draffen. *Pour La Foy.* p. 13. However, the Minutes of Lodge St. Stephen's of that date make no mention of any KT ceremonial. The Minute relates to the conferral of *'the six sundry steps of Masonry - Past the Chair, Excellent and Super Excellent Mason, Arch and Royal Arch Mason and, lastly, Knights of Malta'.* It is surely significant that the 'last step' of Freemasonry in Scotland at that time was the ceremonial of the Knights of Malta and that there was no mention whatsoever of the Knights Templar.

[33] See, for instance, Stevenson, David, *The First Freemasons* (Edinburgh, 2001).

[34] The Seal of Cause does mention St. John the Baptist but this saint is quite secondary to St. John the Evangelist. The aisle is dedicated to St. John the Evangelist.

[35] Those who were dominant in the formation of the Grand Lodge of Scotland were non-operative members (particularly those of Lodge Canongate

Kilwinning) and who appeared to have been unaware of the operative's patron
saint - St. John the Evangelist. There is clear evidence that the founders were
emulating the English pattern and mostly likely also adopted St John the Baptist
from this source. The Grand Lodge's annual meeting was to take place on 24
June, the feast day of St. John the Baptist. It seems that operative masons
revolted against that change in their 'antient landmarks' and the new Grand
Lodge, to avoid upsetting either group, diplomatically rejected both St Johns
and settled on St. Andrew, the Patron Saint of Scotland. Since then the
Installation of the Grand Master Mason takes place on, or near to, that feast day.
[36] *The Sword and the Grail, op. cit.,* p. 46.

[37] It is known that other nationalities were present at the battle and who would
have had no reservations in reporting the facts. In *The Bruce*, p. 408, John
Barbour states that knights from Germany, Gascony, Poitou, Brittany and
France served against the Scots. There were also Welsh and Irish present and it
does seem odd to argue the 'true' cause of the English defeat, the intervention of
KT, is 'proved' by the silence of everyone involved.

[38] This is a dangerous method to use when discussing the past. In effect the
absence of any evidence, a 'negative', can be used to create a 'positive' — a
'fact'. This disingenuous method means that proof can be manufactured from
nothing in order to prove something, anything.

[39] See, for example, *The Chronicle of Lanercost,* which together with some other
primary sources also detail the fighting on 23 June and contains eye-witness
accounts of the battle on that day and the next.

[40] Duncan's introduction to the Canongate Classics edition of *The Bruce*
provides an excellent overview of the life of Bruce as recounted by Barbour.
His discussion of other sources is valuable. Also important is his '*Bannockburn
Commentary*' which analyses the battle succinctly.

[41] *The Hiram Key, op. cit.,* p. 298.

[42] *The Templar Legacy and the Masonic Inheritance within Rosslyn Chapel,*
Wallace-Murphy, T., p. 22.

[43] Barbour, *op. cit.,* p. 490.

[44] *Op. cit.,* p. 496.

[45] E.g. *The Sword and The Grail.* p. 46. *The Head of God.* p. 244.

[46] *Supremely Abominable Crimes,* Burman, Edward (London, 1994), p. 32.

[47] *New Knighthood, The,* Barber, Malcolm (Cambridge, 1995), p. 294.

[48] *Ibid.*

[49] *Op. cit.,* p. 295.

[50] *The Sword and The Grail, op. cit.,* p. 46.

[51] *Ex-Templars in England* by A. J. Forley. 2002. p.34.

[52] A detailed analysis, if possible, of the age, structure and geographic origin of
members of the Order *c.*1307 would be most useful but is beyond the scope of
this chapter. In any event it seems that by this time the Order had no young
knights with experience of battle.

[53] *Ex-Templars in England* by A. J. Forley. 2002. p. 34.

[54] *Sword and The Grail, The, op. cit.,* p. 46.

[55] I am quite sure that my Irish colleagues are frequently confronted with the

same problem!

[56] Professor David Stevenson expressed a similar exasperation in his book *The Origins of Freemasonry — Scotland's Century 1590–1710*, describing the problem as 'Anglo-centric'.

[57] The practice of Christian burial can be traced as a direct consequence of the 'burial' of Jesus Christ in a 'cave' after his crucifixion and as perpetuated by members of the early Christian Church in, for example the catacombs of Rome.

[58] E.g. archaeological evidence from a variety of sites such as Whithorn, Wigtownshire, a very early Christian place of worship and pilgrimage.

[59] See: *Burial Practice in Early England*. Taylor, Alison.

[60] Burgess, Frederick. *English Churchyard Memorials*. Lutterworth Press. 1963. p. 22.

[61] These are known as 'lairs' in Scotland and typically provided for four or five interments (one on top of another) in each lair. The word is suggestive of the cave and catacombs mentioned at 56 above.

[62] Given the low survival rate of graveslabs from 700 years ago one can only speculate as to the original number of such slabs.

[63] The stink of death came to be associated with disease and was a problem for the church which had encouraged burials in consecrated ground. This was an added incentive for the rich and powerful to seek alternative solutions.

[64] One of the most famous Charnel Houses was the Cemetery of the Innocents at Paris.

[65] There were a number of other Scottish families that also built similar churches for the same purpose. For example: the Douglases, Setons and Crichtons.

[66] Although Henry VIII appropriated church land, buildings and money he remained doctrinally conservative. Protestantism in England only triumphed after his death in 1547.

[67] See Appendix X.

[68] Although those adhering to the old faith such as the St. Clairs who owned their own churches continued to do so despite the displeasure of the church and this is why after 1559 members of the St. Clair family could continue to be buried in the family vault.

[69] The use of graveslabs did not cease immediately, especially in places furthest from the centre of church power.

[70] There were many local variations but they remain accepted, and acceptable, Christian symbols, devices, etc.

[71] *Collins Encyclopaedia of Scotland*. p. 577.

[72] For examples and many illustrations see: *Understanding Scottish Graveyards — An Interpretive Approach* by Betty Whillsher.

[73] These invaluable records are the property of the Grand Lodge of Antient Free and Accepted Masons of Scotland.

[74] *The Sword and the Grail*, by Andrew Sinclair (1993). Between page 150 and 151.

[75] *Ibid*. Between page 150 and 151.

[76] There is evidence that this trade, like stonemasons, developed an organisation similar to Freemasonry — Free Wrights or Free Carpenters. This is the subject

of ongoing research.

[77] *Temple and The Lodge, The, op. cit.,* p. 27.

[78] Determining when the interred person died, given that very few of the 600+ medieval graveslabs in the West Highlands bear a name or a date, would be, in any event, difficult. In other words, the vast majority of the graveslabs in that part of Scotland are anonymous. The graveslabs at Kilmartin are not therefore unique in this respect.

[79] *Scotland and the Crusades 1095-1560,* MacQuarrie, Alan. p. 53.

[80] Royal Commission on the Ancient and Historical Monuments of Scotland. (RCAHMS). *East Lothian.* 1924 p.235.

[81] Certainly no later than October 1328 when Robert I was released from the ban of excommunication by Pope John XXII (1316-1334, b. 1249).

[82] *Temple and The Lodge, The, op. cit.,* pp. 24, 30-31.

[83] *Op. cit.,* p. 24

[84] *Op. cit.,* p. 295.

[85] RCAHMS — Argyll. Vol. 7. pp. 131-137.

[86] *Ibid.*

[87] The inclusion of such other devices etc. rather undermines the argument that the simple, unsophisticated, outline of a sword was all that was required to 'identify' an anonymous Knight Templar grave.

[88] A foliated or foliate cross may take a number of forms but is essentially a four armed cross developed into a circular design. The design can be simple with the merest allusion, anything floral or quite elaborate and obviously intended to represent a flower. Such designs have also been described as 'marigold' crosses. Floriate crosses are nearly always mounted on a long shaft, making the whole design suitable for use on an oblong graveslab. The base of the shaft can be a simple line or have no base at all but frequently the design has a 'stepped' base consisting of three steps and less commonly five steps. Crosses with stepped bases are known as Calvary crosses which strictly applies only to the three step variety. A cross consisting of the three elements: 1) a calvary or stepped base, 2) a shaft and 3) a floriate cross head should, therefore, be more accurately described as a 'floriate Calvary cross'. There are a large number of graveslabs with this design in many parts of Britain but they survive in greatest numbers in now isolated areas such as Argyll. It is when this design is claimed to represent the grave of a KT that matters become complicated. If the simple outline of a single sword is that of a KT graveslab then what must a floriate cross together with the outline of a sword, and found in Argyll, represent? There are, therefore, three basic designs which are most commonly claimed to be found on alleged KT graveslabs: 1) the outline of a sword, 2) a floriate cross and 3) a sword with a floriate cross. The question of what such graveslabs represent outside Argyll represents an additional, unresolved difficulty. When other additional designs (i.e. shears [sometimes erroneously claimed to be compasses], armed men, animals, galleys, cups, harps, combs etc.) are also claimed to be found on KT graveslabs then virtually all existing medieval graveslabs can be claimed to be KT. This is clearly unsustainable.

[89] *Forgotten Monarchy of Scotland, The, op. cit.,* p. 63. No other writer claims that this kind of decoration designates a KT grave. It depicts a central floriate cross (without a base), a sword (to the left) and a mythical beast atop an intertwined floral motif (to the right of the cross). It is said to be located on the Isle of Islay. It is, in fact, to be found within Kilmory Chapel, Knapdale. RCAHMS. Mid Argyll and Cowal. Vol. 7. p. 166.

[90] *The Temple and The Lodge, op. cit.,* p. 34.

[91] Some who adopt the Popular Approach also use the term 'Crusaders' rather than 'Templars'. In publications dedicated to the discussion of the medieval KT and an alleged connection between that Order and modern Freemasonry the use of this term means that the conclusion is inevitably drawn that the terms 'Crusaders' and 'Templars' are interchangeable. In other words they are one in the same. This has the effect, without saying so, that the 'stock' of potential KT graves is actually much greater. Examples are the images of armed and armoured warriors at Saddell Abbey, on Skye and in Kilmartin graveyard. For example: *The Sword and the Grail.* See plates between pp. 150-151.

[92] *Medieval Religious Houses — England and Wales,* Knowles, David, & Hadcock, R. Neville (London, 1953), p. 236. Garway was transferred to the Knights Hospitaller during 1308-1312. The alleged KT stones must, therefore, date from after 1307 but before 1312, as there was no need for anonymity prior to 1307. Those who expound the Popular Approach explain that the graveslabs in Argyll are anonymous because the KT were fugitives in hiding. Why KT graves in England, such as those at Garway, were anonymous is not explained.

[93] Royal Commission on Ancient and Historical Monuments England (RCAHME). Monmouthshire — Southwest. Vol. 1. p. 72.

[94] If these 'anonymous' graveslabs in Ireland and England are those of the KT (*because* they are anonymous?) the implication must be that they died only during the period they required to be buried anonymously. If true this has not been taken into account by those adopting the Popular Approach who have not explained the ramifications of these graves. Equally, if they are not the graves of members of the KT their need to be anonymous, explained for those in Scotland, has not been explained for those not located in Scotland.

[95] There were also a number of independent stone workers.

[95] The list is based on the author's own sporadic research which is by no means exhaustive nor is it comprehensive. A systematic search for such graveslabs in the records of RCAHMS, RCAHMW and RCAHME, among others, would provide a great deal of information regarding alleged KT graveslabs throughout Britain.

[97] *The Temple and The Lodge, op. cit.,* p. 34. An image of the stone is provided.

[98] The authors could not have been aware of this at the time of writing their book (1989) as the original location of the cross was not made public until 1992 with the publication of the details by RCAHMS in that year.

[99] *The Celtic Cross,* Pennick, Nigel (London, 1997).

[100] The RCAHMS list 36 graveslabs within Kilmory Chapel but none are of the type said to be KT as at Kilmartin. RCAHMS. *Mid Argyll and Cowal.* Vol. 7. (1992), pp. 161-169.

[101] *The Temple and The Lodge, op. cit.,* pp. 34–35. In addition to the simple outline of a sword, floriate crosses of various types and other devices which, as previously discussed, are said to designate a KT grave, must now be added: a galley, an armed man, a set square, etc.

[102] *Op. cit.,* p. 35.

[103] For fuller details of the events around Loch Sween and Knapdale during the time the fugitive KT were said to be hiding there, see Barrow, Geoffrey W.S., *Robert Bruce and the Community of the Realm of Scotland,* pp. 54 *et seq.*

[104] *Kingdom of the Isles — Scotland's Western Seaboard c.1100-1336, The, op. cit.,* pp. 249 *et seq.* This book would be most useful to those who wish to learn more of the politics, feuds and economy etc. of the western seaboard of Scotland throughout the period concerned.

[105] There are numerous sources for such illustrations. See, for example, *Bannockburn 1314 — Robert Bruce's great victory,* by Pete Armstrong.

[106] A great deal of research into the arms and armour of the period has been published. David Nicolle's *Arms and Armour of the Crusading Era 1050 — 1350* has identified a number of images showing warriors throughout the period and across Europe who are wearing aketons — none are knights.

[107] *Bannockburn 1314 — Robert Bruce's great victory,* by Pete Armstrong. p. 21.

[109] *Arms and Armour of the Crusading Era 1050-1350* by David Nicolle. p. 97.

[110] *The Sword and the Grail, op. cit.,* p. 45.

[111] RCAHMS. Mid Argyll and Cowal. Vol. 7. p.186.

[112] There are round churches at Ophir, Orkney; Church of the Holy Sepulchre, Cambridge; St. John the Baptist, Little Maplestead; St Sepulchre, Northampton and St. Mary Magdalene, Ludlow. None of these have any connection with the medieval Order of the KT.

[113] *Celtic Cross, The op. cit.,* pp.105-108.

[114] *Argyll Volume 7 — Mid Argyll & Cowal Medieval & Later Monuments.* RCAHMS. 1992. pp. 186-187.

[115] *Genealogie of the Sainteclaires* of Rosslyn. p. 45.

[116] The full text, in Latin, is reproduced in the *Account of the Templars* by Father Richard A. Hay. 1828

Chapter 9
Conclusion

Have we been Hoaxed?

At the beginning of this book one claim in particular regarding Freemasons was discussed — that *all* Prime Ministers of England [*sic*] between 1721–1935 were Grand Masters and that *all* Presidents of the United States of America from 1789–1961 were Freemasons of 'a high degree'. Yes, everyone has been hoaxed; not only the public but Freemasons themselves have been victims of a sustained attempt to make them out to be something that they are not:

> *'This pattern of power was repeated throughout Europe. The same situation also existed in America where every President until John F. Kennedy, was a Freemason of high degree ... [they have] domination of power [which] was not just restricted to the Heads of State but also permeated throughout the entire power structure of the judiciary, the police, the armed services and civil administration throughout the Western World. And, in this manner, Freemasonry continues to exercise profound influence, on all aspects of society today.'*[1]

What purpose is served by distortions such as these? As society, rightly, moves away from victimising minorities by holding them responsible for all manner of things the number of groups 'available' to act as society's 'bogey men' has been reduced. Freemasonry, a minority group, is not classed as a politically correct group and so remains 'available' for all sorts of baseless accusations. The blame culture of today leads one to suspect that for the foreseeable future Freemasonry will continue to serve as society's 'whipping boy'.[2]

Is there a Masonic conspiracy as suggested by the quote above? On the contrary the reverse is true. Freemasons have been the victims of a conspiracy of sensationalism, of innuendo, and being used as society's scapegoat.[3] More pointedly the organisation's history, culture and ethos have been hijacked for a variety of purposes. Those purposes can be: to make money; to divert attention; the indulgence in fantasies; the creation of tourist attractions and to support a number of political and theological prejudices.

Here a final crucial point is reached, and it is one that tends to prove the existence of an anti-Masonic conspiracy: all the accusations levelled against

Freemasonry (and therefore all Freemasons) are based on an assumption that exists nowhere else — that individuals act in a certain way *because* they are Freemasons. This means that all members of an organisation known as Freemasonry are guilty as accused (of anything and everything) by virtue alone of being a Freemason.[4] No members of a particular group are so persistently and consistently accused of doing something (often criminal) simply because they are members. No one is accused in the way Freemasons are simply because they are members of, for example, a political party, a particular faith, a particular business or charity.

Although this is something of a digression from the main discussion it is an important digression as it indicates that Freemasons are victims rather than perpetrators of a whole host of alleged crimes and other nefarious activities. In this light the following discussion can be considered from an altogether different perspective. The question that is the title of this book *'The Rosslyn Hoax?'* may be expanded further:

> *'Has the public, especially the reading public, been the subject of a hoax regarding Rosslyn Chapel or any other of the ancillary theories and subjects discussed in this book?'*

The answer must be yes and no. Yes because there has been deliberate manipulation of physical evidence — the carving of the head alleged to be that of the murdered apprentice in Rosslyn Chapel being an example. The misquoting of documents which are the property of the Grand Lodge of Scotland is another 'manipulation' of evidence, in particular, the oft repeated statement that the St. Clair 'Charters' contain references to a Grand Master when they do no such thing. Most crucial of all in respect of the St. Clair family and their alleged status as hereditary Grand Masters is the fact that Charles I (1625–1649, b.1600) denied that the family had been granted any hereditary rights of the 'masons' of Scotland. For this reason this book contains the most crucial documents on the subject — the St. Clair 'Charters', the Schaw Statutes, a typical charter granted to a Masonic Lodge and William St. Clair's *'Deed of Resignation'* along with a number of others. In making the text of these documents available in the public domain for the first time in recent memory more people can have access to them. This will enable those interested to use the documents to compare them against what popular authors say they contain. Finally their publication means that no one who seriously undertakes research in this area can claim to be ignorant of their existence and their contents.

Those responsible for 'manipulation' of evidence are probably long dead but their desire to make the physical evidence support their personal opinions in respect of Rosslyn Chapel etc. is being perpetuated to this day. In that sense their views, right or wrong, are being perpetuated, by proxy. For some, the constant elaboration of the myth, without the critical re-examination of the myth itself, might be considered as a form of hoax but I would argue that the use of the word hoax is too strong in this context and 'unconsciously misleading' might be a better description. In a general sense the answer to the question posed by the title must be 'no' because there is no evidence of a malicious, organised, attempt to foist on the general public any deliberate misrepresentations regarding Rosslyn Chapel, the Knights Templar, the St. Clair family and alleged connections with Scottish Freemasonry. That said, the situation is that error after error, assumption after assumption, is being repeated to the extent that some are hoaxing themselves and in the process convincing others that there is some veracity in what is a myth.

Rosslyn Chapel restored? — A Digression

The analysis of the myth and evidence which allegedly supports it gives rise to a conundrum in respect of Rosslyn Chapel:

> '*Will Rosslyn Chapel be restored to what it is now known to be — a privately owned pre-Reformation Roman Collegiate Church or will the power of an incredibly popular modern myth dictate that the restoration be something else?*'

This raises all sorts of intriguing possibilities. If the chapel is not restored in line with medieval church architecture of pre-Reformation type will it be restored in accordance with the 'Masonic' notions of *non-Freemasons*? If not, will Scottish Freemasons be consulted as to the manner in which the building is to be 'restored' in accordance with *Scottish* Masonic custom and practice? These questions are asked because there is a manifest misunderstanding or ignorance of symbolism in a wide and general sense. More particularly there is a profound ignorance regarding *Scottish* Masonic symbolism, custom and practice most likely due to non-Masons believing, wrongly, that there a unified body of Masonic symbolism which includes Scotland.

In a similar vein — what is to be done regarding the alleged existence of artefacts in the chapel? Most authors presently writing on the subject suggest that there is something buried or hidden in the chapel. The hidden items are claimed to include the Holy Grail; the Ark of the Covenant; the treasure of the Knights Templar (which may or may not be the Holy Grail); the lost writing of Jesus Christ; or perhaps even the embalmed head of the Son of God. Imagine for a moment the implications of these claims. Items of inestimable historical value are 'known' to be within Rosslyn Chapel.[5] Imagine actually finding the Holy Grail and having it on display in Edinburgh? Imagine the information the Ark of the Covenant would provide to historians, theologians and even Freemasons. What is being done to locate some of the most important artefacts in the world? Nothing! That does seem rather incredible. It is akin to Howard Carter (1874–1939) announcing that he knew exactly where Tutankhamun's tomb was but he was not going to open it! There have been three 'non-invasive' investigations — radar ground scans — but these were inconclusive.[6] Why are these relics, arguably some of the most important in the history of the human race, not being actively sought? Rosslyn Chapel is scheduled as a '*monument of national importance*' under the Ancient Monuments and Archaeological Areas Act, 1979. This means that in order to look for the Holy Grail in Rosslyn Chapel prior permission from Ministers of the Scottish Parliament would be required.[7] No doubt such an application would only succeed if supported by respected historians and archaeologists motivated only by the desire to advance human knowledge and understanding.

End of Digression and the conclusion continued

The myth of a direct lineal connection between the medieval Order of the Knights Templar in a Scottish context was invented by a Scottish Freemason, Chevalier James Burnes, for his fellow Freemasons who were interested in creating a Masonic Order which mirrored their own attitudes and their own 19th century chivalric ideals. These attitudes and ideals were almost certainly strongly influenced by the Romantic Movement. That the new Masonic Order was influenced by such ideals is made very clear by Burnes' re-wording and his explanation for the re-writing of the four KT vows. Burnes' work was largely taken from the work others, something he freely admits, the French Masonic historian, Claude A. Thory (1759–1827), being the principal source for a Scottish connection. Thory claimed that Bruce had founded the Masonic Order of Heredom de Kilwinning immediately after the Battle of Bannockburn (1314) (appendix X.) The point here is that Burnes' developed an idea to the point where a Masonic Order of Knights Templar in Scotland was created and that the idea underpinning it originated with a Freemason. Even in the history of the Order in

Scotland written by Burnes, which the Masonic body adopted uncritically, he expressed some doubts — *'But whether the Scottish Templars really joined the victorious standard of Robert Bruce . . .'*, doubts which were brushed aside by subsequent authors.

Since Burnes' piece: *'The Knights Templars of Scotland'*, was published in Scotland (1837) a large number of people, including many Freemasons, have accepted this 'history' as being true. That being so, logic dictates that there may be evidence to prove a whole variety of things — for example that Bruce founded the Order of Heredom de Kilwinning in 1314; that the KT had (and has) a continued existence in Scotland since 1307/1312; that Charles Edward Stuart (Bonnie Prince Charlie) (1720–1788) was not only a Freemason but a member of the Royal Order of Scotland (appendix X) etc., etc. In accepting uncritically the claims of Burnes, Thory and others would have left that 'traditional history' created by a Freemason for Freemasons, in the realm of belief and not history.[8] Burnes was writing merely at the request of romantically inclined Victorian Freemasons who were interested in reviving, in a Masonic mould, the KT. Disregarding that simple fact took many from the realm of using, for moralistic purposes, a traditional history into the realm that it (the traditional history) was historical fact. Burnes himself had begun that process by citing 'evidence' which supported the notion that his traditional history had a factual basis. This in itself indicates that he did not understand the function of a Masonic traditional history. He was therefore predisposed to believe that his research revealed the literal truth about Freemasonry and the KT.

It is therefore appropriate here to explain what a traditional history is and its Masonic purpose and intent. There are a number of branches within Freemasonry. Each has its own 'story', its own traditional history, which underpins that particular part of the Masonic system. In this book we have seen that the traditional history of Masonic Lodges (often erroneously called 'blue' Lodges and all the connotations that that description implies) centres on King Solomon's Temple. The Royal Arch Chapter is concerned with the building of a new or second Temple, often referred to as Zerubabbel's Temple. Another branch of Freemasonry has for its traditional history the story of Helena, wife of Constantine, and her search for the place of Christ's crucifixion.

This is not at all unusual as other, similar, organisations, such as the Free Gardeners, Free Fishermen, Free Carpenters, Free Potters, Free Shipwrights (shipbuilders) and Free Carters each had a traditional history one for each part of the organisation.[9] For example, the ritual of Lodges of Free Gardeners (equivalent to 'blue' or 'Craft' Masonic lodges) was based on a traditional history which concerned the Garden of Eden. Other branches within the Order of Free Gardeners (the Royal Arch and the equivalent of the Knights Templar) focused on horticultural allusions within the Bible such as the Garden of Gethsemane. The Free Gardeners therefore chose the first garden mentioned in the Bible on which to base their ceremonies. The masons (stonemasons) chose the first major stone building mentioned in the Bible — King Solomon's Temple.[10] Without giving anything away I am sure that the reader will intuitively know which Biblical account inspired the Free Shipwrights!

It is interesting that none of these other, similar, organisations such as the Free Gardeners etc. were ever the subject of the myth-making associated with Freemasonry.[11] One reason may be the fact none of these other similar organisations remain in existence. This suggests that this kind of myth making and speculative history is only applicable to an existing organisation — Freemasonry.[12] That is, one which has a membership receptive to material written about them.

All branches of Freemasonry, therefore, have a 'traditional history' on which their ceremonies are based. As well as having considerable colour (the Temple at Jerusalem must have seemed very exotic to the stonemasons of Scotland) KST added a great deal of prestige to a group of honest working men — where could bankers, if they so wished, turn for Biblical inspiration? Again I leave you to answer that question! Each branch of Freemasonry is separate and distinct. At a meeting of a Craft Lodge one would hear nothing about any other branch's traditional history because it would be irrelevant to the purpose of that meeting. In the same way at a meeting of a Royal Arch Chapter one would here nothing of the ceremonies of the Knights Templar. The traditional histories are therefore unique to each separate branch of Freemasonry not only because they provide a specific identity and purpose to each but because they were designed to impart a particular moral lesson, attitude or insight different from each other. In other words, the traditional histories of Freemasonry are always kept separate. It was only when some enterprising authors mixed them all together that a 'unified history' of Freemasonry was presented and it is one which only exists in books and not within Freemasonry.

This popular 'unified history' of Freemasonry, particularly Scottish Freemasonry, did not exist until recently and certainly would not have been recognised or understood by Freemasons of even 50 years ago. However, since the myth (that is, the one containing the essential elements described in the first chapter) was created by Burnes for Scottish Freemasons in 1837 it has been refined and elaborated. It did not reach its final, present, form until the latter part of the 20th century when Rosslyn Chapel came to occupy a central role in terms of evidence presented in support of the myth. It is almost as if there was a conscious decision taken in the early 1980's to deny the previous history of the chapel and replace it with something quite different. Certainly the official, essentially Christian, history (written by the chaplain to the Earl of Rosslyn who was also the official guide) which had been in use for almost 90 years was dropped and was replaced by increasingly speculative and non-Christian interpretations of the chapel.

The desire to show that the myth was not a myth at all but was actually an entirely valid account of the origin and development of Scottish (and therefore all) Freemasonry induced some to present evidence of a variety of types to prove the validity of their account. The central theme has been that modern Scottish Freemasonry is merely a continuation of the Medieval Order of Knights Templar (this means that all Freemasons today are simply Knights Templar in disguise!) The first difficulty to be overcome was to find evidence with which to 'bridge the gap' between the arrest of and subsequent suppression of the Order (1307/1312) and today.

The difficulty in attempting to 'bridge the gap' is that after the suppression of the Order there *was* no evidence available to support that view. The evidence which is now represented is material which has been re-interpreted to make it suitable. It is that evidence, and its re-interpretation, which formed the other substantial part of this book. Rosslyn Chapel must have pride of place given that nearly every proponent of the Popular Approach uses it in some way as evidence in support of their view. As has been seen, that involved a re-classification of what the chapel was into something quite different. Something that was not Masonic has been made to appear Masonic. In a similar way Masonic material has been changed into something which is not Masonic — in particular the Kirkwall Scroll. All sorts of other evidence from Latin charters and documents — the St. Clair Charters; 'anonymous' Scottish graveslabs; carvings within Rosslyn Chapel; Scottish churches; events at the Battle of Bannockburn; Masonic symbolism; Scottish Masonic ritual and practice — have been used in this manner. Even the lives of historical figures (e.g. British Prime Ministers and United States Presidents) have undergone re-interpretation in an effort to change the myth into reality. The physical evidence has been discussed to a greater or lesser extent in the preceding chapters.

Early writers who claimed a connection with the KT and Freemasonry (Barruel etc.) made no attempt to prove the link — the claim was sufficient as they had a political/religious agenda. Even when the Masonic KT themselves (Burnes etc.) claimed the connection they too did not provide any hard evidence — the best they could do was suggest that others (such as Calmet) also supported their claim or referred to evidence that only indirectly supported their claims such as the charter of Larmenius. These historical characters do prove one thing, however — this is not a new 'theory' — it has been around for over 200 years but it is not as old as Freemasonry itself. Only after the Scottish Masonic KT came into existence did the myth come into being and it was elaborated, initially by the KT themselves and then by other authors who (re) discovered the myth.

A variety of techniques used by those of the Popular or Alternative approach have been discussed in Chapter 1. Some might uncharitably suggest that these are mere ploys used to support a claim that would not otherwise be valid. One of the most invidious of these techniques is that which uses the absence of evidence to suggest the opposite — that is, a negative is used to 'prove' a positive. The classic example of this, in the context of this book, is the suggestion (discussed in Chapter 8 — Other Physical Evidence) that because there is no evidence that the Knights Templar were at the Battle of Bannockburn that means that they may have been there! Using that method, creating evidence from nothing, many writers then go on to discuss the subsequent activities of the Knights Templar in Scotland. By embarking on such a discussion means by implication that the KT were present at the battle but avoid the need of presenting any supporting evidence. Another example where this technique is used relates to the graveslabs at Kilmartin which bear the outline of a sword but which bear no names. These are cited as crucially important as they are evidence that the KT hid in Argyll after 1307. The graveslabs, are anonymous — those originally buried there are unknown. The evidence therefore is negative. Yet their very anonymity is used to claim that they are something specific, something positive — the graves of deceased Knights Templar.[13] To further illustrate the shortcoming of this technique is to apply it to other 'evidence' and examine the consequences of doing so. Below is a list of what the KT who allegedly fled to, and hid in, Argyll *did not do*. For example they left no evidence of:

Marriage
Having children
Building churches

Travelling anywhere
Trading with anyone
Buying or selling horses
Buying or selling property
Building farms, mills or homes
Written transactions and records
Impacting on the Gaelic language
Employing anyone (e.g armourers, farriers, etc.)
Fighting any of Bruce's enemies in Argyll during 1307–1314[14]

The situation is therefore that the only evidence that the KT allegedly left of their presence is a few anonymous graveslabs. Doubts about them being KT graveslabs at all have been discussed more fully above. Let us consider just one of the points mentioned in the above list. These knights were French; no one has suggested otherwise. The language of Argyll was Gaelic — one of the most distinctive languages in Europe. Setting aside how French speaking fugitives would have coped with the Gaelic language, it is remarkable that, assuming that they were indeed in Argyll, their presence made no impact whatsoever on the Gaelic language. What is more, Gaelic was well developed at this time and was the language of the area but there is not one trace of the KT in any of the oral traditions of the area. Nor are there any references in any of the documents of the time regarding the sudden and uninvited appearance of non-Gaelic speakers.

The only thing they did in Argyll, according to the evidence presented by the exponents of the Popular Approach, was to arrive, hide and die there, the only trace of their presence being anonymous graveslabs. The Popular Approach only uses a very limited range of evidence (the graveslabs) and, when compared to evidence not used, it becomes clear that the use of 'evidence' has been selective.

Rosslyn Chapel has now gained a central place in the physical evidence presented in support of the myth. An event also holds a central position — the Battle of Bannockburn and its immediate aftermath. Popular writers claim that the battle was the catalyst for a variety of things, particularly the actions of Robert Bruce. It is claimed that he created Freemasonry into which the Knights Templar were integrated or alternatively that he allowed the KT to continue to exist.[15]

These post-Bannockburn organisations have allegedly passed secret knowledge or treasure down to the present day and Freemasonry is frequently cited as being the modern custodian. These claims give rise to some curious consequences. For example, if the Knights Templar continued to exist in Scotland after they were officially suppressed then the Freemasons of Scotland knew nothing about them because they went on to establish — the Order of the Knights Templar! If Freemasonry came into existence in 1314 into which the Knights Templar integrated, the Freemasons who changed stonemasons' lodges into Masonic Lodges did not know that Freemasonry already existed, having been invented in 1314. That being the case there must have been two forms of Freemasonry in existence at the same time: one 'invented' by Robert Bruce and another created from stonemasons' lodges.

One of the consequences of the Popular Approach means that the Freemasons writing during the 17th, 18th and first half of the 19th centuries were ignorant of their true history. The only other alternative would be that they were *not* ignorant — that they did know the truth but decided it must be suppressed. This view suggests that Freemasons were involved in a conspiracy of massive proportions involving many generations over hundreds of years and that the victims were — themselves!

The historical distortions which would be created if the myth were remotely true are rather bizarre and somewhat entertaining: for example, it would mean that Robert the Bruce did not win Scotland's independence at Bannockburn — some renegade French Knights did that for the Scots. It would also mean that until recently all British Prime Ministers and all American Presidents were Knights Templar — because they were Freemasons!

Stimulating and thought provoking though some of the ideas of a variety of writers are, these must be seen as merely one way of attempting to understand the past. What has been attempted here, albeit briefly, has been to examine some of the more common elements of the Scottish version of the myth, by testing them as if they were hypotheses. That testing has been carried out using sources and evidence well known in the academic world but perhaps not so well known elsewhere. The process has revealed some major shortcomings with the Popular Approach. It is somewhat disappointing that so many authors obviously have a limited knowledge of Scottish Freemasonry, or more correctly, a limited knowledge of the difference between Freemasonry in Scotland and that practised elsewhere. More serious is the dismissal, virtually without discussion, of enormous bodies of relevant material. That relating to the Battle of Bannockburn is a prime example.

On the darker side it is of concern to note that the modern myth has its roots in late 18th and 19th century anti-Masonic attacks by Barruel and Robison. Those Freemasons who devised a 'traditional history' in which the medieval KT and modern Freemasonry were intimately connected, had no way of knowing that 'their' myth would be adapted and embellished for purposes other than the innocuous pleasure of their fellow Freemasons. The perversion of the myth into anti-Semitic and anti-Masonic diatribes that led to the Protocols of the Elders of Zion, and ultimately the Holocaust, can be traced from the writings of Barruel and Robison. It is a fact, and a sad one, that this is completely ignored and is perhaps one of the reasons why Freemasonry is not a 'politically correct' group. One wonders where today's constant repetition of the myth might next lead.

This myth is unusual in that it does not appear until *after* the history of Freemasonry itself first appears in print, with the publication of Anderson's *Constitutions* in 1723. Even then the myth does not begin to obviously resemble the myth as it is known today until the late 20th century when it was created from a variety of traditional histories originally developed in the 18th and 19th centuries. The influence of the Romantic Movement, and its promotion of medieval notions of chivalry etc., cannot be underestimated as a major impulse in its creation. This myth is, therefore, part of a long line of mythologising by stonemasons beginning with the 1628 St. Clair 'Charter'. The myth has a dynamism that is markedly different from that of other myths, particularly those of classical antiquity, which demonstrates that it is young and has not, yet, reached the fixed maturity of other myths. Fortunately, the origin and development of this myth took place at a time when it was easily recorded and thus future generations of historians will, hopefully, continue to chart its progress and development.

This survey of material relating to how Scottish Freemasons perceived their past demonstrates that they were as susceptible to outside influence, then as now. Originally Scottish Freemasons had an understanding of their past that was reasonably straightforward and simple, if too fantastic for our modern tastes. Once printed histories began to appear which suggested a more exotic past, especially those with the sanction, tacit or otherwise, of those in authority, these new versions were eagerly consumed and ardently believed. Anderson, Ramsay, Preston, Laurie, Brewster, Hutchinson, Walker Arnott and assorted others were writers who initiated, and perpetuated, a fantastic history of Freemasonry. Each built on, and elaborated, the mythical work of their predecessors but all were Freemasons whose writings were for internal use only. Tragically they never took the opportunity to correct even the most obvious errors. The traditional histories of the various branches of Freemasonry were never intended for public consumption. Over approximately the last twenty years the traditional histories of

Freemasons have been re-interpreted, repackaged and resold to — Freemasons!

All the essential elements of the modern myth were created during the Romantic period when a nostalgic view of the chivalric codes of the Middle Ages was fashionable and which culminated in not only physical displays of chivalry (e.g. the Eglinton Tournament), but also in a host of artistic and literary works. At a time when Scottish culture was fashionable and when there was a widespread belief that chivalry could still be relevant, a romantic Scottish Masonic chivalric Order was synthesised — the present KT.

The myth as we know it today was created by the Masonic KT of Scotland. They appear to have done so for a number of reasons:

To legitimise the newly created Order.

To provide a Traditional History as with other branches of Freemasonry.

To differentiate the Order from other branches of Scottish Freemasonry.

To create an Order superior to 'ordinary' Freemasonry.

To demonstrate a particularly Scottish interpretation of the myth, that is, a different version from the then dominant French version.

Here lies the crux of the matter. None of the traditional histories of *any* of the branches of Freemasonry are, or were, intended to be taken literally. Our forebears in all the Masonic Orders manufactured suitable 'pasts' for allegorical purposes.[16] They did so with romantic notions at heart but understood that these histories manufactured by, and for, themselves were not literal truths.

It seems that, after all, Freemasonry is and always has been:

A peculiar System of Morality,
Veiled in Allegory and
Illustrated by Symbols

Fig. 22:

[1] The use of this particular quote is by way of example only; a whole host of others would have served the same purpose.

[2] This observation is made on the basis of anecdotal evidence only and there is clearly a need for research as to why it is acceptable to attack Freemasonry when it is not permissible to attack other innocent minority groups.

[3] Whilst such a conspiracy may exist, it does not appear to be in any way organised.

[4] Members of true secret societies — criminal and terrorist groups — are condemned in this manner but Freemasonry is neither a criminal nor a terrorist organisation.

[5] Numerous authors have proved this to be so in their writings.

[6] The radar surveys were undertaken by undergraduates from the Mechanical Engineering Department (now the School of Engineering and Electronics) of the University of Edinburgh. Unfortunately the non-academic supervisor and the undergraduates of the surveys are no longer with the university. The results of the surveys have disappeared.

[7] An application to make a physical search of the chapel would require to be submitted via Historic Scotland which is undertaking the work presently under way at the chapel. Historic Scotland is a government agency and the work at the chapel is therefore ultimately being funded by the taxpayer. Historic Scotland looks after much of the built heritage of Scotland and, at the time of writing, has an excellent web site at: www.historic-scotland.gov.uk

[8] Although created by a Freemason for Freemasons it must be remembered the group (the Scottish Knights Templar) had then nothing to do with Freemasonry (other than the fact that its members were all Freemasons) and had been rejected by mainstream Freemasonry in Scotland as being spurious and non-Masonic.

[9] Some of these organisations had but one ceremony whilst others had several which were every bit as complex as those within Freemasonry.

[10] The tower of Babel is the first building mentioned in the Bible but it was made from brick and would not therefore have been built by stonemasons. The fact that it was destroyed by God made it doubly unattractive to Scottish stonemasons.

[11] There are remnants of the Free Gardeners in existence and efforts have been made in the last few years to revive the Order. Others such as the Horsemen, the Free Carters and others lead a much quieter existence.

[12] I have been asked, no doubt rather mischievously, that if the Freemasons originated with the Knights Templar then do the origins of the Free Gardeners lie with the Teutonic Knights or the Knights of Calatrava!

[13] The assertion that the graveslabs are anonymous is itself an assertion without any supporting evidence. If there was a genuine desire that they be anonymous why bother with the carving of the outline of a sword at all? Why bother with any form of grave marker? In addition pause for thought is given by the fact that graveslabs which are not claimed to be Knight Templar graves are also anonymous.

[14] This technique dictates that, like the anonymous graveslabs, the above list should/could also be used as 'evidence' to prove the existence of the KT in Argyll after 1307. Doing so of course reveals the nonsensical nature of this technique.

[15] Some authors appear to be confused regarding the various branches of Freemasonry, suggesting that Bruce was responsible for the creation of the Royal Order of Scotland, The Order of the Rosy Cross, the Masonic Knights Templar, Order of Heredom de Kilwinning, etc.

[16] I can provide no better example of this process than that of the newly created English Masonic Order of Athelstan which is based on the Masonic Legend of Athelstan King of England (c. 895-939) who defeated the Scots and Welsh in 937. See *Freemasonry Today*, Issue 37 (Summer 2006) p. 12.

Bibliography

The amount of material that deals with, or touches on, the subject matter of this book is truly enormous. It would be a mammoth undertaking to list every work, every relevant publication. I have opted, therefore, to list only those works actually consulted by me. To assist the reader further I have separated the works of those of the Popular or Alternative Approach from the rest. Where possible I have quoted the original publisher, as well as the actual volume consulted, in order that a reader wishing to examine, or obtain, either or both publications has, where possible, the necessary details.

In the preparation of this work it became noticeable that very many authors, although writing about Scotland, Scottish Freemasonry, Scottish culture, Scottish buildings (e.g. Rosslyn Chapel) etc. did not quote, and therefore did not consult, Scottish sources or works about Scotland. I have attempted in some small way to redress that imbalance but I cannot claim to provide any comprehensive list of Scottish material. The best that might be hoped is to alert others to the fact that there is a considerable amount of relevant published material about Scotland.

Although it is normal to thank those who have assisted an author in an 'acknowledgements page', I take the opportunity to express additional thanks to my publisher, Lewis [Masonic] Publishing, for indulging my desire to provide such an extensive bibliography.

The Theory of History
The Philosophy of History is a subject that many writers rarely touch on. There are two particular approaches to the history of Freemasonry, the Popular or Alternative Approach and the Academic — both of which are dominant at this time — and some would argue, with justification, always have been! In any event it may be useful detail to a few books which discuss the Philosophy of History. Needless to say, there is extensive literature on this aspect of history and those titles mentioned are merely an indication of the material available.

Ankersmit, Frank and Kellner, Hans. (Eds.) *A New Philosophy of History*. Reaktion Books Ltd. 1995.
Baxter, Loraine, Hughes, Christina, and Tight, Malcolm. *How to Research*. Open University Press. 2001.
Carr, Edward H. *What is history?* The George Macaulay Trevelyan lectures delivered in the University of Cambridge January-March 1961. London. 1961.

Danto, Arthur C. *Analytical Philosophy of History*. Cambridge. 1965.

Elton, Geoffrey R. *The Practice of History*. Sydney: Sydney University Press and London: Methuen. 1967. Recently republished by Blackwell Publishers. 2001.

Gallie, Walter B. *Philosophy and the Historical Understanding*. London. 1964.

Gardiner, Patrick. (Ed.) *Philosophy of History*. Oxford University Press. 1974.

Gardiner, Patrick *The Nature of Historical Explanation*. Oxford University Press. 1968.

Hobsbawn, Eric. *On History*. Abacus. 1998. (First published by Weidenfeld & Nicolson, 1997.)

Marwick, Arthur. *The Nature of History*. Macmillan Press Ltd. 1989 (First published by Macmillan Press Ltd, 1970.)

Walsh, William, H. *Introduction to the Philosophy of History*. London. 1951.

History

Adams, Cecil. *Ahiman Rezon, The Book of Constitutions*. Ars Quatuor Coronatorum (AQC) Vol. 46 (1936). London. 1937.

Addison, Charles Greenstreet. *The History of the Knights Templars*. 1842.

Aitken, R. *The Knights Templar in Scotland*. The Scottish Review Vol. XXXII (1898).

Allen, J. Romilly. *The Early Christian Monuments of Scotland*. Edinburgh. 1903.

Anstruther, Ian. *The Knight and the Umbrella – An Account of the Eglinton Tournament, 1839*. Alan Sutton Publishing Ltd. 1986.

Argyll Castles in the care of Historic Scotland. Royal Commission on the Ancient and Historical Monuments of Scotland. Edinburgh. 1997.

Armstrong, Pete. *Bannockburn 1314 – Robert Bruce's great victory*. Osprey Publishing. Oxford. 2002.

Ashlar Magazine. Various Vols. — 1997 to date. Circle Publications Ltd. Helensburgh.

Ashley, Maurice. *The House of Stuart: Its Rise and Fall*. London. Dent. 1980.

Barber, Malcolm. *The Trial of the Templars*. Canto. 1995. (First published by Cambridge University Press, 1978.)

Barber, Malcolm. *The Two Cities – Medieval Europe 1050–1320*. Routledge. 1993 (paperback edition).

Barber, Malcolm. *The Military Orders; Fighting and Caring for the Sick*. Variorum, 1994.

Barber, Malcolm. *The New Knighthood — A History of the Order of the Temple*. Canto. 1998. (First Published by Cambridge University Press, 1994).

Barber, W. H. et al. (Eds.) *The Age of Enlightenment*. Oliver & Boyd. Edinburgh. 1967.

Barbour, John. *The Bruce*. *c.*1375. Reprinted by Canongate Classics, Edinburgh. 1997.

Barbour, John Gordon. *Unique Traditions Chiefly of the West and South of Scotlan*d. Glasgow. 1969.

Barron, Evan MacLeod. *The Scottish Wars of Independence*. London. 1914.

Barrow, Geoffrey W. S. *Robert Bruce & The Community of The Realm of Scotland*. Edinburgh University Press. 1996. (First published 1988).

Barrow, Geoffrey W. S. *Scotland and its neighbours in the Middle Ages*. The Hambleton Press. London. 1992.

Barrow, Geoffrey W. S. *The Scottish Clergy in the War of Independence*. Scottish Historical Review. Edinburgh Vol. XLI (1963).

Basford, Kathleen. *The Green Man*. D. S. Brewer (Boydell & Brewer Ltd). Ipswich. 1998. (First published 1978).

Bennett, Matthew and Wintney, Hartley. *The Hutchinson Dictionary of Ancient & Medieval Warfare*. Helicon, Oxford. 1998.

Beresford, Maurice W. *New Towns of the Middle Ages — Town Plantation in England, Wales and Gascony*. Lutterworth Press. London. 1967.

Billings, Robert William. *The Baronial and Ecclesiastical Antiquities of Scotland*. Edinburgh. 1852.

Bingham, Caroline. *Robert the Bruce*. Constable and Company Ltd. London. 1998.

Blaikie, Walter B., *Edinburgh at the Time of the Occupation of Prince Charles*. T. & A. Constable. Edinburgh. 1910.

Bonar, Horatius. *Catechisms of the Scottish Reformation*. Reprints of Calvin's, the Heidelberg, and Craig's catechisms and the Rudimenta Pietatis. By Andrew Duncan. Edited, with preface and notes, by Horatius Bonar. London. 1866.

Boulton, D'Arcy. J. D. *The Knights of the Crown – The Monarchical Orders of Knighthood in Later Medieval Europe 1325–1520*. Paperback edition by the Boydell Press 2000. First published by The Boydell Press, Woodbridge and St Martin's Press Inc., New York, 1987.

Brown, Michael. *The Black Douglases*. Tuckwell Press. Phantassie. 1998.

Burgess, Frederick. *English Churchyard Memorials*. Lutterworth Press. London. 1963.

Burman, Edward. *The Templars; Knights of God*. Crucible. 1986.

Burman, Edward. *Supremely Abominable Crimes—The Trial of the Knights Templar*. Allison and Busby. 1994.

Calmet, Augustine. *The Phantom World*. Wordsworth Editions Ltd. Ware. 2001. First published as: *Dissertations sur les apparitions des anges, des démons et des esprits. Et sur les revenans et vampires de Homgrie, de Boheme, de Moravie et de Silésie*. Paris. 1746.

Cameron, James K. (Ed.) *The First Book of Discipline*. Edinburgh. 1972.

Cameron, Sir Charles A. *Note on the Earliest Reference to the Masonic Knights Templar Degree*. Ars Quatuor Coronatorum. Vol. 16. London. 1903.

Cameron, Sir Charles A. *On the Origin and Progress of Chivalric Freemasonry in the British Isles*. AQC Vol. 13. London. 1900.

Campbell, Andrew J. The Rev. *Fifteen Centuries of the Church in Orkney*. Kirkwall. 1938.

Campbell, David G. *Scotland's Story in Her Monuments*. Robert Hale Ltd. London. 1982.

Campbell, Joseph, with Moyers, Bill D. *The Power of Myth*. Doubleday. New York. 1988.

Campbell, Joseph. *The Hero with a Thousand Faces*. Fontana Press. London. 1993. (First published by Princeton University Press, 1949.)

Campbell, J. L. and Thomson D. *Edward Lhuyd in the Scottish Highlands 1699-1700*. Oxford 1963.

Campbell, Marion. *Mid Argyll, a Handbook of History*. Oban. 1974.

Campbell, Neil and Smellie, R. Martin S. *The Royal Society of Edinburgh (1783–1983)*. Edinburgh. 1983.

Carr, Harry. *The Evolution of the Installation Ceremony and Ritual*. AQC Vol. 89 (1976). London. 1977.

Chetwode Crawley, W. J. *Rabbi Jacob Jehudah Leon*. AQC. Vol. 12 (1899). London. 1900.

Christiansen, Eric. *The Northern Crusades*. Penguin Books. 1997. (First published by Macmillan, 1980).

Christie, Alex. H. *The Abbey of Dundrennan*. Thomas Fraser, Dalbeattie. 1914.

Christison, General Sir Philip Bart., G.B.E., C.B., D.S.O., M.C., D.L., B.A., F.S.A. (Scot.). *Bannockburn*. The National Trust for Scotland. 1960.

Clarke, J. R. *A new look at King Solomon's Temple and its connection with Masonic Ritual*. AQC Vol. 88 (1975). London. 1976.

Clarke, J. R. *The Laying Out of the Ground Plan of Early Churches – with some references to Operative Masonry*. AQC. Vol. 91 (1978). London. 1979.

Cohn, Norman. *Warrant for Genocide. The Myth of the Jewish world-conspiracy and the Protocols of the Elders of Zion*. Eyre & Spottiswoode. London. 1976.

Coil, Henry Wilson. *A Comprehensive View of Freemasonry*. New York. Macoy. 1954.

Coil, Henry Wilson, et al. (Eds.) *Coil's Masonic Encyclopaedia*. New York. Macoy. 1961.

Colquhoun, Patrick, Sir. *A concise history of the Order of the Temple with some mention of those Bodies which claim to be derived from it*. Bedford. 1878.

Cooper, Robert L. D. (Ed). *An Account of the Chapel of Roslin – 1778*. The Grand Lodge of Scotland. Edinburgh. 2000. Author: Bishop Robert Forbes. First published, Edinburgh, 1774. Second, pirated, edition in 1778. It is the latter which was reproduced by the Grand Lodge of Scotland.

Cooper, Robert L. D. (Ed.), Wade, John (Trans.). *Genealogie of the Sainteclaires of Rosslyn*. The Grand Lodge of Scotland. Edinburgh. 2002. First published, Edinburgh, 1835.

Cooper, Robert L. D. *Scottish Masonic Aprons, from Operative to Speculative*, in: *The Freemason's Raiment of Light – Spirit and Matter*. Association 5997. Tours, France. 1997.

Cooper, Robert L. D. (Ed.). *The Illustrated Guide to Rosslyn Chapel and Castle, Hawthornden, &c*. Masonic Publishing Co. Glasgow. 2003. Author: The Rev. John Thompson, FSA, Chaplain to the Right Hon., the Earl of Rosslyn. First published in 1892.

Cooper, Robert L. D. *An Introduction to the Origins and History of the Order of Free Gardeners*. QCCC Ltd. London. 2000.

Cooper, Robert L. D. (Ed). *The Voyages of the Venetian Brothers Nicolò & Antonio Zeno to the Northern Seas in the XIVth Century*. Masonic Publishing Co. Helensburgh. 2004. First published for the Hakluyt Society, London, 1873.

Cooper, Robert L. D. (Ed.) *The Church of the Knights Templar in London*. Worley, George. Masonic Publishing Co. Helensburgh. 2006. 2nd Edition. First published, London, 1907.

Cooper, Robert L. D. *Freemasons, Templars and Gardeners*. Melbourne. 2005.

Cooper, Robert L. D. *The Revenge of the Operatives?* In: *Marking Well – 150 Years of Mark Masonry*. Lewis Masonic Publishing. 2006.

Coss, Peter. *The Knight in Medieval England 1000-1400*. Combined Books Inc. PA, USA. 1996.

Cowan, Edward, J. *'For Freedom Alone' – The Declaration of Arbroath, 1320*. Tuckwell Press. Phantassie, East Linton. 2003.

Cowan Ian B., and Easson, David E. *Medieval Religious Houses — Scotland*. Longman. 1957 and 1976.

Cowan, William. *A Bibliography of the Book of Common Order and Psalm Book of the Church of Scotland – 1556–1644*. Edinburgh. 1913.

Craig, John. *A Shorte Summe of the Whole Catechisme*. Edinburgh. 1581.

Facsimile reprint by Law, Thomas Graves, Edinburgh. 1883.

Craven, Rev. J. B. *Kirkwall Kilwinning Lodge No.38² and its Remarkable Scroll.* AQC. Vol. 10 (1897). London. 1897.

Cruden, Stewart. *Scottish Medieval Churches.* John Donald. Edinburgh. 1986.

Davis, William A. *History of the Edinburgh Royal Arch Chapter, No.1.* Edinburgh. 1911.

Day, W. R. *The Kirkwall Scroll.* AQC. Vol. 38. London. 1925.

Deanesly, Margaret. *A History of the medieval Church 590–1500.* Routledge. London. 2002 (paperback). First published 1925.

Denholm-Young, N. (Ed.) *Vita Edwardi Secundi — The Life of Edward the Second.* London. 1957.

Donaldson, Gordon. *The Making of the Scottish Prayer Book of 1637.* Edinburgh University Press. 1954.

Donaldson, Gordon. *Scottish Historical Documents.* Neil Wilson Publishing Ltd. Glasgow. 1997. (First published by Scottish Academic Press Ltd 1970.)

Donaldson, Islay, Dr. *East Lothian Gravestones.* East Lothian District Library. 1991.

Donaldson, Islay, Dr. *Midlothian Gravestones.* Midlothian District Library Service. 1994.

Donaldson, Mary E. M. *Further Wanderings – Mainly in Argyll.* Gardener. Paisley. 1926.

Donnachie, Ian and Whatley, Christopher. (Eds.) *The Manufacture of Scottish History.* Polygon. Edinburgh. 1992.

Douglas, Sir Robert of Glenbervie. *The Baronage of Scotland.* Edinburgh. 1798.

Douglas, William S. *Cromwell's Scotch Campaigns: 1650–51.* London. 1898.

Dowden, John. *The Bishops of Scotland – being notes on the lives of all the Bishops, under each of the Sees, prior to the Reformation.* Glasgow. 1912.

Draffen, George S, M.B.E. *Pour La Foy — A Short History of the Great Priory of Scotland.* David Winter and Son Ltd. Dundee. 1949. (CD-ROM version GLoS. 2000.)

Drummond, James. (Curator of the National Gallery and of the National Museum of the Antiquaries of Scotland) *Sculptured Monuments in Iona & the West Highlands.* Edinburgh. 1881. (Reprinted, in paperback, by Llanerch Publishers, 1994).

Duncan, Archibald A. M. (Ed.) *The Acts of Robert I, King of Scots 1306-1329.* Vol. 5. Edinburgh Unversity Press. Edinburgh. 1988.

Dyer, Colin. *Symbolism in Craft Freemasonry.* Lewis Masonic Publishers Ltd. Shepperton. 1976.

Eched, Sam. *Authentic or Distorted Hebraism.* Privately printed. nd. (A gift to the author for which I am extremely grateful.)

Edwards, John. *The Templars in Scotland in the Thirteenth Century.* Scottish Historical Review. Vol. V. 1908.

Edwards, John. *Rent-Rolls of the Knights of St John of Jerusalem in Scotland.* Scottish History Review Vol. XIX (part 3). 1922.

Evans, Joan. *The Flowering of the Middle Ages.* Barnes & Noble, Inc. 1998. (First published in 1966 and again in 1985 by Thames and Hudson Ltd.)

Farrah, George. *The Temples at Jerusalem and their Masonic Connections.* Central Regalia Ltd. Hinckley. 2003.

Faÿ, Bernard. *Revolution and Freemasonry 1680–1800.* Little. Boston. 1935.

Firminger, Rev. W. K. *The Romances of Robison and Barruel.* AQC. Vol. 50. London. 1940.

Flett, James. *Lodge Kirkwall Kilwinning, No.38² – The Story from 1736.* Lerwick. 1976.

Forbes, Alexander Penrose, Bishop of Brechin. *The Sanctity of Christian art: a sermon...* 1862.

Forbes, Robert. Dr. Bishop of Caithness. *An Account of the Chapel of Roslin.* The Grand Lodge of Scotland. Edinburgh. 2000. (First published in 1774. Second edition 1778).

Forbes-Leith, William. *The Scots Men-at-Arms and Life Guards in France.* Edinburgh. 1882.

Forley, A. J. *Ex-Templars in England.* Journal of Ecclesiastical History. Vol. 53. No. 1. January 2002. Cambridge University Press.

Fullarton, John. *Historical memoir of the Family of Eglinton and Winton.* Ardrossan. 1864.

Gayre, Lt. Col., of Gayre & Nigg. *The Knightly Twilight — A Glimpse at the Chivalric and Nobility Underworld.* Malta. 1973.

Gibson, John. S. *Edinburgh In The '45 (Bonnie Prince Charlie at Holyrood).* The Saltire Society. 1995.

Goldney, F. H. *Knights Templar.* AQC Vol. 16. London. 1903.

Gould, Robert F. *Military Lodges 1732–1899.* London. 1899.

Gould, Robert Freke, *The history of Freemasonry, its antiquities, symbols, constitutions, customs etc. Embracing an investigation of the records of the organisations of the fraternity in England, Scotland, Ireland, British colonies, France, Germany, and the United States.* 6 Vols. Revised by Dudley Wright. New York. 1936.

Graff, Chev. *The Testement of a Free-Macon, ou le Testament.* Bruxelles. 1745. (The Morison Collection – The Grand Lodge of Scotland.)

Graham, Henry Davenport. *Antiquities of Iona.* London. 1850.

Graham, Robert. C. *The Carved Stones of Islay*. Glasgow. 1895.

Grainger, John D. *Cromwell Against the Scots – The Last Anglo-Scottish War, 1650–1652*. Tuckwell Press. Phantassie, East Lothian. 1997.

Grand Lodge of Scotland. *Year Book (1952-)*. Various volumes.

Grand Lodge of Scotland. *The Laws and Constitutions of the Grand Lodge of Ancient and Honourable fraternity of Free and Accepted Masons of Scotland*. Edinburgh. 1836 and 1848.

Grant, Isabel Frances. *The Lordship of the Isles — Wanderings in the Lost Lordship*. Mercat Press, Edinburgh. 1982. (First published by The Moray Press, 1935.)

Grant, James. *Cassell's Old and New Edinburgh, its History, its People and its Places*. 3 vols. London. *c*.1890.

Grant, Katharine W. *Myth, Tradition and Story from Western Argyll*. Oban. 1925.

Grant, Will. *Rosslyn — its Castle, Chapel, and Scenic Lore*. Dysart and Rosslyn Estates. 1954.

Grantham, John A. *An Introduction to Mark Masonry — A Survey of Masonic Evolution in the British Isles*. Buxton. 1935.

Greenhill, Frank. Allen. *Incised Effigial Slabs in Latin Christendom*. London. 1976.

Greenhill, Frank. Allen. *The Incised Slabs of Leicestershire and Rutland*. Leicester. 1958.

Greenhill, Frank Allen. *Monumental Incised Slabs in the County of Lincoln*. Newport Pagnell Francis Coales Charitable Foundation. 1986.

Halloran, Brian M. *The Scots College Paris 1603–1792*. John Donald Publishers. Edinburgh. 1997.

Hamilton, William of Gilbertfield. *Blind Harry's Wallace*. The Luath Press. 1998. (First published as *The Actes and Deidis of the Illustre and Vallyeant Campioun Schir William Walllace*. *c*.1508. William Hamilton's version first published as: *A new edition of the Life and Heroick Actions of the Renoun'd Sir William Wallace, General and Governour of Scotland*. 1722.)

Hamill, John. *The Craft: A History of English Freemasonry*. Aquarian-Crucible. Wellingborough. 1986.

Hannah, Ian C. *The Story of Scotland in Stone*. Oliver and Boyd. Edinburgh. 1934.

Harvey, John. *The Master Builders: Architecture in the Middle Ages*. Book Club Associates. 1973. (First published by Thames and Hudson Ltd, 1971.)

Hay, Father Richard Augustine. (Ed. Maidment, James) *Account of the Templars*. Edinburgh. 1828.

Hay, Father Richard Augustin. (Ed. Maidment, James) *Genealogie of the*

Saintclairs of Rosslyn. Thomas G. Stevenson. Edinburgh. 1835.

Haywood, H. L. *Freemasonry and the Bible*. Contained within The Holy Bible. Collins Bible. (Masonic Edition) 1952.

Heckethorn, Charles William. *The Secret Societies of All Ages and Countries*. 2 vols. New York University. 1965.

Henderson, George David. *Chevalier Ramsay*. Thomas Nelson & Sons Ltd. London. 1952.

Heron, Robert. *Observations made in a journey through the Western Counties of Scotland in the Autumn of 1792, relating to the scenery, antiquities, customs, manners, population, agriculture, manufactures, commerce, political condition, and literature of these parts*. 2 vols. Perth. 1793.

Hillenbrand, Carole. *The Crusades – Islamic Perspectives*. Edinburgh University Press. 1999.

Hobsbawm, Eric and Ranger, Terence, (Eds.) *The Invention of Tradition*. Cambridge University Press. Paperback. Twelfth Printing. 2004. First published 1983.

Hollister, C. Warren; Leedom, Joe. W.; Meyer, Marc A. and Spear, David S. (Eds.) *Medieval Europe – A Short Source Book*. Newbery Award Records. New York. USA. 1982.

Hooker, Alan H. *The Knights Templar – Fact and Fantasy*. AQC. Vol.96 (1983). London. 1984.

Hopper, Sarah. *To be a Pilgrim – The Medieval Pilgrimage Experience*. Sutton Publishing Ltd. Stroud. 2002.

Horne, Alex *Sources of Masonic Symbolism*. Macoy. Richmond. 1981.

Howarth, Stephen. *The Knights Templar*. William Collins Sons and Co. Ltd. 1982.

Hutchinson, William *The Spirit of Masonry*. London. 1775.

Jackson, A. C. F. *English Masonic Exposures 1760–1769*. Lewis Masonic Publishing. Shepperton. 1986.

Jackson, A. C. F. *Early Statutes of the Knights Templar*. AQC. Vol. 89 (1976) London. 1977.

Jones, Bernard E. *Freemasons' Guide and Compendium*. London. 1950.

Jones, Bernard E. *Freemasons' Book of the Royal Arch*. George G. Harrap & Co. Ltd. London. 1957.

Jupp, Peter C. and Gittings, Clare. *Death in England – An Illustrated History*. Rutgers University Press. New Jersey. 2000. First published by Manchester University Press. 1999.

Kahler, Lisa Dr. *Freemasonry in Edinburgh 1721-1746: Institutions and Context*. Unpublished thesis. University of St Andrews. 1998.

Khaler, Lisa. *Andrew Michael Ramsay and his Masonic Oration*. Heredom. Vol. 1 (1992), Scottish Rite Research Society. Washington D.C. 1993 (This paper includes the text of the two known versions of Ramsay's *Oration*.)

Kieckhefer, Richard. *Magic in the Middle Ages*. Canto. 2000. (First published by Cambridge University Press, 1989.)

Kirk, James. (Ed.) *The Second Book of Discipline*. The Saint Andrew Press. Edinburgh. 1980.

Kirk, James. (Ed.) *The Books of Assumption of the Thirds of Benefices – Scottish Ecclesiastical Rentals at the Reformation*. Published for the British Academy by Oxford University Press. Oxford. 1995.

Knoop, Douglas and G.P. Jones. *The Scottish Mason and the Mason Word*. Manchester University Press. 1939.

Knoop, Douglas and G.P. Jones. *A Short History of Freemasonry to 1730*. Manchester University Press. 1940

Knoop, Douglas and G.P. Jones, and Douglas Hamer. (Eds.) *The Early Masonic Catechisms*. Sheffield. 1943.

Knoop, Douglas and G.P. Jones. *The Genesis of Freemasonry*. Manchester University Press. 1947.

Knowles, David and Hadcock, R. Neville. *Medieval Religious Houses — England and Wales*. Longman, Green and Co. London. 1953.

Knowles, David. *The Religious Orders in England – The End of the Middle Ages*. (Vol. 2) Cambridge University Press. 1955.

Lamont, W. D. *Ancient & Medieval Sculptured Stones of Islay*. Edinburgh. 1968.

Lane, John. *Masonic Records 1717–1894* by John Lane. 2nd edition. London. 1895. First published in 1887. Now available online at: http://www.freemasonry.dept.shef.ac.uk/lane/

Lees, Beatrice A. (Ed.) *Records of the Templars in England in the Twelfth Century. The Inquest of 1185 with Illustrative Charters and Documents*. London. Published for the British Academy by Oxford University Press. 1935.

Lenman, Bruce. *The Jacobite Risings in Britain. 1689 – 1746*. London. Eyre & Spottiswoode. 1980.

Lennhoff, Eugene and Frame, Einar. (Trans.) *The Freemasons*. Lewis Masonic Publishing. Middlesex. 1978.

Lepper, John Heron. *Famous Secret Societies*. London. 1932.

Lindsay, Robert Strathern. *The Royal Order of Scotland*. Edinburgh. 1972.

Lindsay, Robert Strathern. *The Scottish Rite for Scotland*. Edinburgh. 1958.

Loder, John de Vere, Baron Wakehurst. *Colonsay and Oronsay in the Isles of*

Argyll. 1935.

Love, Dane. *Scottish Kirkyards*. Robert Hale Ltd. London. 1989.

Lowe, Chris. *Angels, Fools and Tyrants – Britons and Anglo-Saxons in Southern Scotland*. Canongate Books with Historic Scotland. Edinburgh. 1999.

Lyon, David Murray. *History of Freemasonry in Scotland drawn from Ancient Records with special reference to the Lodge of Edinburgh Mother Kilwinning and other Ancient Lodges*. Wm. Blackwood and Sons. Edinburgh. 1873.

Lyon, David Murray. '*History of The Lodge of Edinburgh (Mary's Chapel), No.1. embracing an account of the rise and progress of freemasonry in Scotland*. London. 1900.

McArthur, Joseph Ewart. *The Lodge of Edinburgh (Mary's Chapel), No.1 – Quatercentenary of Minutes 1599 – 1999*. Published by the Lodge. 1999.

McCann, John. *Essays on the Lodge of Stirling, Ancient and Modern – A Quadricentennial Review of Lodge 'Antient' Stirling*. 1998. Privately printed.

MacCormick, John. *The Island of Mull, its History, Scenes and Legends*. Glasgow. 1923.

MacDonald, Alan R. *The Jacobean Kirk 1567–1625. Sovereignty, Polity and Liturgy*. St. Andrews Studies in Reformation History. Aldershot. 1998.

MacDonald, Thomas D. *Gaelic Proverbs and Proverbial Sayings with English Translations*. Stirling. 1926.

MacDougall, Norman. *An Antidote to the English – The Auld Alliance, 1295-1560*. Tuckwell Press. Phantassie, East Linton. 2001.

MacGibbon, David and Ross, Thomas. *The Ecclesiastical Architecture of Scotland, from Earliest Christian Times to the Seventeenth Century*. 3 vols. Edinburgh. 1896–1897.

MacGibbon, David and Ross, Thomas. *The Castellated and Domestic Architecture of Scotland, from 12th to 18th Century*. 5 vols. Edinburgh. 1887–1892.

McGladdery, Christine. *James II*. John Donald Publishers Ltd. 1990.

MacKie, Robert Laird. *King James IV of Scotland*. Oliver and Boyd. 1958.

MacKechnie, Rev. John. (Ed.) *The Dewar Manuscripts – Scottish West Highland Folk Tales. Collected originally in Gaelic by John Dewar, Woodman to the Duke of Argyll*. Glasgow. 1963.

MacKenzie, Norman. (Ed.) *Secret Societies*. New York. Holt. 1967.

MacKenzie, William MacKay. *The Battle of Bannockburn*. Glasgow. 1913.

MacKenzie, William MacKay. *The Bannockburn Myth*. Edinburgh. 1932.

McLynn, Frank. *The Jacobites*. London. Routledge. 1985.

McNamee, Colm. *The Wars of the Bruces – Scotland, England and Ireland*

1306–1328. Tuckwell Press. 1997.

McNeill, F. Marian. *The Silver Bough — Scottish folk-lore and folk-belief*. 4 vols. Glasgow. 1977.

McNeill, Peter, G. B. and MacQueen, Hectore, L. *Atlas of Scottish History to 1707*. The Scottish Medievalists and Department of Geography, University of Edinburgh. 1996.

McNulty, W. Kirk. *Freemasonry – A Journey through Ritual and Symbol*. Thames and Hudson. London. 1991.

McQuarrie, Alan. *Scotland and the Crusades 1095–1560*. John Donald Publishers Ltd. Edinburgh. 1997.

McRitchie, David. *Scottish Gypsies under the Stewarts*. Edinburgh. 1894.

Maidment, James. (Ed.) *Abstract of the Charters and Other Papers recorded in the Chartulary of Torphichen*. Edinburgh. 1830.

Maidment, James. (Ed.) *Templaria: papers relative to the history, privileges, and possessions of the Scottish Knights Templar, and their successors the Knights of Saint John*. From Father Augustine Hay's MSS. Edinburgh. 1828.

Maxwell, Herbert Eustace, the Rt. Hon. Sir (translated with notes). *The Early Chronicles Relating to Scotland*. Glasgow. 1912.

Maxwell, Herbert Eustace, the Rt. Hon. Sir (translated with notes). *The Chronicle of Lanercost, 1272-1346*. Glasgow. 1913.

Maxwell, Herbert Eustace, the Rt. Hon. Sir (translated with notes). *Scalacronica. The Reigns of Edward I, Edward II, Edward III*. Glasgow. 1907.

Maxwell, William D. *A History of Worship in the Church of Scotland*. Oxford University Press. London. 1955.

Mecklenburg, Counseiller du Duc de (?). *The Temple of Solomon with all its Porches, Walls, Gates, Halls, Chambers, Holy Vessels, the Altar of Burnt-Offering, the Molten Sea, Golden-Candlesticks, Shew-Bread, Tables, Altar of Incense, the Ark of the Covenant, with the Mercy-Seat the Cherubims, &c. As also The Tabernacle of Moses…* London. 1725.

Meikle, Henry W. *Scotland and the French Revolution*. MacLehose & Sons. Glasgow. 1912.

Morris, William J. *A Walk through Glasgow Cathedral*. Glasgow. 1995.

Murray, David. *Early Burgh Organisation in Scotland as Illustrated in the History of Glasgow*. Glasgow. 1924–1932.

Mylne, Rev. Robert Scott. *The Master Masons to the Crown of Scotland and their Works*. Scott & Ferguson and Burness & Company. Edinburgh, 1893.

Napier, James. *Folklore or Superstitious Beliefs in the West of Scotland*. Paisley. 1879.

Newton, David E. *Freemason's Cipher*. in the Encyclopedia of Cryptology. Santa Barbara, California. 1998.

Nicolle, David. *Arms and Armour of the Crusading Era 1050-1350*. Greenhill Books. London. 1999.

Nicolson, Helen. *The Knights Templar – A New History*. Sutton Publishing Ltd. 2001.

Nusbacher, Aryeh. *The Battle of Bannockburn — 1314*. Tempus Publishing Ltd. Stroud. 2000.

Oakeshott, Ewart. *Records of the Medieval Sword*. The Boydell Press. Woodbridge. 1991.

Oakeshott, Ewart. *The Archaeology of Weapons – Arms and Armour from Prehistory to the Age of Chivalry*. The Boydell Press. Woodbridge. 2002. First published 1960.

Oldenbourg, Zoe. *Massacre at Montsegur — A History of the Albigensian Crusade*. Phoenix. 1998. (First published in Great Britain by George Weidenfeld & Nicolson Ltd. 1961.)

Omand, Donald. *The Argyll Book*. Birlinn Ltd. Edinburgh. 2004.

Owen, Olwyn. *The Sea Road – A Viking Voyage Through Scotland*. Historic Scotland. Edinburgh. 1999.

Partner, Peter. *The Knights Templar and their Myth*. Destiny Books. 1990. (First published by Oxford University Press. 1981.)

Paterson, Raymond Campbell. *My Wound is Deep – A History of the later Anglo-Scots Wars 1380 – 1560*. John Donald Publishers Ltd. Edinburgh. 1997.

Paterson, Raymond Campbell. *For the Lion – A History of the Scottish Wars of Independence 1296-1357*. John Donald Publishers Ltd. Edinburgh. 1996.

Paton, Henry, M. '*Accounts of the Masters of Works for building and repairing Royal Palaces and Castles. Volume 1: 1529–1615*'. HMSO. Edinburgh. 1957.

Payne, Robert. *The Crusades*. Wordsworth Editions Ltd. 1998. (First published in Great Britain as *The Dream and the Tomb*. 1986. First published in paperback 1994).

Pennant, T. *A Tour in Scotland; MDCCLXIX*, fifth edition, 1790.

Pennant, T. *A Tour in Scotland, and Voyage to the Hebrides; MDCCLXXII*, (new edition), 1790.

Pennick, Nigel. *The Celtic Cross — An Illustrated History and Celebration*. Blandford (A Cassell Imprint). Harvill, London. 1997.

Piatigorsky, Alexander. *Who's afraid of Freemasons? – the phenomenon of Freemasonry*. London. 1997.

Pick, Fred L. and Knight, Norman G. *The Pocket History of Freemasonry*. New

York. 1953.

Prebble, John. *The King's Jaunt – George IV in Scotland, August 1822*. Birlinn Ltd. Edinburgh. 2000. (First published by Collins, 1988.)

Pride, Glen L. *Glossary of Scottish building terms*. Scottish Civil trust. Glasgow. 1975.

Read, Piers Paul. *The Templars*. Weidenfeld and Nicolson. London. 1999.

Ridley, Jasper. *The Freemasons*. Constable, London. 1999.

Riley-Smith, Jonathan. *The First Crusade and the Idea of Crusading*. The Athlone Press. London. 1993. (First published 1986.)

Riley-Smith, Jonathan. *The Atlas of the Crusades*. Times Books. London. 1991.

Riley-Smith, Jonathan. (Ed.). *The Oxford History of the Crusades*. O.U.P. 1995.

Riley-Smith, Jonathan. *The Hospitallers: The History of the Order of St. John*. Hambelton Press. London. 1999.

Rixson, Denis. *The West Highland Galley*. Birlinn Ltd. Edinburgh. 1998.

Roberts, J. M. *The Mythology of Secret Socities*. Scribners. New York. 1972.

Robinson, Martin. *Scared Places, Pilgrim Paths – An Anthology of Pilgrimage*. Harper Collins. London. 1997.

Rosslyn, The Earl of. *Rosslyn — Its Chapel, Castle and Scenic Lore*. Dysart and Rosslyn Estates. No date.

Rosslyn, The Earl of. *Rosslyn Chapel*. Roslin. 1997.

Rothwell, Harry, (Ed.) *The Chronicle of Walter of Guisborough*. London. 1957.

The Royal Commission on the Ancient and Historical Monuments of Scotland. *Argyll. An Inventory of the Ancient Monuments. Vol. 2. Lorn*. Edinburgh. 1975.

The Royal Commission on the Ancient and Historical Monuments of Scotland. *Mid Argyll and Cowal Medieval and Later Monuments, Vol. 7*. Edinburgh. 1992.

Runciman, Stephen, Sir. *A History of the Crusades*. 3 vols. Penguin, Harmondsworth, London. 1971.

Ryder, Peter. *'Medieval Cross Slab Grave Covers in Northumberland'*. Archaeologia Aeliana 5th series, XXVIII. (2000). (The Journal of the Society of Antiquaries of Newcastle upon Tyne.)

Saul, Nigel. *Age of Chivalry – Art and Society in Late Medieval England*. Brockhampton Press. 1995. (First published by Collins & Brown 1992.)

Scott-Moncrieff, George. (Ed.) *The Stones of Scotland*. London. 1938.

Scott, Ronald M. *Robert the Bruce – King of Scots*. Canongate Books Ltd. 1996. (First published by Hutchinson & Co. Ltd. 1982.)

Scott, William W. C. *Bannockburn Revealed. BANNOCKBURN: The Problems, Sources, Solutions, Status of the Arguments and Discoveries in Topography.*

Elenkus. Rothesay. 2000.

Scottish Borders Council. *Christian Heritage in the Borders*. Melrose. 1998.

Selwood, Dominic. *Knights of the Cloister*. The Boydell Press. Woodbridge. 1999.

Seward, Desmond. *The Monks of War — The Military Religious Orders*. Penguin Books Ltd. 1995. (First published 1972.)

Shane, A. Lewis. *Jacob Judah Leon of Amsterdam (1602–1675) and his models of the Temple of Solomon and the Tabernacle*. AQC. Vol. 96 (1983). London. 1984.

Simon, Edith. *The Piebald Standard*. London. 1919.

Simpson, W. *The Three-fold Division of Temples*. AQC Vol. 1 (1888). London. 1889

Sire, H. J. A. *The Knights of Malta*. Yale University Press. 1994.

Skene, William F. (Ed.) and Skene, Felix J. H. (Trans). *John of Fordun's Chronicle of the Scottish Nation*. Llanerch Publishers. 1993.

Slezer, John. *Theatrum Scotiæ*. London. 1693.

Smith, Jack. *Torphichen*. Torphichen. 1997.

Smith, Robin. *The Making of Scotland – A Comprehensive Guide to the Growth of Scotland's Cities, Towns and Villages*. Edinburgh. 2001.

Smout, Thomas C. *A History of the Scottish People 1560–1830*. Fontana Press. London. 1985. (First published by Harper Collins Publishers, 1969.)

Smyth, Frederick. *Brethren in Chivalry*. Lewis Masonic Publishing Ltd. 1991.

Steer, K. A. and Bannerman, J. W. M. *Late Monumental Sculpture in the West Highlands*. Edinburgh. 1977.

Stevenson, David. *The First Freemasons — Scotland's Early Lodges and their Members*. Second Edition. The Grand Lodge of Scotland. 2001. (First published by the Aberdeen University Press. 1988).

Stevenson, David. *The Origins of Freemasonry — Scotland's Century 1590-1710*. Cambridge University Press. 1988.

Stewart, Trevor. *English Speculative Freemasonry: Some Possible Origins, Themes and Developments*. Prestonian Lecture 2004. Privately printed. Sunderland. 2004.

Stones, Alison; Krochalis, Jeanne; Gerson, Paula and Shaver-Crandell. *The Pilgrim's Guide to Santiago De Compostela*. (2 vols.) Harvey Miller Publishers. London. 1998.

Stones, Edward L. G. *Anglo-Scottish Relations 1174-1328*. Clarendon Press. 1970.

Stuart, J. *Sculpured Stones of Scotland*. 2 vols. Spalding Club. Aberdeen. 1856.

Sutherland, Elizabeth. *Five Euphenias – Women in Medieval Scotland*

1200–1420. Constable and Company Ltd. 1999.

Tannenbaum, Samuel Aaron. *The Handwriting of the Renaissance: being the development and characteristics of the script of Shakspere's time*. London. 1930.

Taylor, Alison. *Burial Practice in Early England*. Tempus Publishing Ltd. Stroud. 2001.

Thompson, Rev. John. *The Illustrated Guide to Rosslyn Chapel and Castle, Hawthornden, &c*. MacNiven & Wallace. 1934.

Thomson, Oliver. *The Great Feud – The Campbells and & the MacDonalds*. Sutton Publishing Ltd. Stroud. 2000.

Thomson, William P. L. *History of Orkney*. Edinburgh. 1987.

Tobin, Stephen. *The Cistercians — Monks and Monasteries of Europe*. The Herbert Press Ltd. 1995.

Todd, Margo. *The Culture of Protestantism in Early Modern Scotland*. Yale University Press. USA. 2002.

Traquair, Peter. *Freedom's Sword — Scotland's Wars of Independence*. Harper Collins. 1998.

Tuchman, Barbara W. *A Distant Mirror — The Calamitous 14th Century*. Macmillan. 1997.

Tull, George F. *Traces of the Templars*. The King's England Press. 2000.

Upton-Ward, J. M. *The Rule of the Templars*. The Boydell Press. 1998. (First published 1992.)

Vernon, W. Fred. *History of Freemasonry in the Province of Roxburgh, Peebles and Selkirkshires from 1674 to the Present Time*. George Kenning. 1893.

Wallace-James, R. E. *The Minute Book of the Lodge of Aitcheson's Haven, 1598–1764*. Grand Lodge of Scotland Year Book. Edinburgh. 1981. pp. 58–59.

Warren, Sir Charles. *On the Orientation of Temples*. AQC. Vol. 1. London. 1895.

Wartski, Lionel. *Freemasonry and the Early Secret Societies Acts*. Privately printed. Natal, South Africa. 1983.

Watson, Fiona, *Under the Hammer — Edward I and Scotland 1286–1307*. Tuckwell Press. Phantassie, East Lothian. 1999.

Webb, Diana. *Pilgrims and Pilgrimage in the Medieval West*. I. B. Tauris. London. 1999. Paperback edition published 2001.

Whillsher, Betty and Hunter, Doreen. *Stones – A Guide to some remarkable Eighteenth Century Gravestones*. Canongate Publishing Ltd. Edinburgh. 1978.

Whillsher, Betty. *Understanding Scottish Graveyards – An Interpretive*

Approach. W. & R. Chambers Ltd. Edinburgh. 1985.

White, T. P. Capt., *Archaeological Sketches in Scotland, District of Kintyre*. Edinburgh. 1873.

White, T. P. Capt., *Archaeological Sketches in Scotland, Districts of Knapdale and Gigha*. Edinburgh. 1875.

Williams, Ronald. *Sons of the Wolf — Campbells and MacGregors and the Cleansing of the Inland Glens*. House of Lochar. Isle of Colonsay. 1998.

Williams, Ronald. *The Lords of the Isles. The Clan Donald and the early Kingdom of the Scots*. House of Lochar. 1997. (First published by Chatto & Windus 1984.)

Wilson, George Washington. *Photographs of Scottish scenery — Edinburgh and Rosslyn*. Edinburgh. 1871.

Wilson, John. Prof. *Scotland Illustrated*. Edinburgh. 1845.

Wise, Terence. *Knights of Christ*. Osprey Publishing Ltd. Oxford. 1984.

Woodhouse, F. C. *The Military Religious Orders of the Middle Ages — The Hospitallers, The Templars, the Teutonic Knights, and Others*. London. 1879.

Wormald, Jenny. *Court, Kirk and Community – Scotland 1470–1625*. Edinburgh University Press. 2001. (First published by Edward Arnold Publishers Ltd. 1981.)

Year Book of the Grand Lodge of Scotland (from 1952-). Various volumes.

Yeoman, Peter. *Pilgrimage in Medieval Scotland*. Historic Scotland. Edinburgh. 1998.

Speculative History

Titles which fall into this category are numerous and this list does not attempt to be in any way comprehensive. Those titles quoted must be taken as merely indicative of the huge range of books which fall into the Alternative, Popular or Mythological school of history.

Andrews, Richard. *Blood on the Mountain*. Weidenfeld and Nicolson. 1999.

Auld and Smellie. *The Free Masons Pocket Companion*. Edinburgh. 1765.

Baigent, Michael and Leigh, Richard. *The Temple and the Lodge*. Corgi Books. 1997. (First published by Jonathan Cape, 1989.)

Baigent, Michael; Leigh, Richard and Lincoln, Henry. *The Holy Blood and the Holy Grail*. Jonathan Cape Ltd. London. 1982.

Baigent, Michael, Leigh, Richard and Lincoln, Henry. *The Messianic Legacy*. Arrow Books. 1996. (First published by Jonathan Cape Ltd, 1996.)

Baigent, Michael and Leigh, Richard. *The Elixir and The Stone — Unlocking the Ancient Mysteries of the Occult*. Penguin Books Ltd. 1998. (First published by Viking, 1997.)

Baigent, Michael and Leigh, Richard. *The Inquisition*. Viking. London. 1999.

Bennett, John R. *Origin of Freemasonry and Knight Templar*. Kessinger Publishing Company (Reprint, no date). Originally published 1907.

Brydon, Robert. *Rosslyn — A History of the Guilds, The Masons and the Rosy Cross*. The Friends of Rosslyn. 1994.

Brydon, Robert. *Rosslyn and the Western Mystery Tradition*. Roslin. 2003.

Burnes, James. *A Sketch of the History of the Knights Templars*. Edinburgh. 1837.

Calcott, Wellins. *A Candid Disquistion of the Principles and Practices of the Most Ancient and Honourable Society of Free and Accepted Masons*. London. 1769.

Cheyne, W. *The Free-Mason's Pocket Companion*. Edinburgh. 1752.

Cotterell, Maurice. *The Tutankhamun Prophecies — The Sacred Secret of the Mayas, Egyptians and Freemasons*. Headline Book Publishing. 1999.

Flanders, Judith. (Ed.) *Mysteries of the Ancient World*. Seven Dials. 1999. (First published by Weidenfeld & Nicolson. 1998.)

Gardener, Laurence. *Bloodline of the Holy Grail — The Hidden Lineage of Jesus Revealed*. Element Books Ltd. 1996.

Gardener, Laurence. *The Shadow of Solomon – The Lost Secrets of the Freemasons Revealed*. Harper Element. London. 2005.

Gilbert, Adrian. *The New Jerusalem – Rebuilding London: The Great Fire, Christopher Wren and the Royal Society*. Bantam Press. London. 2002.

Grand Conclave [of Scotland]. *Statutes of the Religious and Military Order of the Temple as Established in Scotland*. Privately printed. 1843.

Hancock, Graham. *The Sign and the Seal — A Quest for the Lost Ark of the Covenant*. Book Club Associates. 1992. (First published by William Heinemann Ltd, 1992.)

H.R.H. Prince Michael of Albany. *The Forgotten Monarchy of Scotland — The True Story of the Royal House of Stewart and the Hidden Lineage of the Kings and Queens of Scotland*. Element Books Ltd. 1998.

Hunter, C. Bruce and Ferguson, Andrew C. *Legacy of the Sacred Chalice*. Macoy Publishing & Masonic Supply Co. Inc. Virginia. 2001.

Hunter C. Bruce. *Inner Workings – The Origin and Meaning of the Master's Word*. Macoy Publishing & Masonic Supply Co. Inc. Virginia. 2002.

Knight, Christopher and Lomas, Robert. *The Hiram Key. Pharaohs, Freemasons and the Discovery of the Secret Scrolls of Jesus*. Century Books Ltd. 1996.

Knight, Christopher and Lomas, Robert. *The Second Messiah — Templars, the Turin Shroud and the Great Secret of Freemasonry*. Century Books Ltd. 1997.

Knight, Christopher and Lomas, Robert. *Uriel's Machine*. Century Books Ltd. 1999.

Knight, Stephen. *The Brotherhood: The Secret World of the Freemasons*. Granada. London. 1984.

Laidler, Keith. *The Head of God — The Lost Treasure of the Templars*. Weidenfeld & Nicolson. 1998.

Laidler, Keith. *The Divine Deception – The Church, the Shroud and the Creation of a Holy Fraud*. Headline Book Publishing. 2000.

Laurie W. Alexander. *The history of Free Masonry and the Grand Lodge of Scotland. With chapters on the Knight Templars Knights of St. John Mark Masonry and R. A. Degrees to which is added an appendix of valuable papers*. Edinburgh. 1859.

Lawrie, Alexander. *The history of free masonry drawn from authentic sources of information with an account of the Grand Lodge of Scotland from its institution in 1736 to the present time compiled from the records; and an appendix of original papers. Edinburgh*. 1804.

Lomas, Robert. *The Invisible College – The Royal Society, Freemasonry and the Birth of Modern Science*. Headline Book Publishing. 2001.

Picknett, Lynn, and Prince, Clive. *The Templar Revelation – Secret Guardians of the True Identity of Christ*. Bantam Press. (Transworld Publishers Ltd.) London. 1997.

Pohl, Frederick J. *Prince Henry Sinclair. His Expedition to the New World in 1398*. Nimbus Publishing. Halifax, Canada. nd. (First published by C. N. Potter, 1967.)

Robinson, John J. *Born in Blood — The Lost secrets of Freemasonry*. M. Evans and Company, Inc. 1989.

Rosslyn, The Earl of. (Peter St. Clair-Erskine) *Rosslyn Chapel*. The Rosslyn Chapel Trust. 1997.

Ruddiman, Auld and Company. *The Free Masons Pocket Companion*. Edinburgh. 1761.

Sinclair, Andrew. *The Discovery of the Grail*. Century. 1998.

Sinclair, Andrew. *The Sword and the Grail. The Story of the Grail, The Templars and the true discovery of America*. Random House UK. 1993. (First published by Crown Publishers Inc. New York, 1992.)

Sinclair, Andrew. *Rosslyn – The Story of Rosslyn Chapel and the True Story behind the Da Vinci Code*. Birlinn. Edinburgh. 2005.

Sinclair Andrew. *The Secret Scroll*. Christopher Sinclair-Stevenson. London. 2001.

Smart, George. *The Knights Templar Chronology – Tracking History's Most*

Intriguing Monks. Authorhouse. Bloomington, Indiana. 2005.

Sora, Steven. *The Lost Treasure of the Knights Templar — Solving the Oak Island Mystery*. Destiny Books. 1999.

Tait, Peter; Brown, James and Tait, John. *The Freemasons Pocket Companion*. Glasgow. 1771.

Wallace-Murphy, Tim. *The Templar Legacy & The Masonic Inheritance within Rosslyn Chapel*. The Friends of Rosslyn. nd.

Wallace-Murphy, Tim. *An Illustrated Guide-Book to Rosslyn Chapel*. The Friends of Rosslyn. 1993.

Wallace-Murphy, Tim and Hopkins, Marilyn. *Rosslyn — Guardian of the Secrets of the Holy Grail*. Element Books. London. 1999.

Other Books — Fiction

It would be unfair not to mention other books, mainly works of fiction, which have assisted in the continuance of the myth of a link between the Knights Templar and Freemasonry or which touch on either subject. The reader might find these to be of interest and indirectly relevant to the matter discussed here.

Brown, Dan. *The Da Vinci Code*. Corgi. 2004. (First published by Bantam Press, 2003.)

Eco, Umberto. *Foucault's Pendulum*. Trans., Weaver, W. London. 1989.

Follett, Ken. *The Pillars of the Earth.* Signet. 1990.

Jeck, Michael. *The Last Templar*. Headline. 1995.

Khoury, Raymond. *The Last Templar*. Orion Books. 2006.

Kurtz, Katherine. *Two Crowns for America*. Bantam Books. 1997. (First published by Bantam Books, 1996.)

Kurtz, Katherine and Harris, Deborah T. *The Adept*. Ace Books. 1991.

Kurtz, Katherine and Harris, Deborah T. *The Lodge of the Lynx*. Ace Books. 1991.

Kurtz, Katherine and Harris, Deborah T. *The Templar Treasure*. Ace Books. 1991.

Kurtz, Katherine and Harris, Deborah T. *Dagger Magic*. Ace Books. 1991.

Kurtz, Katherine and Harris, Deborah T. *Death of an Adept*. Ace Books, 1997.

Kurtz, Katherine (Ed.) *Tales of the Knights Templar*. Warner Books, Inc. 1995.

Rutherford, Edward. *Sarum*. Arrow Books, 1988. (First Published by Century, 1987.)

Scott, Walter, Sir. *Ivanhoe, A Romance*. 1819.

Scott, Walter, Sir. *The Talisman*. 1825.

Shea, Robert. *All Things Are Lights*. Ballantine Books. 1986.

Appendix I
Schaw Statute of 1598

At Edinburgh the xxviij day of December, The zeir of God V` four scoir awchtene zeiris.

The statutis ordinanceis to be obseruit be all the maister maissounis within this realme, Sett doun be Williame Schaw, Maister of Wark, to his maiestie And generall Wardene of the said craft, with the consent of the maisteris efter specifeit.

Item, first that they obserue and keip all the gude ordinanceis sett doun of befoir concernyng the priviligeis of thair Craft be thair predicesso" of gude memorie, And specialie

That thay be trew ane to ane vther and leve cheritablie togidder as becumis sworne brether and companzeounis of craft.

Item, that thay be obedient to thair wardenis, dekynis, and maisteris in all thingis concernyng thair craft.

Item, that thay be honest, faithfull, and diligent in thair calling, and deill uprichtlie w` the maisteris or awnaris of the warkis that they sail tak vpoun hand, be it in task, meit, & fie, or owlklie wage.

Item, that name tak vpoun hand ony wark gritt or small quhilk he is no` abill to performe qualifeitlie vnder the pane of fourtie pundis money or ellis the fourt pairt of the worth and valor of the said wark, and that by and attor ane condigne amendis and satisfactioun to be maid to the awnaris of the wark at the sycht and discretioun of the generall Wardene, or in his absence at the sycht of the wardeneis, dekynis, and maisteris of the shrefdome quhair the said wark is interprisit and wrocht.

Item, that na maister sail tak ane vther maisteris wark over his heid, efter that the first maister hes aggreit w` the awnar of the wark ather be contract, arlis, or verbail conditioun, vnder the paine of fourtie punds.

Item, that na maister salt tak the wirking of ony wark that vther maisteris hes wrocht at of befoir, vnto the tyme that the first wirkaris be satisfeit for the wark quhilk thay haif wrocht, vnder the pane foirsaid.

Item, that thair be ane wardene chosin and electit Ilk zeir to haif the charge over everie ludge, as thay are devidit particularlie, and that be the voitis of the maisteris of the saids ludgeis, and consent of thair Wardene generall gif he happynis to be pn', And vtherwyis that he be aduerteist that sic ane wardene is chosin for sic ane zeir, to the effect that the Wardene generall may send sic directionis to that wardene electit, as effeiris.

Item, that na maister sail tak ony ma prenteissis nor thre during his lyfetyme w 'out ane speciall consent of the haill wardeneis, dekynis, and maisteris of the schirefdome quhair the said prenteiss that is to be ressauit dwellis and remanis.

Item, that na maister ressaue ony prenteiss bund for fewar zeiris nor sevin at the leist, and siclyke it sail no` be lesum to mak the said prenteiss brother and fallow in craft vnto the tyme that he haif seruit the space of vther sevin zeiris efter the ische of his said prenteischip w`out ane speciall licenc granttit be the wardeneis, dekynis, and maisteris assemblit for the caus, and that sufficient tryall be tane of thair worthynes, qualificatioun, and skill of the persone that desyirs to be maid fallow in craft, and that vnder the pane of fourtie punds to be upliftit as ane pecuniall penaltie fra the persone that is maid fallow in craft aganis this ord`, besyde the penalteis to be set doun aganis his persone, accordyng to the ord' of the ludge quhair he remanis.

Item, it sail not be lesum to na maister to sell his prenteiss to ony vther maister nor zit to dispens w' the zeiris of his prenteischip be selling y` of to the prenteisses self, vnder the pane of fourtie punds.

Item, that na maister ressaue ony prenteiss w'out he signifie the samyn to the wardene of the ludge quhair he dwellis, to the effect that the said prenteissis name and the day of his ressauyng may be ordlie buikit.

Item, that na prenteiss be enterit bot be the samyn ord`, that the day of thair enterer may be buikit.

Item, that na maister or fallow of craft be ressauit nor admittit w'out the numer of sex maisteris and twa enterit prenteissis, the wardene of that ludge being ane of the said sex, and that the day of the ressauyng of the said fallow of craft or maister be ord`lie buikit and his name and mark insert in the said buik w' the names of his sex admitteris and enterit prenteissis, and the names of the intendaris that salbe chosin to everie persone to be alsua insert in thair buik. Providing alwayis that na man be admittit w'out ane assay and sufficient tryall of his skill and worthynes in his vocatioun and craft.

Item, that na maister wirk ony maissoun wark vnder charge or command of ony vther craftisman that takis vpoun hand or vpoun him the wirking of ony maissoun wark.

Item, that na maister or fallow of craft ressaue ony cowanis to wirk in his societie or cumpanye, nor send nane of his servands to wirk w' cowanis, under the pane of twentie punds sa oft as ony persone offendis heirintill.

Item, it salt no' be lesum to na enterit prenteiss to tak ony gritter task or wark vpon hand fra a awnar nor will extend to the soume of ten punds vnder the pane foirsaid, to wit xx libs, and that task being done they sail Interpryiss na mair w'out licence of the maisteris or warden q` thay dwell.

Item, gif ony questioun, stryfe, or varianc salt fall out amang ony of the maisteris, servands, or entert prenteissis, that the parteis that fallis in questioun or debait, sail signifie the causis of thair querrell to he perticular wardeneis or dekynis of thair ludge w'in the space of xxiiij ho' vnder the pane of ten pnds, to the effect that thay may be reconcilit and aggreit and their variance removit be thair said wardeneis, dekynis, and maisteris; and gif ony of the saids parteis salhappin to remane wilfull or obstinat that they salbe deprivit of the privilege of thair ludge and no' permittit to wirk y`at vnto the tyme that thay submit thame selffis to ressoun at the sycht of thair wardenis, dekynis, and maisteris, as said is.

Item, that all maisteris, Inte priseris of wirkis, be verray cairfull to sie thair skaffellis and futegangis surelie sett and placeit, to the effect that throw thair negligence and slewth na hurt or skaith cum vnto ony personis that wirkis at the said wark, vnder pain of dischargeing of thaim y`efter to wirk as maisteris havand charge of ane wark, bot sail ever be subiect all the rest of thair dayis to wirk vnder or w ane other principall maister havand charge of the wark.

Item, that na maister ressaue or ressett ane vther maisteris prenteiss or servand that salhappin to ryn away fra his maisteris seruice, nor interteine him in his cumpanye efter that he hes gottin knawledge yrof, vnder the paine of fourtie punds.

Item, that all personis of the maissoun craft conuene in tyme and place being lawchfullie warnit, vnder the pane of ten punds.

Item, that all the maisteris that salhappin to be send for to ony assemblie or meitting sail be sworn be thair grit aith that thay sail hyde nor coneill na fawltis nor wrangis done be ane to ane vther, nor zit the faultis or wrangis that ony man hes done to the awnaris of the warkis that they haif had in hand safer as they knaw, and that vnder the pane of ten punds to be takin vp frae the conceillairs of the saidis faultis.

Item, it is ordanit that all thir foirsaids penalteis salbe liftit and tane vp fra the offendaris and brekaris of thir ordinances be the wardeneis, dekynis, and maisteris of the ludgeis quhair the offendaris dwellis, and to be distributit ad pion vsus according to gud conscience be the advyis of the foirsaidis.

And for fulfilling and observing of thir ordinances, sett doun as said is, The haill maisteris conuenit the foirsaid day binds and oblisses thaim heirto faithfullie. And thairfore hes requeistit thair said Wardene generall to subscriue thir presentis w' his awn hand, to the effect that ane autentik copy heirof may be send to euerie particular ludge win this realme.

WILLIAM SCHAW, Maistir of Wark.

Appendix II
Schaw Statute of 1599

xxviii Decembris, 1599.

First It is ordanit that the warden witin the bounds of Kilwynning and vther placeis subject to thair ludge salbe chosin and electit zeirlie be monyest of the Mrs voitis of the said ludge vpoun the twentie day of December and that wn the kirk of Kilwynning as the heid and secund ludge of Scotland and yrefter that the generall warden be advertysit zeirlie quha is chosin warden of the ludge, immediatlie efter his electioun.

Item it is thocht neidfull & expedient be my lord warden generall that everie ludge wtin Scotland sail have in tyme cuming ye awld and antient liberties yrof vse and wont of befoir & in speciall, yt ye ludge of Kilwynning secund ludge of Scotland sail haif thair warden pnt at the election of ye wardenis wtin ye bounds of ye Nether Waird of Cliddsdail, Glasgow Air & bounds of Carrik; wt powar to ye said wairden & dekyn of Kilwynning to convene ye remanent wardenis and dekynis wtin ye bounds foirsaid quhan thay haif ony neid of importance ado, and yai to be judgit be ye warden and dekyn of Kilwynning quhen it sail pleis thame to qvene for ye tyme ather in Kilwynning or wtin ony vther pt of the west of Scotland and bounds foirsaid.

Item it is thocht neidfull & expedient be my lord warden generall, that Edr salbe in all tyme cuming as of befoir the first and principall ludge in Scotland, and yt Kilwynning be the secund ludge as of befoir is notourlie manifest in our awld antient writts and that Stirueling salbe the third ludge, conforme to the auld privileges thairof.

Item it is thocht expedient yt ye wardenis of everie ilk ludge salbe answerabel to ye presbyteryes wtin thair schirefdomes for the maissonis subiect to ye ludgeis anent all offensis ony of thame sail committ, and the thrid pt of ye vnlawis salbe employit to ye godlie vsis of ye ludge quhair ony offens salhappin to be committit.

Item yt yr be tryall takin zeirlie be ye wardenis & maist antient maisteris of everie ludge extending to sex personis quha sail tak tryall of ye offenss, yt punishment may be execut conforme to equitie & iustice & guid conscience & ye antient ordor.

Item it is ordanit be my lord warden generall that the warden of Kilwynning as secund in Scotland, elect and chuis sex of the maist perfyt and worthiest of memorie within (thair boundis,) to tak tryall of the qualificatioun of the haill masonis within the boundis foirsaid of thair airt, craft, scyance and antient memorie; To the effect the warden deakin may be answerable heiraftir for sic p(er)sonis as Js qmittit to him & wthin his bounds and jurisdictioun.

Item commissioun in gewin to ye warden and deakon of Kilwynning as secund luge, to secluid and away put furthe of yr societe and cumpanie all p(er)sonis disobedient to fulfil & obey ye haill acts and antient statutts sett doun of befoir of guid memorie, and all p(er)sonis disobedient eyr to kirk craft counsall and uyris statutts and acts to be mayd heireftir for ane guid ordour.

Item it is ordainit be my lord warden generall that the warden and deakyn to be pnt of his quarter maisteris elect cheis and constitut ane famous notar as ordinar clark and scryb, and yat ye said notar to be chosinge sail occupye the office, and that all indentouris discharges and vtheris wrytis quhatsumevir, perteining to ye craft salbe onlie wrytin be ye clark and that na maner of wryt neyther tityll nor other evident to be admit be ye said warden and deakin befoir yame, except it be maid be ye said clark and subscryuit wt his hand.

Item It is ordanit be my lord generall that ye hale auld antient actis and statutis maid of befoir be ye predicessrs of ye masonis of Kilwynning be observit faithfullie and kepit be ye craftis in all tymes cuminge, and that na prenteis nor craftis man, in ony tymes heireftir be admittit nor enterit Bot onlie wthin the kirk of Kilwynning as his paroche and secured ludge, and that all bankatts for entrie of prenteis or fallow of crafts to be maid wthin ye said lug of Kilwynning.

Item It is ordanit that all fallows of craft at his entrie pay to ye commoun bolds of ye luge the soume of ten punds monie, wt x s. worthe of gluiffis or euire he be admttit and that forthebankatt, And that he be not admitit wthout ane sufficient essay and pruife of memorie and art of craft be the warden deacon and quarter mrs of ye lug, conforme to ye foirmer and qrthrow yai may be ye mair answerable to ye generall warden.

Item that all prentessis to be admititbe not admittit qll first pay to ye commoun bankat foiresaid the sowme of sex punds monie, utherwyes to pay the bankat for ye haill members of craft wthin the said ludge and prentessis yrof.

Item It is ordanit that the warden and deakis of ye secund luge of Scotland pnt of Kilwynning, sail tak the aythe, fidelitie and trewthe of all mrs and fallowis of craft wthin ye haill bounds committit to yr charge, zeirlie that thai sail not accumpanie wth cowans nor work with thame, nor any of yr servands or prenteisses wndir ye paine of ye penaltie contenit in ye foirmer actis and peying yrof.

Item It is ordanit be ye generall warden, That ye warden of ye lug of Kilwynning, being the secund lug in Scotland, tak tryall of ye airt of memorie and science yrof, of everie fellowe of craft and everie prenteiss according to ayr of yr vocations; and in cais yat yai haue lost ony point yrof dvied to thame To pay the penaltie as followis for yr slewthfulness, viz., Ilk fallow of craft, xx s., Ilk prentess, x s. , and that to be payit to ye box for ane commoun weill zeirlie & yat conforme to the commoun vs and pratik of the commoun lugs of this realm.

And for the fulfilling, observinge and keping of thir statutis and all oyr actis and statuttis maid of befoir and to be maid be ye warden deaconis and quarter mrs of ye lugis foirsads for guid ordor keping conform to equitie justice & antient ordor to ye makinge and setting doun qrof ye generall warden hes gevin his power and commission to the said warden and yrs abouevrtn to sett doun & mak actis conforme as accords to ye office law. And in signe and taking yrof I the generall warden of Scotland hes sett doun and causit pen yir actis & statutis And hes sybscryuit ye smyis wt my hand eftr ye testimoniale on this syd and on the uther syd.

Be it Kend to the warden dekyn and to the mrs of the ludge of Kilwynning That Archibald Barklay being directit commissioner fra the said ludge comperit in Edr the twentie sevin & twentie awcht of December Instant quhair the said Archibald — in pns of the warden generall & the mrs of the ludge of Edr, producit his commissioun, and behaifit himself verie honestlie and cairfullie for the discharge of sik thingis as was committit into him; bot be ressone of the absence of his Maitie out of the toun and yt thair was na mrs bot the ludge of Edr convenit at this tyme, We culd not get ane satlat order (as the privileges of the craft requyris) tane at this tyme, bot heirefter quhan occasioun sal be offerit we salt get his Maities warrand baith for the authorizing of the ludgeis privilegeis, and ane penaltie set down for the dissobedient persones and perturberis of all guid ordor. Thus far I thocht guid to sgnifie vnto the haill brether of the ludge, vnto the neist commoditie In witnes heirof, I haif subscriuit this pnt wt my hand at Halyrudhous the twentie awcht day of December The zeir of God P"V' fourscoir nynetene zeirs.

WILLIAM SCHAW, Maistir of Wark, Wairden of ye Maisons.

Appendix III
Schaw Tomb Translation

To his most upright Friend,
WILLIAM SCHAW,
Live with the Gods, and live for ever, most excellent man;
This life to thee was labour, death was deep repose.
ALEXANDER SETON, Erected
DEO OPTIMO MAXIMO
(To God the Best and Greatest.)

This humble structure of stones covers a man of excellent skill, notable probity, integrity of life, adorned with the greatest of virtues — William Schaw, Master of the King's Works, President of the Sacred Ceremonies and the Queen's Chamberlain. He died on 18 April 1602.

Among the living he dwelt fifty-two years; he had travelled in France and other kingdoms for the improvement of his mind; he wanted no liberal training; skilful in architecture; was early recommended to great persons for the singularity of his mind; and was not only unwearied and indefatigable in labours and business, but constantly active and vigorous, and was most dear to every good man who knew him. He was born to do good offices and thereby to gain the hearts of men; now he lives eternally with God.

Queen Anne ordered this monument to be erected to the memory of this most excellent and most upright man, lest his virtues, worthy of eternal commendation, should pass away with the death of his body.

Appendix IV
Charter Granted by the Masons of Scotland to William St. Clair of Roslin in 1601

BE IT kend till all men be thir present letters ws Deacons Maistres and freemen of the Masons within the realme of Scotland with express consent and assent of Wm Schaw Maister of Wark to our Sou^{ane} Lord ffor sa meikle as from aige to aige it has been observit amangis that the Lairds of Rosling has ever been Patrons and Protectors of us and our priviledges likeas our predecessors has obey'd and acknowledged them as Patrones and tectoris while that within thir few years throwch negligence and sleuthfulness the samyn has past furth of vse whereby not only has the Laird of Rosling lyne out of his just rycht but also our hail craft has been destitute of ane patron and protector and overseer q^{lk} has genderit manyfauld corruptions and imperfections, baith amangis ourselves and in our craft and has given occasion to mony persones to conseve evill opinioun of ws and our craft and to leive off great enterprises of policie be reason of our great misbehaviour w^tout correction whereby not only the committers of the faults but also the honest men are disapoyntit of their craft and ffeit. As lyikwayes when divers and sundrie contraversies falls out amangis ourselfs thair follows great and manyfald inconvenientis through want of ane [Patron and Protector] we not being able to await upon the ordinar judges and judgement of this realme through the occasioun of our powertie and langsumness of process for remeid q^rof and for keeping of guid ordour amangis us in all tymes cumyng, and for advancement of our craft and vocatioun within this realme and furthering of policie within the samyn We for ourselves and in name of our haill bretherene and craftismen with consent foresaid agrees and consents that Wm Sinclar now of Rosling for himself & his airis purchase and obtene at ye hands of our Sou^{ane} Lord libertie fredome and jurisdictioun vpone us and our successors in all tymes cummyng as patrons and judges to us and the haill fessoris of our craft w^tin this realme quhom off we have power and commission sua that hereafter we may acknawlege him and his airis as our patrone and judge under our Souerane Lord without ony kind of appellation or declynyng from his judgement with power to the said Williame and his airis to depute judges ane or mae under him and to use sick ampill and large jurisdictione upon us and our successors als Weill as burghe as land as it shall pleise our Souerane Lord to grant to him & his airis

WILLIAM SCHAW, Maistir of Wark

Edinburgh -   ANDRO SYMSONE JHONE ROBESOUNE

St Androse -   *   *   *   *   *   *

Hadingtoun -   P. CAMPBELL takand ye burdyng for JON. SAW

                     J. VALLANCE WILLM. AITTOUN

Achiesone Heavin - GEORG AITTOUN Jo. FWSETTER THOMAS PETTICRIF

Dunfermling - ROBERT PEST
Thomas Weir mason in Edr. THOMAS ROBERTSOUN wardane of the Ludge of
Dunfermling and Sanct Androis and takand the burding upon him for the brethren
of the Mason Craft within they Lwdges and for the Commissioners efter
mentionat viz. DAVID SKOWGALL ALEXANDER GILBERT and DAVID
SPENS for the Lwdge of Sanct Androis ANDREW ALISONE and ARCHIBALD
ANGOUS Commissionaris for the Lwdge of Dwmfermling and ROBERT
BALZE of Haddington with our handis led on the pen be the notaris underwritten
at our commandis because we can nocht write

Ita est LAURENTIUS ROBESOUN notarius publicus ad praemissa requisitus de
specialibus mandatis dict. personarum scribere nescien. ut aseruerunt testan.
manu mea propria
(Ita est) HENRICUS BANNA(TYNE) connotarius ad premissa (de mandatis)
antedictarum personarum (scribere nescientium ut aseruerunt teste) manu mea
propria

Appendix V
Charter Granted by the Masons of Scotland to Sir William St. Clair in 1628

BE IT KEND till all men be thir present letters ws the Deacones Masteris friemen of the Maissones and Hammermen within the kingdome of Scotland That forsameikill as from aidge to aidge it has been observet amangis us and our predecessors that the Lairdis of Rosling has ever been patrons and protectors of us and our priviledgis Likeas our predecessors has obeyit reverencet and acknowledget them as patrons and protectors q^r of they had letters of protection and vtheris richtis grantit be his M^{aties} most noble progenitors of worthy memorie q^{lkis} with sindrie vtheris of the Lairdis of Rosling his writtis being consumet and burnt in ane flame of fire within the Castle of Rosling in an .... The consumation and burning qrof being clearly knawin to us and our predecessors deacons maisteris and freemen of the saidis vocations, and our protection of the samyn and priviledgis thereof (be negligence) and slouthfulness being likely to pass furth of us where throw not only Wald the Lairdis of Rosling lyne out of their just richt but also our hail craftis Wald haif bene destitute of ane patrone protector and oversear quhilk wald engenner monyfald imperfectionis and corruptionis baith amangis ourselves and in our craft and give occasione to mony persones to conceive evill opinioun of us and our craft and to leave af many and grit enterpryces of policie whilk wald be vndertaken if our grit misbehaviour were suffered to goe on without correctioun For remeid q^r of and for keeping of good ordour amangis us in all time coming and for advancement of our craft and vocation within his Hienes kingdom of Scotland and furdering of policie yaireintill the maist pairt of our predecessors for themselves and in name and behalfe of our bretherene and craftsmen with express advice and consent of William Schaw Maister of Wark to Hienes umq^{le} darrest father of worthy memorie all in ane voce agreit consentit and subscryvet that William Sinclar of Rosling father to Sir William Sinclar now of Rosling for himself and his airis should purches and obtain at the hands of his Majestie libertie freedome and jurisdictioun upon us and our predecessors deacons maisteris and freemen of the saidis vocation, as patrones and judges to us and the haill professors thereof within the said kingdom q^{r}of they had power and commission sua that they and we micht yairafter acknowledge him and his airis as patrone and judge under our Soverane Lord without any kind of appellation or declinatour from thair judgement forever, as the said agreement subscryvet be the said M^r of Wark and our predecessors at mare length proportis In the whilk office priviledge and jurisdictioun over us and our said (voca)tioun the said William Sinclar of Rosling ever continuit to his going to Ireland q^r he presently reamanes sen the quhilk (time) of his departure furth of this realme there are very many corruptiounes and imperfectiounes risen and ingennerit baith amangis ourselfis and in our saidis vocatiounes in defect of ane patrone and oversear over us and the samyn Sua that our saidis vocatiounes are altogether likely to decay And now for safety thereof we having full experience of the efauld good skill and judgement whilk the said Sr William Sinclar now of Rosling has in our said craft and vocatioun and for reparation of the ruines and manifold corruptiounes and enormities done be unskilfull persones thereintill WE all in ane voce have ratified and approven and be thir presentis ratifies and approves the foresaid former letter of jurisdictioun and libertie made and sub' be our brethrene and his Hienes umq^{le} M' of Wark for the time to the said Williame Sinclar of Rosling father to the said Sr William whereby he and his airis are acknowledget as our patrone and judge under our Soverane Lord over us and the haill professors of our said vocatioun within this his Hienes kingdom of Scotlande without any appelation or declinator from their judgements in ony (time hereafter) forever And further we all in ane voce as said is of new have made constitute and ordainit and be thir presentis makis constitutes and ordanes the said Sir William Sinclar now of Rosling and his airis maill our only patrones protectors and overseers under our Soverane, Lord to us and our successors deacons maisteris and freemen of our saidis vocatiounes of Masons harnmermen within the haile kingdome of Scotland and of our haille priviledges and jurisdictiounes belonging thereto wherein he his father and their predecessors Lairdis of Rosling have been in use of possessioun thir many aidges bygain with full power to him and them be themselves thair wardens and deputis to be constitute be them to affix and appoint places of meeting for keeping of good ordour in the said craft als oft and sua oft as need shall require all and sundry persones that may be knawin to be subject to the said vocatioun to be called absentis to amerciat transgressuris to punish unlawes casualities and vtheris duties whatsomever pertaining and belonging or that may fall to be pait be whatsornever persone or persones subject to the said craft to aske crave receive intromet with and uplift and the samyn to their own proper use to apply deputtis under them in the said office with clerkis seruandis assisteris and all other officers and memberis of court needfull to make create substitute and ordain for whom they shall be holden to answer all and sundry plenum actions and causes pertaining to the said craft and vocation and against whatsornever person or persones professors thereof to hear discuss decerne and decyde acts duties and sentences thereupon to pronunce And the samyn to due execution to cause be put and generallie, all and sundrie other priviledges liberties and immunities whatsornever concerning the said craft to doe use and exerce and cause to be done and exercet and keipit siklyke and als freely in all respects as any vyeris thair predecessors has done or might have done themselves in anytime bygane freely quietly well and in peace but any revocatioun obstacle impediment or again calling quhtsomevir IN WITNESS of the qlke thing to thir presenttis wtin be Alexander Aikinheid servitor to Andrew Hay wrytter we have subt thir nts with our handis at . . .]

The Ludge of Edinburgh.
WILLIAM WALLACE decon JOHN WATT THOMAS PATERSONE

The Ludge of Glasgow.
JOHN BOYD deakin Rorr. BOYD ane of the mestres

    *   *   *   *   *   *

HEW DOUOK deikon of the Measounes and Vrichtis off Ayre and GEORGE LID(ELL) deacan of quarimen and nov quartermaster

The Ludge of Stirlinge
JOHN THOMSONE JAMES RIND

The Ludge of Dunfermlinge
(ROBERT ALISONE one of the masters of Dunfermling)
The Ludge of   *   *   *   *

The Ludge of Dundee
ROBERT STRACHOUNE master

ROBERT JOHNSTONE M^r of (−) DAVID MESONE M^r of (−)

THOMAS FLEMING wardane in Edinburgh and HUGH FORREST with our hands att the pen led be the notar under sub^d for us at our command because we cannot wryt. A. HAY notarius asseruit

ROBERT CALDWELL in Glasgow with my hand at the pen led be the notar under subscrywand for me because I cannot writt myself J. HENRYSONE notarius asseruit

I JOHN SERVEITE Mr of ye Craftis in Stirling with my hand att ye pen led be the notar under subscryvand for me because I cannot writt J. HENRYSONE notarius asseruit

I JOHN BURNE ane of the mris. of Dumfermling with my hand att the pen led
be the notar under subscrywand. for me at my command because I cannot writ
myself J. HENRYSONE notarius asseruit

DAVID ROBERTSON ane of ye mesteris ANDREW WELSONE master and
THOMAS (W)ELSONE varden of the sed Ludg of Sant Androis ANDREW
WAST and DAVID QUHYIT maisteris in Dundee with our hands att the pen led
be the notar under subscryvand att our commands because we cannot writt
THOMAS ROBERTSON notarius asseruit

Appendix VI
Deed of Resignation of
William St Clair of Rossline, 1736

I, William St Clair of Rossline, Esquire, taking into my consideration that the Massons in Scotland did, by several deeds, constitute and appoint William and Sir William Sinclair is of Rossline, my ancestors, and their heirs, to be their patrons, protectors, judges, or masters; and that my holding or claiming any such jurisdiction, right, or privilege, might be prejudiciall to the craft and vocation of Massonrie, whereof I am a member, and I being desirous to advance and promote the good and utility of the said craft of Massonrie to the utmost of my power, do hereby for, for me and my heirs, renounce, quit, claim, overgive, and discharge, all right, claim, or pretence that I or my heirs, had, have, or any ways may have, pretend to, or are claimed, to be patron, protector, judge, or master of the Massons in Scotland, in virtue of any deed or indeed made and granted by the said Massons, or of any grand or charter made by any of the Kings of Scotland to and in favour of the said a William and Sir William St Clairs of Rossline, or any others of my predecessors, or any other manner of way whatsomever, for now and ever: and I bind and oblige me, and my heirs, to warrand and this present renunciation and discharge at all hands; and I consent to the registration hereof in the books of Councill and Session, or any other judge's books competent, therin to remain for preservation; and thereto I. constitute ... my procurators, etc. In witness whereof I have subscribed these presents (written by David Maul, Writer to the Signet), at Edinburgh, the twenty-fourth day of November one thousand seven hundred and thirty-six years, before these witnesses, George Fraser, deputy-auditor of the Excise in Scotland, Master of the Canongate Lodge, and William Montgomery, merchant in Leith, Master of the Leith Lodge, *Sic Subscribitur*, Wm, St Clair. – George Frazer, Canongate Kilwinning, witness.   Wm. Montgomerie, Leith Kilwinning, witness.'

Appendix VII
Charter of Lodge Kirkwall Kilwinning, granted 1st December 1740

To all and Sundrie

To whom this presents shall come Greetings William Sinclair of Rosslyn late grand master of the free and accepted Masons in Scotland in the absence of the most worshipful and Right Honourable the Present Grand Master thereof Captain John Young Esqr. Deputy Grand Master and thereof Henry David Lord Cardross Senior grand Warden and George Drummond Esqr. Junior Grand Warden pro tempore for ourselves and with Consent underwritten Know ye That –

Whereas a Petition was presented to the Grand Lodge at their Quarterly communication the Twelfth day of November 1740 By the right worshipfull James Baikie of Tankerness Esqr. present Master, Robert Sutherland Senior Warden signed by them and fourteen other brethren belonging to the Mason Lodge kept at Kirkwall in Orkney for themselves and behalf of other members belonging to the said Lodge Setting forth That there are the good many brethren in that County of good Character who are desirous of being formed into a regular Lodge owning [of] the Grand Lodge and that they are ready and willing to pay all dues and pre[re]quisites to the Grand Lodge ordinary in the like Cases and praying the most worshipfull the Grand Master Grand wardens and other brethren of the Grand Lodge to grant a Charter Erecting them into a regular Lodge with all the Privileges belonging thereto on payment of the ordinary fees and therefore which being read and considered by the Grand Lodge at their said quarterly communication They granted and hereby grants the desire thereof and appointed the said Lodge to be inrolled in the books of the Grand Lodge and a Charter of Constitution and Erection to be made out accordingly **Therefore** witness [.] By the Advice and with the Consent of the grand Lodge To have Constituted Erected and Appointed and by their presents with the Advice and Consent foresaid Constitute Erect and Appoint the worshipfull brethren Petitioners above named and their Successors to be hereafter in all time Coming a true and regular Lodge of Free and Accepted Masons under the Title and Designation of the Lodge of Kirkwall in Orkney and ordains all other regular mason Lodges in Scotland to hold and respect them as such for the future [.] **Hereby** Giving, granting and Committing to them and their Successors full and ample power to meet and conveen conveen [*sic*] as a True and regular Lodge and to enter and receive Apprentices Pass fellow Crafts and raise Master Masons upon payment of such regular and reasonable Composition as they shall think proper for support of the brewer distressed brethren Widows and Orphans agreable to their stations with power also to them to collect and make choise of Masters wardens and other office bearers annually or other ways they shall have occassion and wee [*sic*] with consent foresaid Hereby Recommend to the said brethren to hereby Constitute to Obey their Superiors in all things Lawfull and Honest as becomes the honour and Harmony of Masonry and they hereby become bound and engaged not to desert their said Lodge (hereby Constituted and Erected) and that none of them presume upon any pretext whatsoever to make any separate or schismaticall meetings among themselves without the consent and approbation and presence of their Masters and wardens for the time nor yet shall they or any of them presume to collect money or other funds separate from the common stock of their Lodge to the hurt and detriment of the poor thereof the said a Worshipfull brethren being always bound and obliged as by their acceptance hereof they faithfully bind and obliged themselves and their successors in all time coming to submit to, observe [?] and obey the whole statutes acts and regulations of the Grand Lodge as well as those already made as those hereafter to he made for the Utility and Welfare and prosperity of Masonry in general and to pay and perform what ever is stipulated or demanded from them for supporting the dignity of the grand Lodge and shall record in their books (which they are hereby appointed to keep) of this present charter of constitution and erection with the regulations or by laws already made or hereafter to be made by them from time to time with their other proceedings and annuall elections as the shall happened to the occur to the effect the same may be the more readily seen and observed by their brethren subject nevertheless to the review of the Grand Lodge **And in Like manner** the said brethren and their aforesaids are hereby appointed and required punctually to attend the whole general meetings And quarterly communications of the Grand Lodge by their Representatives being their Master and Senior and Junior Wardens for the claim or by proxies in their place duly authorised by Commission from their Lodge providing the said proxies be master masons or fellow Crafts belonging to some Established Lodge to the end the said brethren may be duly certiorate apprised of the proceedings of the grand Lodge to whom they may represent their grievances from time to time as they shall see cause **Declaring** here by the said brethrens precedancy in the grand Lodge and shall commence from the day and date of their presents and to the effect this present Charter of Constitution and Erection may be the more securely kept and preserved we hereby appoint the same to be recorded in the books of Grand Lodge conform to the regulations thereof made there anent [.] Given under our hand at Edin^r. in the presence Grand Lodge held in St Maries Chapple there this first day of Decem^{br} **1740** in the presence of the right Worshipfull brethren aforementioned and John Douglas Esqr. present master of the Lodge Cannongate [*sic*] Kilwinning, Alex^r. Drummond Es^{qr}. present Master of Lodge Greenock Kilwinning Samuel Beresford master and present master [*sic*] of the Lodge of Cannongate [*sic*] and Leith, Leith and Cannongate [*sic*] and Mr David Kennedy Advocate present master of the Lodge of Leith Kilwinning Captain Arthur Forbes of Pittincrieff Esqr. present master of the Lodge of Edinburgh Kilwinning Archibald Kennedy writer in Edin^r present master of the Lodge of Maybole and John M'Dougall secretary to the Grand Lodge *Sic Subs^{cr}* Wm Stclair A.G.M [acting Grand Master] John Young D.G.M [Deputy Grand Master] Cardross S.G. Warden Geo. Drummond J.G.W. [Junior Grand Warden] John Douglas Canongate Kilwinning Alex^r Drummond Greenock Kilwinning Samuel Beresford Master Cannongate [*sic*] and Leith Leith and Cannongate [*sic*] David Kennedy Leith witness Arthur Forbes Edin^r Kilwinning Arch^d Kennedy Maybole Jn M'Dougall Secretary.

Note: Charters issued by the Grand Lodge generally followed the same formula. That granted to Lodge Kirkwall Kilwinning can be safely taken as a standard specimen from the 18th century. It is the internal evidence which is of importance here. The document has been transcribed from the Grand Lodge of Scotland Chartulary (which contains copies of many, but by no means all, of the charters issued to Daughter Lodges.)

Appendix VIII
Ramsay's Oration 1737

The noble ardour of which you show to enter into the ancient and very illustrious order of Freemasons, is a certain proof that you already possess all the qualities necessary to become members. These qualities are philanthropy, inviolable secrecy, and tasteful the fine arts.

Lycurgus, Solon, Numa, and all other political legislators have failed to make their republics lasting. However wise their laws may have been, they have not been able to extend through all countries and through all ages. As they were founded on victories and conquests, on military violence, and the elevation of one people above another, they were not able to become universal nor to make themselves acceptable to the taste, spirit, and interest of all nations. Philanthropy was not their basis. Patriotism badly understood and pushed to excess by men who inhabited a small portion of the Universe, destroyed in al these warrior republics the love of humanity in general. Mankind is not essentially distinguished by the tongues spoken, the clothes worn nor by the corners of this busy world that they occupy. The world is nothing but a huge republic, of which every nation is a family, and each individual a child. It was, gentlemen, for the purpose of reviving and spreading these ancient maxims borrowed from the nature of man, that our Society was established. We desire to unite all men of enlightened minds, gentle manners, and agreeable wit, not only by a love of the fine arts, but much more by the grand principles of virtue, science, and religion, where the interests of the Fraternity shall become those of the whole human race, whence all nations shall be enabled to draw useful knowledge, and where the subjects of all Kingdoms shall learn to cherish one another without renouncing their own country. Our ancestors, the Crusaders, gathered together from all parts of Christendom in the Holy Land, desired thus to reunite into one sole Fraternity the individuals of all nations. What obligations we do not owe these superior men who, without gross selfish interests, without even listening to the inborn tendency to dominate, imagined such an institution, the sole aim of which is to unite minds and hearts in order to make them better, and form in the course of ages spiritual empire where without derogating from the various duties which different States exact, an new people shall be created, which composed of many nations, shall in some sort cement them all into one by the tie of virtue and science.

The second requisite of our Society is sound morals. The religious orders were established to make perfect Christians, military orders to inspire a love of true glory, and the Order of Freemasons, to make men lovable men, good citizens, good subjects, inviolable in their promises, faithful adorers of the God of love, lovers of virtue rather than of reward.

> *Polliciti servare fidem, sanctumque vereri*
> *Nomen amicitae, mores non munera amare*

> (Having made a promise, to keep faith, to respect the sacred
> name of friendship, to prefer a good character to wealth)

Nevertheless, we do not confine ourselves to purely civic virtues. We have amongst us three kinds of brothers: Novices or Apprentices, Fellows or Professed Brothers, Masters, or Perfected Brothers.

To the first are explained the moral virtues; to the second the heroic virtues; to the last the Christian virtues; so that the institution embraces the whole philosophy of sentiment and the complete theology of the heart. This is why one of our brothers has said -

> Freemason, illustrious Grand Master,
> Received my first transports
> In my heart the Order has given them birth,
> Happily I, if noble efforts
> Cause me to merit your esteem
> By elevating me to the sublime,
> The primeval Truth,
> To the Essence pure and divine
> The celestial Origin of the soul,
> The source of life and love.

Because a sad, savage, and misanthropic philosophy disgusts virtuous men, our ancestors, the Crusaders, wished to render it lovable by the attractions of innocent pleasures, agreeable music, pure joy, and moderate gaiety. Our festivals are not what the profane world and the ignorant vulgar imagine. All the vices of heart and soul are banished there, and irreligion, libertinage, incredulity and debauch[ery] are prescribed. Our banquets resemble those of virtuous symposia of Horace, where the conversation only touched what could enlighten the soul, discipline the heart, and inspired a task for the true, the good, and the beautiful.

> *O noctes coenaeque Deum ...*
> *Sermo oritur, non de regnis domibusve alienis*

... sed quod magis ad nos
Pertinet, et nescire malum est, agitamus uitrumne
Divitiis homines, an sint virtute beati
Quidve ad amicitias usus rectumve trahat nos

(O nights and suppers of gods ... The talk begins, not about other
men's kingdoms or houses ... but what concerns us more, and it is
ill not to know, we discuss: whether men are happy from riches or
virtue; or what draws us into friendship – utility? or rectitude?, and
what is the nature of good, and what is its highest point.)

Thus the obligations imposed upon you by the Order, are to protect your brothers
by your authority, to enlighten them by your knowledge, to a edify them by your
virtues, to succour them in their necessities, to sacrifice all personal resentment,
and to strive after all that meet contribute to the peace and unity of society.

We have secrets; they are figurative signs and sacred words, composing a language sometimes mute, sometimes very eloquent, in order to communicate with
one another at the greatest distance, and to recognise our brothers of whatever
tongue. These were words of war which the Crusaders gave each other in order
to guarantee them from the surprises of the Saracens, who often crept in amongst
them to kill them. These signs and words recall the remembrance either of some
part of our science, or of some moral virtue, or of some mystery of the faith.

What has never been known in any other Society is that our Lodges have been
established of old and today are spread throughout all civilised nations and nevertheless amongst this great multitude of men, no brother has ever betrayed our
Secret. Those natures most trivial, most indiscreet, least accustomed secrecy, then
learn this great art on entering our Brotherhood.

It seems at that time to transform them and to make new men of them, men both
impenetrable and perceptive.

Such is the power over all natures of the idea of a fraternal bond. This inviolable secret contributes powerfully to unite the subjects of all nations and to render the communication of benefits easy and mutual between us. We have many
examples in the annals of our Order. Our brothers, travelling in diverse lands,
have only needed to make themselves known in our Lodges in order to be there
are immediately overwhelmed by all kinds of succour, even in time of the most
bloody wars, and illustrious prisoners have found brothers were the only expected to meet enemies.

Should anyone fail in the solemn promises that bind us, we have no penalties other than remorse of conscious and exclusion from our Society, according to those words of Horace

> *Est et fideli tuta silentio*
> *Merces; vetabo qui Cereris sacrum*
> *Vulgarit arcanae, sub iisdem*
> *Sit trabibis, fragilemque mecum*
> *Solvat phaselon ...*

(There is a sure reward for trusty silence, too, I will forbid the man who has divulged the sacred rites of mystic Ceres, to abide beneath the same roof or to unmoor with me the fragile bark.)

Yes, sir, the famous festivals of Ceres at Eleusis, of Isis in Egypt, of Minerva at Athens, of Urania amongst the Phoenicians, of Diana in Scythia were connected with ours. In those places mysteries were celebrated which concealed many vestiges of the ancient religion of Noah and the Patriarchs. They concluded with banquets and libations, and neither that intemperance nor excess were known into which the heathen gradually fell. The source of those infamies was the admission to the nocturnal assemblies of persons of both sexes in contravention of the primitive usages. It is in order to prevent similar abuses that women are excluded from our Order. We are not so unjust as to regard the fair sex as incapable of keeping a secret. But their presence may insensibly corrupt the purity of our maxims and manners.

The fourth quality required in our Order is the taste of useful science and the liberal arts. Thus, the Order extracts of each of you to contribute, by his protection, liberality, or labour, to a vast work for which no will Academy can suffice, because all these societies, been composed of a very small number of men, their work cannot embrace an object so extensive. All the Grand Masters in Germany, England, Italy, and elsewhere, exhort all the learned men and all the artisans of the fraternity to unite to furnish the materials for a Universal Dictionary for the liberal arts and useful sciences, excepting only Theology and Politics. The work has already been commenced in London, and by means of the Union of our Brothers, it may be carried to a conclusion in a few years. Not only are technical works and their etymology explained, but the history of each art and science, its principals and operations, are described. By this means the lights of all nations will be united in one single work, which will be a universal library of all that is beautiful, great, luminous, solid and useful in all the sciences and in all noble arts. This work will augment in each century, according to the increase of knowledge, it will spread everywhere emulation and the taste for things of beauty and utility.

The word Freemason must not therefore be taken a literal, gross, and material sense, as if our founders had been simple workers in stone, or merely curious and geniuses who wished to perfect the arts. They were not only skilful architects, desirous of concentrating their talents and goods to the construction of material temples; also religious and warrior princes who designed to enlighten, edify, and protect the living Temples of the Most High. This I will demonstrate by developing the history or rather the renewal of the Order.

Every family, every Republic, every Empire, of which the origin is lost in obscure antiquity, has its fable and its truth, its legend and its history. Some ascribe our institution to Solomon, some to Moses, some to Abraham, some to Noah, and some to Enoch, who built the first city, or even to Adam. Without any pretence of denying these origins, I pass on to matters less ancient. This, then, is it part of what I have gathered in the annals of Great Britain, in the Acts of Parliament, which often speak of our privileges and in the living traditions of the English people, which has been the centre of our Society since the eleventh century.

At the time of the Crusades in Palestine many princes, lords, and citizens associated themselves, and vowed to restore the Temple of the Christians in the Holy Land, to employ themselves in bringing back their architecture to its first institution. They agreed upon several ancient signs and symbolic words drawn from the well of religion in order to recognise themselves amongst the heathen and Saracens. These signs and words were only communicated to those who promised solemnly, and even sometimes at the foot of the altar, never to reveal them. This sacred promise was therefore not an execrable oath, as it has been called, but a respectable bond to unite Christians of all nationalities in one confraternity. Sometime afterwards our Order formed an intimate union with the Knights of St. John of Jerusalem. From that time, our Lodges took the name of Lodges of St. John. The union was made after the example set by the Israelites when they erected the second Temple, who, whilst they handled the trowel and the mortar with one hand, in the other held the sword and the buckler.

Our Order, therefore, must not be considered a revival of the Bacchanals, but as an order founded in remote antiquity, renewed in the Holy Land by our ancestors in order to recall the memory of the most sublime truths amidst the pleasures of Society. The Kings, princes, and lords returned from Palestine to their own lands, and there established divers Lodges. At the time of the last Crusades many lodges were already erected in Germany, Italy, Spain, France, and from thence in Scotland, because of the close alliance between the French and the Scots. James, Lord Steward of Scotland, was Grand Master of a large established at Kilwinning, in the West of Scotland 1286 shortly after the death of Alexander III, King of Scotland, and one year before John Balliol mounted the throne. This lord received as Freemasons into his lodge the Earls of Gloucester and Ulster, the one English, the other Irish.

By degrees, over Lodges and our Rites were neglected in most places. This is why of so many historians only those of Great Britain speak of our Order. Nevertheless, it preserved its splendour amongst those Scotsmen to whom the Kings of France confided during many centuries the safeguard of their royal persons.

After the deplorable mishaps in the Crusades, the perishing of the Christian armies, and the triumph of Bendocdar, Sultan of Egypt, during the eighth and last Crusade, that great Prince Edward, son of Henry III, King of England, seeing there was no longer any safety for his brethren in the Holy Land, whence the Christian troops were retiring, brought them all back, and this colony of brothers was established in England. As this prince was endowed with all the high and noble qualities which constitute heroes, he loved the fine arts, and in particular our noble science.

The fatal religious discords which embarrassed and tore Europe in the sixteeth century caused our Order to degenerate from the nobility of its origin. Many of our rites and usages which were contrary to the prejudices of the times were changed, disguised and suppressed. Thus it was that many of our Brothers forgot, like the ancient Jews, the spirit of our laws, and only retained only the letter and shell. The beginnings of a remedy have already been made. It is necessary only to continue and, at last, to bring everything back to its original institution. This work cannot be difficult in a State where Religion and the Government can only be favourable to our laws.

From the British Isles, the royal art is now repassing into France, under the reign of the most amiable of Kings, whose humanity animates all his virtues and under the Ministry of a mentor [Cardinal Fleury], who has realised all that could be imagined most fabulous. In this happy age when love of peace has become the virtue of heroes, this nation [France], one of the most spiritual of Europe, will become the centre of the Order. She will clothe our work, our statutes, our customs with grace, delicacy and good taste, essential qualities of the Order, of which the basis is the wisdom, strength, and beauty of genius. It is in the future in our Lodges, as it were public schools, that Frenchman will learn, without travelling, the characters of all nations and that strangers will experience that France is the home of all peoples. *Patria gentis humanae* (The native land of the whole human race.)

Note: Ramsay's *Oration* exists in two forms – the Grand Lodge and Epernay versions. The above is the Grand Lodge version and is reproduced, with permission, from: *Andrew Michael Ramsay and his Masonic Oration*, by Dr Lisa Kahler in: Heredom, Vol. 1 (1992) – the annual Transactions of the Scottish Rite Research Society, Washington DC. Readers are directed to that journal where the two versions are compared.

Appendix IX
A Funeral Lodge

Edinburgh, 14th February 1778
In honour of WILLIAM ST CLAIR OF ROSLIN.
Formerly Hereditary Grand Master Mason of Scotland.
By Sir WILLIAM FORBES, The Present Grand Master Mason.

Right Worshipful Masters,
Worshipful Wardens, and Worthy Brethren

I should have been greatly wanting in my duty, had I not called you together on so solemn an occasion as the death of our Late Most Worshipful Grand Master, and worthy Brother ST CLAIR OF ROSLIN, to whom our Craft lies under very high and peculiar obligations.

Funeral orations are but too often perverted from their proper purposes; and instead of exhibiting faithful portraits of departed merit, are prostituted to the arts of pompous declamation and unmeaning panegyric. It would be no very difficult task for me in this manner to ring changes on a set of well-sounding words, and to make a display of all the epithets, and all the virtues, that can adorn a human character. But this would neither do honour to my audience, nor to myself; far less to the person whose death we now meet to commemorate. As something, however, is probably expected from me, in the office which I now have the power to fill, I shall beg leave to lead your attention for a few minutes, whilst I recall to your remembrance what he was, and the gratitude which we owe to the memory of this worthy Brother.

Descended from an ancient and illustrious House, whose heroes have often bled in their country's cause, he inherited their intrepid spirit, united with the milder virtues of humanity, and the polished manners of a gentleman. Athletic and active, he delighted in all the manly exercises; and in all of them excelled most of his contemporaries. Ardent in his pursuits, he steadily persevered in promoting the interests of every public society, whether of business or amusement, of which he was a member, and thereby justly obtained pre-eminence in each.

Of this laudable spirit on the part of our worthy Brother, no society can afford a more remarkable instance than our own. Among other marks of royal approbation conferred on his ancestors, for their faithful and valuable services, they enjoyed the dignity of Grand Master Mason, by charters of high antiquity, from the Kings of Scotland. This hereditary honour continued in the family of Roslin under the year 1736; when, with a disinterestedness of which there are a few examples, he made a voluntary resignation of the office into the hands of the Craft in general; by which from being hereditary, it has ever since been elective: and in consequence of such a singular act of generosity it is, that, by your suffrages, I have now the honour to fill this chair. His zeal, however, to promote the welfare of our society, was not confined to this single instance: for he continued almost to the very close of life, on all occasions where his influence, or his example, could prevail, to extend the spirit of Masonry, and to increase the number of the Brethren. It is, therefore, with justice that his name should ever be dear to the Craft, and that we lament the loss of one who did such honour to our institution.

To these more conspicuous and public parts of his character, I am happy to be able to add, that he possessed in an eminent degree the virtues of a benevolent and good heart; virtues which ought ever to be the distinguishing marks of a true Brother. Though those ample and flourishing possessions which the house of Roslin once inherited, had, by the mutability of human things, extensive domains; yet he not only supported with decent dignity the appearance of a gentleman, but he extended his bounty to many; and, as far as his fortune permitted, was every ready to assist those who claimed the benefit of his protection. — If in the course of his transactions in business, his schemes were not always successful; if a sanguine temper sometimes led him too far in the pursuit of a favourite plan; whatever might be urged against his prudence, none ever suspected the rectitude of his principles; and if at any time he was unintentionally the cause of misfortune to others, it was never without his being, at the same time, himself a sufferer.

After this brief, but I hope just and well-merited eulogy, permit me to claim your attention a little longer, to some few reflections which naturally present themselves on such an occasion; and, which, therefore, I hope, will not be thought foreign to the purpose of our present meeting — I need hardly remark, that commemorations, such as this, are meant not solely in honour of the dead, but chiefly for the advantage of the living. Our worthy Brother is now gone to that land, where, in respect of the passions and prejudices of mortals, "all things are forgotten;" where he is far removed from the applause or censure of the world. But whatever can tend to enhance the value of departed merit, must, to an ingenuous mind, prove an incitement to the performance of praise-worthy actions; and if we make the proper use of this recent instance of morality, our Brother's death may prove of higher utility to us, than all those advantages for which in his lifetime we stood indebted to him.

My younger Brethren will permit me to remark to them, that although this our Most Worshipful Brother attained to that age which David has marked at the boundary of human life*, at the same time without experiencing any great degree of that "labour and sorrow" which the Royal Prophet has recorded as the inseparable concomitants of so advanced a period; although his mental faculties remained unimpaired to the last; and even his bodily strength had suffered but slight and very late decay; we are not to look on this as a common instance nor to expect that we shall certainly be indulged with an equal longevity: for hair so grey as his are permitted but to a few; and few can boast of so singular an exemption from the usual uneasiness of advanced age. Let us not, therefore, vainly flatter ourselves, that we have still many years unexhausted, in which we shall have time sufficient to our respective stations; nor from this idea delay those talks which, although of infinite importance, we may be disposed to postpone a little longer, because they are not perhaps of a very pleasing nature.

If this instance of our aged Brother should seem to contradict my assertion, I am able to confirm it by another recent event, which but too fully proves the justness of my observation. The hallowed earth is but newly laid over the remains of a Noble Lady†, cut off in the morning of her days. Blest with health, with youth, with beauty, riches, titles, beloved by all who knew here; yet all these "blushing honours" could avail her nothing; they quickly vanished, and "like the baseless fabrick of a vision, left not "a wreck behind." So sudden, so unsuspected was her fate, so little thought she of her instant dissolution, that she drew her last breath without a moment's time to say, "May Heaven receive my parting spirit." An awful warning this! May it strike such forcible conviction on our minds, of the uncertainty of all sublunary things, that we may study to live with innocence like hers, lest our fate may steal upon us equally sudden, and equally unlooked for.

To my Brethren, who, like myself, have passed the middle period of life, allow me to say, that by having already spent thirty or forty years in this world, our chance of making a much longer residence in it is greatly diminished: and even the longest life with which our hopes may flatter us, will shortly come to an end. When we look forward to the years to come, the space indeed, in fancy's eye, seems almost immeasurable; but when we look back on the same space already past, how does it appear contracted almost to nothing! — Happy! if we can look back on something better than a total blank. — If we can discover, on a careful and impartial review, that the general tenor of our conduct has been virtuous, our anxiety to live many more days should be the less: but it we find nothing by which to mark our former years, but scenes of guilt or folly, the time we have yet to spend on earth may prove too short too expiate them, and we may be called out of the world before the great business of life be finished, perhaps even before it be properly begun. It is therefore our indispensable duty to employ well that period which may yet be granted to us, and not to waste in idleness those precious hours that Heaven has lent us for the noblest purposes; and of which we must one day render a severe account.

My Brethren who are farthest advanced in years, will not, I hope, be offended if they are reminded of their mortality by a Brother younger than themselves; because it is by one who has but lately escaped from the gates of the grave; and exhibited, in his own person, a striking instance in how few hours the highest health and strength may be reduced to a state of the lowest debility. It has pleased Heaven, however, to spare me a little longer, in order to show, perhaps, that in the hands of the Almighty alone are the issues of life and death; and that not a single moment of our mortal existence, but the present, can we call our own. This uncertainty of life is, indeed, of all reflections the most obvious; yet, though the most important, it is unhappily too often the most neglected. What a damp would come over our spirits, what agitations would be raised even in this assembly, were the book of Fate to be unrolled to our view! If Providence should permit us to penetrate this moment into futurity, and to foresee the fate of ourselves and others, only to the end of the present year, some of us, who, perhaps, suppose death to be at a great distance, would see him already at the very door; some who in full security are dreaming of a long course of years yet to come, would find that they have already entered on their last*; and that before it came to a close, they, like our departed Brother, shall be mingled with the dust. A great part of this assembly, by the course of nature, will probably survive a little longer; but it is morally certain that some of us, before the sun has made another annual revolution, will be removed hence, to that unchangeable state, where our doom will be fixed for ever. And although Heaven has wrapt in impenetrable darkness who they are that shall pass through the vale of the shadow of death during that short period, in order that we may all live in a state of habitual preparation; yet who can have the presumption to say, that he himself shall not be the first to visit "that undiscovered country, from whose bourne no traveller e'er returns?"

How careful, therefore, ought we to be, not to disappoint the wise design of this mysterious secrecy, nor pervert what is meant to keep us perpetually on our guard, into a source of fatal security: for the day will most assuredly come, (whether sooner or later is of little importance to us), when we likewise shall be numbered with those that have been. May we all endeavour, therefore, so to live daily, as we shall fervently wish we had lived when that awful moment overtakes us, in which our souls shall be required of us. May we study to act in such a manner, that our practice may prove the best comment on the principles of our Craft, and thereby teach the world that charity and brotherly love, integrity of heart, and purity of manners, are not less the distinguishing characteristics of Masonry than of Religion. Then may we piously hope, that when a period even still more awful than the hour of our dissolution shall arrive, when the last trumpet shall sound, and the dead shall be raised incorruptible, when our scattered atoms shall be collected, and we shall appear in the presence of the Lord God Omnipotent, "the high and lofty One who inhabiteth eternity," that our transgressions will be mercifully forgiven; and that the GRAND ARCHITECT of the universe will be graciously pleased to give us rest from all our labours — by an admission into the celestial fraternity of angels, and the spirits of just men made perfect.

To HIM be glory, honour and praise for ever and ever. AMEN.

*78 years
*The Countess of Eglintoune, who died at the age of 21
*Fide Riddoch's Sermon

Appendix X
Extract of the Lay of the Last Minstrel

XXII

And much of wild and wonderful
In these rude isles might fancy cull;
For thither came. in times afar,
Stern Lochlin's sons of roving war.
The Norsemen, train'd to spoil and blood,
Skill'd to prepare the raven's food;
Kings of the main their leaders brave,
Their barks the dragons of the wave.
And there in many a stormy vale,
The Scald had told his wondrous tale;
And many a Runic column high
Had witness'd grim idolatry.
And thus had Harold in his youth
Learn'd many a Saga's rhyme uncouth—
Of that Sea-Snake, tremendous curl'd,
Whose monstrous circle girds the world;
Of those dread Maids, whose hideous yell
Maddens the battle's bloody swell;
Of Chief, who, guided through the gloom
By the pale death-lights of the tomb,
Ransack'd the graves of warriors old,
Their falchions wrench'd from corpses' hold,
Wak'd the deaf tomb with war's alarms,
And bade the dead arise to arms!
With war and wonder all on flame,
To Roslin's bowers young Harold came,
Where, by sweet glen and greenwood tree,
He learn'd a milder minstrelsy;
Yet something of the Northern spell
Mix'd with the softer numbers well.

XXIII

Harold

O listen, listen, ladies gay!
No haughty feat of arms I tell;
Soft is the note, and sad the lay,

That mourns the lovely Rosabelle.

- —"Moor, moor the barge, ye gallant crew!
And gentle ladye, deign to stay!

Rest thee in Castle Ravensheuch,
Nor tempt the stormy firth to-day.

"The blackening wave is edg'd with white:
To inch and rock the sea-mews fly;

The fishers have heard the Water-Sprite,
Whose screams forebode that wreck is nigh.

"Last night the gifted Seer did view
A wet shroud swathed round ladye gay;

Then stay thee, Fair, in Ravensheuch:
Why cross the gloomy firth today?"

" 'Tis not because Lord Lindesay's heir
To-night at Roslin leads the ball,

But that my ladye-mother there
Sits lonely in her castle-hall.

" 'Tis not because the ring they ride,
And Lindesay at the ring rides well,

But that my sire the wine will chide,
If 'tis not fill'd by Rosabelle."

O'er Roslin all that dreary night
A wondrous blaze was seen to gleam;

'Twas broader than the watch-fire's light,
And redder than the bright moonbeam.

It glar'd on Roslin's castled rock,
It ruddied all the copse wood glen;

'Twas seen from Dryden's groves of oak
And seen from cavern'd Hawthorn-den.

Seem'd all on fire that chapel proud,
Where Roslin's chiefs uncoffin'd lie,

Each Baron, for a sable shroud,
Sheath'd in his iron panoply.

Seem'd all on fire within, around,
Deep sacristy and altars pale;

Shone every pillar foliage bound,
And glimmer'd all the dead men's mail.

Blaz'd battlement and pinnet high,
Blaz'd every rose-carved buttress fair—

So still they blaze when fate is nigh
The lordly line of high St. Clair.

There are twenty of Roslin's barons bold
Lie buried within that proud chapelle;

Each one the holy vault doth hold—
But the sea holds lovely Rosabelle!

And each St. Clair was buried there,
With candle, with book, and with knell;

But the sea-caves rung, and the wild winds sung
The dirge of lovely Rosabelle.

XXIV

So sweet was Harold's piteous lay,
Scarce mark'd the guests the darken'd hall,

Though, long before the sinking day,
A wondrous shade involv'd them all:

It was not eddying mist or fog,

Drain'd by the sun from fen or bog;
Of no eclipse had sages told;

And yet, as it came on apace,

Each one could scarce his neighbour's face,
Could scarce his own stretch'd hand behold.

A secret horror check'd the feast,

And chill'd the soul of every guest;

Even the high Dame stood half aghast—

She knew some evil on the blast;

The elvish page fell to the ground,

And, shuddering, mutter'd, "Found! found! found!"

Appendix XI
The Knights Templars of Scotland by
Chevalier James Burnes (1837)

The Knights of the Temple were introduced in to Scotland before 1153 by King David the First, who established them at Temple on the Southesk, and who was so attached to the brotherhood, that we are told by an old historian "*Sanctus David de preeclara Militia Templi optimos fraters secum retinens, eos diebus et noctibus morum suorum fecit esse custodes.*"[1] Malcolm, the grandson of David, conferred on the brethren "*in liberam et puram Elymosynam unum plenarium Toftum in quolibet Burgo totius terse,*" which foundation was enlarged by his successors, William the Lion and Alexander the Second. The charter of the latter is still in the possession of Lord Torphichen, whereby he grants and confirms "*Deo et fratribus Templi Salomonis de Jerusalem omnes illas rectitudines, libertates et consuetudines quas Rex DAVID et rex Malcolm et decessus pater meus Rex Willielmus eis dederunt et concesserunt, sicut scripta eorum authentica attestant.*" This curious document, after enumerating certain of these rights and liberties, scilicet, — the king's sure peace; the privilege of buying, selling, and trading with all his subjects; freedom from all tribute and toll, &c. proceeds "*Et nullus eis injuriam faciat, vel fieri consentiat super meam defensionem. Et ubicunque in tota terra mea ad judiorum (q. judicium) venerint, causa eorum primum tractata, et prius rectum swum habeant, et postea faciant. Et nullus ponat hominem predictorum fratrum nostrorum ad foram judicii si noluerint, &c. Et omnes libertates et consuetudines quas ipsi per alias regiones habent in terra mea ubique habeant.*"

These general privileges, throughout Europe, were very extensive. The Templars were freed from all tythes to the church, and their priests were entitled to celebrate mass, and to absolve from sins to the same extent as bishops, a privilege which was strongly objected to by the latter. Their houses possessed the right of sanctuary or asylum for criminals. They could be witnesses in their own cause, and were exempted from giving testimony in the cause of others. They were relieved by the papal bulls from all taxes, and from subjection and obedience to any secular power. By these great immunities the Order was rendered in a manner independent, but it would appear, nevertheless, that both the Templars and Hospitallers considered themselves subjects of the countries to which they belonged, and took part in the national wars, for we find by the Ragman Roll, "*Freere Johan de Sautre, Mestre de la Chevalerie del Temple en Ecoce,*" and another Brother, swearing fealty to Edward I. in 1296; and the author of the

Annals of Scotland, taking notice of the Battle of Falkirk, 12th July 1298, informs us that the only persons of note who fell were Brian le Jay, Master of the English Templars, and the Prior of Torphichen in Scotland, a Knight of another Order of religious soldiery. The former of these Chevaliers met his death by the hand of the redoubted Sir William Wallace, who advanced alone from the midst of his little band, and slew him with a single blow, although the historian adds, that Sir Brian Le Jay was a Knight Templar of high military renown, who had shewn himself most active against the Scots.

Little is known of the farther History of the Knights Templars in Scotland from the time of Alexander II down to the beginning of the 14th century, excepting that their privileges were continued to them by succeeding kings, whose bounty and piety were in those ages continually directed towards the religious orders. By their endowments, and the bequests of the nobles, the possessions of the Order came to be so extensive, that their lands were scattered "*per totum regnum Scotiæ, a limitibus versus Angliam, et sic discendo per totum regnum usque ad Orchades.*" Besides the House of the Temple in Lothian, the following establishments or Priories of the Order are enumerated in Keith's Catalogue, viz. Ballantradock, now called Arniston, in Edinburghshire; St. Germains, in East Lothian; Inchynan, in Renfrewshire; Maryculter, in Kincardineshire; Aggerstone, in Stirlingshire, and Aboyne, in Aberdeenshire.

The date of the spoliation of the Templars of Scotland, corresponds of course with that of the persecution of the Order in other countries, and it is to the credit of our forefathers that we can obtain no account of any member of the brotherhood having been subjected to personal torture or suffering amongst them; while, on the contrary, it is believed that some of the fugitive brethren of the Order from other countries, found peaceful refuge in Scotland. In reference to this subject, tradition mentions that Peter de Bologna, Grand Prelate of the Order, and Procurator General at the Court of Rome, fled from Germany along with others, and arrived on the coast of Scotland, where, together with the Templars Aumont and Harris, he continued to carry on the mysteries of the Order.[2]

In December 1309, John de Soleure, the Papal Legate, and William, Bishop of St. Andrews, held an inquisitorial Court at the Abbey of Holyrood to investigate the charges against the Templars, but Walter de Clifton, the Preceptor of the Order in North Britain, and William de Middleton, were the only two Knights who appeared before the Tribunal, the proceedings of which, as recorded at length in Wilkins' Consilia, make no allusion to any punishment being inflicted, so that we may fairly conclude they were soon set at liberty.[3] The Preceptor, in his examination, readily confessed that the rest of the Brethren had fled, and dispersed themselves *propter scandalium exortum contra ordinem*, and we are told by a learned French writer, that having deserted the Temple, they had ranged themselves under the banners of Robert Bruce, by whom they were formed into a new Order, the observances of which were based on those of the Templars, and became, according to him, the source of Scottish Free Masonry.[4] This statement corresponds with the celebrated Charter of Larmenius already referred to, in which the Scottish Templars are excommunicated as *Templi desertores*, *anathemate percussos*; and along with the Knights of St. John, *dominiorum Militiæ spoliatores*, placed for ever beyond the pale of the Temple, *extra gyrum Templi nunc*, *et in futurum*; and it is likewise supported in some measure by the authority of the accurate historian of Free Masonry, M. Thory, who, in his "Acta Latomorum," states that Robert Bruce founded the Masonic Order of Heredom de Kilwinning, after the battle of Bannockburn, reserving to himself and his successors on the throne of Scotland, the office and title of Grand Master. Scottish tradition has, moreover, always been in favour of this origin of the Ancient Mother Kilwinning Lodge, which certainly at one time possessed other degrees of Masonry besides those of St. John; and it is well known to our Masonic readers, that there are even in our own days at Edinburgh, a few individuals claiming to be the representatives of the Royal Order established by Bruce, which, though now nearly extinct in this country, still flourishes in France, where it was established by Charter from Scotland, and even by the Pretender himself, in the course of last century, and is now conferred as the highest and most distinguished grade of Masonry, sanctioned by the Grand Orient, under the title of the Rose Croix de Heredom de Kilwinning. It may be interesting to add, that the introduction on the Continent of this ancient branch of our national Masonry, has been commemorated by a splendid medal struck at Paris, bearing, amongst other devices, the Royal Arms and Motto of Scotland; and that the Brethren of the Lodge of Constancy at Arras, still preserve with reverence, an original charter of the Order, granted to their Chapter in 1747, by Charles Edward Stuart, and signed by that unfortunate Prince himself as the representative of the Scottish Kings.[5] Nor can anything indicate more strongly the high estimation in which the chivalry of the Rosy Cross of Kilwinning is held in France, than the fact that the Prince Cambaceres, arch-chancellor of the Empire, presided over it as Provincial Grand Master, (the office of supreme head being inherent in the crown of Scotland,) for many years; and that he has been succeeded in his dignity, if we mistake not, by the present head of the illustrious family of Choiseul.

But whether the Scottish Templars really joined the victorious standard of Robert Bruce, and with him, as our countrymen would fain hope, fought and conquered at Bannock-burn, or whether the majority of them transferred themselves along with the possessions of the Order, to the Knights of St. John of

Jerusalem, certain it is, that from the time of the persecution, the Order of the Temple, together with all its wealth, became merged in that of the Hospitallers, though certainly not to such a degree as to obliterate all distinct traces of the Red Cross Knights. On the contrary, we find by a public document recorded entire in the Register of the Great Seal of Scotland, and dated two centuries after the incorporation of the Orders, that King James the Fourth confirmed all former grants *sancto Hospitali de Jerusalem, et fratribus ejusdem militiæ Templi Salomonis*, a satisfactory proof that the Order, although proscribed by the Pope, was still retained conjointly with that of the Hospital, in law papers at least.

The Knights of St. John had also been introduced into Scotland by King David the First, and had a charter granted to them by Alexander the Second, two years after that to the Templars. The Preceptory of Torphichen, in West Lothian, was their first, and continued to be their chief residence, and by the accession of the Temple lands and other additions, their property at the time of the Reformation came to be immense. When that event took place, the chief dignitary or Grand Preceptor of the Order in Scotland, with a seat as a Peer in Parliament, was Sir James Sandilands of the family of Calder, who, as is well known to readers of Scottish History, was the private friend of John Knox, and one of the first persons of distinction to embrace the reformed religion. We might suspect, that even before the promulgation of the statute of 1560, prohibiting all allegiance within the realm to the See of Rome, this eminent personage had become in-different to the charge confided to him by the Order; for a rescript from the Grand Master and Chapter at Malta, dated so early as the 1st of October 1557, and addressed to him, is still on record, wherein they complain "that many of the possessions, jurisdictions, &c. were conveyed or taken away from them contrary to the statutes and oaths, and to the damnation of the souls, as well of those who possessed them, as of those who, without sufficient authority, yielded them up; producing thereby great detriment to religion and the said Commandery;" but be this as it may, we are certain that the conversion of Sir James Sandilands, or as he was termed, the Lord of St. John of Jerusalem in Scotland, was followed by his surrender to the Crown of the whole possessions of the combined Templars and Hospitallers, which having been declared forfeited to the State on the ground that "the principal cause of the foundation of the *Preceptory of Torphichen, Fratribus Hospitalis Hierosolinaitani, Militibus Templi Salomonis*, was the service enjoined to the Preceptor on oath to defend and advance the Roman Catholic Religion," were by a process of transformation well understood by the Scottish Parliament of those days, converted into a Temporal Lordship which, the unfortunate Queen Mary, then only twenty years of age, and newly established amongst her Scottish subjects, in consideration of a payment of ten thousand crowns of the Sun, and of his *fidele, nobile, et gratuitum, servitium, nobis nostrisgee patri et matri boræ memoriæ*, conferred on, or rather retransferred to the Ex Grand Preceptor himself and his heirs with the title of Torphichen, which, although the estate is much dilapidated, still remains in his family.[6] All this was transacted on the petition of Sir James Sandilands himself, with the formal approbation of the national legislature; and after renouncing the profession of a soldier-monk, we find that the last of Scottish Preceptors of St. John became married and lived to a good old age, having died so late as 1596 without issue, when the title of Torphichen passed to his grand nephew, the lineal descendant of his elder brother, Sir John Sandilands of Calder.

We shall not pause to consider whether a body of Masonic Templars unconnected with the Hospitallers, and representing the Royal Order which Bruce is said to have instituted from the relict of the ancient Knights, has been perpetuated in Scotland since the days of Bannockburn, having no means of illustrating so obscure a subject; but, with all due respect to the learned French writer, whose authority we have already quoted, we may observe, that the Masonic tradition of the country does not connect the Templars with Bruce's Order in any way whatever, but, on the contrary, invariably conjoins those Knights with the Hospitallers, and consequently points to the period of the renunciation of Popery, as the time when they first sought refuge, and a continuance of their Chivalry among the "Brethren of the Mystic Tie." The Chevaliers also of the Rosy Cross of Kilwinning in France, own no alliance with Masonic Templary, which they consider a comparatively modern invention; nor do there exist, so far as we know, any authentic records anterior to the Reformation, to prove a connection between the Knights Templars and Free-Masons in any part of the world, though we must not omit to mention, that a formal document in the Latin language is said to be deposited in a Lodge at Namur on the Meuse, purporting to be a proclamation by the Free-Masons of Europe, "of the venerable Society sacred to John," assembled by representatives from London, Edinburgh, Vienna, Amsterdam, Paris, Madrid, Venice, Brussels, and almost every other Capital City, at Cologne on the Rhine in 1535; and signed, amongst others, by the famous Melancthon, in which, after declaring that "to be more effectually vilified and devoted to public execration, they had been accused of reviving the Order of the Templars," they solemnly affirm, that "the Free-Masons of St. John derive not their origin from the Templars, nor from any other Order of Knights; neither have they any, or the least communication with them directly, or through any manner of intermediate tie, being far more ancient, &c." - all of which would imply, that some sort of connection was understood in those days to exist between certain of the Masonic Fraternities and the Knights

Templars. A copy of this document was sent to Edinburgh in 1826, by M. de Marchot, an Advocate at Nivelles, and a translation of it has been inserted under the attestation of a Notary Public in the Records of the Ancient Lodge, Mary's Chapel; but we have little faith in German documents on Free-Masonry, unless supported by other testimony; and as no historian of the Craft makes the slightest allusion to the great Convocation of the Brethren at Cologne, in the sixteenth century, rather than ask the reader to believe that it ever took place, we shall presume that M. de Marchot may have been deceived.

From the era of the Reformation, the combined Order appears in Scotland only as a Masonic body; but there are some records to indicate that, so early as 1590, a few of the brethren had become mingled with the Architectural Fraternities, and that a Lodge at Stirling, patronised by King James, had a Chapter of Templars attached to it, who were termed cross-legged Masons; and whose initiatory ceremonies were performed not in a room, but in the old Abbey, the ruins of which are still to be seen in the neighbourhood. The next authentic notice we can find on this subject, is in M. Thory's excellent Chronology of Masonry, wherein it is recorded, that about 1728, Sir John Mitchell Ramsay, the well-known author of Cyrus, appeared in London with a system of Scottish Masonry, up to that date, perfectly unknown in the metropolis, tracing its origin from the Crusades, and consisting of three degrees, the *Ecossais*, the *Novice*, and the *Knight Templar*. The English Grand Lodge rejected the system of Ramsay, who, as is well known, along with the other adherents of the Stuart Family, transferred it to the Continent, where it became the corner-stone of the *hauts grades*, and the foundation of those innumerable ramifications into which an excellent and naturally simple institution has been very uselessly extended in France, Germany, and other countries abroad.[7]

In pursuing the very curious subject of the hauts grades, we may observe, however, that they never obtained much consideration during the lifetime of Ramsay, although they are invariably traced to him and to Scotland, the fairy land of Foreign Masonry, but gathered their chief impulse from the disgraceful dissentions in the Masonic Lodges at Paris, about the middle of last century, which induced the Chevalier de Bonneville, and other distinguished persons at the Court of France, to form themselves into a separate institution, named, in honour of one of the Princes of the Blood, Louis de Bourbon, Prince de Clermont, then presiding over the Masonic Fraternities, the *Chapitre de Clermont*.[8] In this Chapter they established, amongst other degrees, Ramsay's system of the Masonic Templars, which, along with other high grades, was soon conveyed into the Northern Kingdoms of Europe, by the Officers of the French Army, but especially by the Marquis de Bernez, and the Baron de Hund, the latter of whom made it the ground-work of his Templar *Regime de la Stricte Observance*, which occupied, for several years, so prominent a place in the Secret Societies of Germany. This adventurer appeared in that country with a patent, under the sign-manual of Prince Charles Edward Stuart, appointing him Grand Master of the seventh province; but although he had invented a plausible tale in support of his title and authority, — both of which he affirmed had been made over to him by the Earl Marischal on his death-bed, — and of the antiquity of his order, which he derived, of course, from Scotland, where the chief seat of the Templars was Aberdeen, the imposture was soon detected, and it was even discovered that he had himself enticed and initiated the ill-fated Pretender into his fabulous order of Chivalry.[9] The delusions on this subject, however, had taken such a hold in Germany, that they were not altogether dispelled, until a deputation had actually visited Aberdeen, and found amongst the worthy and astonished brethren there, no trace either of very ancient Templars or Free-Masonry. From some of the Continental States, it is conjectured that Masonic Templary was transplanted into England and Ireland, in both of which countries it has continued to draw a languid existence, unconnected with any remnant of the Knights of St. John, whose incorporation in the Scottish Order, is one of the most remarkable features of that Institution. We are happy to add, nevertheless, that the most fraternal feelings and the intercourse subsist between the Scottish brethren and the Templars of the sister kingdoms, and we can ourselves testify to the cordiality with which the former are received in the encampments of London.

During the whole of the eighteenth century the combined Order of the Temple and Hospital in Scotland can be but faintly traced, though I have the assurance of well-informed Masons that thirty or forty years ago they knew old men who had been members of it for sixty years, and it had sunk so low at the time of the French Revolution, that the sentence which the Grand Lodge of Scotland fulminated in 1792 against all degrees of Masonry except those of St. John, was expected to put a period to its existence. Soon after this, however, some active individuals revived it, and with the view of obtaining documentary authority for their chapters, as well as of avoiding any infringement of the statutes then recently enacted against secret societies, adopted the precaution of accepting charters of constitution from a body of Masonic Templars, named the Early Grand Encampment, in Dublin, of whose origin we can find no account, and whose legitimacy, to say the least, was quite as questionable as their own. Several charters of this description were granted to different Lodges of Templars in Scotland about the beginning of the present century, but these bodies maintained little concert or intercourse with each other, and were certainly not much esteemed in the country. Affairs were in this state when, about 1808, Mr. Alexander Deuchar was elected Commander, or

Chief of the Edinburgh Encampment of Templars, and his brother, Major David Deuchar of the Royals, along with other Officers of that distinguished Regiment, was initiated into the Order. This infusion of per-sons of higher station and better information gave an immediate impulse to the Institution, and a General Convocation of all the Templars of Scotland by representatives having taken place at the Capital, they unanimously resolved to discard the Irish Charters, and to rest their claims, as the representatives of the Knights of old, on the general belief of the country in their favour, and the well-accredited traditions handed down from their forefathers. They further determined to entreat the Duke of Kent, who was a Chevalier du Temple, as well as the chief of the Masonic Templars in England, to become the Patron Protector of the Order in North Britain, offering to submit themselves to His Royal Highness in that capacity, and to accept from him a formal Charter of Constitution, erecting them into a regular Conclave of Knights Templars, and Knights of St. John of Jerusalem. The Duke of Kent lost no time in complying with their request, and his Charter bears date 19th of June 1811. By a provision in it, Mr. Deuchar, who had been nominated by the Brethren, was appointed Grand Master for life.

These wise and vigorous measures rescued the Order from in-significance; and in its improved condition, we find that it continued rapidly to flourish, numbering, in the course of a few years, no less than forty encampments or lodges in different parts of the British dominions holding of its Conclave.[10] Dissentions, however, unfortunately occurred, and from 1830 to 1835, it may be said to have again almost fallen into abeyance. For reasons perfectly well understood at the time, it was resuscitated in the end of the latter year, when a committee of ten gentlemen was appointed by all parties to settle the differences, as well as to frame proper regulations for the future government of the Order. Under their arrangement and arbitration, the present statutes were established, and a satisfactory reconciliation effected between the contending parties.[11] Mr. Deuchar having resigned the Grand Mastership in January.

1836, Admiral Sir David Milne, K. C. B. was unanimously elected to that high office, and at a general election in the same month, Lord Ramsay was appointed Depute Grand Master, the various other offices in the Order being filled by gentlemen, generally well known, and of a respectable station in society. In the course of three months after the reconciliation, not fewer than a hundred persons, chiefly men of fortune, officers, and members of the learned professions, had been received into the Order in the Edinburgh Canongate Kilwinning Priory or Encampment alone. Since then, other Priories have been established in the country, and the institution has assumed an importance and dignity worthy of the highest class of gentlemen connected with the Masonic Institutions of Scotland.

FINIS.

[1] Book of Cupar quoted in Father Hay's MS.

[2] *Wilckes Geschichte des Tempelherrenordens.*

[3] It appears by the following extract from Clifton's examination, that the Preceptor of Scotland was a subordinate officer to the Master, or Grand Prior in England. — *"Interrogatus; quis recepit emir ad dictum ordinem et dedit ei habitum? dixit, quod Frater Willielmus de la More oriundus de Comitatu Ebor. tune et nune Magister dicti Ordinis in Anglia et Scotia."*

[4] *Apres la mort de Jacques de Molay, des Templiers ecossais etant de venus apostats, a l'instigation du roi Robert Bruce, se rangerent sous les bannieres d'un novel Ordre institue par ce prince, et dans lequel les receptions furent basees sur celles de l'Ordre du Temple. C'est la qu'il faut chercher l'origine de la Maconnerie ecossaise, et meme elle des autres. Rites maconiques.—Du schisme qui s'introduisit en Ecosse naquit un grand nombre de sectes. Presque toutes ont la pretention de deriver du Temple, et quelques une Celle de se dire l'Ordre lui-meme. Manuel des Chevaliers de l'Ordre du Temple.* Paris, 1825.

[5] The medal alluded to was struck at the expense of the Chapitre du Choix at Paris, to celebrate the establishment in France of a Provincial Grand Lodge of Heredom de Kilwinning, by a charter, dated Edinburgh the 1st of May 1786, constituting Mr. John Mattheus, a distinguished merchant of Rouen, Provincial Chief, with very ample powers, to disseminate the order. The Chapitre du Choix was itself erected by a charter from Edinburgh in the same year, addressed to Nicholas Chabouille, avocat en parlement, and other brethren. Both these documents bear the signatures of William Charles Little, Deputy Grand Master, William Mason, and William Gibb. At a later date, a Provincial Grand Master was also appointed for Spain, in the person of Mr. James Gordon, a merchant at Xeres de da Frontera, whose commission was signed by Deputy Grand Master Dr. Thomas Hay, and Messrs. Charles Moor and John Brown, as heads of the Royal Order. In 1811, there were no less than twenty-six Chapters of Heredom holding of the Provincial Grand Lodge of the Order in France, including some in Belgium and Italy. *Histoire de la Fondation du Grand Orient de France.* Paris 1812.

[6] Sir James Sandilands only followed the fashion of the time, and the reader will find his motives and proceedings explained in an authentic family document printed from a manuscript copy in the Advocates Library, in a little work named, "Templaria. Edinburgh, 1828." We extract from it the following account of the surrender of the Preceptory:- "He personally compeirit in presence of the Queen's Majesty, the Lord Chancelour the Earles of Murray, Marischall, and diuers others of her Hiehnes Privy Council, and ther, as the only lawful

undoubted Titular, and present possessor of the Lordship and Precabortorie of Torphephen, which was never subject to any Chapter or Conuent whatsomever, except only the Knights of Jerusalem and Temple of Solomon, *Genibus flexis et reverentia qua decuit*, resigned and ouergave in the hands of our Souerane Lady, his undoubted Superior, *ad perpetuam remanentiam*, all Right, Property, and Possession, which he had, or any way could pretend to the said Precabortorie, or any part thereof, in all time Coming; to the effect the same might remain perpetually, with her Hyeness and her Successours, as a Part of Property and Patrimony of her Crown for ever. After this resignation in the Queen's Majesty's hands, *ad Remanentiam*, of this Benefice, be the lawful Titular thereof, her Hyeness, in remembrance of the good service of the said Sir James Sandilands, gave and grantid and dispon'd, in feu-farme heritably, to the said Sir James, his heirs and assignies, All and Haill, the said Precabortorie and Lordship."

[7] *Il est certain que l'invention des hauts grades maconniques a fait le plus grand tort a l'institution, en denaturant son objet, et en l'aflhblant de titres pompeux et de cordons qui ne lui appartiennent pas. On conviendra que jamais elle n'eut ete proscrite, dans une partie d'Allemagne, si les dissentions occasionees par la Stricte-Observance, le pretentions de soidisant successeurs des Freres de la Rose-Croix, et surtout l'invention de l'illuminatisme qu'on introduisit dans quelques L. n'eussent rendu "l'association suspecte aux gouvernemens." - Acta Latomorum.*

[8] There have been at least a hundred grades of Continental Masonrye denominated "Ecossais."

[9] On this subject we shall let the Baron de Hund speak for himself:- *Les Freres de la Stricte-Observance se disent les successeurs des Templiers, et leur doctrine consiste a perpetuer l'existence de l'Ordre sous le voile de la Franche Maconnerie. Voici l'Histoire de l'Institution, selon le baron de Hund; Dans l'annee 1303, deux Chevaliers, nommes Noffodoi et Florian, furent punis pour crimes. Tons deux perdirent leurs commanderies et particulierement, le dernier, celle de Montfaucon. Ils en demanderent de nouvelles au Gr.-Maitre provincial de Mont-Carmel; et comme il les leur refusa, ils l'assassinerent date sa maison de campagne, pres de Milan, et cacherent son corps dans le jardin, sous des arbrisseaux. Ils se refugierent ensuite a Paris, ou its accuserent l'Ordre des crimes le plus herribles, ce qui entrains sa perte, et par suite le supplice de J. Molay. Apres la catastrophe, le Grand-Maitre provincial de l' Auvergne, Pierre d'Aumont, s'enfuit avec deux Commandeurs et cinq Chevaliers. Pour n'etre point reconnus, ils se deguiserent en ouvriers macons, et se refugierent date une ile Ecossaise, ou its trouverent le Grand-Commandeur Haupton-court, Georges de Hasris, et plusieurs autres Freres aver lesquels ils resolurent de continuer l'Ordre. Ils tinrent, le jour de St.-Jean 1313, un Chapitre dans lequel Aumont, premier du nom, fut nomme Grand-Maitre. Pour 'se soustraire aux persecutions, ils emprunterent des symboles pris dans art de la Maconnerie, et se denommerent Mums libres…. En 1361, le Grand-Maitre du Temple transporta son siege a Aberdeen, et par suite l'Ordre se repandit, sous le voile de la Fr.-Maconnerie, en Italie, en Allemagne, en France, en Portugal, en Espagne et ailleurs. Der Signatstern, etc., p. 178.*

[10] "Neglected, and almost unknown, as the Order of Knights Templars has hitherto been in Scotland, it was requisite that some patron like your Royal Highness should interpose, to prevent its annihilation." Address of the Conclave to the Duke of Kent, on receiving the Charter of Constitution, 2nd November 1811."

[11] "The following gentlemen formed the committee, with the addition of the writer of these pages:- Sir Patrick Walker; Captain J. D. Boswall of Wardie, R.N.; John Wilson, Advocate; James Graham of Leitchtown; Edward MacMillan, S.S.C.; James Macewan, Lieutenant James Deans, David Deuchar, and John Forbes, all of whom were appointed to high offices in the Order, at the election in January 183G. For information on the subject of the statutes, &c. of the Scottish Order, vide "Statutes of the combined Masonic Order of the Temple, and of St. John of Jerusalem in Scotland, with the Charter of Constitution, and a list of the Grand Office-bearers and Members of Conclave. Edinburgh, printed by authority of the Grand Conclave, January 1837."

Index

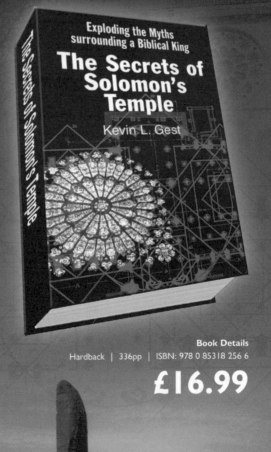